05/07

Harrison Learning Centre
City Campus
University of Wolverhampton
St Peter's Square
Wolverhampton
WV1 1RH
Telephone: 0845 408 1631
Online renewals:
www.wlv.ac.uk/lib/myaccount

ONE WEEK LOAN

Telephone Renewals: 01902 321333 or 0845 408 1631
Please RETURN this item on or before the last date shown above.
Fines will be charged if items are returned late.
See tariff of fines displayed at the Counter.   (L2)

WOMEN, PRIVILEGE, AND POWER:
BRITISH POLITICS,
1750 TO THE PRESENT

THE MAKING OF MODERN FREEDOM

General Editor: R. W. Davis
Center for the History of Freedom
Washington University in St. Louis

WOMEN, PRIVILEGE, AND POWER
BRITISH POLITICS, 1750 TO THE PRESENT

Edited by Amanda Vickery

STANFORD UNIVERSITY PRESS
STANFORD, CALIFORNIA
2001

Stanford University Press
Stanford, California
© 2001 by the Board of Trustees of the
Leland Stanford Junior University

Library of Congress Cataloging-in-Publication Data

Women, privilege, and power : British politics, 1750 to the present / edited by Amanda Vickery.
   p. cm. — (The making of modern freedom)
   Includes bibliographical references and index.
   ISBN 0-8047-4284-7 (acid-free paper)
   1. Women in politics—Great Britain—History. 2. Great Britain—Politics and government. I. Vickery, Amanda. II. Series.
HQ1236.5.G7 W67   2001
306.2'082—dc21   2001020017

This book is printed on acid-free, archival-quality paper.
Original printing 2001

Typeset in 10/13 Trump Mediaeval

Printed and bound in Great Britain by
Marston Book Services Ltd, Oxfordshire

Series Foreword

THE STARTLING AND moving events that swept from China to Eastern Europe to Latin America and South Africa at the end of the 1980s, followed closely by similar events and the subsequent dissolution of what used to be the Soviet Union, formed one of those great historic occasions when calls for freedom, rights, and democracy echoed through political upheaval. A clear-eyed look at any of those conjunctions—in 1776 and 1789, in 1848 and 1918, as well as in 1989—reminds us that freedom, liberty, rights, and democracy are words into which many different and conflicting hopes have been read. The language of freedom—or liberty, which is interchangeable with freedom most of the time—is inherently difficult. It carried vastly different meanings in the classical world and in medieval Europe from those of modern understanding, though thinkers in later ages sometimes eagerly assimilated the older meanings to their own circumstances and purposes.

A new kind of freedom, which we have here called modern, gradually disentangles itself from old contexts in Europe, beginning first in England in the early seventeenth century and then, with many confusions, denials, reversals, and cross-purposes, elsewhere in Europe and the world. A large-scale history of this modern, conceptually distinct, idea of freedom is now beyond the ambition of any one scholar, however learned. This collaborative enterprise, tentative though it must be, is an effort to fill the gap.

We could not take into account all the varied meanings that freedom and liberty have carried in the modern world. We have, for example, ruled out extended attention to what some political philosophers have called "positive freedom," in the sense of self-realization of the individual; nor could we, even in a series as large as this, cope with the enormous implications of the four freedoms invoked by Franklin D. Roosevelt in 1941. Freedom of speech and freedom of the press will have their place in the narrative that follows, certainly, but not the boundless calls for freedom from want and freedom from fear.

We use freedom in the traditional and restricted sense of civil and political liberty—freedom of religion, freedom of speech and assembly, freedom of the individual from arbitrary and capricious authority over persons or property, freedom to produce and to exchange goods and services, and the freedom to take part in the political process that shapes people's destiny. In no major part of the world over the past few years have aspirations for those freedoms not been at least powerfully expressed; and in most places where they did not exist, strong measures have been taken—not always successfully—to attain them.

The history we trace was not a steady march toward the present or the fulfillment of some cosmic necessity. Modern freedom had its roots in specific circumstances in early modern Europe, despite the unpromising and even hostile characteristics of the larger society and culture. From these narrow and often selfishly motivated beginnings, modern freedom came to be realized in later times, constrained by old traditions and institutions hard to move, and driven by ambition as well as idealism: everywhere the growth of freedom has been *sui generis*. But to understand these unique developments fully, we must first try to see them against the making of modern freedom as a whole.

The present volume differs from those that precede it in that it is not primarily concerned with rights and formal liberties. It cannot be, because before the last century, though women possessed privilege and power, they enjoyed them not so much by virtue of constitutional principles and legal guarantees as from their social position, or from the strength of their own characters and intellects.

Until recently the orientation of the historiography of Women's History was toward what women *could not do*, constrained as they supposedly were by "separate spheres" for men and women, the women's sphere, at any rate in the middle and upper classes, tending to be that of household deity, whose realm did not reach into the wider world where men and greater gods held sway: the "Angel in the House" was meant to be, for all practical purposes, just that.

In the last half dozen years this orthodoxy has begun to be reexamined, and a new question is being asked: What *could* women do?

A great deal of the credit for this shift of emphasis belongs to Amanda Vickery. In a seminal article and a much acclaimed book she challenged the orthodoxy of the separate spheres and argued that women, though they could not reach equality with men, could in fact do most of the things men did, and very effectively.* What they could not do was to reap the tangible rewards or enjoy the credit; but, short of those admittedly important benefits, they could make for themselves rewarding, and even satisfying lives. In this volume Vickery and a talented group of colleagues reveal how women managed this.

The Making of Modern Freedom grows out of a continuing series of conferences held at the Center for the History of Freedom at Washington University in St. Louis. Professor J. H. Hexter was the founder and, for three years, the resident gadfly of the Center. His contribution is gratefully recalled by all his colleagues.

R.W.D.

*A. J. Vickery, "Golden Age to Separate Spheres: A Review of the Categories and Chronology of English Women's History," *Historical Journal* 36, 2 (1993):383–414; id., *The Gentleman's Daughter: Women's Lives in Georgian England* (London, 1998).

Contents

Contributors	xi
Introduction AMANDA VICKERY	1
1. "To Serve my friends": Women and Political Patronage in Eighteenth-Century England ELAINE CHALUS	57
2. 1784 and All That: Aristocratic Women and Electoral Politics JUDITH S. LEWIS	89
3. British Women and Radical Politics in the Late Nonconformist Enlightenment, c. 1780–1830 KATHRYN GLEADLE	123
4. From Almack's to Willis's: Aristocratic Women and Politics, 1815–1867 PETER MANDLER	152
5. John Stuart Mill, Liberal Politics, and the Movements for Women's Suffrage, 1865–1873 JANE RENDALL	168
6. Contesting the Male Polity: The Suffragettes and the Politics of Disruption in Edwardian Britain JON LAWRENCE	201
7. The Privilege of Power: Suffrage Women and the Issue of Men's Support ANGELA V. JOHN	227
8. What Difference Did the Vote Make? PAT THANE	253
9. "Behind Every Great Party": Women and Conservatism in Twentieth-Century Britain DAVID JARVIS	289

Abbreviations	317
Notes	319
Index	395

CONTRIBUTORS

Elaine Chalus
Bath Spa University College

Kathryn Gleadle
London Guildhall University

David Jarvis
Emmanuel College, Cambridge University

Angela V. John
University of Greenwich

Jon Lawrence
Liverpool University

Judith S. Lewis
University of Oklahoma

Peter Mandler
London Guildhall University

Jane Rendall
University of York

Pat Thane
Sussex University

Amanda Vickery
Royal Holloway, University of London

WOMEN, PRIVILEGE, AND POWER:
BRITISH POLITICS,
1750 TO THE PRESENT

Introduction

AMANDA VICKERY

THE HISTORY OF women's politics and unfolding political rights can easily be told in the heroic voice. The first significant history of the British women's movement, written by the activist Ray Strachey in 1928, is a thrilling history of repression and rebellion, with opening chapters entitled "The Prison House of Home, 1792–1837," "The Stirring of Discontent," "The Widening Circle, 1837–1850," and so on. It is a story that still exercises a powerful influence on histories of women's political emancipation. In its barest essentials the story goes like this. The late eighteenth and early nineteenth centuries were the nadir of women's public and political assertiveness. The repressions of the 1790s gave voice to that lone pioneer Mary Wollstonecraft, but "as part of a national mood of political conservatism, feminism was quiescent in England in the early nineteenth century."[1] The Great Reform Act of 1832 introduced a new standardized franchise, but one that was for the first time explicitly restricted to men. In the boroughs of England and Wales the franchise was restricted to male householders with property worth at least ten pounds per annum in rent, and in the counties to the forty shilling male freeholder and the ten pound male copy holder. Any remaining radical female ambitions for reform were crushed and it was not until the 1850s that the women's movement recovered. The campaign for women's suffrage gained a focus in the 1860s around the political career of John Stuart Mill. When Mill stood for election in Westminster in 1865, he included votes for women in his election address and three heroines of the early women's movement—Barbara Bodichon, Emily Davies, and Bessie Rayner Parkes—publicly campaigned for him. In 1866, Mill agreed to present a petition of 1,499 names in favor of women's suffrage, collected by the first women's suffrage committee. Mill's proposed amendment was not carried and the Second Reform Act of 1867 simply extended the vote to all male householders and men paying more than ten pounds in annual rent in the boroughs. But Bodichon, Davies, and Parkes went on to establish the *Englishwomen's Review* in 1868 as a forum for feminist debate on a range of topics. From these small beginnings, the Victorian women's movement gathered momentum and claimed a series of stunning victories in the creation of opportunities for female education, the reform of women's legal status, and so on. However, in popular memory it is the spectacularly militant campaign of the Edwardian and Georgian Women's Social and Political Union (WSPU), the "suffragettes," which looms largest, while the dedicated work of the constitutionalists, like the National Union of Women's Suffrage Societies (NUWSS) hardly registers at all. Partial victory came in 1918 with the extension of the franchise to women householders over 30 years of age. Complete victory came with the Equal Franchise Act of 1928, which extended the vote to all adult women.

This well rehearsed tale of an ultimately triumphant 60-year battle for political rights should not, however, be allowed to mask the continuous threads and the diverse changes in British women's political roles, responsibilities, and preoccupations from the eighteenth century to the present. As Jane Rendall pointed out over a decade ago, "The symbolic importance of the vote to generations of feminists and subsequent historians has meant the obscuring of women's broader political culture."[2] Although the issue of rights and votes runs throughout this volume, the chapters explore the many different ways that women enjoyed public standing and exercised political purchase. The volume draws on five major revisions underway in recent historiography. Firstly, the chapters reflect a renewed interest in the way rank, property, and inheritance could confer de facto political power on privileged women. Heiresses' inheritance rights before 1832 often entitled them to prerogatives and appointments (not least the nomination of MPs to rotten boroughs). Across the centuries the arrogance of birth and title empowered aristocratic women to overawe enfranchised, but lesser men. Meanwhile a lady's own place in a political family and her proximity to powerful men meant she was often a crucial link in the chains of political patronage and had little choice but to be active in the maintenance of electoral power.

Secondly, this volume contributes to an ongoing "rethinking of the political," a consequence in part of the rediscovery of the work of Jürgen Habermas by political and social historians.[3] Habermas famously incarnated the notion of the public sphere of politics, "a forum in which the private people, come together to form a public, readied themselves to compel public authority to legitimate itself before public opinion."[4] For Habermas, the public consisted most prominently of readers of the printed word and members of voluntary associations, and certainly this volume stresses the extent of female engagement in political culture broadly conceived and an interest in the political implications of female associational life. However, the work here of Kathryn Gleadle, Rendall, and Angela John suggests we should extend this definition of the public sphere of politics further still to include the supposedly "private" world of family connections and friendship networks—fora within which political ideas were debated and new social practices played out.

Thirdly, many of the chapters are inspired by a related project, the effort to reintegrate the radical female activists within their political context. Although feminist hagiography has accustomed us to see female activists as heroic outsiders rising *sui generis* from a hostile environment, new research restores them to their contexts both intellectual and familial.

Fourthly, the volume responds to the growing interest in the way that political identities and political propaganda are entwined with ideas about sex and gender. In particular, politics and manliness have been seen to walk hand in hand. Keith McClelland was one of the first to point out that mid-Victorian working-class radicals came to set great store by a distinctly masculine vision of "independence." By this view, a man achieved political adulthood when he could support his dependents and represent them, a belief which denied women "an independent political subjectivity," according to Sally Alexander. It was this vision of responsible manly independence (and female dependence) which found expression in the limited householder franchise of 1867.[5] Futhermore, masculinity was also to the fore in Tory ideology. Jon Lawrence has shown the extent to which late nineteenth-century urban Toryism was built around a masculinist defense of male pleasures, like the pub and the race track.[6] What we are seeing here is a new confluence between political history and gender history; but in particular, we benefit from the emergence of the history of masculinity, which has emphasized that male political life needs to be located in a broader domestic, private hinterland. Revival and modernization of the political biography has had an impact here, helping to broaden our conception of the political life. Many biographers are more prepared to reflect on the political consequences of unhappy marriages, sexual and spiritual crises, and so on.[7] If politics could suffuse the supposedly private world of home, family, and relationships between men and women, then conversely personal issues of sexuality and sexual difference informed politics, even at Westminster. Not only was the political personal, but there was more to politics than Parliament. Accordingly, our fifth theme is exploration of the limits and possibilities of citizenship both before and after the winning of the vote.

Much of the work in this volume focuses on the political experiences of privileged women in Britain. It was they who, for much of the period under discussion, were in the strongest position to test the limits of women's political engagement. Their experience enables us, therefore, to map the outer boundaries of the politically possible at key moments. Most of the material is drawn from England, though some Scottish and Welsh examples are offered. A subject not covered here is the playing out of female ambitions in an imperial context; nor is there a discussion of the part women played in foreign affairs in general, though it is more than likely that diplomacy left great scope for elite female influence, since hospitality and social ties were crucial to success. There were, of course, women of color in Britain before the arrival of the Windrush in 1947, but their activism is not researched here.[8] The claims of birth, rank, and title are explored most fully by Elaine Chalus, Judith Lewis, and Peter Mandler; the impetus for political participation provided by religion, conscience, and enlightenment progressivism is recreated in the chapters by Gleadle, Rendall, and Mandler again; while the meanings of female citizenship both for women and the polity are explored by John, Lawrence, Pat Thane, and David Jarvis.

Inevitably with such a long span of time, questions of chronology, change, and continuity come to the fore. For some seventeenth-century historians, the Glorious Revolution of 1688 and its aftermath led to a tighter definition of political rights which excluded women. "By the end of the [seventeenth] century, both political theory and political institutions were more clearly defined as male. After 1690, women were explicitly excluded from parliamentary suffrage because of their sex."[9] Uncannily, an identical argument is made by several nineteenth-century scholars for the Great Reform Act. Clearly the Reform Acts of 1832, 1867, and 1884–85 were significant in that they defined the politically excluded ever more precisely, making the vote ever more important as a symbol of civil and political personality. It may be that as Sarah Mendelson and Patricia Crawford have argued, "democratic paradigms of the rights of men and brothers excluded women more decisively than did patriarchal discourses in which lineage and inheritance provided grounds for the formal political privileges of elite property-holders of both sexes."[10] However, as we will see, women were still able to carve a place within Enlightenment cultures and were quick to borrow the radical rhetoric of unjust exclusion and to apply it to their own case. Moreover, as Mandler stresses, the nineteenth-century valorization of "a new liberal subjectivity" which melded morality and rationality "was a shift to which women could and did contribute," if anything somewhat more convincingly than their aristocratic menfolk.[11] Still it is worth noting that historians' assumptions about the leading edge of political change have often configured our vision of the substantive *content* of politics in each era: a matter of aristocratic patronage, corruption, and riotous popular theater between 1688 and 1832; of religious lobbying and Liberal individualism from 1832 to the 1880s; of mass politics, party machines, and tumultuous streets from the Corrupt Practices Act to the First World War; and of citizenship, committees, and smoke-filled rooms from 1918 to the present. Such an effective teleology makes late nineteenth-century charity administrators or twentieth-century members of the National Childbirth Trust appear irrelevant to "real politics," blinding us to the continuation of older forms of political relationship and engagement.

For everyone for all of the period covered by this volume, political experience was broader than Parliament and political parties. An awareness of this provides a firmer context for an understanding of the achievements of the suffragettes and the colonists of state offices since 1945, but also for the continuities in the political experience and activities of women despite the dramatic ruptures. The feminists of Parliament might seal the revolution sought by the suffragists and suffragettes, but doing so would represent a transformation of one aspect, rather than the totality of women's political experience. Embracing other aspects of that experience makes for a more complex chronology and a more nuanced account of modulation in the political opportunities available to women between 1750 and 2000.

≺ I ≻

Women's Political Rights before 1832

The historic constraints on women's citizenship are well known but bear repetition here, for it is not our purpose to argue that legions of women exercised formal political power before the 1880s. However, as Mendelson and Crawford have pointed out, "if we ask to what extent women could participate as citizens in the early modern English polity, we are being deliberately anachronistic . . . It was not clear to contemporaries (nor is it yet clear to historians) precisely what citizenship meant for men. Women's civil rights and privileges were even more ambiguously defined."[12] In practice, a woman's "rights" varied according to inherited privileges, royal grants, local "liberties," and competing legal and religious jurisdictions, as did men's. That said, it is possible to sketch out a general picture of women's political powers and civil responsibilities. Unlike a number of European states, England allowed women to rule as monarchs after 1553 (Mary was the first acknowledged Queen regnant),[13] but in almost every other respect the political position of women was highly disadvantageous. *The Lawes and Resolutions of Women's Rights* published in 1632 was unequivocal on English women's political rights, or rather on the lack of them: "Women have no voice in Parliament. They make no laws, they consent to none, they abrogate none."[14] All the institutions of the eighteenth-century state were dominated by men. It may be obvious, but it is worth noting that women could not be Members of Parliament, nor could they hold offices of state. Women played no direct role in county government or in the administration of criminal justice, as they could not serve as Justices of the Peace, deputy lieutenants, or high sheriffs. Indeed, women could not even serve as ordinary jurors until 1919.[15]

At the level of parish, the occasional female householder may have enjoyed formal opportunities to be heard, but the picture must be reconstructed from legal fragments. Scattered court rulings demonstrate that there were occasional English women who were allowed to vote in meetings of the parish vestry (the basic unit of parish administration) and to serve as church sextons, overseers of the poor, constables, church wardens, reeves of manors, parish clerks (an office which principally involved washing the church linen), and so on.[16] But those women who tasted local power were mostly widows and householders, whose dead husbands had held the same office before them. Their nomination to office was often greeted by local fuss, many were disqualified, and many enlisted a male deputy to act for them. The only significant position that women filled with any regularity was that of jailer, but jails were seen as businesses, so widows inherited the job in much the same way that they took over the family shop. Female jailers were *not* seen as the representatives of local government. Commentators continued to argue that the mentally defective, infants, and women were unsuitable for local office, while "every gentleman of rank and property in the country" had it in him to be the model eighteenth-century justice.

Experts on eighteenth-century parish government estimate that less than two percent of local offices were held by women at any one time, while research on women and criminal justice in seventeenth-century Yorkshire delivered only one example of a female parish officer in the whole century, and that was in the lowly post of parish dog whipper.[17] Leonore Davidoff and Catherine Hall argue that it was Evangelical intolerance which expunged the female parish officer in the early nineteenth century. A woman in office smacked too much of vulgarity, disorganization, and Methodism.[18] Be that as it may, female office-holding before the nineteenth century was hardly extensive or prestigious.

Whether women voted in parliamentary elections in the seventeenth and eighteenth centuries is a trickier question. Before 1832 there was no actual statute which decreed that women could not vote in national elections. In the Suffolk election for the Long Parliament in 1640 some women tried to vote, but D'Ewes the high sheriff disallowed "what might in law have been allowed" because it was "very unworthy of any gentleman and most dishonourable in such an election to make use of their voices." In Richmond, Yorkshire, in 1678, women were stopped voting themselves, but allowed to assign their votes to male deputies acting for them. However,

George Peyt's *Lex Parliamentaria* of 1690 explicitly excluded women from the freehold franchise because of their sex, and for Crawford and Mendelson this was a defining moment in the political exclusion of women.[19]

That women should vote was certainly not unthinkable to contemporaries. After all, female property holders voted in Sweden, and the state of New Jersey briefly enfranchised women. Mary Wollstonecraft and Abigail Adams wistfully pondered the possibility and ladies' debating societies wrestled with the issue in London in the 1780s. Charles James Fox, a supporter of universal manhood suffrage, in 1797 floated the idea that well-educated women were worthy of the franchise. Nevertheless, in her survey of politically active elite women between 1754 and 1790, Elaine Chalus found no evidence whatsoever of women voting in parliamentary elections. The weight of custom prevented the vast majority of eligible women from approaching the ballot.[20] The passing of the Great Reform Act of course enshrined a tacit exclusion and parliamentary convention in law. However, it could not be said that a customary use-right was thereby wrenched from women's hands. The very mention of the possibility of votes for women was "an insult to common sense" for Josiah Tucker, Dean of Gloucester, an implacable opponent of democracy in the 1780s.[21] Not that the vast majority of the male population voted either: only 440,000 had the right to vote before 1832 (and the turnout was normally around 340,000).[22] Women, like the millions of unenfranchised men, had to use other strategies to affect political decision-making.

≺ II ≻

Women and Old Corruption

What then were the qualifications and strategies women used to claim power? How did women exert political power in the absence of technical rights? Linda Colley has argued that cohorts of patrician women enjoyed political clout in unreformed Britain, by virtue of their rank, family, and property; that is as a consequence of the same privileges which delivered authority into the hands of patrician men. In fact, the work of Colley, combined with that of Elaine Chalus and Judith Lewis, argues for the uncontroversial, not to say deeply ordinary, involvement of patrician women throughout the political process.[23] All three have called upon the work of Lawrence Stone or John Cannon or both to demonstrate that the eighteenth-century demographic regime benefited female authority over land. According to Stone, the eighteenth and early nineteenth centuries saw a marked tendency for male lines to die out. In the decades up to 1700 roughly ten percent of all family seats passed to women, or passed down the female line; but this figure rose in the eighteenth century, peaking at about a third by 1760–1769, and remained high to 1840.[24] Colley also reminds us that in the mid-eighteenth century the average age of noblemen at marriage was about 33—at its highest ever—while their brides tended to be considerably younger [and to live longer], a situation which aided the production of merry widows and long minorities. John Cannon finds that 59 out of the 84 families who held a peerage in the eighteenth century endured at least one minority, and one third of all successions were by minors.[25] Hence heiresses and female heads of families simply inherited power. Indeed Colley estimates that there were at least 21 different constituencies between 1790 and 1820 in which women exercised control.

The power that women from rich, well-connected, and exalted families disposed as patrons has a long history, reaching back at least to the Tudors, but doubtless beyond.[26] While few political historians would now accept the thesis that eighteenth-century politics was *solely* a matter of patronage, most would concede that patronage was still central to political life and crucial to individual advancement. In fact, women's historians have tended self-consciously to reinforce Sir Lewis Namier's view that eighteenth-century politics was above all a social activity, governed as much by friendships, alliances, and compromise as by events and ideology. Thus patronage was the very stuff of political power. And patronage as a system was one which ideally suited women, argues Chalus in this volume, since it operated as effectively at home and in the country, as at Westminster.

Moreover, women were held to have a duty to further the interests of family, kin, and connections. There was no hostility expressed to women doing this and indeed there is no lack of women's correspondence in male politicians' papers. Chalus looks in detail at women's patronage requests in the Newcastle papers during the period when the duke was First Lord of the Treasury, from 1754 to

1762. Roughly ten percent of patronage requests were authored by women. Though the number is small, women's aims were the same as men's; they requested places, pensions, preferment, access to Parliament, and peerages. They wrote on their own behalf, on behalf of their sons, and for other men. Moreover, they deployed the same language as men and obtained similar results. On the whole, "rank and relations ... appear to have mattered more than gender in shaping patronage requests and expectations, and in determining responses and outcomes."[27] Interestingly, married women usually left it to their husbands to request patronage unless they themselves were more socially exalted or better connected; thus there were occasions when rank outweighed gender in the scale of public regard. This conclusion is reinforced by the language of patronage. The submissiveness of the tone used was entirely subject to rank, whatever the sex of the writer: the lower the rank of the pleader, the more supplicatory the stance; the more equal the supplicant and the patron, the greater the informality. Some female correspondents had clearly carved out a role for themselves as "brokers" of patronage who forwarded the requests of others, "frequently women who were members of leading territorial political families" like Lady Yarmouth, Lady Katherine Pelham, the duchess of Newcastle, Lady North, and Mrs. Boothby Scrimshaw.

However, it was women's proximity to powerful men which accorded them their important, but admittedly nebulous status. "While claims of kinship or obligation and promises of reciprocity or political service, liberally supported by sheer determination and perseverance, could result in success ... in the end, the right to dispense patronage lay with the patron."[28] Of course, women did dispense copious private patronage in their own right, but as they were barred from positions of state no government patronage was in their direct gift. However, as heiresses and widows, they inherited the right of nomination to various local offices, from the mastership of Oxbridge colleges to church livings, and often were solicited by both women and men. In sum, patronage as a system lays bare the extent to which social expectations were structured by rank, and also lays bare the power both direct and indirect that birth entailed on the privileged female few.

Patronage was but one aspect of the political lives of the patrician elite. Chalus argues that women from politically active families had little choice but to be involved throughout the political process. She has itemized the drudgery of pleasures that ladies had to undergo between elections in order to maintain and consolidate family influence in the constituency—attendance at balls, assemblies, breakfasts, dinners, and race meetings was obligatory. They had to host public days in their own homes, make formal calls on mayoresses and aldermanesses, and generally treat the corporations of local boroughs. At election times the working unit of the political family went into overdrive. Heiresses often expected to control the family influence, to manage the electoral campaign, while most female relatives were expected to dispense yet more hospitality and to canvass for their menfolk. Chalus concludes that women's involvement was an accepted and expected part of the electoral responsibilities of women whose families were involved in elections. Indeed, though it is a subject little studied, ladies' involvement in electioneering certainly dates back to the seventeenth century.[29] And moreover, Chalus finds that women's involvement was taken for granted in political correspondence and often evoked little discussion. As Lewis reminds us in chapter 2, it was the *men* in the duchess of Devonshire's family who urged her to take part in the Westminster election of 1784.

This notorious election has played a totemic role in traditional accounts of the decline of women's political power before Victoria. The salacious opprobrium heaped upon Georgiana, Duchess of Devonshire, for her highly publicized canvassing of the male voters of Westminster (the largest and most prestigious constituency with the most democratic franchise in Britain) in support of the flamboyant Charles James Fox has fed the assumption that her activities were extraordinary and outrageous, and that the furor resulted in new boundaries on autonomous female action in public. However as Lewis emphasizes, "at the very moment Georgiana and her sister were canvassing the streets of Westminster, their mother, Lady Spencer, was managing the Spencer electoral interest in St Albans."[30] And moreover there were other noble canvassers in Westminster, both Whig and Tory, so as she concludes it is not the duchess's canvassing which needs to be explained, but the opposition to it.

Why was the press so hostile? Colley has argued that the duchess laid herself open because she broke with precedent in canvassing for a candidate who was not a blood relative, in a constituency which could hardly be presented as the family borough. Thus she exposed herself to the suggestion that Fox was her lover and that she acted out of ideological conviction rather than duty to her menfolk.[31] However, Amanda Foreman has countered that this explanation does not explain the fact that Mrs. Crewe and the duchess of Portland, as well as fifteen other Whig ladies who trafficked the streets for Fox, as well as Lady Hobart and Mrs. Salisbury, who canvassed for the government, emerged blameless. As the duchess of Devonshire said herself "it is very hard they should single me out when all the women of my side do as much." Foreman attributes the public castigation to the fact that the duchess of Devonshire challenged convention on two fronts: her direct style and apparent autonomy breached contemporary notions of femininity, while in forgetting her rank with male electors over ale and gin, she was seen "committing lese majesté," thereby threatening hierarchy.[32]

Yet what gets too little emphasis, argues Lewis, is the crucial point that Georgiana's efforts were *successful*. As Dorothy George pointed out nearly 50 years ago, "The gross abuse heaped upon the Duchess is a measure of her achievement." Charles James Fox retained his seat despite the best efforts of Admiral Lord Hood and Sir Cecil Wray, but throughout the campaign the Pittites feared that the duchess, armed with her massive celebrity, was personally winning the election for him. (*The Morning Herald and Daily Advertizer* alone was publishing at least one story a week about Georgiana from 1781, estimates Foreman.) As one newspaper put it, "all advertisements relative to the Westminster election should be in the Duchess of Devonshire's name. She is the candidate to all intents and purposes."[33] Although the Pittites generated a snowstorm of damaging literature excoriating the duchess in particular and censuring female political assertiveness in general, the Foxites ran a rival discursive campaign, particularly through *The Morning Chronicle* which affirmed women's claims to political autonomy. In fact, as the storm grew and the duchess wavered, she was pressed by members of the Whig cousinhood to continue;[34] but since the Pittite cartoons were so numerous, so colorful, and so obscene, history has bequeathed a Pittite view of the case.

Not that the Foxites helped Georgiana's reputation when they raised the issue of virility, arguing that Pitt's spleen originated in his frigid virginity; "that a real man would be happy to have his passion and his vote swayed by a lovely woman."[35] The Whigs were ever conscious of Georgiana's sex, and hoped to exploit it, using her to lure voters rather than persuade them. Nobility did not wipe away inferiority of sex; womanhood, feminine weakness, and sexuality were always the easiest targets of attack. However, it would be wrong to suggest that in venturing in public the duchess was bursting out of her sphere. As Lewis reminds us, "the duke of Devonshire's highly critical family, who had the previous year attacked Georgiana's breast feeding as an unnecessary romantic affectation, had no qualms about her political activities."[36] It was her *conduct* in public, not her *presence* there, that was at issue. Like Foreman, Lewis finds that the duchess's greatest sin was against hierarchy; she had stooped to familiarities with plebeians. So, for Lewis, the real threat that the duchess of Devonshire posed was a political one. Westminster was a scot-and-lot borough, wherein all ratepayers including many artisans had the vote. The duchess's free and easy encouragement of the butchers of Westminster, combined with Foxite politics, looked too democratic to be borne. (The butcher has to be one of the most pugnacious symbols of plebeian masculinity on which the satirists could draw, although it was not a new one. The butcher was a long-standing icon of red-blooded Britishness—carving his roast beef—in caricatures which often contrasted him with a frenchified effeminate.)[37] Hence the pamphlet war speaks to conservative fear of the male elector, bloody knife in hand.

The impact that the Westminster election had on public politicking by patrician women is far from clear cut. Foreman, the duchess of Devonshire's latest biographer, believes that the duchess had discredited both herself and her style of canvassing and that she never appeared on the hustings again. She did canvass once more in 1788 at the Westminster by-election, by letter and at private gatherings, but she "did not go about the streets" as she had before. Still, ladies' debating societies found in her favor ("it was determined that the Fair Sex deserved praise rather than censure for their interference in elections") and women of rank continued to canvass in family seats. And indeed Foreman has argued that though forced to exhibit more self-conscious propriety, the duchess "nevertheless . . . remained at the forefront of Whig political life" until her death in 1805. She continued to act as "confidante, spy, messenger and even party whip for her colleagues" and pulled off propaganda coups through copious use of the Whig colors, the blue and the buff.[38]

⊰ III ⊱
Continuity and Change, 1780 and 1884

The story of women's political lives between 1780 and 1850 is often told as a series of defeats. The Westminster election is often seen as marking new boundaries on female behavior in public. Foreman says "It would be another hundred years before women once more ventured boldly into street politics as Georgiana had not been afraid to do in 1784."[39] Conservative reaction in the wake of the French Revolution is seen as reducing public tolerance of female as well as plebeian assertiveness, while the solemn march of Evangelicalism forced women of rank into further retreat. The growing professionalization of politics closed committee room doors in the face of aristocratic women. These currents are taken to be crystallized in the Great Reform Act of 1832—which formally excluded women for the first time and removed the rotten boroughs wherein the power of many an aristocratic heiress had resided.

It would be perverse to suggest that these dramatic years of war, revolution, reaction, and reform saw no alternation in women's political lives; but it remains the case that for all our assumptions there has been little open debate about the precise extent of continuity or change. Clearly in extending the franchise to the ten pound male householder in the boroughs, in explicitly defining the political nation as male, the Great Reform Act had important discursive power. For James Vernon, "the significance of this can not be overplayed," since, as Catherine Hall has argued, the creation of "the official male political subject" cast the distinction between public male politics and private female domesticity into sharp relief thereafter. "Thus for women, but also for many men," argues Vernon, "the 1832 Reform Act represented a retreat, one which had given them less of a chance to be included within the official political nation than the unreformed electoral system."[40]

Certainly the complacency with which women were excluded is striking. James Mill, writing "On Government" for the *Encyclopaedia Britannica* in 1820, airily concluded "all those individuals whose interests are included in those of other individuals may be struck off from political rights without inconvenience. In this light women may be regarded."[41] Moreover, it was smarting for interested women to see new rights of citizenship extended to their fathers, brothers, and husbands while they were so conspicuously overlooked. However, we should be careful not to exaggerate women's customary rights in the unreformed polity. Indeed there are many examples in the statute book of eighteenth- and early nineteenth-century legislation that appears innovatory, but on closer examination is found merely to provide new statutory authority for long-established practices.[42] The explicit exclusion of women from the franchise by the Great Reform Act appears to fall into this pattern.

It would also be mistaken to see 1832 as a serious blow to landed political power. Despite the vociferous attack on corruption, the statute did not attempt to eliminate aristocratic influence on elections, but rather to circumscribe it. Indeed the legislators explicitly disavowed taking "away that [legitimate] influence [of landlords] over the vote which preserves the representative system ... from being of too democratic a character." "Legitimate influence" was still seen as appropriate and beneficial. Although most rotten boroughs were abolished, there were still 73 boroughs with electorates smaller than 500 which were highly susceptible to local landed influence. Moreover the ring-fencing of the boroughs (however imperfect) also tended to reinforce landed authority in the counties, and as voting was still a very public act dependants were easily accountable. Even after 1832, with an expanded electorate of 650,000, not many more men exercised the vote than had been the case under Queen Anne. In many boroughs, moreover, standardization meant the electorate was actually reduced by reform (for instance Preston, Lancaster, Coventry, and Westminster). Nor was there much change in the background of MPs; even in the new constituencies, the majority of candidates were still wealthy and leisured.[43] As Kim Reynolds summarizes, "Rather than viewing the Reform Act of 1832 as an irrevocable break with the past, ushering in an age of political modernisation, bureaucracy, and ultimately and inexorably democracy," there is much to be said "for viewing the first 40 years of Victoria's reign as belonging to a tradition with its roots in the Glorious Revolution of 1688, rather than as a precursor of the twentieth century."[44]

It is in this context that Reynolds has argued for the strong continuities in the role and function of aristocratic women between 1688 and 1884–85, albeit mitigated by the gradual decline of aristocratic power.[45] Despite the increasing bureaucratization of politics, the overlap between social and political life remained a generous one. Consequently political hostessing and the furtherance of family projects through patronage remained important. Despite 1832, the Second Reform Act of 1867, the secret ballot of 1872, and growing public concern about the limits of "legitimate influence," Reynolds finds aristocratic women continuing to play a significant part in the return of MPs to the House of Commons. However, Reynolds does suggest a fluctuating pattern of political engagement. The generation which came of age before the Great Reform Act (which included Lady Jersey, Lady Palmerston, Lady Londonderry, the duchess of Sutherland, and Lady Charlotte Guest) "took an unequivocally public stance in the electoral process" until their deaths. Still, the following generation (Lady Milton and Lady John Russell) seemed to adopt a self-consciously lower political profile. Yet the next generation, including such stalwarts as Lady Derby, Lady Salisbury, Lady Randolph Churchill, and Louisa Athol, sallied forth again in the 1870s and 1880s, both as individuals and as members of organizations. Reynolds speculates that propaganda about domestic womanhood may have deterred a generation from public politicking between 1840 and 1870, yet by the time the grandmothers were ready to pass the torch, the granddaughters were anxious to take it from them.

But it was a dimmer torch. The radical extension of the franchise of 1884–85 and the Corrupt Practices Act (1883) ushered in a new political world. The Women's Liberal Federation (1886) and the Conservative Primrose League (1883) institutionalized aristocratic female management in electoral politics, but the lady's influence was both diluted and circumscribed. According to Reynolds, she was left with "an attenuated role, controlled to an extent by the parallel male organizations and dominated by women of other classes." Ladies like the duchess of Marlborough (president of the ladies grand council of the Primrose League), or Rosalind, Lady Carlisle (a stalwart of the Women's Liberal Federation), wielded less power than the likes of Lady Palmerston in the 1830s and 1840s, though in canvassing support for their chosen candidates, they were doing much the same thing. "Ironically the criticisms levelled against the new breed of female canvassers were little removed from those aimed at the Duchess of Devonshire in the previous century: women were going among strangers to seek support for political ideas, not among personal connections to seek support for family."[46] Thus Reynolds suggests that the practical contribution to politics made by these prominent aristocratic women in the new organizations was far from novel in terms of actual content. Nor, Reynolds concludes, did many see their activities as a step on the road to feminism. She argues that aristocratic women defined themselves as *aristocratic* first and foremost, and saw little to gain from the women's movement. "Any increase in the electorate whether from women's votes or from working-class votes, diminished the political importance of the aristocracy, and muted the voice of the aristocratic woman."[47]

However, we should be careful not to exaggerate the formal power that aristocratic women enjoyed at any time before or after 1832. Peeresses were not summoned to take a seat in the House of Lords after the fourteenth century (indeed the first women did not enter the Lords until 1958!). Ministers of the Crown, Members of Parliament, election officials, and electors were all and always male. In chapter 4, Peter Mandler reminds us that aristocratic women were not even allowed to witness parliamentary debates after 1778; the intrepid few managed to listen in the notorious "ventilator," a sordid niche in the roof of the old House of Commons. Consequently the political power of the peeress was always indirect. Rank may have outweighed sex when a duchess patronized a butcher, but sex was still pre-eminent within the aristocracy itself. Though in relation to the world at large aristocratic women were "aristocrats first and last," "in relation to their own families, and to an extent their own class, aristocratic women were first and foremost women."[48] And aristocratic men were not always sympathetic to the ambitions of their womenfolk. George Canning, for instance, deplored his aunt's tendency to take issue with him over matters of state and clutched at any hope of abatement.

... had no political differences—insomuch that I really thought Hetty had come to her senses, and seen that a woman has no business at all with politicks, or that if she thinks at all about them, it should be at least in a feminine manner, as wishing for the peace and prosperity of her country—and for the success and credit of those of her family (if she has any) who are engaged in the practical part of politicks.[49]

As Chalus has acknowledged, there was always "an impenetrable ceiling" on elite female power.[50] Mandler goes even further to suggest that a powerfully "masculinized culture of political virtue" drawing inspiration from Republican Rome and martial Sparta infected the governing families, severely curtailing male tolerance of female assertiveness.[51] He finds much evidence of snide misogyny in male aristocratic correspondence of the Regency period. Although new work on the aristocracy has evoked the shared concerns and ambitions of the men and women of the leading political families, further research would do well to explore the issues that divided them.

It also remains to be seen whether the aristocratic woman was altogether exceptional in her particular brand of political behavior. It may be stating the obvious but we should remember how unrepresentative was the experience of the nobility; unrepresentative not only of the political agency of working and tradeswomen, but even of the lesser gentry, professional and mercantile elites. (The nobility comprised about 300 families in the late eighteenth century and its prominent families enjoyed princely wealth. The duke of Devonshire's annual income in the 1760s was believed to be in excess of £60,000, while the local elite of Lancashire and Yorkshire got by on £300 a year. Maids managed on a sorry £4–5 per annum.[52]) How far female canvassing, election management, or explicitly political hospitality extended down the social hierarchy remains an open question. Although I found no evidence of it among the local elite of Lancashire and the West Riding of Yorkshire in the later eighteenth and early nineteenth centuries, this is not surprising since these counties witnessed so few elections in the period. Research on female politics *below* the level of the greater gentry in other areas is lacking. We know that the *York Herald* hailed "the FAIR SEX" as the best canvassers for Wilberforce in the Yorkshire election of 1807; and that lesser gentry Anne Lister acted as a minor political patron in Halifax in the 1830s, threatening with characteristic self-confidence to evict tenants who did not promise for the Tories. But we do not yet know, for instance, whether the wives of mayors and aldermen canvassed in borough elections before the Great Reform Act.[53]

Whether in their tactics aristocratic women resembled their less fortunate sisters is a question which also deserves exploration—the furtherance of family projects, the orchestration of kin, a heroic rate of letter-writing, the patronage of certain tradesmen, the manipulation of symbols were activities pursued by a wide range of women. Yet, on the other hand, a recognized gulf yawned between those great families born into public life and the rest of humanity confined to the private. Risqué behavior that was legitimated by noble rank was usually repugnant in subordinates. It seems most unlikely that the duchess of Devonshire was seen as a useful role model—an icon yes, but one so removed from ordinary women and men by her exalted rank and fabulous wealth that she was inimitable. After all, ultra-successful female politicians have long presented themselves as exceptions "who were superior to the usual disabilities that afflicted ordinary women." Tellingly, Elizabeth I, the Virgin Queen, was represented as inimitable, a "phoenix, matchless and unique," and her successful reign did not lead to a general reassessment of women's fitness to rule.[54] Lesser mortals had to find other claims to political authority than blood and lineage, and other fora for political activity.

≺ IV ≻

Women and the Political Nation

In emphasizing women's part in the patronage, alliances, and electoral management of aristocratic government there is a danger that we reintroduce the impoverished vision of politics promulgated by Lewis Namier. Back in 1976, John Brewer countered that "the political nation [of the 1760s] was never coterminous with the parliamentary classes. Political argument . . . bound together whether the elite liked it or not, the two political nations of those who were excluded from institutionalised politics, and those who dominated its formal structures. Men might not be entitled to vote, and might not exercise political power, but they could not be prevented from developing political attitudes, engaging in political argument, and giving forceful expression to their views." And one might add that women could not be prevented from developing and giving vent to political views either. By the 1760s, Brewer argues, it had become impossible for the parliamentary factions to succeed without addressing themselves to popular debate. Whether a politician believed his own utterances is neither here nor there, since he was still constrained by his own rhetoric.[55]

Subsequent research has endorsed Brewer's view, but demonstrated that it applies earlier and earlier. Kathleen Wilson, looking at provincial politics in Newcastle and Norwich between 1715 and 1785, has found that "electoral evidence, excluding as it does the vast majority of the population, is a wholly inadequate gauge of the extent of popular political involvement." Like Brewer, Wilson has cast her research net wider, trawling across newspapers, ballads, sermons, broadsheets, pamphlets, and cartoons to conjure the many extra-parliamentary sites of political involvement and expression—"both formal and informal activities, from street theatre, club life and print culture, to instruction and petitioning movements, demonstrations and reforming campaigns."[56] It is against this background that Linda Colley has recently cautioned "we should not feel obliged to argue that politically involved women, of whatever social background, achieved more than in fact they did. What is needed is to reconfigure our image of past politics in the very broadest sense, so as legitimately to include female as well as male actors."[57]

If the eighteenth-century press was crucial in the construction of the political nation in its broadest sense, then women's engagement with print is of the essence. Paula Macdowell found dozens of female producers of political pamphlets and books active in London between the 1670s and the 1730s and convincingly argues that the expansion of the book trade offered unprecedented opportunities for public political expression of every stripe, from High Church Toryism and radical Whiggery to Jacobitism. Indeed many women were notorious for the editing and transmission of seditious literature and were frequently prosecuted for libel and even treason.[58] But it was as readers that the female political nation swelled to tens of thousands, though research on the female consumption of print is sketchy to say the least.[59] Newspapers were clearly interested in fostering a female audience and to this end included fashion news from the 1760s; but we need not assume that women readers perused only what the printers targeted at them. A reader like merchant's wife Elizabeth Shackleton who studied the height of the duchess of Devonshire's bonnet was equally capable of fuming about the loss of the American colonies, or applauding the release of John Wilkes—"I wish he may be Good & Honest & true to his friends & Liberty & Remember

45."[60] Some acquaintance with politics and public affairs was an essential component of that polite general knowledge, the purveying of which was one way the Enlightenment inheritance was spent outside radical coteries.

The expansion of club life was an important element in the growth and sustenance of extra-parliamentary politics. In 1750, the novelist Edward Kimber estimated that "perhaps Twenty Thousand people in London" met every night at clubs.[61] Formally at least, the majority of these clubs were within the purview of men, and many were marked by an aggressively masculine exclusivity. Wilson reminds us that sexual as well as political libertarianism flourished in Radical club life in the 1760s. Wilkes, after all, was a self-confessed libertine, an adulterer, a pornographer, and an alleged participator in orgies—in the words of one awed male admirer he was "free from cock to wig."[62] However, club life took other forms, and at this early stage of research it would be unwise to pronounce too emphatically on the dearth of public intellectual life for women. A surprisingly large number of ladies' and mixed debating societies were active in London in the 1770s, 1780s, and 1790s. Not that women's public speaking met with universal approval. *The Times* of 1788 maintained that "the debating ladies would be much better employed at their needle and thread, a good sempstress being a more amiable character than a female orator." But to little avail. There were at least 48 sets of rooms in the metropolis hired out to mixed or ladies' debating societies in this period, Donna Andrew has found. However, debating societies in general, like combinations of all kinds, fell foul of Pitt's terror in the 1790s. Only societies debating nonpolitical topics endured.[63] Nevertheless, the popularity and scope of debating societies suggests the potential of a public culture both rational and entertaining to which metropolitan women could lay claim. Further research must test the vitality of this culture in the provinces, although it is already clear that there were "female coffee-houses" and conversation clubs sprinkled about the growing cities and resorts.[64] It remains to be seen whether debating societies (male and female alike) revived in the more relaxed legal climate of the 1820s. In any case, if radical voices were muzzled, female loyalism found considerable public expression during the revolutionary war—no fewer than 50 anti-Jacobin novels written by women hit the shelves of the circulating libraries.

But words were not the only medium of political expression. The increasing commercialization of politics offered other opportunities for female participation at all levels of the social hierarchy, most obviously through the purchase of political artifacts. Teapots, bowls, tankards, plates, medals, and handkerchiefs could all be used to advertise political opinion since they could be had decorated with scenes of British victories, patriotic champions, popular election candidates and opposition heroes. The Lancashire gentlewoman Elizabeth Shackleton flirted with Jacobitism in her youth, tempted by racy tartan garters proclaiming "when you see this think of me," and in later life fancied purchasing a chamber pot with a likeness of Wilkes on it. Women proved adept at the manipulation of symbols to demonstrate political affiliation. Kathleen Wilson has discovered that in London and Norwich Whig women formed loyal associations against the Pretender, wearing orange cockades to the theatre as a riposte to the blue ribbons and white roses of the Tory and Jacobite ladies. In Norwich, York, and Worcester in 1733 female opposition supporters laid table cloths commemorating the defeat of the excise bill. In the 1740s, the opposition hero Admiral Vernon was celebrated in ballads, garlands, and snuff. And so on.[65] The duchess of Devonshire, of course, was adept at political symbolism. Journalistic acclaim greeted her efforts; fans with her likeness on them sold by the hundred.[66]

Women's independence from men as consumers had long been recognized, though their role in political manipulation through boycotting and exclusive dealing remains to be studied, especially for the eighteenth century. Boycotting as a political tactic had a long history, stretching back at least as far as the Irish boycott of English imports during the "Wood's half pence" agitation of the 1720s. American female patriots were central to the colonial boycott of British products, especially tea, in the 1760s and 1770s, while the ladies of Lincolnshire attended "stuff balls" in the 1780s at which only worsted fabrics made in the county could be worn. The duchess of Devonshire and her squadrons made princely purchases from the shopkeepers of Westminster during the 1784 election. Perhaps most famously, the early nineteenth-century women's anti-slavery societies forwent slave-grown sugar. And, of course, the tactic lived on in the Chartist women's exclusive dealing campaign and the female boycott of feathers from endangered birds in late-Victorian department stores. In fact, the power that disenfranchised consumers had in influencing the vote of enfranchised retailers is notorious.[67]

It is also worth emphasizing the obvious but important point that as integral members of their community, women had a role to play in most community actions and crowd protests. Most famously, women played a practical and symbolic role in food riots. Banging pans and with children in tow, plebeian women made it clear that moral economy began at home.[68] Court records suggest that women played only a minimal role in political riots such as those surrounding Sacheverell, Wilkes, and Gordon, and few women's names appear in the lists of those prosecuted after conscription or election riots. However, Nicholas Rogers believes female marginality is more apparent than real, a consequence of the peace officers' interest in "ring-leaders" and women's exploitation of magisterial belief in their naivety.

Women were undoubtedly central to "the infrastructure of community action, disseminating ballads and broadsides, emboldening men to collective protest, rallying neighbourhoods in their defence, flamboyantly displaying the symbols of sedition, and as the Gordon riots revealed using their knowledge of local networks and reputations to influence the course of the action." The political crowd was never exclusively male. Given the hurly burly of electoral politics was played out on the streets, plebeian and middling women were vocal, often heckling, participants in most contests. Though it seems women rarely marched in huge electoral parades or ate at special election dinners, they were present at election treatings, open air nomination meetings, victory parades and election chairings, and the like.[69] Moreover, middling women and gentlewomen usually played a prominent symbolic role in civic processions and official pageantry (often parading in white dresses personifying peace, health, royalty, nation) and were part of the throng of spectators at state ceremonials. In fact, Colley argues that the conservative backlash of the 1790s offered opportunities for greater female participation in a refurbished public life of loyalist parades, petitions, and patriotic subscriptions.[70] And certainly women played a role, albeit secondary, in radical protest and popular politics across the nineteenth century, from their iconographic sufferings under the saber at Peterloo, to their merciless barracking of electioneers and painting of faces in party colors in the late-Victorian and Edwardian periods.[71]

< V >
The Politics of Philanthropy

If the turn of the nineteenth century saw a decline in opportunities for public political debate on radical subjects, it witnessed a remorseless rise in institutional opportunities for public action through charity, female associational life, and reforming campaigns. Of course, religious activism has a long history. Mendelson and Crawford maintain that in early modern England "the most significant impetus for political participation among ordinary women was religious."[72] The language of conscience, built on the doctrine of equal souls, has given dissenting women the confidence to speak since at least the Reformation, while the eighteenth-century doctrine of works urged practical intervention on pious Anglican women. Informal, individualized charity was an ancient Christian obligation entailed upon property holders. Yet alongside this old tradition, often championed by devout women, grew up the great eighteenth-century associative charities directed by men, such as the Foundling Hospital and the Marine Society. Comparable charities and self-help associations sprang up in most prosperous provincial cities. Less is known, however, of the increasing number of societies set up and run by women. According to Donna Andrew, the first institutional charity organized by women (as opposed to charities run by men in which they participated) was the Ladies Charitable Society, or the Society for Charitable Purposes, which began its activities in London in the early 1770s. It provided employment and care for the women of the lower classes in the West End, especially the old and widowed, mainly by giving clothing and bedding.[73]

In the absence of systematic research, scattered instances must suffice to suggest the potential range of early female associative life in the provinces. Take the Bedale Ladies Amicable Society begun in Yorkshire in 1783. Essentially a self-help association set up to relieve its 123 members in illness, disability, and old age, it also offered the pleasures of participation in club life. A president and two stewards were appointed every six months, as was a clerk "which may be male if thought proper by the society," along with a standing committee of seven members to transact business. The members met on the last Saturday of every month, except December, between six and nine in the evening at rented club rooms and paid eight pence into the communal box. On club nights, the ladies were each given a ticket which they could exchange for a glass of wine or a pint of ale. On feast days, the members processed into church together to hear a sermon upon the occasion. All its members were demonstrably women of "sober life and conversation," but some were in greater need than others. Doubtless the likes of the Honourable Mrs. Pierce, Mrs. Jane North, and Mrs. Ann Burgess attended in a spirit of gracious patronage, or Christian responsibility, or even female solidarity, rather than financial expectation. Beyond its immediate monetary benefits, membership of such a society offered women the gratifications of institutional importance. By 1820, few were the provincial towns which lacked new public platforms for female right-doing. Certainly, archival evidence survives for female societies in York, Bradford, Leeds, Whalley, Wakefield, Carlisle, Workington, Hawkshead, Chester, Liverpool, and doubtless elsewhere should one care to look.[74] Indeed if Margaret Hunt is right in her plausible suggestion that there were "very powerful and long-standing taboos against women meeting together in a formal manner,"[75] then the emergence of female-dominated voluntary organizations is a very significant breakthrough.

Although detailed research on the late eighteenth century is lacking, so to an extent we are arguing from silence, it does appear that female associational life expanded most markedly in the 1810s and 1820s.[76] Hence, while some historians have stressed the extent to which respectable women were marginalized in nineteenth-century associative life, what is more remarkable from the eighteenth-century perspective is the extraordinary *explosion* in the number of philanthropic ventures authored and administered by women. As F. K. Prochaska has concluded of the early nineteenth-century boom in "feminized" philanthropy: "The welling up from below of female power produced, among other things, the rapid growth of district visiting, with its emphasis on the moral and physical cleansing of the nation's homes; the prominence of institutions for servants, widows and 'ladies'; the application of the family system in orphanages, ragged schools and other institutions; and the expansion of children's charity."[77] The public lives and profiles of even the most fastidious Anglican women, not to mention more radical dissenters, were therefore enhanced by the nineteenth-century multiplication of organizations which gave a little consequence.

Moreover, though we have been accustomed to read Evangelical awakening as a distinctively bourgeois phenomenon, the lure of personal religion was felt in aristocratic circles as well. As Mandler notes, the reform of upper class mores from within was a major element of the Evangelical project.[78] Personal religion led many aristocratic wives to embark on attempts to reform their men, to save their souls and light some home fires, but the attempted moralization of aristocratic men can even be seen as a far-sighted response to the writing on the wall. "The long-term political and social predominance of the aristocracy required a de-emphasis on gradations of status and birth, which were patently offensive and not long defensible, and a shift to new grounds for hierarchy, based on service to the nation, personal worthiness, and good conduct as judged on a universally-acceptable barometer." Mandler acknowledges that Hannah More called for women to renounce politics, but argues that this was a function of her critique of the content of Regency politics, and moreover the long-term consequence of her mission was in effect a rethinking of the political. "[i]t can hardly be argued that evangelicalism induced [aristocratic women] to withdraw from the public sphere: on the contrary, it put them far more visibly within it."[79]

Aristocratic women never saw philanthropic work as a retirement to the private; the most extrovert and politically ambitious ladies were often the ones most engaged. Frustrated with obstruction in formal political life, the duchess of Sutherland involved herself in a servants' training school on her estate, a campaign to relieve the Spitalfields silk weavers, and the anti-slavery campaign of the 1850s. Lady Noel Byron established model schools on her estate in the 1830s. Henrietta, wife of the second Lord Stanley of Alderley, ran estate schools and campaigns to improve ventilation and was a founder of Girton College, the Girls' Public Day School Company, the Medical College for Women, and the Women's Liberal Unionist Association. Even if philanthropy is assigned by historians to a separate female sphere, then that sphere is so extraordinarily expansive it stretches the metaphors of boundaries and containment to breaking point.

Not only did associational life attract women from aristocratic as well as commercial and professional backgrounds, it also galvanized women across the political spectrum. The movement for the abolition of slavery, for instance, though embracing and influencing many self-conscious radical proto-feminists, drew in support from conservative Evangelicals like Hannah More, Whig grandees like the duchess of Sutherland, and feminist advocates of political economy like Harriet Martineau. Though from the first female abolitionists canvassed door to door, engaged in debates, and raised funds in antislavery societies, they were barred from sitting on committees and signing petitions. In response, the first specifically female antislavery society was formed in 1825 and by 1830 there were ladies' anti-slavery societies in virtually every British town. Significantly, the women began signing separate petitions, and in 1833 presented half a million signatures, the largest anti-slavery petition of the lot, a gesture reminiscent of the mass female petitions of the 1640s and 1650s.[80] The women may have been forced to set up a separate organization from men (which for some is read as proof enough of the power of the ideology of separate spheres), but the campaign nevertheless offered thousands of women a new administrative training and an expanded field of public endeavor. For Claire Midgley, antislavery offered the "skills, self-confidence, connections, sense of collective identity, and commitment to public political activism" that supplied the basis for organized feminism.[81] This is doubtless true, but it also offered the same gifts to non-feminists and could be said like other organized charities to have furnished a training for Tory constituency organization and local government. In either case, it is clear that the experience of institutions is something that properly belongs within an expanded definition of the political.

The religious awakenings of the late eighteenth and early nineteenth century undoubtedly encouraged the role of mild guardian of the hearth, but they also could empower women to act as soldiers of Christ both at home and abroad. The temperance movement in Wales, the Salvation Army, and the missionary movement represent but three crusades which engaged Victorian women in enormous numbers, and however unsavory some aspects of these campaigns appear to us now, there can be no doubt of their message that British women had urgent public duties to perform.[82] The assumption that anything we might identify as progressive for women languished in the early nineteenth century owes much to the sympathies of modern secular feminism. An allergy to Evangelicalism and a tendency to counterpose serious religion and emancipation have been widespread in women's history.

⋖ VI ⋗
Politics, Religion, and the Radical Intelligentsia

The interplay of politics and religious practices in the revolutionary years is to the fore in Kathryn Gleadle's chapter on women and the nonconformist enlightenment, 1780–1830. Her work gives the lie to the received wisdom that feminism languished between the death of Mary Wollstonecraft in 1796 and the Langham Place circle of the 1850s. "It is generally accepted that feminist debate and discussion ceased completely at this time. The French Revolution and the wars that followed them brought a powerful conservative reaction which made any suggestion of political and social reform all but impossible."[83] Gleadle's excavations reveal a more complicated and interesting chronology. Certainly the initially enthusiastic pamphleteering on liberty by the likes of A. L. Barbauld, Catherine Macauley, Mary Robinson, and H. M. Williams in the early 1790s was petering out by the end of the decade in face of growing hostility to radical ambitions of all kinds. Gleadle finds that many Radical women looked to "less politically threatening ideological outlets,"[84] like Quakerism and Romanticism. Unitarians of both sexes eschewed questions of democracy in favor of humanitarian issues like peace and antislavery, while other Unitarian women sought to fulfill their "civic duties" through philanthropy, giving their charity a radical tinge.

But we should not exaggerate the extent of political quiescence. Interested women still played a public role in elections in the first two decades of the nineteenth century; some, like Rachel Lee, A. L. Barbauld and Eliza Heyrick, circulated and published their political pamphlets, and female dissenters in general continued to be crucial players in the rich intellectual subculture of radical nonconformity. Moreover one of Gleadle's most interesting departures is her insistence that the domestic sphere (so often invoked as the prison of female politics) was itself construed in terms of political space. "The home was the site of salons, informal discussion groups, political correspondences, ideologically motivated consumer choices, politically inspired child-rearing methods and so on, all of which were crucial to the emergence of specific radical political cultures."[85] Consequently, the common truism that the dread shadow of the guillotine eclipsed the radical aspirations of a generation is both a gross simplification and an exaggeration. And in any case, as Gleadle has already shown, by the early 1830s "stimulated by the growing ferment of co-operative ideologies, a new alignment of progressive reformers, the 'radical unitarians,' began to revive debate upon the position of women within society." All of which raises the interesting possibility that historians have taken what was a temporary recession in some forms of explicitly political female activity to be an epochal shift, the major sea-change in women's political history.

The significance of these years for radical middle-class dissenters lies rather in the combined impact of the repeal of the Test and Corporation Acts (1828) and the Great Reform Act (1832). Whereas before dissenting women "had perceived themselves to labor under the same legal discrimination as their menfolk, this was no longer the case. It was now the legal position of women, and not that of the dissenters as a whole, which loomed as a stark and anomalous grievance,"[86] a hardship which rankled with feminists thereafter. Gleadle's chapter here, combined with her published work on the 1830s and 1840s, shows how the ideologies and personnel networks which determined mid-Victorian feminism were laid.[87] (Bessie Rayner Parkes and Barbara Bodichon, who established the path-breaking *English Women's Journal* in 1858, were both from politically radical Unitarian families.[88]) Gleadle broadens her sights not only to consider collective female action, but also to recreate a reforming *outlook*, shared by progressives of both sexes. Men, of course, were dominant, but prided themselves on the contribution of their womenfolk, seeing their own commitment to feminism as an element in a wider radical philosophy.

As Gleadle summarizes, "originally a small and frequently maligned coterie, by the 1840s many radical unitarians were beginning to assume a more prominent position within contemporary culture. Their visionary agenda had led them to embark upon a number of specific campaigns to elevate women's position—including the reform of women's legal position, an attempt to secure female suffrage on the Chartist program, efforts to tackle the problem of prostitution; and the launching of a unique experiment in adult education. It was these early feminists who were the pioneers of the Victorian women's rights movement." However Gleadle is at pains to stress that for the radical unitarians the emancipation of women was to be but a part of a wider cultural revolution. Women deserved equal treatment to men, but their mothering should be protected, while men should accept their duty to care. Radical humanitarianism demanded the creation of a more equal, caring society. It is to the entire philosophy that attention should be paid, concludes Gleadle.

Indeed the existence of a broader radical political milieu embracing both women and men has become the focus of creative research. Sarah Richardson reveals the importance of letter-writing, hospitality, European travel, cosmopolitan salons, translation, and the reading of *avant garde* literature in the creation of a political culture for radical women in the 1830s and 1840s. Debate in letters and salons certainly focused on questions such as political reform and the repeal of the Corn Laws and slavery, but it also extended to the rights of oppressed nationalities, such as the Italians and Hungarians, the need for educational reform, crusades against cruelty to animals, vegetarianism, and homeopathy.[89] Moreover, the middle-class radical culture of the 1850s excavated by Margot Finn was "centred on family life, private houses, Nonconformist chapels and liberal salons" and was characterized by the same weakness for Mazzini.[90] Taken together, such research promises an entirely new take on nineteenth-century women's politics *and* the proposal of a new paradigm for political history—one that demands we look as seriously at the politics of lifestyle (such as the promulgation of vegetarianism and alternative therapies), as at agitation around issues such as the rights of oppressed nationalities and minorities in Europe. As Gleadle and Richardson conclude, radicals at the time drew no distinction between hard and soft politics, so neither should we.[91]

The reconstruction of an ideological milieu embracing *both* men and women is also to the fore in Jane Rendall's work. Elsewhere Rendall has emphasized the extent to which female campaigners for the suffrage in the 1860s appropriated the languages of advanced radicalism and liberalism: British constitutionalism, a Gladstonian stress on the industry and intelligence of the woman rate payer, a claim to the rights and duties of citizenship, and a stress on social progress.[92] In her chapter here, Rendall focuses not so much on the arguments and activities of the women campaigners, as on the contexts in which they flourished. Thus she offers a painstaking reconstruction of the network of liberal and radical alliances which facilitated the reform agitation of 1866–67 and the election of the Liberal government of 1868–74, finding that these were the same networks that lent support to the women's suffrage movement.

When John Stuart Mill proposed an amendment to the Reform Bill of 1867 he was defeated by 196 votes to 73; but it is not the defeat that is surprising, rather it is the support given to the proposal of women's suffrage in its first parliamentary hearing. Those 73 votes were hailed at the time as "a great triumph." Where did this support come from? Rendall finds that radical Unitarians, Christian socialists like the Reverend Charles Kingsley, Manchester Liberals like Jacob Bright, some academic liberals, elements of the National Reform Union and the Social Science Association were all broadly in favor of enfranchising women (especially pure, upright, ladylike women) on the same terms as men. Of course, the relationship of feminism and liberalism in all its varieties is not a simple one, and Mill's own role and attitudes were far from unambiguously supportive. Still this coalescence of "progressive" opinion in favor of suffrage is suggestive of the ways in which an acceptance of the virtue of the female claim to citizenship became disseminated across the political class. As Rendall concludes, "John Stuart Mill brought to the cause of women's suffrage an attractive intellectual influence and reputation, an unexpectedly effective parliamentary voice, and a willingness to court ridicule in its name. Yet the power of his name and personal commitment have tended to obscure developments already at work within some liberal and radical circles by the 1860s, and evident to an extent in the support he received in the House of Commons in 1867."[93]

However, the increase in support for women's citizenship over the nineteenth century was neither steady nor linear; the encouragement of the 1860s was very much of its moment. It appears that the debates over extending male suffrage created the discursive space for a whole raft of radical discussions to flourish, including House of Lords reform and republicanism, as well as the rights of women. But the Third Reform Act of 1884 seemed to have closed the book on franchise issues for a generation, and drew a line under radical debate. The coalescence of support for women's citizenship 1865–70 was in reality a shifting and uncertain set of connections—a tissue of alliances that did not survive the death of Mill in 1873 and Liberal defeat in 1874 absolutely intact. In the wake of the Irish fiasco and faddism, the intellectual hegemony of high Victorian Liberalism dematerialized. The increasing importance of Ireland's claims for Home Rule also divided and deflected support. Numerous of Mill's acolytes shifted ground. Several former advocates of female suffrage became implacable enemies. "The positivist view of women as too likely to be an anti-progressive force gained ground among many Liberals, who came to share the views of Goldwin Smith; among them was William Randall Cremer, once a supporter, who by 1886 believed that 'giving the suffrage to women would have a reactionary effect and prevent progress for many years to come.'"[94] Gladstone, whose Liberalism owed much to Peel and Tory traditions, sympathized little with the cause.

The ground gained by Social Darwinism also made for a less receptive ideological climate, exaggerating as it did the biological differences between men and women, rather than a shared capacity for reason and enlightenment. The rise of the Independent Labour Party (ILP) and the new trades unionism increased the potential for division among radicals between those supporting equal suffrage for women and those seeking universal suffrage for men, although Hardie, Lansbury, and many of the ILP rank and file supported militancy on principle and equal suffrage as an achievable goal. However, even among feminists themselves there was disagreement about the virtue of the equal suffrage goal because it excluded married women. Impatience with the glacial pace of reform led some activists to work at immediate goals like women's higher education, or to aim at other targets like the sexual double standard, the notorious Contagious Diseases Acts, and male brutality to women and children in general.[95] The passage of the Third Reform Act in 1884, which increased the male electorate from three million to five million (60 percent of the male population), was another galling blow (though in fact there is little or no research on the debates around women's exclusion here).

However, the mid-Victorian liberal coalition could claim one important success. Jacob Bright did manage to establish the right of female rate payers (therefore unmarried or widowed) to vote in local elections in boroughs in 1869; they made up some 10 to 15 percent of the local electorate. Furthermore, women consolidated their rights of membership of local school and poor law boards in the early 1870s, so that by the 1900s women provided respectively over 500 and over 1000 of the representatives on these bodies in England and Wales. However, the significance of women's participation in local government could be read in a variety of ways. "Invariably and inevitably, women members spoke the language of separate spheres," finds Hollis, but this language "should not be dismissed as necessarily conservative and confining." Though the language of separate spheres could certainly be deployed in reactionary ways, for many the flourishing of this vocabulary of separate spheres was part of an attempt to push the boundaries of local action further out and to recast local government in a humanitarian mold. It was a sign neither of limited goals nor of an acceptance of a masculine reading of local government. As Rendall concludes, "In these settings middle-class women activists were to put into practice a view of citizenship which transcended sharp boundaries between domestic, social, and political responsibilities."[96] Suffragists could offer female participation as proof that here was a trained electorate who would wield the franchise responsibly. On the other hand, the anti-suffragist Mrs. Humphry Ward argued that since women now influenced local government through the "domestic" vote they had no need of the national or "imperial" vote.[97]

Meanwhile the establishment of party electoral machines in the wake of the Corrupt Practices Act (1883) extended opportunities for the political participation of late Victorian women—notably through the Primrose League (1883), the Women's Liberal Federation (1886), and the Women's Labour League (1906). Strikingly, the Socialist Democratic Federation (1884) and the Independent Labour Party (1893) admitted women as equal members from the outset, something the Liberals and Conservatives failed to do until after the war.[98] Of course, the existence and activities of these subsidiary women's party organizations further problematized the issue of female citizenship: how was it that thousands of women were authorized by their political parties to educate themselves in political affairs, to make political speeches, to preach politics on the doorstep, and to help get the voters out at election time, while those same parties did not recognize them as citizens in their own right? On the other hand, although much was made of the back-room quality of women's constituency work and many workers felt compelled to emphasize that their activities were yet another extension of that remarkably elastic entity, the woman's sphere, Linda Walker nevertheless finds that Conservative organizations like the Primrose League "cultivated a sense of political responsibility" and educated women in the operation of political machines. Unlike the Primrose

League, Liberal women's organizations retained an ideological engagement with women's issues per se, and "came to share a sense of solidarity with a wide network of feminist organizations who attempted to apply pressure from without."[99] By the early 1900s, Martin Pugh concludes, politicians of every stripe were prepared to concede that election campaigns could hardly function without female legwork.[100]

≺ VII ≻

The Women's Suffrage Movement in Edwardian England

Jon Lawrence and Angela John look in this volume at the resurgence of the women's suffrage movement in the Edwardian era. Their approaches reflect the revisions underway in feminist historiography about the suffrage. With new research on women's suffrage campaigns in the regions, some of which were led by working-class women, it is no longer possible to caricature the movement as an isolated, purely middle-class, metropolitan, and liberal phenomenon. Historians are now aware that "votes for women" was not a simple equal rights demand, but an appeal which concentrated a range of challenges to the male dominated polity and symbolized a new way of being of a woman.

Attempts have been made to restore the full range of pro-suffrage activity, giving more weight to the comparatively unexciting work of the constitutionalist NUWSS, an organization which benefited in increased numbers from militant publicity and often shared members with the WSPU. Recently, there has been a concerted attempt to reconstruct the activities of mixed sex societies like the United Suffragists and of men's suffrage societies like the Men's League for Women's Suffrage or the Men's Political Union for Women's Enfranchisement. Finally, there has been a re-examination and reinterpretation of the spectacular militancy of the WSPU. Perhaps the most welcome departure has been the effort to situate the female activist in her familial, social, and cultural contexts and thus restore the famous story of suffrage campaign to the new social history of Victorian and Edwardian women. Sandra Holton finds that activists like Helena Swanwick, Hannah Mitchell, and Mary Gawthorpe all portrayed "an involvement in politics as neither an abnormal aberrant aspect of a woman's life in the communities and subcultures of which they were a part, nor as a deliberate departure from, a rejection of their place therein." Assuredly, "the atypicality of suffragists lay principally in their articulateness and public visibility, but this did not render them absolutely different or completely separated from other women as a caste apart. Equally their feminism drew its meaning from experiences that were the commonplaces of women's lives. Not surprisingly then the suffragist and the average woman may often be found in one and the same person."[101]

The Edwardian suffrage campaign deployed the full gamut of political tactics and props: banners, colors, pageantry, artifacts, shop displays, and exclusive dealing; posters, cards, and handbills; novels and plays; lectures and speeches; discreet lobbying, committee work, and the careful building of alliances one person at a time; as well as the militant disruption of political meetings, assaults on property, and hunger strikes. It is in the context of new work on the meanings and philosophy of suffragette militancy that Jon Lawrence places his analysis of the evolving feminist campaign to disrupt meetings addressed by Liberal cabinet ministers in the years after 1905. Thereby Lawrence is able to draw conclusions about both the nature of the suffragette challenge to the male polity and the continued male domination of public political space. The "rough and tumble" of street politics, the violence and alcohol which were integral to elections, had long been offered as reasons why nice women should eschew election politicking, although the presence of women as municipal electors after 1869 may have "tamed" some of the worst excesses there. Lawrence argues that violent and disorderly crowd behavior and the assertion of manly authority from the platform was central to the English political meeting in the era of partial male democracy 1867–1914. By embarking on a campaign of disruption, therefore, the suffragettes were not breaking with political convention, rather they were interacting creatively with the robust customs of street politics. For all the increase in female public speaking in organizations like the Primrose League, the Women's Liberal Federation, and the early socialist groups, party political meetings "remained powerfully male environments," despite the fact that women were not formally excluded.

Suffragette disruption commenced in 1905 with a relatively decorous wait for question time but swiftly progressed to random interruption, heckling, and outright disruption, which brought down the violence of the crowd on the women's heads. Somewhat paradoxically, disruption was viewed both as an appropriation of male rights and customs *and* as a strategy designed to expose the ugly brutality and raw misogyny of Edwardian politics. Of course, violence done to women had great symbolic power. If the male monopoly of the franchise was justified by men's superior power, then here was brute force in all its shaming glory; if this was chivalric manliness, then perhaps men could not be trusted with power? The crying need for a feminization of politics for the sake of the nation as a whole was therefore vividly suggested. Of course, the symbolic message of the suffragette campaign was not always so coherent—in soliciting aggressive protection from supportive men, the suffragettes imitated the conventions of "masculinist popular politics" rather than contesting them.

Moreover, the physical cost of offering oneself as a sacrifice to male violence was increasingly seen as too expensive; and though disruption continued until 1914, its importance faded because newer, more challenging tactics were developed. Force-feeding offered straightforward martyrdom, in a way that was easier to read than the confusing world of street politics. However, the experience of disruption and its reception strengthened a growing determination to transform the male political world, not just to claim a place in it; "to reform not just the franchise and the culture of Westminster, but popular politics as a whole."[102] Indeed this "vision of a democracy transformed" was one to which many across the political spectrum were sympathetic and in fact foreshadowed the comparatively tamed culture of mainstream party politics between the wars. Of course, it was recoil from the excesses of industrialized warfare which did most to reduce public acceptance of male violence in political life after 1918. Still, the sustained feminist critique of hypermasculine posturing, combined with the inauguration of an entirely new and alien female constituency, also played an important role in the transformation of the conduct of politics.

Angela John's research also broadens our understanding of the much celebrated struggle for the vote. Although male opposition to female suffrage is notorious, the activities of supportive men have until very recently been lost to view. Of the societies which John, Clare Eustance, and their colleagues have studied, the most important were the Men's League for Women's Suffrage, the Men's Political Union for Women's Enfranchisement, and the United Suffragists. The Men's League for Women's Suffrage, active from March 1907 to the outbreak of war in August 1914, was headed by Herbert Jacobs, a middle-aged Jewish banker. It was a non-party constitutionalist organization which aimed to promote women's enfranchisement on the same terms as men's. Its ranks were swelled by Tories, Socialists, Independents, and frustrated Liberals—a number of whom had been formed politically by mid-Victorian Liberalism, John Stuart Mill, and indeed the early women's suffrage campaigns of the 1860s. The Men's Political Union for Women's Enfranchisement was a more militant organization of younger men which drew inspiration from Christabel Pankhurst's WSPU and even adopted the purple, white, and green of the suffragettes. It was smaller than the Men's League and shorter lived, falling foul of Christabel Pankhurst's intolerance of male interference as the militant campaign escalated after November 1911. But even less well known is the patient work of the United Suffragists, active from 1914 to partial victory on February 6, 1918. It was run by equal numbers of men and women, in what John considers a "constructive alliance," putting informal pressure on key government figures, canvassing in elections, and pursuing a damage limitation policy with the media. In offering a united forum for previously disparate activists, the society represented an important departure, successfully consolidating the campaign for the vote and playing a crucial role in driving in the thin end of the wedge—the Representation of the People Bill.

John considers that although male support could be problematic, it was nevertheless invaluable to the cause in organizational and propaganda terms—channels of influence were open to men through clubs, career structures, and institutional activities which few women enjoyed. For many male supporters, women's suffrage was one cause among many, one element in a broader radical commitment. As Eustance and John crisply observe elsewhere, "the public platform was familiar to them."[103] Some were striking in their commitment to marriage as a progressive project itself, a public partnership. Not that it was always easy for men to face the taunt of henpecked effeminacy from opponents, or the charge that they had deserted the working man in support of privileged women. Nor did playing a secondary, auxiliary role in a movement organized by women for women come naturally to all. The Liberal newspaper editor and proprietor John Gibson sat on the council of the Women's Franchise League in 1889, yet still found it in himself to propound that "women are not organized and do not seem to have the power of men to organize" and to denounce the "foolish, nagging policy of the WSPU."[104]

Male self-importance was never utterly extinguished, indeed such public progressivism could take it to new heights. An exquisite sense of moral superiority was held out as the key prize of pro-suffrage work by Israel Zangwill in an address to the Men's League for Women's Suffrage. "If ever a person had a right not only to a quiet hearing, but to an almost pharisaic self-satisfaction—if anybody could exclaim 'I am not as other men,' it would be a member of this league."[105] Many women remained equivocal about the virtue of male interference. And although initially sympathetic, Christabel Pankhurst found any intervention by men increasingly hard to stomach and inimical to her vision of an heroic female rebellion. Her understandable efforts to spotlight women's struggles as women have bequeathed to us the potent image of the bravely broken suffragette at war with and sometimes crushed by a male establishment. But the enduring pictures of martyred suffragettes starving in cells or falling under hooves should not obliterate the fact that much suffrage agitation was an entirely traditional matter of demonstrations, processions, petitions, and lobbying. Moreover, even "terrorist" activists were often nurtured in an encouraging family context, growing up with the assumption that they were fit for the franchise. Indeed considerable organized male support for the cause was forthcoming, however difficult condescending male sympathy was to swallow at the time.

Both in continuing beyond the conventional 1914 watershed and in its focus on wider networks of support, John's chapter aims to counter the tendency to see the pre-war suffrage campaign as, in Cheryl Law's words, "an isolated political pantomime characterised by eccentric middle class women, unrepresentative of their sex, propelling their cause with a flash onto the historical stage before disappearing into satisfied anonymity."[106] As John concludes, a broader history of the movement, combined with careful attention to the changing parameters of politics before and after 1918, should also help us "move away from the labels of 'First Wave' and 'Second

Wave' feminism which not only somehow suggest that feminism is a fashion but also can camouflage the continuities, developments, and complexities of adapting needs and demands to shifting political circumstances."[107]

≺ VIII ≻

The Limits of Citizenship, 1918 to the Present

For the children of the Victorians, the years after the First World War delivered both "emancipation" and "modernity," though both fell short of complete equality of the sexes. Nevertheless, when judged against the long history of women's legal subordination and political exclusion, women's twentieth-century gains are stunning and bear repetition here. The Representation of the People Act of 1918 enfranchised 8.4 million female voters, joined by another 5 million after the Equal Franchise Act of 1928; thereafter the majority of the electorate was female. With the passing of the 1919 Sex Disqualification (Removal) Act, for the first time in history women had an explicit statutory right to be Members of Parliament, jurors, and Justices of the Peace. Technically this act also opened the doors of the universities and the professions to women. In the same year, on December 1, 1919, the first woman MP, Lady Nancy Astor, took her seat in the house, while 1929 saw Margaret Bondfield made Labour Minister for Labour, the first woman ever to enter the cabinet. Although Viscountess Rhondda failed in her attempt to take her place in the House of Lords, female life peers finally entered the upper house in 1958.[108]

Wives were at last enabled to sue for divorce on the same terms as men thanks to the Matrimonial Causes Act of 1923, while changes in the law of property in 1926 and 1935 increased women's financial independence from men. Notoriously, the non-working, dependent wife and mother was basic to the Beveridge report of 1942 and thus the provisions of the post-war Welfare State. As Kingsley Kent summarizes, "under the provisions of the National Insurance Act [of 1946], the breadwinner ideal enjoyed official sanction: unemployed, ill or disabled men received benefits from the state to make up their lost wages; unemployed, ill, or disabled married women received (fewer) benefits from the state only when the provider of first resort—their husbands—were unable to support them."[109] Nevertheless, married women's employment increased markedly from the 1940s onward, ironically much of it in the rapidly expanding bureaucracy of the Welfare State. Furthermore, the hated marriage bar was suspended for teachers during the Second World War and finally abolished in 1944, as an amendment to the Butler Education Act. The marriage bar was abolished in the civil service in 1946. Women were recognized as a permanent part of the police force in 1945 and finally admitted to the diplomatic and foreign service after the war. Women's individual citizenship gained further recognition in the British Nationality Act of 1948, which allowed for women to keep their nationality on marriage. The first measures of equal pay (for civil servants and teachers) were passed by a Conservative government in 1954 and 1955, but the removal of striking (though by no means all) anomalies awaited the passing of the Equal Pay Act of 1970 and the Sex Discrimination Act of 1975 by Harold Wilson's Labour governments. Unforgettably, the first female prime minister came to power in 1979.

Despite all these real gains in women's rights, the years between 1918 and 1968 for many delivered a frustrating lack of excitement. In popular mythology and in much historiography the impact of partial female suffrage in 1918 and universal female suffrage in 1928 is seen as profoundly anti-climactic. Disappointment pervades much writing. There was no revolution in gender roles. Indeed if anything, domesticity was reimposed on women all the more crushingly in a wide-ranging, post-war backlash.[110] The women's movement splintered and abandoned the dramatic activism of the pre-war years. "By the end of the 1920s," concludes Susan Kingsley Kent, "feminism as a distinct political and social movement had become insignificant."[111] Meanwhile, the female impact on party politics was superficial and on policy minor—and where women did shape legislation they tended to focus on women's traditional roles, reinforcing the conventional sexual division of labor. As Harold Smith somberly concludes,

Some of the legislation which appeared to be an important victory for feminism was phrased in such a way as to give the appearance of substantial reform while actually impeding change. Most of the legislation enhanced the status of mothers, thus encouraging women to view motherhood as a woman's primary function, rather than facilitating new roles. What seems most striking about this burst of legislative activity is the extent to which non-feminist forces guided the pressure for reform into channels which preserved women's traditional place in society."[112]

Further, the Second World War brought few unambiguous, long-term gains for women, and even the great challenge of "second wave" feminism in the 1960s and 1970s hardly revolutionized the fundamental structures of family life.

Pat Thane's chapter is a useful counter to these excessively pessimistic views of women's concrete political achievements post 1918. As she emphasizes, we must ask how realistic are our expectations: would the structures of a millennium be overthrown in the first 100 days of power? History suggests a long lag between enfranchisement and effective dominance. Middle-class men did not command British politics for some decades after enfranchisement in 1832; working-class men did not wield true leverage until some 50 years after partial enfranchisment in 1867. Eleanor Rathbone for one was conscious of the gritty difficulty of the task faced by women activists who no longer sought the comparatively easy goal of "a big elemental ... simple reform," but the "difficult re-adjustments of a complicated ... antiquated structure of case law and statute law."[113] Inter-war feminist activity might appear a sad falling away from the great days of passionate militancy, proof enough of the evaporation of feminist ardor, but in the scaling-down of public protest, feminists shared in the general taming of British politics after 1918. After the grisly horror of Paschendael and the Somme, violence was no longer an accepted part of *mainstream* party politics. It is in the context of this cooler climate that the scale of women's political achievement needs to be judged.

The disintegration of an allegedly cohesive feminism is a common lament, but as Cheryl Law insists, "No movement or party working out ideas and beliefs on its journey from oppression to emancipation, while devising campaign policies to effect that transition in the face of continued opposition could realistically expect to avoid conflict." Furthermore, one can see the efflorescence of different women's organizations (such as the National Union of Societies for Equal Citizenship, the Six Point group, the Women's Institute and the Townswomen's Guilds, the National Union of Women Teachers, the Council of Women Civil Servants, the Women's Sanitary Improvement and Health Visitors Union, the Women's Co-operative Guild, and so on) as a sign of strength not weakness. For Law, far from "duplicating effort and diluting effectiveness," the range and spread of organizations "was essential to cope with the enormity of the task in hand which concerned itself with every aspect of women's lives."[114] Similarly Thane sees no splintering of the movement, rather proof of the general permeation of public life by groups attempting to better women's lives. Moreover, despite the well-researched internecine conflict between "new feminists" and equality feminists, women's organizations worked together on issues such as the welfare of women and children and equal pay and against the marriage bar.

And indeed the impact women made on public policy was striking and significant. A surge of reforms demanded by organizations such as the Women's Co-operative Guild reached the statute book after 1918, including the Maternity and Child Welfare Act (1918), divorce on equal terms (1923), and Widows' and Orphans' Pensions (1925). For some, such welfare reform seems disappointingly lacking in revolutionary feminist fervor, yet to undervalue these efforts in Law's words "marks a failure to recognize the wretchedness of the poverty, dismal housing and lack of health care which burdened large numbers of women and children in particular." Here, Law insists, was "no dereliction of the feminist credo."[115] As Thane makes clear, though such reforms acknowledged women principally as mothers and homemakers, the intention was often to lighten the load of maternity in order that women might embrace life outside the home, not to incarcerate them. Freedom, Health, Reasonable Leisure, and Useful Public Service were all treasured aims of Labour women. In any case, reforms did mean real improvements in the quality of life as most women lived it. Improving the conditions of childbirth was particularly dear to the heart of organizations with large working-class membership such as the Women's Co-operative Guild and the Labour Party's women's sections. The Sex Disqualification (Removal) Act, as we have seen, enabled women to become magistrates. Though the history of female Justices of the Peace has long been neglected, their significance is worth noting. As Thane reports, by 1927 there were 1600 female J.P.s in England and Wales. "As well as admitting women to an influential area of public life, this change brought to an end the situation in which, throughout time, women involved in the legal processes, such as those concerning marital or family matters or cases of physical and sexual assualt, had faced courtrooms wholly composed of men."[116] Of course, the doors of all the professions were hardly flung open. The marriage bar certainly spread between the wars, but recorded numbers of women in paid employment increased in the 1930s, though as Thane emphasizes the chronic unemployment and laissez-faire response of the inter-war years militated against *any* section of the population gaining improved conditions in the labor market.

There is no firm evidence to suggest that once the vote was achieved the vast majority of women were uninterested in it, disengaged from political debate, or in any sense simply deferential to the opinions of husbands and fathers. Of course, party activism is always a minority pursuit for men or women, but thousands joined the three major parties in the 1920s. One might imagine that the Labour Party, as the party of the dispossessed, was the natural home for politicized, newly enfranchised, idealistic women, and certainly by 1927 there were 300,000 female members.

The Labour Party's receptiveness to women and the impact women had (and have) on the party is still open to debate. As Martin Francis concludes, there was always a contradiction between Labour as the standard bearer of a broad-based humanitarianism, emphasizing dignity and emancipation for all, and Labour as the defender of the interests and privileges of male manual workers. This conflict led to frustration for women as well as success. For Francis, "women made a vital contribution to shaping the character and programmes of the party (especially in regard to welfare) but found progress in some areas (such as equal pay) unsatisfactorily slow." Nor did women members find much institutional reward within the people's party. The overwhelming power of the trade union block vote at the annual conference offset the influence of female Labour Party members (roughly half of the individual membership), and stemmed any radical feminization of party policy. While there were always more female MPs in the Labour Party than in the other parties, their numbers were still unimpressive. "There were the same number of women standing for parliament in 1964 as there had been in 1935 (thirty three), and that figure had risen to only fifty by 1974." And until the 1980s, if not beyond, Labour women were mostly marginalized from centers of power within the party.[117]

Thane's emphasis is more optimistic. Though we should not underestimate male resistance to new party members, Thane stresses that there is evidence to suggest the particular importance of women to a redefinition of Labour goals between the wars. In Preston, for instance, the women's section of the local Labour Party made up of mill workers persuaded their representatives to support a wide-ranging welfare program of maternity and child welfare, educational improvement, public baths, housing, and health care. Michael Savage credits this reorientation with the transformation of this archetypal cotton town from a Conservative to a Labour stronghold.[118] Though they often found it difficult to be heard or selected as candidates, female members sought a political education through organizations aiming to teach campaign skills in all three parties. Still there is no denying the depth of hostility to women at Westminster. As the first serving MP, the Conservative Lady Astor concluded "If I'd known how much men would hate it, I would never have dared do it."[119] But the acknowledgment of how "profoundly inhospitable" to women was political culture should not be read as a comment on how little female politicians have achieved, rather as an index of how hard they have struggled.

As Thane concludes, to assume that the achievement of the vote had no effect just from an examination of the 1920s and 1930s is to expect too much too fast. To expect an absolute revolution in gender roles at any time in the twentieth century as a consequence of the vote is to mistake the ambitions of the women's movement, and perhaps the vast majority of the female population. Nevertheless, she argues, there "was change in the ways in which women lived their lives, which enabled successive generations to imagine a wider range of possibilities and a greater sense of their capacity to control their own lives. The feminists of the 1960s, after all, were the daughters of the first generation of women who grew up knowing that they could control the size of their families, that they had the vote on equal terms with men, and that they had effective equality before the law."[120] Indeed it was the celebration of 50 years of female enfranchisement which occasioned the full flowering of second-wave feminism in 1968—a powerful testimony to the continuing symbolic power of the vote.

If the tamer female politics of the twentieth century caused disappointment, the vitality of female Conservatism has bred fatalistic despair. Although the Labour Party has done much to champion equal rights and humanitarianism, women have been seen to vote Tory in appalling numbers. The essentialist view that women are innately Conservative and conservative has become lodged in popular political understanding—a belief that eighteen years of Tory hegemony between 1979 and 1997 did much to feed. But for all our assumptions, there has been little academic examination of the motivation behind female Conservative voting, or study of the Conservative Party's construction of an ideological appeal to a female constituency, or serious measurement of the importance of female membership within the party, or an assessment of their influence on policy. It is in response to this research vacuum that David Jarvis offers in this volume a wide-ranging assessment of the interaction of women and the Conservative Party in the twentieth century and a thoroughgoing assault on essentialist readings of a natural female political character. In a three-pronged argument, Jarvis considers female voting, party membership, and the changing construction of the party's ideological appeal to women.

If Conservatism is often seen today as a latent female vice, it is ironic that late-Victorian Tories were far from complacent about the impact the enfranchisement of women would have on their party's fortunes. In fact, even as the Primrose Dames surged forth on their bicycles, there was considerable apprehension and ambivalence within the party about the prospect of a female electorate, an anxiety which was not unjustified. Though the evidence produced by political scientists on the persistence of the gender gap is often invoked to buttress the view that women as a group simply and always vote Tory, on closer examination female support for the party can be seen to fluctuate markedly and to vary according to age and social class. Indeed, Ina Zweiniger-Bargielowska reveals that in 1945 and 1966 a majority of women supported Labour, while since the 1970s the differences in male and female voting have narrowed.[121] In 1997, young women deserted the Conservatives in droves—ironically a breed similar to young working women who so appalled and perplexed the Tories in the 1920s. As Jarvis concludes, the "evident volatility and social and generational variables inherent in the gender gap should now lay finally to rest tired essentialist assumptions about the 'innate' or natural conservatism of women."[122]

Of course, from the aristocratic Primrose Dames of the 1880s and 1890s to the blue-rinse constituency workers of today, formal female membership of the Conservative Party has been impressive in comparative terms. Yet the relative success of the Conservative Party does not mean that female membership over the twentieth century was static and faithful, or that membership translated into executive power. The National Union, the club movement, and the Primrose League successfully integrated the party into working-class communities by 1900. In fact, the Primrose League with its conspicuously large female membership was particularly important in weaving Conservatism into the very stuff of local life, since active leaguers usually held prominent roles within community associations and charities. Undoubtedly, the experience of political cooperation with women between 1880 and 1918 helped sections of the Tory party come to terms with female enfranchisement, or in Jarvis's phrase "sugared the impending pill of full female citizenship,"[123] although there was still horror in some quarters as late as 1931. While the Primrose League declined rapidly in the 1920s, Conservative associations established separate women's sections after 1918. Although there was traditional male hostility to female party workers, the party increasingly saw the benefit of indefatigable female fund-raising and canvassing. The women's unionist association had over four thousand branches by 1924. In 1928, female membership of the party reached an impressive peak of one million. Even though numbers fluctuated subsequently, active female Tories were always more numerous than their Labour or Liberal counterparts. Female involvement continued on a splendid scale in the 1950s, but by the mid-1960s concern was expressed about the hemorrhage of younger women and in the 1970s and 1980s about the absence of professional women in the party. By the early 1990s, it was estimated that the average age of constituency activists was 62. In Jarvis's words "It is therefore clear that women's active membership of the Conservative Party has been no more static or 'reliable' than their votes."[124]

Undoubtedly, female party workers played an invaluable role in the vigor of the Conservative Party, particularly at a local level, raising money, canvassing, and serving politically ambitious men. Perhaps their most important contribution was through their links with non-political charitable organizations like the Women's Institute. But despite the conspicuous prominence of Margaret Thatcher, women's reward has not been impressive and it cannot be said that respect for female political acumen is a deep-seated Tory tradition. Indeed there is a continuing condescending tendency to attribute any female success to feminine allure. In the 1920s and 1930s, women's associations had to go out of their way to convince Tory men they were not feminists, and women rarely achieved senior elected office within full constituency association bodies. Women were often "marginalized, patronized, and ignored" and appreciated most for supplying tea, cakes, and walk-on glamor.[125]

To understand the shifting patterns of female loyalty to the Conservatives it is crucial to consider the party's ideological appeal to women, argues Jarvis. Here he follows historians of the nineteenth century like Jon Lawrence, who has urged that in trying to explain why men have tended to vote Labour and women Conservative "we must focus, not on the peculiarities of men and women, but on the peculiarities of political parties. That is we should analyse the gendered language and practice of political parties in an attempt to understand why they should have appealed differentially to men and women."[126] For all the disclaiming of high theory, Jarvis finds that Conservative ideology "has been very sensitive to, indeed was originally predicated upon, idealized gender roles, and the salience of this discourse ... has played a crucial role in determining the Party's success with that audience."[127] From the very first, mass female participation in Tory politics prompted an uneven process of ideological adaptation—a winding journey away from a libertarian defense of "masculine" popular culture and pleasure, in favor of a more woman-friendly celebration of hearth and home. Inter-war Conservative propaganda tried to make electoral capital out of a "female alienation from a 'beer and butty' culture of Labour and trade union politics [which] equated socialism with machismo and the unacceptable face of male aggression."[128] However, this adaptation reinforced the party's championing of negative models of political freedom. Party propaganda emphasized the socialist threat to domestic tradition and the well-being of children, invoking the unnatural horrors of such things as Russian baby farming. Increasingly, propagandists idealized women as mothers, their biological experience uniquely conditioning them to appreciate the inescapable realities of human nature. Women were also idealized as compassionate nurturers smoothing the way down the primrose path to caring capitalism.

But Tory woman was tough as well as tender, proof against self-indulgent, sentimental claptrap, for above all else she was a bastion of common sense. She sought the traditional personal freedom of bringing up her family without excessive intervention from busy-body organizations. Essential to this was the economic freedom of shopping and saving, not the false freedom of liberation in all its lurid modern forms. Though ideologues realized that promoting consumer freedom was a potentially dangerous strategy, as in practice the party could not always deliver on the standard of living, this was an even more prominent element in the party's appeal to women in the late 1940s, when housewives were promised freedom from the shortages and queues of Labour austerity.[129]

However, despite the fact that the Conservatives briefly championed several feminist demands for equal treatment in the 1950s (as a deliberate attempt to steal a march on Labour), underlying changes in women's lives and roles were deeply threatening to the party. There was little place for young female workers in Conservative propaganda between the wars, but at least the party could look forward to the days when flighty flappers became sensible married housewives balancing a domestic budget. But the massive increase in the numbers of married women moving into the labor market in the 1950s was profoundly disturbing to the traditional Tory vision of gender roles and home life. Hence the endorsement of the notorious view that married women's work resulted in broken marriages and juvenile delinquency. As Martin Francis stresses, the Conservative pursuit of freedom in the 1940s and 50s (and 1920s) was always tempered by a concern to preserve conventional morality, even if this required authoritarian policing by the state to banish deviancy.[130] But as the right to work replaced the right to shop at the top of the hierarchy of Conservative economic freedoms, the latent contradictions within the party's ideological system emerged in sharp relief. Thatcherite ideologues were forced into unconvincing attempts to reconcile libertarian economics with the traditional dream of the non-working wife and mother as moral guardian, through such ill-judged efforts as John Major's back-to-basics campaign. But in promoting a model of family life so at odds with facts of female work and child-care patterns the Tories were seen to deny women the very economic freedoms which they claimed to offer all. As Ian Crowther pithily confirmed, "Conservative freedom is not about freeing women from the home."[131] The party signally failed to adapt its ideology to the realities of life for 80 percent of the adult female population. As we have seen, younger women have deserted the party in droves. It remains to be seen whether the party can remake an alliance which has always been crafted and contingent. Conservative womanhood could turn out to be an oxymoron after all.

≺ IX ≻
Conclusion

The great story of women's battle for political rights in the late nineteenth and early twentieth centuries deserves to be set in a much larger historical context than the one it usually inhabits, a context that extends further both in its chronology and in its definition of the political. It is with this task that this volume is centrally concerned.

It begins by considering the power unenfranchised patrician women were able to wield by virtue of their rank and wealth in the period when aristocratic government was at its apogee. However, the limits on elite female power both before and after 1832 are worth remembering. Only heiresses and widows personally gripped the reins of power through unusually direct control of their wealth and patronage, and even they had to work within a system operated at virtually every level by men. There was an iron ceiling on the political participation of even the most privileged women. Further research must also ascertain whether the well-documented and highly-publicized party political activities of aristocratic women were exceptional. How far female canvassing, election management, or explicitly political hospitality extended down the social hierarchy is debatable, though it is clear that some noble tactics were shared more widely, such as the manipulation of kin, ceaseless letter-writing, deliberate consumerism, and the flaunting of symbols.

An implicit question which follows is to what extent female politicians might be said to have developed a distinctively female political style? Or is it more fruitful to see patrician women as simply deploying class privilege in a manner identical to that of their men? After all, in a society inured to hierarchy, there were plenty of opportunities for women to wield power over inferiors. In seventeenth- and eighteenth-century common law, women were authorized to mete out moderate corporal punishment to children and servants for instance, just as men were allowed to dole out the same to their wives. Indeed one could argue that female aristocrats benefited from a hierarchical system which accepted a delegatory view of political authority; essentially they wielded power as surrogates for the men in their families, as honorary males. Whether this matters to the substance of their authority is not clear, but surely in the end it is the political effect of their power that is more significant than the name in which it was wielded. It remains to be seen, however, whether aristocratic women pushed different political imperatives to their men, or whether noblewomen's political ideas were simply subsumed within the ambitions of the great political families. Yet patronage, alliances, and electoral management were not the totality of political life. Reintegrating aristocratic women within the traditional analysis of eighteenth- and early nineteenth-century high politics is long overdue, but we should still retain an awareness of the importance of extra-parliamentary opinion in the shaping of political argument and policy making at Westminster. The changing contours of female ideological engagement and participation in political culture remain to be mapped, particularly for the eighteenth and early nineteenth centuries.

The long history of charity and associational life also cries out for a broader treatment which thinks through their relationship to political change. Organized female charity predated the repressions of the 1790s and Hannah More's clarion call in *Coelebs in Search of a Wife* of 1809, but the 1810s and 1820s witnessed a sea change in terms of both exploding numbers and heightened meaning. Yet we must remember that philanthropic associations and reform campaigns attracted women from aristocratic as well as a wide range of commercial and professional backgrounds, and moreover galvanized women *across* the political and religious spectrum. Of course, women's associational life was typically a segregated one, but it nevertheless offered thousands of women a new administrative training and an expanded field of public endeavor, all the while cultivating a sense of civic responsibility. Though we are familiar with the argument that here was the training ground for organized feminism, we must also recognize that here too are the antecedents of Tory constituency organization and municipal government. In both cases, it is clear that the experience of associations is something that properly belongs within an expanded definition of the political. What is suitably feminine philanthropy in one generation becomes local government in the next, both still unpaid.

Moreover it is through associational life that at last women asserted a legitimate authority over public questions as women, albeit as properly feminine, domesticated, and maternal women. When the Manchester Abolitionists appealed in 1787 for female aid in the *Manchester Mercury*, they promised that benevolent public action would be the ultimate expression of sensitive femininity, not its negation.

If any public Interference will at any TIME become the Fair Sex; if their Names are ever to be mentioned with Honour beyond the Boundaries of their Family, and the Circle of their Connections, it can only be, when a public Opportunity is given for the Exertion of those Qualities which are peculiarly expected in, and particularly possessed by that most amiable Part of the Creation—the Qualities of Humanity, Benevolence and Compassion.[132]

To modern ears, such an assertion of feminine difference sounds profoundly reactionary. Still as Claire Midgeley, Peter Mandler, Pat Hollis, and Linda Walker (among others) have pointed out, the much-flaunted mission of the fair sex turned out in practice to be remarkably all-embracing in its scope. And moreover, female association was not seen as a mild, genteel, or trivial venture at the time; for some the prospect was deeply unsettling. Gleadle finds that Eliza Fletcher's female benefit society affronted the Edinburgh authorities in the 1790s, appalled that ladies of "democratic principals" should be leading a public institution. Indeed they were convinced that this was "so novel and extraordinary 'proceeding as ought not to be countenanced.'"[133] Since the language of feminine conscience was so hard for men to disparage, it must have been one of the first rhetorical gambits that cynics and realists pressed into service. Linda Colley is also convinced of its effectiveness. "When British women posed as ... selfless activists who had left their customary domesticity only in order to further the greater good, they put on powerful armour against the lances of misogyny and condescension. In this guise, female voices could be heard in Westminster."[134] Of course, this emphasis on feminine difference had potential drawbacks. Still, as I have argued elsewhere, insofar as the language of separate spheres became more powerful and pervasive in the first half of the nineteenth century, women became more adept at deploying or subverting it to justify an enormous range of institutional activities and public endeavors.[135]

Another message of this book is the need to widen our definition of the political sphere to incorporate not just the reading public and voluntary associations evoked by Habermas, but also politicized households, family connections, and friendship networks—fora within which political ideas were thrashed out and new social practices developed and lived out. Although political subcultures and counter-cultures were probably only named and celebrated as such in the 1960s, they have existed for centuries. The importance of a broader radical political milieu which embraced both women and men is emphasized by Gleadle, Rendall, and John. The feminist heroic mode has accustomed us to see female activists as unique, defiant outsiders rebelling against their crushing families, but new research reveals many of them nurtured in comparatively congenial familial and social networks. Certainly there were many coteries which supported a more enlightened attitude to female political rights, as one element in a broader radical commitment, across the nineteenth century. However, the increase in general sympathy for women's citizenship over the nineteenth century was not a steadily rising tide. It ebbed decisively after the death of John Stuart Mill. Meanwhile, for all the late nineteenth-century increase in female public speaking in organizations like the Primrose League, the Women's Liberal Federation, and the early socialist groups, party political meetings "remained powerfully male environments," despite the fact that women were not formally excluded. Indeed the suffragette disruption campaign was as much an attempt to indict male political customs as to appropriate them, demonstrating the pressing need for a feminization of politics for the good of all; a campaign which reminds us that definitions and characterizations of politics can themselves be politically charged.

Finally, let us take stock of the limits of citizenship and political victory. In terms of direct political involvement, women have remained a minority of the membership of the major political parties. Women party activists in all parties have faced considerable obstacles at every level, as the tiny number of women who have ever served as MPs demonstrates. But, as Pat Thane makes clear, to assume that the vote should have changed everything would be to ignore a central message of this book: that women's political engagement always involved more than simply the struggle for the suffrage, however dominant that struggle became in the first two decades of the twentieth century. Male suspicion and condescension to politically active women continued after the vote was won. The post-1918 political establishment was hardly universally receptive to female emancipation (as late as 1931, the Conservative Party old guard were still appalled by the prospect of the fully enfranchised woman) or tolerant of women on their platforms and in their smoke-filled rooms. The political culture of the inter-war years may have become less brutally masculine than its predecessor, but men continued to see women primarily in their roles as housewives, mothers, and consumers. So it is not surprising that it was in the area of welfare that women political activists were able to score signal successes in the post-suffrage era. Moreover marriage, motherhood, and provisioning the household remained central to the experience of most women voters, so it is equally unsurprising that the Conservatives often succeeded with women by dignifying these roles in their rhetoric and promising real benefits in the shopping basket. Conspicuously lacking in Conservative ideology, however, has been an acceptance of the implications of married women's work, although accommodating the working mother has not proved an easy task for Labour either, whether in old or new guises.

A muted theme in this volume is the extent to which political performance was inevitably bound up with different constructions of manliness—from the sexual and political libertarianism of Wilkes and the generous freewheeling heterosexuality of Charles James Fox (contrasted to the fastidious frigidity of the younger Pitt), to the self-conscious uxoriousness of the radical unitarians, the chivalrous superiority of "the suffragettes in trousers," and the robust machismo of the electioneers of late Victorian and Edwardian street politics.[136] The culture of Westminster has long been powerfully masculine. Indeed it is striking and perhaps significant that while most of the female writers in this volume have stressed the potentialities of female politics and instances of effective co-operation between men and women, the male contributors have emphasized male resistance and deep-seated misogyny. Of course, that the palace of Westminster functioned as a gentleman's club, a bastion of self-important masculine conviviality, is a truism. It was an old nineteenth-century joke that marriage transformed the lazy MP into a keen attender. When Grantley Berkeley recalled in 1866 his thwarted attempts to improve the Ladies' Gallery he presented curmudgeonly masculine opposition with affectionate humor.

> One dear, gallant old soldier now no more, who served on [the Ladies' Gallery Committee] asked me "what could I be thinking of to propose a gallery for women; you're married," he continued, "and you ought to have remembered that when a man is in Parliament the business of the house is always an excellent excuse for not being at home. If you get a comfortable gallery, and make attendance at debates a fashion among women, we shall have our wives looking us up." "Then why don't you move a skulking room for men?" I retorted. "But at all events you have got the library where you can be supposed to be reading or writing if your better half should be scanning the benches and not see you; so old boy you may do 'em yet."

When Nancy Astor, MP for Plymouth, braved the male sanctum in 1919, Winston Churchill later admitted "I felt like a woman had entered my bathroom and I had nothing to protect myself with except a sponge."[137] Given the fear and resentment of women among Conservative Party activists uncovered by David Jarvis, and their deep desire to preserve real politics for real men untainted by the advancing tide of allegedly fussy, spiteful, and hysterical women, with their whist drives and fetes, the Conservative Party seems hardly more welcoming to women than the union-dominated Labour Party.[138] We should not underestimate male support for female political ambitions before 1918, but neither should we assume that male resistance melted away with progressive legislation.

Of course, female political engagement was always broader than Westminster party politics and women's issues as defined at Westminster. No less than in the nineteenth century, the enfranchised women of the twentieth remained vigorously active in unpaid public service, pressure groups, campaigns, and counter cultures, some of which they shared with men, but others of which were characteristically female. Many of the issues that exercised radical women in the 1830s according to Sarah Richardson—sexual politics, humanitarianism, the claims of children, the rights of oppressed minorities throughout the world, cruelty to animals, vegetarianism, and alternative medicine—continue to engage tens of thousands of women very powerfully today. That so much of this engagement thrives outside the official machinery of politics is testimony to the vitality of a distinctively female (probably middle-class) political practice. It also suggests the continuing limits of the alleged desire of Westminster politicians to embrace the whole range of women's political concerns.

However, the hopes of many were raised high in 1997. As Pat Thane reminds us, "the general election of May 1997 brought an unprecedented number of women into the House of Commons and into ministerial office, as a result of a commitment to greater gender equality on the part of influential sections of the victorious Labour Party."[139] Although the press mocked "Blair's babes," the sight of so many younger female MPs did contrive to make the Labour Party appear the standard bearer of a modern, progressive culture, with the Tories reduced to a gerontocratic rump. With hindsight, however, the Labour Party does not appear so "woman friendly" as on that sunny day in 1997 when Tony Blair walked onto College Green and was photographed with 101 women MPs. Leading Labour stateswomen—Mo Mowlam, Harriet Harman, and Claire Short—have been marginalized, and the cabinet office's women's unit has been frustrated. Harman has complained at the way the party has fallen back on "militaristic, macho, hierarchical language and behaviour," MPs who are mothers have found the House anything but family-friendly in its hours and practices, while female voters have expressed disappointment that a new type of politics has not been delivered after all.[140] Is "real politics" by its nature always on the armed defensive, looking for a stronghold against the emasculating presence of women? As ladies toilets are now being built in the Palace of Westminster, let us hope that the House of Commons gun club will finally be its last redoubt.

"To Serve my friends": Women and Political Patronage in Eighteenth-Century England

ELAINE CHALUS

IN JANUARY 1759, Lady Henry Beauclerk first addressed the duke of Newcastle in his role as first lord of the Treasury in what was to become an extended campaign for patronage:

> As your Grace possobly may not give me an opertunety of Speaking to you before you See the King, I beg leave to tell you: I have wrote to His Majesty to beg an addition to My Pension. I have no reason to doubt of His Majestys good Intention towards me: but cannot hope to Succeed So well as by your Graces assistance. Therefore My Lord Duke flatter Myself you will on this occasion, recollect the many pretentions I have to the Royal Favour. I Shou'd not prehaps have wanted this Instance of It had not my Father risqued with the Late Lord Lincoln & others all His fortune in Supporting the Succession of the House of Hanover: I Value myself on the Honour of My family, who ventured, & was ruin'd. In So glorious a Cause but let not me & mine, be the only unprovided of that Sett. I dare not name a Sum: your Grace will find me now Stand, I believe the Lowest on the List. but I will hope Through your favour to receive from the Kings Bounty, a proper Maintainance, for Lord Lovelaces Daughter, a Servant of the late Queen's; and the Wife of Lord Henry Beauclerk.[1]

Lady Beauclerk's appeal is representative of patronage requests made by many eighteenth-century women and men: she appealed first for herself (to have her pension augmented) and then for her children; she made her requests both directly to patrons and indirectly through brokers, by letter and in person; and she was firm in her belief that she was owed patronage on personal and familial grounds. She based her arguments on a combination of factors, including rank, lineage, honor, loyalty, and service. Like most suppliants, she had no guarantee of success—immediate, or even eventual. Her arguments carried weight, however, and her determination and sheer dogged obstinacy finally produced results.

While it is a historical commonplace that the patronage system was central to eighteenth-century English politics, the fact that it involved women and that it was eminently suitable to women, especially women of the political elite, has received little attention. A unique, intermediate area of political involvement, patronage linked together social and electoral politics, providing women with an important way of participating in political life. Not only did it thrive in the gray areas between formal and informal political participation, public and private life, and the political and social arenas, but it also operated primarily through personal contact, "connexion," and persuasion. It operated as readily face-to-face in the dining room and ballroom as it did at politicians' levees, in the lobbies of Westminster, or at Court. It was in this very personal, socio-political world that women were likely to move most comfortably and be most active.

The flexibility of the patronage system, with its multiplicity of points of access and degrees of involvement, facilitated women's participation, allowing them to shape their actions to suit their inclinations or circumstances. The most informal and personal patronage requests were made, granted, or refused verbally; consequently, they appear only tantalizingly and anecdotally in surviving sources. It is rather through the more formal aspects of patronage, particularly women's written requests preserved in political correspondences, that we can come to some understanding of their motivations and methods, as well as an appreciation, albeit necessarily impressionistic, of the extent of their involvement.

Fortunately, plenty of patronage requests from women survive. Letters from women, many of whom have left no other historical records, pepper MPs' correspondences. The more patronage that a politician controlled personally, the better his connexions, greater his influence, or wider his networks, the more likely he was to be solicited by men and women alike. A rich and powerful aristocrat serving as first lord, thus having direct access to the king and the rich pickings of Crown patronage, was certain to be inundated with requests. And, when it came to patronage, the duke of Newcastle was arguably unequaled among eighteenth-century first lords.[2] By the time

Newcastle became first lord in 1754, he had nearly 50 years of political experience and was a past master of patronage and electoral management. His voluminous correspondence contains the most comprehensive collection of eighteenth-century patronage requests. Taken together, these requests provide an unrivaled insight into the workings of the patronage system and into eighteenth-century political life itself.

By examining women's patronage requests in the Newcastle papers during Newcastle's time as first lord, 1754–62, this chapter throws new light on an almost unrecognized aspect of eighteenth-century women's involvement in English political life. It reveals that a small but diverse group of women took an active part in patronage even at this highest of political levels. Moreover, it demonstrates that women took part in patronage for many of the same reasons, in much the same way, and with similar results, as their male counterparts. Women, like men, sought the five Ps of patronage—place, pension, preferment, Parliament, and peerage—with the object of obtaining something for themselves, something for their family members, or something for others (usually their friends, relatives, clients, or retainers). Operating as they did in what was still a predominantly familial political world, where a degree of female political involvement for family ends was accepted and often expected, they often turned their family roles as wives/widows, mothers, and daughters to patronage ends. While there were always more women who were clients than brokers or patrons, the Newcastle papers reveal that women in the latter two categories were by no means as rare as has been assumed. What is more, the avidity with which men and women sought the influence or patronage of female brokers and patrons testifies to the practical acceptance of women as political actors.

This, in turn, raises questions about patronage, about women's place in political society and, more generally, about the relationship between eighteenth-century politics and society. We need to restore due weight to those personal and social aspects of politics, like patronage, which have frequently been trivialized or dismissed, if we want to come to a more comprehensive understanding of eighteenth-century political culture. In order to do this, we need to reintegrate women into political life, paying careful attention to the complicated ways that the societal ideal of an apolitical femininity was modified or even confuted in reality. The picture that emerges from this study of women's involvement in patronage is of a sociopolitical world that was tightly knit, ambitious, and highly politicized; and that included a significant amount of involvement from women.

≺ I ≻

The Patronage System

Before turning to a general examination of women's patronage requests in the Newcastle papers, it is necessary to put the patronage system itself into context. There is no denying the importance of patronage in eighteenth-century political life. The expansion of the state and the growing importance of Parliament saw a significant rise in the amount of patronage available and in its importance as a tool of political management. In a political society where modern notions of professional, meritocratic, public service had yet to make any significant impact, and where access to the trinity of power, place, and profit remained personal and idiosyncratic, patronage operated through linked networks of individuals by means of such nebulous concepts as "interest" and "influence." Political patronage was only one manifestation of a universal phenomenon. As a means of recruitment and advancement, patronage also pervaded the eighteenth-century domestic, cultural, social, and economic domains. It was replete with meaning, as Linda Levy Peck's description of seventeenth-century patronage makes clear:

> At once symbiotic and symbolic, these private, dependent, deferential alliances were designed to bring reward to the client and continuing proof of power and standing to the patron. The establishment of patron-client relationships came about in many different ways: through appeal to mutual friends, to kinship ties, and to neighborhood bonds. Often, important courtiers and officials served as brokers to carry out patronage transactions. The language of patronage, situated in a theory of mutual, indeed, social benefits, and the practice of gift-giving, strongly marked political and social behavior.[3]

Despite its importance, eighteenth-century political patronage has frequently attracted more polemic than analysis. For many historians, especially those grounded in reforming or Whig traditions, it was simply something to be reacted against: a symbol of the "old corruption" of pre-Reform, pre-modern politics. Mary Bateson, for instance, writing in 1892, was representative in describing the "appetite for promotion" found in Newcastle's papers (and in eighteenth-century political correspondence in general) as both a "vice" and an "evil." Nor was she alone in smugly believing that it had been expunged by the forces of progress over the course of the nineteenth century.[4] It was not until the 1920s that Lewis Namier revealed the limitations of patronage in the eighteenth century and undermined the link between patronage and corruption. Not only did he demonstrate that the Crown and Treasury had less control over patronage than had often been assumed, but he was also able to show that patronage was generally used to reward past service or relieve current need. It was not a guarantee of future political support.[5]

With the rise of social history and the subsequent shift away from high politics, compounded perhaps by a modern distaste for the self-seeking sycophancy of client-patron relationships, patronage has received only sporadic and limited attention.[6] Intriguingly, the most comprehensive recent study of patronage and society has concentrated on the nineteenth century. In it, J. M. Bourne uncoupled the belief that nineteenth-century modernization spelled the death of patronage. He argued instead that while political reform gradually removed rotten boroughs and the most obvious forms of Crown and Treasury patronage, other opportunities for patronage actually increased in the nineteenth century. The growth of local and national government (especially the proliferation of boards, commissions, and committees), the creation of the civil service, the growing importance of empire (particularly India), the development of the honors system, and so on, all provided new possibilities for patrons and clients alike.[7]

Bourne's conclusions, those of an historian, echo those of social scientists, who have concluded that patronage adapts instead of disappearing with modernization.[8] Indeed, most of the recent research into patronage arises from social scientists' interest in the nature and operation of patronage as a system of transactions, relationships, and power. Their insights are useful to keep in mind when considering patronage in the eighteenth century. They see patronage as based upon "a certain logic of social exchange," structured around transactions which are unequal and open ended, but mutually beneficial. It is a system particularly well suited for apportioning resources in stratified societies.[9]

Patronage arrangements are made through networks of individuals, with clients approaching patrons directly or through brokers. The brokers' value is strategic, resting in the size of their networks, their access to information, and their proximity to (and influence over) patrons.[10] All of the parties enter into and end patronage relationships voluntarily, usually preferring to keep them indeterminate and long-term. A sense of debt and credit provides leverage for future transactions and allows the balance of power to shift with circumstances.[11] The gains offered by patronage may be tangible (jobs, money, position, votes) or intangible (good will, reputation, honor, promises of support, reciprocity, loyalty). The vertical connections created by patronage may predicate against the formation of strong horizontal ties, but the system as a whole is seen to encourage a sense of inclusivity or cohesion that might not otherwise be present in the society.[12] Paradoxically informal yet binding, patronage is at best quasi-institutional. It is also simultaneously public and private. Deals forged in private are displayed in public;[13] patron-client relations depend upon the public and the private spheres being inextricably intertwined.[14]

Eighteenth-century women's involvement in patronage, other than cultural patronage, has thus far received little attention from political or women's historians.[15] Still, there has been some important work on early modern women and patronage which demonstrates that eighteenth-century women's involvement had strong historical precedents. Recent publications by Barbara Harris and Linda Levy Peck[16] reveal that early modern English women used their positions as members of political families to seek cultural, ecclesiastical, or political patronage for themselves, their kin, or their clients. Harris's and Peck's publications show that these women operated through a multiplicity of connexions and patronage networks in much the same way as their male counterparts. Peck's work also suggests that early modern women made the transition from magnate-centered to Court-centered patronage by capitalizing on the societal acceptance of their earlier activities and quietly extending their activities into the new arena. A similar shift may well explain women's subsequent transition to parliamentary patronage in the eighteenth century.[17] Furthermore, in revealing that the institutional powerlessness of women could mask significant patronage power, both Harris and Peck echo a conclusion reached by Sharon Kettering in her study of the patronage power of early modern French noblewomen.[18]

≺ II ≻

Women's Requests to the Duke of Newcastle

A closer examination of the twists and turns of Lady Beauclerk's request for patronage, with which this chapter opened, serves as an instructive starting point to a study of women's requests in the Newcastle papers. Although Lady Beauclerk was a widow by the time that she finally achieved her goal, her husband, Lord Henry Beauclerk, was still alive in 1759 when she first wrote to Newcastle. The fact that she and not her husband conducted the campaign for patronage, and the arguments that she chose to support her claim, are significant. The Beauclerks were in a difficult position in 1759. Lord Henry's health was worsening and his limited income left him unable to make satisfactory provision for his growing family after his death. The family's financial problems were at least partly of his own making, however. He had incurred George II's lasting anger by quitting his regiment when it had been posted to Minorca for three years (ostensibly because he had not been able to obtain leave to settle his affairs in advance). As a result, he had been stripped of his military rank. Nor had his subsequent efforts to get back into the army—the patronage of which was jealously controlled by the king—been successful. Given these circumstances, it is not surprising that it was Lady Beauclerk who approached Newcastle for patronage or that she emphasized her claim to patronage through her own and her family's service to the Crown. She seldom mentioned her husband. In the end, she succeeded only after both Lord Henry and George II had died.[19]

When Lady Beauclerk learned that the king had refused her initial request, supposedly because he feared it would set a precedent and result in a flood of claims, she swiftly recast it. Within three days, she wrote again. This time, she shifted attention away from herself and onto her husband's inability to provide for their children;

she asked for a pension in the children's names or for a place for her husband. She drew upon a rhetoric of responsible motherhood and laid the blame for her situation at Newcastle's feet:

your Grace might propose Some thing in my Children's Name which wou'd be of the Same Service. My Son will be no troble to the Crown, nor wou'd my Daughters had Lord Hen: Beauclerk had the Common Chances, his Rank demanded: but unless your Grace can find Some employment he is worthy of. I fear I must Still be troblesome for myself & Girls. for you may believe, my Lord I must Suffer, whilst They are unprovided, and If I Suffer must apply for redress, To whom can I apply but to the King. & Through your Grace—.[20]

A little more than two weeks later, she wrote again. She promised to allay Newcastle's fears of setting precedents if he allowed her to wait upon him in person.[21] This was unnecessary, according to Newcastle, as the king was aware of her case. Newcastle promised, however, that he would support her request if she wrote directly to the king and he proved amenable.[22] A month later she wrote to tell him that she had just applied to the king for the Orchard Keeper's place for her daughter.[23] This too was refused.

After this letter there is a gap of nearly a year in their correspondence. A letter in March 1760 reveals that she made at least one attempt in the intervening period to obtain the place of Lieutenant of the Tower for her husband.[24] By 1760, though, she had become frustrated with what she interpreted as Newcastle's inaction. She modified her request yet again, resubmitting her request for the Orchard Keeper's place at Whitehall for her daughter and her initial application for an increased pension.[25] To persuade Newcastle that she was serious, she threatened to embarrass him at his own levee—traditionally a male event—if he continued to ignore her "pretentions": "[I] beg you will reflect How little Honour my Attendance at your Levee will do You: for There I must Come. However, disagreble to me, & However unused to Such attendance."[26] Newcastle must have believed that there was some chance that she would do just this, as he responded immediately: "If Your Ladyship has any Commands for me, which cannot be explained by Letter, I will, with great Pleasure, do Myself the Honor to wait upon Your Ladyship at Your own House." Adopting an injured tone, he promised that he would, if she was adamant, bring the matter up with the king yet again. But, he argued, the king simply "did Absolutely refuse to comply with it. And, that being the case, It is not possible for me to alter His Majesty's Resolution."[27] She, in turn, insisted that her case was unique:[28] "you can find no other person so Slenderly provided whose family has been So great Sufferers for The Crown."[29] In setting out her case for the king, she returned to this argument, reminding him that he had thought highly enough of her family to award her mother a pension, of which she still received £200 per annum (although she hastened to add that this was now worth little more than £100 after taxes). A larger pension would not only ease her financial situation, but also help her to instill loyalty to the Crown in her children: "an addition ... will enable us to bring up a Family by Nature attach't to your Majesty and by example most faithfull Subjects."[30]

While no further correspondence survives between Lady Beauclerk and Newcastle, she did not give up. Instead, she persuaded the young duke of Grafton to act as a broker. He was a relative of hers and a political supporter of Newcastle's. This time, she wanted her eldest daughter to be appointed a Maid of Honour at George III's wedding. Grafton made a very early application, writing shortly after George III came to the throne and reiterating arguments about the young woman's suitability. He stressed both her rank and her family history, reminding Newcastle that she had been educated "in the best manner," notwithstanding the financial difficulties posed by a large family and her father's limited fortune.[31]

Eventually, Lady Beauclerk's requests were granted. When the new Queen's household was finally settled in 1761, Miss Beauclerk was made one of the Maids of Honour.[32] Even more importantly, Lady Beauclerk also achieved her ultimate goal; she secured her daughters' financial security. An entry for "Martha, Ly Beauclerk, widow of Ld Henry Beauclerk in trust for her daughters £400 [p.a.]" appears on the Irish establishment in 1761 (at pleasure).[33] Success, however, did not come as a result of her requests to Newcastle. His unpopularity with the new king, his mother, and the favorite, Lord Bute, spelled a loss of influence and the end of his ability to secure Crown patronage.[34] But then, Lady Beauclerk had never confined her patronage requests to Newcastle alone. She had also approached other leading politicians, including William Pitt, whose wife acted as her broker.[35] Her patronage request was finally granted when Lord

Bute was at the height of his power. He was an old acquaintance of her late husband's and someone whose influence they had sought in the past. In 1761, he was closer to the king than any other politician.

Lady Beauclerk's case serves as a useful introduction to a study of women's involvement in patronage. It reinforces the notion that patronage operated, at least at the level of the political elite, in a familial political world. This, and the contemporary understanding of patronage as transactional, diffuse, and open-ended, facilitated both women's involvement and contemporary male acceptance of it. Lady Beauclerk's interactions with Newcastle reveal that women could have a sophisticated understanding of the workings of the patronage system and use their knowledge to make calculated requests. These requests could then be modified and supported by a variety of political, familial, or gendered arguments, as appropriate.

This suggests significant political acuteness. In order to make effective requests, women had to know what patronage was available and what would be suitable to their social status and personal circumstances. They also had to be astute enough to know which relatives, friends, or acquaintances—male or female—had influence with the patron and could either lend support or act as brokers. Finally, they had to be alert to changes in the political climate that might prejudice their chances of success by threatening patrons' access to favor or power.

While any attempt at quantifying the extent of women's overall participation in patronage is fraught with difficulties, a study of Newcastle's surviving patronage requests between 1754 and 1762 reveals that approximately ten percent of his total requests came from women.[36] This is a small proportion, but it is not insignificant. Moreover, it also considerably underrepresents women's overall involvement. Not only does it omit entirely that portion of patronage that was negotiated face-to-face in predominantly social situations, but it is also an incomplete record of women's written requests. As extensive as the Newcastle papers are, anecdotal references in other politicians' correspondences indicate that a variety of women's requests have gone astray over time. Still, Newcastle's requests serve as a snapshot of patronage at the very highest level of the political world in the middle of the eighteenth century. The papers of leading local families, backbench MPs, and leading politicians who were in charge of other, more specialized forms of patronage (Lord Hardwicke, Lord Holdernesse, and Henry Fox, to name only a few) all reveal additional requests. Some of these come from women who also wrote to Newcastle and were simply trying to elicit extra official support for their cases, but many are from women who are entirely unrepresented in the Newcastle papers. This is due, in part, to different networks of acquaintances and political affiliations, but it is also a reflection both of the decentered nature of power and patronage, and of women's knowing and selective applications.

The demand for patronage in eighteenth-century England always outstripped supply. Considering that women's ability to benefit directly from patronage was circumscribed by their inability to hold most government appointments or places, to serve in the Church, or sit in Parliament, it is perhaps remarkable to find them participating at all. Yet they did, both for themselves and for the men in their lives. As we have seen, their requests fell into the same five general categories as men's. Their requests used the same kind of political language as men's, were structured in the same ways, and obtained comparable results. It is a telling point about the relationship between class, gender, and politics in the eighteenth century that rank and relations (kin and others) appear to have mattered more than gender in shaping patronage requests and expectations, and in determining responses and outcomes.

Figures 1 and 2 compare women's and men's patronage requests to the duke of Newcastle at the beginning and end of his period in office. They reveal that, like men, women requested patronage for themselves, their family members, or others (their more distant relations, clients, or retainers). This is both unremarkable and revealing. It is not surprising to find women making requests for their male family members, particularly their sons. What is striking is the extent to which they used the system for themselves and for other men, who were not members of their nuclear families.

Women's requests for the men in their immediate families generally reflected a desire for social and financial improvement. They tried to secure patronage appointments for their sons, and occasionally their sons-in-law, which would provide financial security, wealth, or status (or all three, if possible). Since it was assumed that husbands could plead for themselves, women consistently made fewer requests for them than for their sons. Wives did step in, however, when their husbands were ill, obstinate, shy, or lacked the nec-

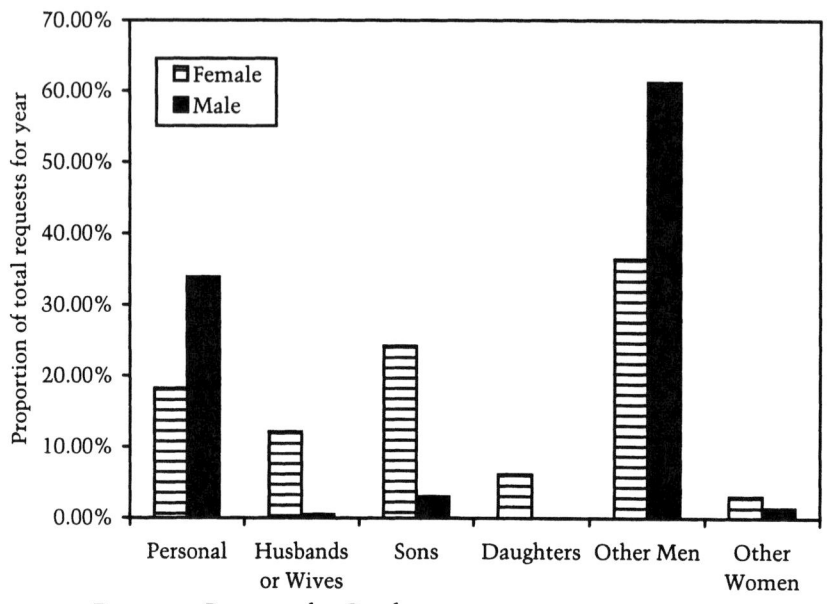

FIG. 1. Patronage Requests by Gender, 1754–55

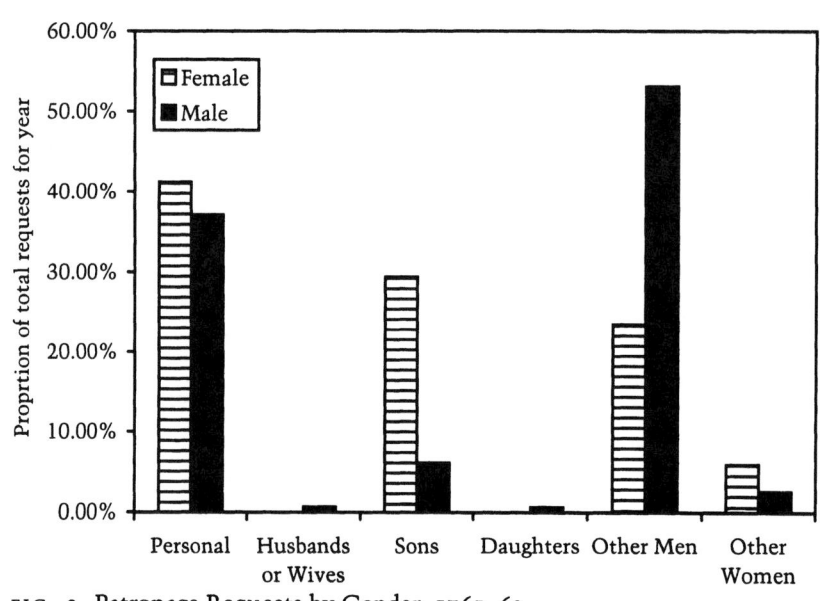

FIG. 2. Patronage Requests by Gender, 1761–62

essary connexions to achieve success. They were most likely to get involved in patronage if they were of higher social status than their husbands, if they came from politically active families, or if they had personal political connexions that provided them with more direct access to patrons and better chances of success.

Women's patronage requests for other men form a significant proportion of their total requests throughout Newcastle's time in office. These applications, which were usually for places or preferments, demonstrate that women's involvement in patronage extended beyond the narrow boundaries of their immediate families. Although women's motivations for involvement varied, their requests for other men reveal a widespread assumption that women who had political connexions or influence, or both, should use them to forward the applications of those who were deserving but less fortunate. Harriett Lane used exactly this argument when requesting the place of "Historiographer to the Kingdom" for a Mr. Arnott, a fellow of Clare Hall, Cambridge, who had a good education but little fortune, and little chance of increasing it save through patronage. The place was currently held by a Mr. Phillips, who, she claimed, "is said to be in a most declining state of health." She emphasized that Arnott would be "Perfectly contented with Gratitude to his Benefactor" if he was successful—in other words, he would not be seeking additional patronage in the future. She added that she wanted nothing herself: her request stemmed solely from her "desire to Serve my friends."[37]

Women's requests for other men frequently feature women with some degree of political influence operating as brokers. Yet, even here, the personal dimension of patronage remained important. Brokers seldom made requests for people they did not know personally. When they did, it was usually on the strength of recommendations from people they did know, and whose judgment they trusted.

What is perhaps the most interesting aspect of women's patronage requests to Newcastle between 1754 and 1762 is the extent to which they made applications for themselves. Their suits reflect the limited range of patronage opportunities open to women: close to two-thirds are concerned with financial arrangements, mainly pensions or annuities; places or peerages constitute the remainder. Not only did women deal with these issues themselves, but they also drew knowingly upon familial and political circumstances in order to justify their claims.

The pattern of women's requests between 1754 and 1762 suggests that they were aware of the larger political context in which patronage operated and made their requests accordingly. Newcastle's strong political position after the 1754 election was reflected in a large number of requests. When he resigned and was briefly out of office in 1756–57, the number of requests plummeted, only to rise again when he returned to power. Women's involvement peaked during the 1758–59 parliamentary season. This was the high point of the Seven Years War and the year before a general election; consequently, military and electoral patronage dominated requests. After George II died in October 1760, Newcastle's political position became increasingly tenuous. Although he continued in office under George III, he did so in the face of open hostility from the king and Lord Bute. As a result, his ability to deliver patronage diminished and he received fewer requests. Conversely, people who were in favor with the king and Lord Bute, or had direct access to them, such as Charles Jenkinson and the duke and duchess of Northumberland, received a growing number of requests.[38]

This suggests a significant level of female politicization. While it might be assumed that the female members of the aristocracy would be this politically aware, they were by no means the only women who wrote to Newcastle for patronage. Instead, patronage requests from women constitute a cross-section of English political society: 53 percent come from titled women (knights' wives upward); the remaining 47 percent come from untitled women (from women of the gentry down into the artisanate). They also appear to be demographically representative. At least 40 percent of Newcastle's female correspondents were married; at least as many were widows; only 8 percent can clearly be identified as unmarried.

In terms of structure, motivation, and supporting arguments, women's requests differ little from those of their male counterparts. The letters themselves conform to the same basic formula, with little regard to gender. They open with a brief apology for troubling the reader, followed by a passage setting out the writer's parentage and any pre-existing connexions with socially or politically important people (especially the reader). Special care is then taken to establish the claimant's worthiness by pointing out records of personal or familial political allegiance and service. Only after this is the case in question presented, complete with whatever extenuating circumstances make it particularly unique, worthy, or distressing. More apologies—rhetorical or otherwise—then ensue. The letters usually end in a flourish of expressions of thanks and subtle (or not-so-subtle) attempts to flatter the reader into action, usually by praising his or her reputation and public character.

≺ III ≻
Women as Clients

As clients, women, like men, sought patronage for a wide variety of reasons. Self-interest, duty, necessity, greed, and social or political aspirations all played their parts. Some women's requests were tentative, obsequious, and overly apologetic, but so too were some men's. Indeed, if a "sphere" existed with regard to patronage, it was one defined first and foremost by status and connexion, not gender. The less acquainted or lower in rank the clients, the more formal, self-deprecatory, or flattering the requests.

Exceptional circumstances could demand extra deference, however, even from people of equal rank. Compare, for example, the following excerpts from requests to the duchess of Newcastle. In the first, the correspondent approaches the duchess as a broker to Newcastle: "Your Grace's known goodness & Charitable Disposition makes us Humbly Hope, that You will Compassionate our unhappy Case, & be our Advocate with His Grace, since you cannot imploy those Noble Qualities upon Objects who stand more in need of Your Powerful Protection, then my Sister & My Self."[39] In the second, written two years after the duke's death, the correspondent approaches the duchess as a patron in her own right: "I can make no apology for the very great trouble I presume to wish Your Grace to give yourself, as it is solely upon my own account that I venture to request it, & feel but too conscious of my own unworthiness to imagine that I deserve so much favor at Your Graces hands."[40] The humility of the first writer is understandable: the client was a woman much lower in rank than the duchess and not well known to her. That of the second is more intriguing. The client in this instance was the young duke of Portland, a man who equaled the duchess in rank and knew her well. His deferential tone can be attributed, instead, to a number of factors: the disparity in their ages;

his respect for her personally and as the widow of his first political leader; and, finally, his desire to secure the three votes that she directed in the House of Lords as the acting head of the Pelham family.

Not all clients were especially humble. Older and more experienced women, and women of rank or fortune, were often the most confident. On the whole, however, the most assertive and knowledgeable patronage requests came from men and women who were members of politically active families and knew Newcastle personally, or were connected to him through family or politics. Most of these women had extensive and useful personal networks which provided them with valuable information and contacts. They were usually socially active and based in or around London during the parliamentary season. By background and experience, they were political insiders. They knew how the political world worked and used their knowledge and connexions to get what they wanted. In terms of patronage, they knew the proper channels of application and how best to present a case to get action.

Katherine, Duchess of Gordon, was especially highly skilled at turning her personal and political situation to patronage advantage.[41] As a young widow with four children, the eldest of whom was only nine, she had assumed control of the vast Gordon estates and political interest for her son and heir in 1752. A firm Whig supporter and an active politician, she was a force to be reckoned with in Scottish politics. Her patronage requests were clever and usually ended with some twist of service that made a refusal to comply seem like ingratitude. For instance, when she wanted to secure a place in the exclusive Guards for her second husband in 1759, she included several subtle hints about her political importance with her request. She reminded Newcastle that she would be directing the Gordon family interest for the upcoming election by telling him that she had already been approached by several candidates, but was awaiting his "Commands," "as I have always Acted in the way I thought was most agreable to Your Grace." She also pointed out that her brother, Lord Aberdeen, another leading Scottish Whig, supported her suit.[42]

Just over a month later she sent Newcastle another request. This time she wanted to assert her claim to a £400 per annum pension that Newcastle's late brother, Henry Pelham, had promised her would come to her on Lady Stair's death. To this end, she combined an encomium on Pelham with information calculated to please the king and show her patriotism: she sent a glowing report of her success in raising the first Gordon regiment.[43] In the spring of 1760, when this regiment was unexpectedly posted to the East Indies, she used every argument at her disposal to get it reassigned. She pointedly called Newcastle's attention to "that Unwearied Zeal I have always show'd to his Majestys Person and Government." She emphasized the part that she had played in raising the regiment and the steps that she had taken to ensure that it was done quickly and well—including taking her young son to Scotland to boost recruitment among the tenants. She stressed that sending the regiment to the East Indies would color the way that her "young Family" viewed "this first Essay of their early Zeal for His Majestys Person & Government." And, astutely, given Newcastle's electoral concerns in this election year, she argued that it would upset the tenants' confidence and have dire political consequences, both for her family's political interest and for the Whig interest in Scotland: "I can assure your Grace no measure could be more hurtfull to Government in our Part of the World, as well as to my Sons Interest."[44]

Some correspondents were less likely to craft their requests. Aristocrats of both sexes could be brief to the point of brusqueness. They frequently even dispensed with salutations and most social niceties. A request from Anne, Duchess of Hamilton, would have left Newcastle in no doubt that she wanted to have a Mr. Carter appointed to the next vacant stall in Windsor, Westminster, or Canterbury: "I repeat the next as his advanced time of life leave him no view to distant prospects." To encourage a notoriously dilatory Newcastle into action, she brought her political position to bear— "if all my Weight & interest merit your Grace's regard, I hope this application will succeed." She also took more practical steps, empowering the man who took the letter to Newcastle to "enforce" her request "in the strongest manner."[45]

Personal political credentials were undeniably valuable in the quest for patronage, as they held out the promise of a direct return for the patron, but women and men also placed overwhelming emphasis on status, real or fabricated family membership (by birth or marriage), and traditions of service. Consequently, Maria Constantia Nethercott, whose family background was more noteworthy than her husband's, made much of it when she applied to have either her pension renewed or a place for her husband. She was Admiral

Rodney's sister and she brought the full weight of the Rodney family's tradition of loyalty and service to the Crown to bear in supporting her request: "my Family for many Generations past of both sides have been Servants of the Crown, the Rodneys always in the Navy & Army, & my Grandfather Sir Henry Newton was twenty one Years Minister at Genoa & Florence."[46] Lady Forbes deployed a variation on this familial argument when she used her position as a widow and matriarch to support her petition for the reinstatement of a pension which had been inexplicably stopped after her husband's death. Since pensions were not normally recalled unless the receivers had forfeited them through bad behavior, it was her duty as the head of the family to protect the family's reputation and have the pension restored. She was particularly concerned about the damage being done to her family's reputation by "being treated, on a foot, with those who do not entertain, Greatfull, and Loyal Sentiments for our Royal Benefactor."[47]

This familial emphasis was due to the familial nature of politics at mid century and to the flexible, long-term nature of patronage. "Debts" incurred in the past could be paid by patronage in the present; conversely, patronage in the present could create obligations for the future. When Lady Deskfoord wrote to inform Newcastle that Lord Kintore was dying and to ask that her husband be awarded Kintore's pension of £400 per annum and his position of "Knight Marischal" (worth another £400 per annum), she did so because her husband refused to write "about any thing he himself may possibly be concern'd in."[48] Lord Kinnoull, one of Newcastle's trusted advisers on Scottish affairs, gave his hearty approval. The appointment, he told Newcastle, would make sound political and financial sense. It would give Newcastle, "an Oppertunity of terminating an Affair which has given you so much Trouble, to the Satisfaction of the Person's concerned, without any Additional Charge to the King's Revenue."[49]

The more complicated the case, the greater the sense of obligation. When Ladies Jane and Margaret Leslie submitted their memorial for a pension, they set out their case along conventional lines. They wanted support from the state because the expenses that their father had incurred during the reigns of Queen Anne and George I, "in the Service of the Government, and in Support of the Whig Interest in Scotland," had made him unable to provide for them.[50] A covering letter from their eldest brother, Lord Rothes, set out the complicated familial machinations which underlay their petition. What the family actually wanted was the revival of a pension of £400 per annum, formerly held by an aunt and her son, now both deceased. If granted, the pension would be split among the sisters and another brother. The entire amount had to be issued in the women's names, however, as the brother's employment would be compromised if he was awarded anything openly. Success in this undertaking, Rothes assured Newcastle, would lay "a Lasting obligation on me & my family."[51]

Determining the outcome of patronage requests—men's or women's—and ascertaining what made some requests successful is difficult. This is due in part to the decentralized nature of the patronage system and the varying quality of surviving sources. It is further complicated by the fact that even the most complete sources contain far fewer responses than requests. Some answers simply have not survived; others were given verbally or were not recorded. Answers are also difficult to trace, because patronage was so open ended. The period between requests and responses could vary greatly. In some rare instances Newcastle received and answered requests on the same day. Most, however, took much longer; sometimes even years.

Women would not have submitted as many requests as they did, or phrased them as commandingly, if they had not stood a chance of achieving their goals. Of the 51 responses that survive for women's requests between 1754 and 1762, 57 percent were successful and a further 24 percent were potentially successful (that is, promises were given that they would be filled as soon as possible). This is a small sample and it is unlikely that all of the promises materialized, but it does confirm that women's applications were taken seriously, even at the highest political levels, and that there was enough chance of being successful to justify involvement.

Indeed, this conclusion is borne out by the number of women on the English and Irish establishments. Newcastle records 119 women receiving pensions of £10 to £1,000 per annum on the English civil list between 1754 and 1762. Similarly, Lord North's register for the period up to 1761 includes 122 women receiving between £15 and £1,000 per annum. An identical exercise for the Irish civil list, carried out in 1763 not long after Newcastle left office, identifies yet another 71 women, chiefly English. Amounts on the Irish establishment were usually larger than those on the English, and women's pensions, ranging from £18 5s. to £5,000 per annum, were no exception. The largest of the Irish pensions went to Princess Amelia and Princess Mary of Hesse (£1,000 and £5,000 per annum, respectively), and to George II's mistress, Lady Yarmouth (£4,000 per annum).[52] The number of women on the English and Irish establishments was not a mid-century anomaly. Lord Gage's accounts as paymaster for 1755–63 and 1765–83 reveal that women were the recipients of three-fifths of all pensions.[53] In part, this reflected a growing belief that the state should provide some degree of maintenance for those who were unable to support themselves. It also marked the development of an official form of recognition for certain types of civil or military service to the state. The detailed claims for pensions that continued to be submitted even by the widows of admirals, high-ranking military officers, and diplomats suggests that this system was not yet fully institutionalized at midcentury.

≺ IV ≻

Women as Brokers

Most women—and most men—took part in patronage as clients. Some, however, were brokers; yet others were patrons. Although the category of "broker" is a creation of modern social scientists, it identifies the intermediary position in eighteenth-century patronage. Brokers inhabit an amorphous place in the middle of any patronage system. Their power is nebulous and strategic, as they do not have the resources to grant clients' requests. But it is nonetheless real. It is founded upon access to information and individuals, sound personal and political judgment, and a reputation for getting results.[54] Brokers are always in a somewhat precarious position. The very personal nature of their power, the methods that they use to attain their goals, and the extent that they profit personally from their involvement lay them open to accusations of corruption.

In the eighteenth century, the alleged corruption of the patronage system provided opposition politicians with a convenient platform from which to attack other politicians, the current administration, or even the monarch. When women were involved, historical precedents (real or mythical) could be dredged up to give examples of influential women—specifically kings' mistresses—who had sold, or were presumed to have sold, places or secured patronage for favorites through illegitimate sexual influence. These sorts of accusations were usually little more than political ploys which evaporated once they had served their immediate political purpose, but their existence reflects widespread concerns about "undue" influence and the lack of accountability in politics in general. Where women were concerned, these anxieties were wrapped up with long-standing concerns about female venality and sexuality, and, equally, with fears about women's sexual power over men.

Early in the eighteenth century, accusations of corruption were regularly leveled at the two leading female brokers at the Court, George I's mistress the duchess of Kendal and his half-sister the countess of Darlington.[55] Much later, two highly publicized legal cases brought the issue to the fore again. The first, in 1773, saw Lord Sandwich's mistress, Martha Ray, charged with corruption as part of an Opposition attempt to discredit him. The charges could not be substantiated and the case failed miserably.[56] The second, in 1809, was more damaging. It saw Opposition politicians succeed in discrediting the duke of York and forcing him to resign by revealing that his ex-mistress, Mary Anne Clarke, had taken money for influence.[57] This was a gift for reformers who equated patronage with corruption and, eventually, led to the passage of the Sales of Offices Prevention Act, which made seeking money for offices a penal offense. For women, the Wardle affair, as it came to be known, was particularly unfortunate, as it reinforced negative stereotypes about women, patronage, and corruption.

Undoubtedly some degree of venality did exist among brokers of both sexes in the eighteenth century. However appealing, the connection of female brokers with rapacity, illicit sexuality, and corruption is conspicuously absent in the sources. It is impossible to know what went on in person behind closed doors, but the very absence of gossip and rumor in as tightly knit and highly competitive a society as that of the eighteenth-century political elite suggests that the activities of female brokers were largely unremarkable. Certainly those of Newcastle's female brokers—most of whom were the middle-aged and wives or widows of politically active families—seem not to have generated a ripple of scandal. Instead, their participation appears to have been taken for granted. Their backing was often enthusiastically sought and their aid was openly acknowledged. On the whole, they appear to have shared a common belief that it was their duty to use their family membership or their social or political positions to secure patronage for worthy but unconnected candidates. Their choices, however, and the timing of their requests were often more calculated than altruistic. Acting occasionally for clients of low social status or no political interest may have given the broker little more than personal satisfaction, but it was also sure to add to her reputation and create a fund of good will for the future. Backing the applications of clients who were higher in rank, or were actual or potential political supporters, was often more purposeful. It helped to establish networks of obligation that might later be turned to personal or political advantage. Thus, attempts to secure patronage for voters was especially common in advance of elections.

In general, the applications that brokers received fell into two groups. A few came from people who were genuinely unsure about the merits of their requests and wanted to have them vetted by someone who understood the system. The majority came from people who believed that the broker's support improved their chances of success. It was ostensibly Ann Boscawen's unfamiliarity with the best way to present her request for her husband that prompted her to enlist the duchess of Newcastle as broker: "Your Grace's goodness to me on many occasions, encourages me to beg the favour of your assistance at this time; I realy am greatly distressed in what manner to address myself to the Duke of Newcastle, in behalf of Mr. Boscawen (who is now in Ireland and therefore cannot plead for Himself) and as the Duke of Marlborough assured Mr. Boscawen that the Duke of Newcastle was so kind to tell Him that He would assist Mr. Boscawen the first opportunity."[58] On the other hand, it was the previous "proofs of your Laps: goodness and humanity," which encouraged Lady Cromertie to approach the duchess again over patronage. This time, she wanted the duchess to plead her case for the arrears on her annuity, albeit in a roundabout fashion. She informed the duchess that she had already written to Lord Hardwicke, but she wanted the duchess to use her influence with him, so that he, in turn, would use his influence with Newcastle.[59]

Men applied to female brokers for the same reasons that women applied to male brokers. Both tended to choose brokers with whom they had some kind of link and whose reputations, rank, political importance, or access to power increased the likelihood of success. While some male brokers had stronger claims to support or were more politically influential, the sex of the broker does not seem to have been crucial to the bestowal of patronage. The decision-making process was so complicated by a whole range of concerns, including petty rivalries and political expediency, and so dependent upon circumstances, that it was never simply gendered.

In instances where the personal interest of brokers was involved, husbands and wives, or mothers and sons, might work together. Each then made applications through his or her own network of contacts. This double-barreled approach could yield results, as it did when the Marlboroughs sought to have Dr. Pitt appointed Professor of Physick at Oxford in 1758. In this case, Newcastle was able to grant the request the following day: "Immediately on the Dutchess of Marlborough's Letter to the Dutchess of Newcastle, and in Consequence of my Promise to the Duke of Marlborough I applied to the King, in favor of Dr. Pitt."[60]

Brokers were frequently women who were known to have useful connexions and who were members of leading territorial political families. Wives or matriarchs who spent a good deal of their time in the country, where they served as their families' agents, were ideal candidates. The dowager Lady Howe was a formidable example. Newcastle approached her with caution.[61] A woman of the highest social standing, she had been a member of the Court since birth, and politically active for nearly as long as Newcastle himself. At midcentury, her position as a Lady of the Bedchamber to the Princess of Wales placed her at Leicester House, the heart of opposition politics. Furthermore, her management of the Howe family interest at Nottingham between 1735 and 1745, and again in 1758 after her eldest son was killed at Ticonderoga, placed her in direct opposition to Newcastle, who had his own interest in the borough.[62] Consequently, there may well have been a distinct political edge to her decision in 1757 to champion the case of a Nottingham man who had been waiting for over a year to have the paperwork for his baronetcy completed. Her letter to Newcastle was polite but succinct: he was to see to it that the Clerk of the Crown produced the "order or warrant" as soon as possible.[63]

The eighteenth-century assumption that the women who were

the closest to politically powerful men would have access to and influence over them ensured that the women in politicians' immediate family circles were regularly enlisted as brokers. At the very top of the political world, George II's mistress, Lady Yarmouth, was regularly appealed to by politicians, including Newcastle, to use her influence with the king.[64] In Newcastle's own case, his wife and his widowed sister-in-law, Lady Katherine Pelham, were his chief brokers.

The duchess of Newcastle remains a shadowy figure. Her chronic bad health prevented her from taking an active part in society or even spending much time in London. Newcastle's correspondence with her demonstrates that he valued her political judgment highly and that she took particular interest in ecclesiastical patronage. Unfortunately, as little of her own correspondence for this period survives, the extent of her involvement must remain impressionistic. Fortunately, some sense of her involvement can be gained from Newcastle's letters to her. He seems to have kept her informed of successful applications, so that she could complete her brokership by informing petitioners of their success. Thus, after a round of ecclesiastical appointments in 1756, he wrote to tell her that her clients had been appointed the bishops of Bristol and Bangor, respectively.[65] Being Newcastle's wife was no guarantee of rapid action or success, however. Like many of Newcastle's other brokers, she too was sometimes frustrated by the time that it took to get things done. Then, we find an apologetic Newcastle protesting, "My Dearest sees that by degrees I do all she wishes," or, "My Dearest Het. I do things when I can."[66]

For sheer volume of requests and reminders, and for stark brevity, few of Newcastle's brokers could match Lady Katherine Pelham. As a daughter of the duke of Rutland and the widow of Newcastle's brother and predecessor as first lord, Henry Pelham, she had unquestionable social and political credentials. As a broker, she was similarly unrivaled. Birth, connexions, and character were key contributory factors in the make-up of politically active eighteenth-century women—and Lady Katherine had them all in abundance.

She appears to have dealt mainly in applications for places or preferments. Her influence was solicited regularly, if the frequency of her letters to Newcastle is any indication. Indeed, she assured Newcastle in 1759 that she forwarded far fewer requests than she received: "I seldom attend to people who desire me to sollicite you for places."⁶⁷ Her relationship with Newcastle was often stormy and her impatience with him is mirrored in varying degrees of impatience in her correspondence. She kept herself informed of potential vacancies and was quick to remind Newcastle if he had promised her that she would have the next "turn" to make a particular appointment. Curt and to the point, such a note from Lady Katherine was designed to elicit action: "Ly Kath: Pelham was orderd by ye D: of Newcastle to remember him to provide for John Heath as soon as possible: She therefore acquaints his Grace, that there is likely to be a vacancy in the Stamp Office, one of the Stampers being thought adying; and it is the D: of Newcastles turn to put me in."⁶⁸

Lady Katherine's lengthy and ultimately successful campaign for John Roberts to secure a parliamentary seat at Harwich sheds light on the difficulties and frustrations inherent in being broker and not a patron—even for a highly political woman. Roberts had been Henry Pelham's assistant in managing government boroughs and he had stayed on after Pelham's death. Harwich was just such a government borough. It was torn by animosities between the Treasury and the Post Office and, in good eighteenth-century fashion, Roberts had taken advantage of his position to build up his own political interest in the borough.⁶⁹ He had been approached by Pelham to stand for Parliament as early as 1754, but it was not until 1758 that he was ready to do it.

One of the seats at Harwich became vacant in July 1758 when the sitting member, Lord Duncannon, succeeded his father to the Lords. Lady Katherine quickly sent a terse note to Newcastle recommending that Roberts be chosen in his place.⁷⁰ In December 1759, after much local wrangling and rivalry, Newcastle promised to bring Roberts in at the next election. Problems arose when the new king decided that his candidate, Charles Townshend, should get Harwich. As Namier astutely remarked, this put Newcastle in a real dilemma, "between the upper and nether millstone, the King and Lady Katherine Pelham, and he hardly knew which was the more formidable."⁷¹

By February 1761, Newcastle was having to justify his lack of success to a decidedly irritated Lady Katherine: "I disputed it, combated it, and oppos'd it, as much as I could; I did not prevail; But yet I don't despair, but I shall at last be able to get Mr. Roberts in at Harwich. But If I can't, It is not my Fault."[72] She would have none of it. As far as she was concerned, Roberts was to have both the seat at Harwich and the first vacancy at the Board of Trade; and Newcastle should secure the vacancy immediately. His predicament elicited little sympathy: "I am really sorry for the distresses you are in, and shall always wish to diminish, not increase them; but you must give me leave to say, that you bring them chiefly on your self."[73] In the end, Newcastle succeeded in placating both the king and Lady Katherine. He installed Roberts and Townshend at Harwich and moved the sitting members elsewhere.

Lady Katherine's frustration at having to work through Newcastle was due in large part to the differences in their personalities, exacerbated by her position as an intermediary in the patronage system. Interestingly enough, gender does not seem to have been an issue. At no point in her extensive correspondence with Newcastle or other politicians, on this or other patronage matters, does it appear to have played a part in shaping either her requests or the responses which she received. Arguably, her personal circumstances—her character, rank, family, Whig credentials, extensive personal and political networks, and years of experience at the heart of politics—ensured her a privileged position and encouraged male politicians to take her seriously. The eagerness with which predominantly male clients employed female brokers from less elevated socio-political backgrounds and the pragmatic, case-by-case consideration that patrons usually accorded their requests suggests that female brokers played an accepted and effective part in the patronage system.

While claims of kinship or obligation and promises of reciprocity or political service, liberally supported by sheer determination and perseverance, could result in success for brokers of either sex, the influence of the broker was intrinsically unstable. This was especially true at the highest levels of political patronage, where patrons moved in and out of favor and appointments. When, for instance, George III's distaste for his grandfather's ministers and measures finally succeeded in driving Newcastle from office, Lady Katherine's importance as a broker fell; conversely, that of the duchess of Northumberland, who was closely related to Lord Bute through marriage, rose. Brokers who hedged their bets by cultivating a number of patrons or potential patrons and who were astute enough to know when to shift requests among them tended to be the most successful over time. Yet even a shrewd and well-connected broker could only do so much; in the end, the right to dispense patronage lay with the patron.

≺ V ≻

Women as Patrons

Lady Katherine would certainly have been happier if she had been a patron in her own right. Women were patrons of art, architecture, music, literature, and drama in the eighteenth century, but we still know little about their roles as ecclesiastical or political patrons. While the customary constraints which prevented women from holding official political positions (lord lieutenancies, ministerial posts, and the like) meant that they could not distribute patronage that was in the gift of the Crown or in specific ministers of state, the vast majority of eighteenth-century patronage remained in private hands, where it could well be controlled by women. Indeed, women may have benefited from the prevailing understanding of patronage as private property: it was usually jealously guarded and passed down carefully through families. If nothing else, the vagaries of birth and sex-specific infant mortality would have ensured the existence of female patrons in the eighteenth century. There were undoubtedly fewer female patrons than female brokers or clients, but they were not anomalies. Nor were they confined solely to the upper strata of the political elite. While there were always a few women who were patrons by right of appointment, calculation, or purchase, there were more who were patrons through inheritance (including widowhood). There were also always some women, usually widows with underage sons, who were patrons by proxy.

It is something of a commonplace that eighteenth-century ecclesiastical patronage was put to political ends, with patrons tending to prefer candidates who shared or reflected their political outlooks.[74] Considering that 53.4 percent of the livings in England and Wales were in the gift of private patrons and that the Crown itself appointed to only 9.6 percent of livings (the remaining 26 percent being in the hands of churchmen), the complexion of the eighteenth-century church was largely determined by private patronage.[75] That women controlled some of this patronage is tacitly acknowledged, if perhaps best remembered through the activities of the heterodox Queen Caroline and the reforming Lady Huntingdon.[76]

A brief examination of two contemporary analyses of ecclesiastical patronage, *The Clergyman's Intelligencer* (1745) and John Ecton's *Thesaurus Rerum Ecclesiasticarum* (1754),[77] suggests that while female patrons were always in the minority, they were present in significant enough numbers to be a common feature in the localities. Although these texts are not comprehensive and not all discrepancies between them can be explained away by the nine-year gap between their publications, they record hundreds of female patrons at midcentury. Most parishes appear to have had at least one female patron, and many had several. Some were unmarried, others were married, yet others were widowed; some were titled, more were not.[78]

In the diocese of Oxford, the *Thesaurus* lists nine female patrons, only two of whom were titled.[79] They presented, in total, to four rectories, six vicarages, and one curacy. Mrs. Dorothy Dashwood, who had the largest individual gift, presented to two vicarages and a rectory, the most valuable of which was worth £75 12s. Mrs. Newell, who presented to the rectory of Adwell St. Mary in 1747, may well have been either the daughter or wife of the William Newell, Clerk, who had presented there in 1729. Women who were co-heirs inherited shares in ecclesiastical appointments. Presentments were then made either by consensus or in turn. Mrs. Loder and Mr. Hammersley, who presented jointly to the rectory of Kencote St. George, may well have been kin, either brother and sister or cousins.

The same pattern is revealed in the much larger diocese of Norwich. There, the *Thesaurus* lists 55 women as the sole patrons of 66 livings. Four women shared the patronage of the same number of livings with other women; six shared with their husbands; twelve with more than one man; and seven sets of unspecified heirs shared yet another eight livings. Although some appointments would have been to decrepit, impoverished curacies in out-of-the-way locations, and would have done little to increase the status or influence of the patron, good livings also existed. Appointments to these were usually keenly pursued. It is also worth bearing in mind that by the middle of the eighteenth century many livings were worth a good deal more than their recorded value in the King's Books. In the Norwich diocese, the rectory at Edgfield to which the widow Rebeccah Harbord presented was listed at only £11 6s. 8d. Its clear yearly value was actually £120, which would have made it eminently desirable. Similarly, John Hase and his wife presented to the rectory of Sparham St. Mary, valued at only £9 17s. 11d. in the King's Books. It was really worth £100.[80]

The degree to which female ecclesiastical patrons put their patronage to political ends must have varied widely, but their right to make political appointments was undisputed. Unmarried women and widows were at least theoretically free to do as they wished, while married women seem to have had anything from no control at all to total control over their patronage. A woman with a vacant living in her gift in the lead-up to an election, just like a woman with any other form of political interest, would have been approached by political agents and candidates, and encouraged to appoint someone who held the "right" sort of political sentiments.[81]

There were far fewer women than men with electoral patronage, but like men, they were scattered across the country and throughout the political nation. At one end of the spectrum, there was a small group of elite women who controlled boroughs or managed family political interests. For instance, when Newcastle made a register of political interests in the country in 1754 and 1760, he included as a matter of course the dowager Lady Orford, who controlled the Cornish boroughs of Callington and Ashburton.[82] Nor was he allowed to forget that the valuable Gordon interest in Scotland was being maintained by the duchess of Gordon for the young duke. When a contest loomed in Aberdeenshire in 1760, one of Newcastle's most important Scottish contacts, Lord Deskfoord, made it clear that she would play a central role in the election: "Your Graces Friend the Dutchess of Gordon, and her brother Lord Aberdeen will be of Consequence in determining that Matter."[83]

At the other end of the spectrum were women who were freeholders in freeholder boroughs or owned burgages in burgage boroughs.[84] Newcastle included five such women, paying rentals of between £1 and £5 16s. 6d., in his list of 43 voters at Aldborough, c. 1754; similarly, Lord Irwin's political agent indicated that 12 women owned 19 of the 83 votes in the burgage borough of Horsham in 1764.[85] These women were, in effect, small-scale electoral patrons. They had the legal right to vote but in practice chose male proxies to vote for them. *Douceurs* offered by opposing political camps in the lead-up to an election could make choosing a proxy a lucrative business. While husbands seem to have automatically served as their wives' proxies, unmarried women's and widows' votes were generally exercised by their tenants. It was not unheard of for women to select tenants according to political preference.[86] Records of controverted election cases throughout the century indicate that women used a variety of means to influence their tenants' votes, including threats of eviction.[87]

Women's ability to become patrons and appoint whom they wished to the places in their gift is perhaps best illustrated by Newcastle's dealings with Lady Portsmouth in 1760. As one of the three co-heirs of the earl of Suffolk (d. 1745), she had gained a share of his estate, including "a joyn'd right to the nomination" of the mastership of Magdalene College, Cambridge.[88] As early as 1746, she was taking steps to become the sole patron. Since the patronage was tied to the ownership of the manor of Brooks Walden and the house Audley End, she needed to buy out the other owner, Lord Effingham. The negotiations were protracted because Effingham demanded a high price (£15,000 at one stage in 1751). By March 1752, however, she had acquired the property and the patronage.[89]

Newcastle, who was chancellor of the University of Cambridge as well as first lord, was particularly concerned about university appointments. He believed that it was important to place politically congenial individuals (that is, dedicated Whigs) in key university posts. The mastership was one of these. When it fell open in 1760, he sent a patronage request to Lady Portsmouth. Like any other client, he set out his credentials before requesting that she appoint the man that he had in mind:

being an old Friend, and Humble Servant, to My Lord Portsmouth, & My Particular Relation to the University of Cambridge, as having the Honor to be their Chancellor, will, I hope be my Excuse, for giving your Ladyship this trouble, most earnestly to beg the Favor of You, to Suspend determining anything upon the vacancy of the Mastership of Magdalen College If, (as I understand,) the Appointment is in your Ladyship, 'till I have the Honor to lay before you the Wishes, and Inclinations, of the principal Members of the University . . . If I ask too much, I heartily beg your Ladyships' Pardon; But, as I know Your Ladyship's Zeal for the King, and His Interest, And as I have no View but His Majesty's Service, & that of the University, I flatter Myself you will excuse me.[90]

His exquisite politeness was wasted. Lady Portsmouth had already decided to appoint an Oxford man to the post.[91] This left Newcastle fretting, as Oxford's reputation as a Tory stronghold made it distinctly possible that the new appointee would have Tory leanings or—worse—be one. In either case, there was nothing that he could do about it.[92] Fortunately for his peace of mind, Lady Portsmouth's choice turned out to be a hearty Whig. Within two weeks, Newcastle was writing to Portsmouth, praising his wife's choice: "As My Lady Portsmouth did not take one of our own Body, I am persuaded, Her Ladyship could not have made a better Choice, than that of Mr. Sanby."[93]

Even when he had been the most worried about the appointment, Newcastle had never questioned Lady Portsmouth's right to be a patron or to choose whom she wished. She had gone to significant effort and expense to gain the patronage, and it was legitimately hers. Moreover, the decision appears to have been hers alone. Her husband never appears in more than a supporting role in any of the correspondence.[94]

≺ VI ≻

Conclusion

Patronage supplied women with a variety of forms of political involvement in an assortment of milieus. It was intrinsically flexible, non-institutional, and decentralized. It linked the political and social arenas together and operated in the overlap between the public and the private domains. It allowed women to deal with public affairs from the comfort of their own homes, or private affairs through personal contacts in public places. It enabled them to control the type and degree of their involvement, and shape it to fit their lives. They could choose to take part in person, in writing, or at one remove through male, female, or mixed-sex networks of friends and connexions.

As this examination of women's requests in the Newcastle papers has shown, women made up approximately ten percent of Newcastle's total patronage requests between 1754 and 1762. Given the personal nature of patronage and the under-recording of requests, women's overall involvement in patronage was clearly far greater than has hitherto been imagined. Women's requests reveal that they believed they had the right to solicit patronage for themselves or for others, and that they did so in much the same way and for many of the same reasons as their male counterparts. The responses they received indicate that politicians, even at the very uppermost echelons of the political world, accepted their involvement and treated their requests in much the same way as those from men of similar rank and connexion.

While more women were clients than brokers or patrons, the Newcastle papers show us that female brokers and patrons were not anomalies. Their influence and support were eagerly sought by men and women alike. Recognizing this adds a new gendered dimension to our understanding of the way that patronage operated in the eighteenth century. It also illustrates the way that the reality of politics might contradict the contemporary ideal of apolitical, domestic femininity. This is not to deny that both personal and institutionalized misogyny existed in the eighteenth century, or to denigrate contemporary ambivalence about female political involvement. Rather, it is to suggest that where political relationships between men and women were concerned, the translation of belief into practice, rhetoric into reality, was invariably complicated, and could be compromised or subverted by a range of factors, including greed, self-interest, deference, respect, affection, or personal or political expediency. Some of the avenues to political involvement through patronage which Newcastle's female correspondents enjoyed would have been lost with parliamentary reform and the gradual removal of Crown and Treasury patronage in the nineteenth century, but just how much they were offset by new forms of patronage, and how much women were active in them, still remains to be discovered.

≪ 2 ≫

1784 and All That: Aristocratic Women and Electoral Politics

JUDITH S. LEWIS

THE 1784 WESTMINSTER ELECTION has served historians for over two hundred years as the exception to prove the rule that politics was no place for a lady. In what has been called "the most famous of all political contests,"[1] Fox's local victory over his Pittite opponent, Sir Cecil Wray, owed much to the canvassing of Georgiana, Duchess of Devonshire. Nevertheless, it is the hostility shown the duchess, rather than her success, that has become legendary. "I had rather kiss my Moll than she," began one typical ditty,

> With all her paint and Finery;
> What's a Duchess more than Woman?
> We've sounder flesh on Portsmouth Common.[2]

Historians traditionally argued that the duchess's conduct was so unorthodox, and public castigation so severe, that women were effectively intimidated from political participation for another century. Even as recently as 1989, the distinguished historian Joan Perkin told us that "canvassing and other subsidiary work of elections" was historically done only by men. With the exception, she pointed out, "of the occasional aristocratic lady who traded kisses for votes, no woman had taken an open part in elections at all" prior to the passage of the Corrupt Practices Act of 1883.[3]

As historians have come to focus more on women and on upper-class women specifically, Perkin's judgment has begun to look premature.[4] But the full significance of the Westminster election still eludes us. We have forgotten—if we ever knew—some important features of this campaign: that it was perfectly normal for women of rank to campaign in elections; that the duchess of Devonshire did so, not in rebellion against, but at the behest of, her family; and that Fox's campaign openly asserted women's right to participate in the political life of their nation. Most importantly of all, of course, we seem to have forgotten that Fox and the duchess actually *won* the election for the great constituency of Westminster. Even as astute a commentator as Linda Colley appears to disregard this most salient point when she asserts that "Georgiana's champions were unable to construct a satisfying way of legitimising and explaining her endeavors."[5] It seems more likely that they were.

While valuably situating the episode in the mainstream of political history,[6] Colley's account of the Westminster campaign in fact errs in several important ways: she incorrectly assumes that aristocratic women of 1784 only canvassed on behalf of male relations, and then out of family loyalty rather than political conviction; and that aristocrats like the duchess may have maneuvered privately, but they never took action publicly. If this were so, the duchess of Devonshire's conduct would indeed be anomalous. Following these assumptions, Colley posits, as many have before, that Georgiana was indeed so intimidated by the understandable hostility directed against her unorthodox conduct that she withdrew from all political activity ever after. Ultimately, then, although Colley's account is useful in taking the Westminster campaign seriously, her ultimate interpretation, in focusing on the negative and the unique, varies little from the two-hundred-year-old master text which positioned Georgiana as an aberration—though at least to Colley, she is a serious rather than an amusing one.

Amanda Foreman, however, has recently demonstrated that the duchess of Devonshire, far from being intimidated, in fact remained politically active throughout her life.[7] But while Foreman has a great deal to tell us, it is difficult from her account to draw larger conclusions about the patterns of gender which typified late eighteenth-century politics. As a biographer, Foreman highlights her subject by decontextualizing her. With one woman in the foreground, others retreat into the shadows. In evaluating the full significance of the Westminster election, therefore, historians must bring the other participants back into the light. Only then can we begin to understand what was and was not unique about the Westminster campaign of 1784, and what was and was not unique about its most famous participant, the legendary Georgiana.

Like pottery shards scattered about the surface, the evidence for more balanced interpretations of this election has been hiding in plain sight. For one thing, all the negative material with which we are familiar was simply partisan campaign literature generated by Sir Cecil Wray, Fox's opponent, hardly an adequate source for received historical wisdom. Indeed, as long ago as 1939, Dorothy George noted that all the negative campaigning had become necessary only because the duchess was so successful a campaigner, giving Fox the narrow margin of victory he needed to secure his election for Westminster.[8] Would this have been true had she been the social freak, feminist rebel, or frivolous femme normally depicted?

Dirty doggerel provides us with other, highly decorative shards of evidence. The simple fact is that the nasty stuff was by no means directed at the duchess alone. Nor was it limited to this campaign, or even to women. Though some campaigns were dirtier than others, no politician was beyond the reach of the smutmongers. In his 1805 campaign for County Down, for instance, the foreign secretary Lord Castlereagh was attacked for his reputed sexual impotence, "so useless a fellow at home," it was said, "that he seldom minds even to wind up the family clock." According to one address to the freeholders of County Down,

> There is only one virtue I see in this peer,
> A bounty from heaven, this county to cheer;
> His vices must cease, when his sun it has set,
> For tis not in his breeches, a son to beget.[9]

The most numerous shards of evidence, however, are those that testify to the presence of other politically engaged women in British electoral contests. Georgiana was not even the only upper-class woman on the Westminster campaign trail in 1784. She was joined, at a minimum, by her sister, Harriet, Lady Duncannon; her sister-in-law, the duchess of Portland; the latter's mother-in-law, the dowager Duchess; and some lesser lights of the Whig party, such as the Ladies Waldegrave, Mrs. Damer, Mrs. Bouverie, and Mrs. Crewe. The Wray campaign, so vituperative against Georgiana, was not itself above the use of female canvassers, the duchess of Rutland, Lady Salisbury, and Mrs. Hobart among them. Indeed, at the very moment Georgiana and her sister were canvassing the streets of Westminster, their mother, Lady Spencer, was managing the Spencer electoral interest in St. Albans. Such political activity was in fact welcomed at the time: at the ceremonial chairing celebrating Fox's great victory, a banner proclaiming "Sacred to Female Patriotism" was carried in the procession to the Devonshire House courtyard.

Nevertheless, as Linda Colley has suggested, the 1784 Westminster campaign was the first election in British history in which the position of women became a contentious political issue.[10] There is indeed much left to unpack. In other elections of the time, such as the one at St. Albans, the gender of the campaigner was so incidental as to be beneath notice. In the Westminster campaign, it became central. Why? And why, of all the female canvassers present, was Georgiana, Duchess of Devonshire, the one who was remembered? It was a mystery that confounded even its principal player. "It is very hard they shd single me out," the duchess complained to her mother during the course of the campaign, "when all the women of my side do as much."[11]

We will begin by examining the factors that made this contest a unique one: Fox was not just any candidate, Westminster was not just any constituency, the 1784 election was not just another election, and the duchess of Devonshire was not just another pretty face. But the participation of upper-class women in an election was not in itself unusual for the time. It was, however, their participation in this otherwise unique context that catalyzed pre-existing anxieties about class and gender. By first exploring what was and was not unusual, we will be better able to understand why these are the campaign and the canvasser that became legendary, and most importantly, how it was that issues of gender became central to this critical contest.

≺ I ≻

The 1784 General Election

First, a quick look at what happened. The 1784 general election was one of the most important in the eighteenth century, turning as it did on the constitutional division of powers between king and Parliament, as well as on the personal animosity between George III and the Whig leader, Charles James Fox. The election had come about after George III had let it be known to members of the House of Lords that he wanted them to defeat Fox's East India Bill, which had just passed in Commons. Sure enough, Lords did the king's bidding and defeated the bill, providing George III with an excuse to dismiss the Fox-North Coalition ministry and invite the young William Pitt to form a new government. To the Whigs, this represented an unconstitutional and unwarranted abuse of power on the part of the king, who had interfered with the independent deliberations of the legislature. It was not only wrong, but it also represented a continuation of the disastrous policies which had just led to the loss of the American colonies. The Whigs, led by Fox, cried tyranny. They wanted an election fought on the issue of king and constitution: the king and his supporters, however, wanted an election fought on the issue of Fox's character. As one chronicler aptly phrased it, the election represented "the culmination" of the king's dislike, "the antipathy every unconsciously dull man feels towards his keener-witted neighbour."[12]

Keen wit notwithstanding, Fox's loss nationwide cast the Whigs into the political wilderness, where they would remain, with the exception of a brief coalition ministry, until 1830. By that time, the 1784 election itself had come to be part of Whig mythology, the event which proved George III's despotism and Pitt's treachery. Meanwhile, Pitt's victory, with the king's support, helped to create what Linda Colley has called the apotheosis of the monarchy.[13] Despite the losses of Fox's martyrs around the country, however, his personal victory in the constituency of Westminster enabled him to carry on as the "Man of the People," fighting against what he saw as a despotic monarchy. And he was not all wrong there. "No tactics were to be ruled out," George III had informed Pitt, when it came to defeating Fox in Westminster.[14]

Fox is one eighteenth-century man who needs no introduction.[15] Large both in bulk and in appetites, financially, and to much of England morally, bankrupt for most of his life, Fox was a rake and a gambler, though also widely beloved as a reforming Friend of the People. The previous year's coalition with Lord North, with whom he had disagreed over the conduct of the recently concluded American war, was in many ways his undoing. To Fox's opponents, it appeared he was willing to sacrifice even the most basic political principles for the sake of political ambition. The immediate issue on which the 1784 election was fought, the India Bill, provided further grist to the mill. The argument that Fox, now nicknamed "Carlo

Khan" by his opponents, was turning the wealth of India into a fund for political corruption, was readily believed, Joanna Innes asserts, "only because Fox's reputation was already so badly tarnished."[16]

Nor did it help that Fox came from a family known as much for their financial and sexual irregularities as for their intellectual gifts. A political advertisement of April 12, 1784, directed to "all canvassing Duchesses and Ladies," gleefully warned them of Fox's moral shortcomings:

> To cover this Season (at any price) that *infamous* Stallion, called CARLO KHAN, well-known among the *deep* ones of King's and Duke's Places, &c. He won, by hard running, one City Plate, and walked over the course for a second; but in attempting a *third*, is so strained and broke down, that it is hourly expected *he must give it in*. He will never be able to *enter* again, unless for the *private* amusement of all canvassing wives, who are determined to make the *most* of him whenever he is *entered* for the future. *Carlo Khan was got by* Public Defaulter *out of Unaccounted Millions*, whose dam, great dam, and great, great dam ought to be *d—d* till the national debt is paid off.[17]

At least in the minds of political opponents, then, Fox's female canvassers were automatically tainted by their connection with him. Given his reputation and her beauty, many people of the time assumed that he and the duchess of Devonshire in particular were lovers and supposed this sufficient to explain her motivation. But in fact, even if that were the case, politics would have made them compatible bedfellows.

Georgiana, Duchess of Devonshire, was one of the world's first celebrities, someone famous for being famous. In the spring of 1784 she was just short of her 27th birthday, a great beauty who had become very much of a public figure since her marriage to the duke ten years earlier. As one of her biographers astutely claimed, "She suffered the fate of all who attract public attention without appearing to deserve it."[18] The press was happy to satisfy the public's voracious appetite for news about her. As early as 1781, according to Foreman, *The Morning Herald and Daily Advertiser* alone published a story a week about her,[19] eagerly dissecting the tiniest details of her conduct and appearance. The duchess's forays into fashion particularly attracted attention. Although women had been painted in riding costumes since at least the seventeenth century, the *London Chronicle* of May 1778 credited the more masculine look to the duchess of Devonshire, who, while attending military reviews brought on by the American war, had patriotically adapted her husband's Derbyshire uniform to her own attire.[20] Though she was barely 21 years old in 1778, it was then that Georgiana became the target of a 100-page pamphlet by the self-styled moralist William Combe, who took her publicly to task for the sin of wearing too tall a plume.[21] He begged her to put her talents and fame to more serious purposes, without, however "entering into the laborious talk of Society and Government."[22]

But society and government it was, and not surprisingly, for a woman who had been weaned on Whiggery. Born Lady Georgiana Spencer, she both came from, and married into, a family distinguished for its political activity. Spencer women expected to participate in society and politics, a tradition established by her great-great-grandmother, the formidable Sarah, Duchess of Marlborough. Georgiana's political views were both independent of and consistent with those of Fox. Even a month before George III's controversial dissolution of Parliament, Georgiana wrote her mother, the dowager Countess Spencer, of her fears for Britain's balanced constitution:

> If Mr. Pitt succeeds, he will have brought about an event that he himself as well as every Englishman will repent ever after—for if the King and the House of Lords . . . conquer the House of Commons he will destroy the consequence of that House and make the government quite absolute . . . those who are interested in the Wellfare of their Country—cannot without some degree of Warmth and disdain see a young Man take upon him—and rest upon its being his *opinion* the entirely changing the happy constitution of his country. This is an odious subject and yet considering all things do what one will it is a subject one must think and feel about.[23]

These staunchly Whiggish views were shared by the men of her family, who begged Georgiana to campaign. "Everyone is convinced," the duke of Portland wrote to her during the course of the campaign, "that your exertions have produced the very material alteration which has appeared in Fox's favor." Her efforts, he told her, were essential to the success of the Whig party. Without her, the "Triumph of the Court would be the inevitable Consequence."[24]

For all that, Georgiana was most famous for her beauty. "I could light my pipe by her eyes," one workman is reported to have said.[25] Along with her fresh, guileless personality, her warmth, intelligence, and political passion, the duchess of Devonshire was a natural campaigner, as one anecdote from the St. Albans campaign, where she went to assist her mother, illustrates. "As she stepped out of her carriage to go into the house of a butcher," it was reported, "by some accident her shoe was torn, in so much that it was with difficulty she could keep it on her foot. In this embarrassment, the beautiful politician acquitted herself with great vivacity and good humour; she kicked the shoe from her, and said, 'I gladly serve my friends, even bare-footed.'"[26]

≺ II ≻

St. Albans Holds an Election

The 1784 St. Albans campaign is worth examining in some detail for many reasons. As obscure as the Westminster contest is famous, St. Albans was a far more typical eighteenth-century constituency. The ancient abbey town had only about 500 voters and was dominated by two old families of the neighborhood, the Spencers and the Grimstons. The concurrent experience of St. Albans will therefore help us establish a baseline against which Westminster can be measured.

That the Evangelical dowager Lady Spencer, the duchess of Devonshire's mother, did not consider politics beyond "women's sphere" can best be gauged by her management of the St. Albans election. This was a campaign which functioned very much like a "dress rehearsal" for Westminster: Lady Spencer's principal opponent was Lady Salisbury, who was active in Westminster politics as well. And it was in St. Albans that Georgiana and her younger sister, Harriet, Lady Duncannon, assisted William Sloper's candidacy without attracting the vitriol and notoriety that followed them in Westminster.

Georgiana's father, the first Earl Spencer, had died in October 1783, leaving her 25-year-old brother in charge of a vast network of political interests on the eve of a major election. Although he would later prove to be a capable and distinguished administrator, at this point the young second earl was overwhelmed by his new responsibilities.[27] Northampton, which he would ultimately lose, was more than enough to keep him occupied. Since his mother had decided to make the family residence at Holywell in St. Albans her dower house, it made sense for the dowager Lady Spencer to take up the cudgels there on behalf of Sloper, "a violent advocate of reform,"[28] and one of the few Foxites who, like the party leader himself, managed to win in the general election of 1784.

Two major interests dominated the borough of St. Albans. In addition to the Spencers, who had inherited a substantial estate there from Sarah, Duchess of Marlborough, there were the Grimstons of Gorhambury. Generally the two families had been able to agree that each would return one member, thus precluding the need for an election. In fact, St. Albans had not had a contested election since 1761. The Cecils of nearby Hatfield House also had some influence, though they tended to concentrate their political efforts instead on the borough of Hertford and in the County. The head of the family, the earl of Salisbury, was the lord-lieutenant of Hertfordshire. But it was his wife, the ambitious 34-year-old countess of Salisbury, who would prove to be Lady Spencer's major adversary in the election.

Mary Amelia, Lady Salisbury, the daughter of the first marquess of Downshire and his Fitzgerald wife Margaretta, had married the earl in 1773. Most of their children were not yet born at the time of the 1784 general election.[29] The earl and countess of Salisbury zealously pursued politics. Recognizing her talents in the St. Albans campaign, Pitt's government brought Lady Salisbury forward to oppose the duchess of Devonshire in the Westminster election. "Acknowledging her services," according to *The Complete Peerage*, Pitt made her husband lord chamberlain, and in 1789, awarded him a marquessate. Always a fierce competitor and an enthusiastic horsewoman, Lady Salisbury eventually came to be known as "Old Sarum," recalling both the Latin derivation of her title and the most infamous of rotten boroughs. She assumed the management of her husband's foxhounds in his declining years, and "attired in a habit of the hunt livery, hunted the hounds"[30] to within a few years of her grisly death in the famous Hatfield House fire of 1835. She was by then 85.

In 1784, however, the Spencers expected that the incumbents, Sloper and Lord Grimston,[31] would once again be elected for St. Albans without a contest. But before the month of March was out Lady Salisbury had brought her brother Lord Fairford from Ireland to stand in opposition to Sloper, his politics, and the Spencer interest. "Lady Salisbury came this morning to Canvass for Lord Fairford," Lady Spencer wrote a friend on March 30. "She has been very active has canvass'd the whole day—throwing handfulls of Silver about her."[32]

Perhaps Lady Salisbury used the same velvet bag, held by an accompanying groom, with which she customarily scattered guineas to the poor of her neighborhood.[33]

It must have been about this time that Lady Spencer asked her two daughters, the duchess of Devonshire and Lady Duncannon, to come up to St. Albans to help her. On April 1 Lady Spencer reported to her son that her opponent, Lady Salisbury, "has canvassed the town we were told with amazing success, and she threw a sort of spirit upon their party that depressed ours. So last night I sent for your two sisters who set out an hour ago with Mr. Sloper and a very large body of friends to make a regular canvass. It is amazing what this has already done."[34] Lord Spencer was "much obliged" to his sisters for their assistance, he replied. "I wish I could persuade Lavinia to do the same at Northampton," he added regarding his young wife, "but I do not think she has spirits enough to go through with it."[35] By the next day Sloper had pulled ahead of Fairford, and as Lady Spencer told Mrs. Howe, "I really believe Georgiana and Harriet in great measure turned the election."[36]

Lady Spencer was actively involved in the election, meeting daily with her committee at a little past five.[37] But Lady Salisbury was proving a fierce and energetic competitor, with unlimited financial resources, little scruple, and a large body of active supporters. "This morning about eleven," Sloper himself reported to Lord Spencer on April 8, "Lady Salisbury, with Mr. Nicole, Mrs. Sam Nicole and Miss Nicole began a canvass for Lord Fairford, Her ladyship scattering half Crowns and shillings as she went along. She continued the Canvass till six o'clock."[38] Nevertheless, Lady Salisbury had more than met her match in Lady Spencer. Ultimately, Sloper pulled out a narrow victory over Fairford, which the successful candidate attributed entirely to Lady Spencer's efforts. "She is the most admirable woman I know," Sloper reported to her son, "and she is as superior in the conduct of an Election as in the rest of her Conduct."[39] Already planning for the next election, on May 3 Lady Spencer met with one of her political agents to make out a more precise list of the St. Albans voters, annotated with their political inclinations, while these were still fresh in her mind.[40]

On the basis of this campaign, it appears that women played highly visible parts in election contests, appeared in public, and consulted and maneuvered in private. And they did so without generating gender-based hostility. Female politicians were unremarkable in this rather unremarkable constituency. Women canvassed both for relatives and for those unrelated to them. The Spencer campaign in St. Albans was fought on behalf of the family interest, though not on behalf of a family member as candidate.[41] And although Lady Salisbury was canvassing for her brother, this was not merely an apolitical effort on behalf of a much-beloved sibling. Instead, Lady Salisbury's specific intention was to defeat the Spencers and the cause they represented. She was quite simply an ambitious politician who strove to advance the political fortunes of her family and the Pittites more generally.

What we also learn from the example of St. Albans is how false would be a dichotomy between family loyalty on the one hand, and political conviction on the other. Far from precluding each other, these political families seem to stand for particular ideologies. When the Spencers began to fear they might need another candidate for the next election, Lady Spencer suggested a Mr. Lewis, a popular resident of the borough. "I like the idea very much," her son replied, "but how are his politicks?"[42] The family's arduous support of Mr. Sloper's candidacy was a matter *both* of supporting their own interests *as well as* promoting the cause of Fox and reform. In their minds, the two were inextricably entwined.

Thus the notion that "family" belongs in the private sphere and "politics" in the public makes little sense.[43] It is not merely that women refused to stay home, but also that politics refused to stay "in public." Politics, like charity, often began at home. But while these great families functioned in what we would call the public sector, they were still families. Most of the Spencers' correspondence, even during the spring of 1784, is concerned with "private" matters: Lord Spencer is more interested in the health and antics of toddler Jack—the future Lord Althorp of the Reform Bill—than he is in politics. The dowager Lady Spencer is preoccupied with a troublesome knee, while taking delight in the visit of the duchess of Devonshire's first child, who accompanied her mother to St. Albans for the duration of that campaign. And once Duchess Georgiana was "comforted"[44] by the successful results of the St. Albans election, she and her sister Harriet returned to the very different contest still underway in Westminster.

≺ III ≻

In Darkest Westminster

The borough of Westminster was unique. Much of its singularity is readily apparent: located at the political heart of the country, it was bound to attract more attention from Fleet Street than did provincial constituencies like St. Albans. And with the fashionable town houses of so many grandees located there, Westminster provided a ready battleground for competing political interests. But in the metropolis the aristocracy lacked many of the social and economic controls which sustained the sinews of deference in most county and borough electorates. Consequently in Westminster there were both many interests and none: certainly there was nothing like the power exercised in St. Albans by the Grimstons, Cecils, and Spencers, the "settled natural interests."

The real flavor of a Westminster election, then, came from its electorate, the most independent and democratic in England, often humble in station yet politically sophisticated. It was a scot-and-lot borough, which meant that the vote was vested in those who paid the local rates. Consequently many small shopkeepers and artisans were enfranchised. Westminster was Britain's largest and most prestigious borough, with an estimated 18,000 voters in 1784.[45] Her chosen member could justly claim the title "Man of the People."

As in every other constituency, Westminster had only one polling site. In 1784 the hustings were located in Covent Garden, famous not only for its opera house and produce market, but also as the haunt of prostitutes. Covent Garden's distinctive flavor created an unusually favorable environment for smutmongers, who accused the duchess of Devonshire of putting working girls out of business, now that men could kiss duchesses for free.[46] One seamy squib, liberally and typically supplied with italics to keep every one abreast of the *entendres*, insinuated that "Considering the frequent visits they pay to Covent Garden, it is no wonder that the Ladies catch the *contagion* of party spirit and are so *warm* in support of their favorite *member*."[47] This then provided the context for the famous story of Georgiana kissing a butcher for a vote, an episode more mythic than real, though the myth was established immediately. "My S[iste]r and Ly [Horatia?] were both kiss'd," the duchess wrote her mother plaintively, "so it is very hard I who was not shd have the reputation of it."[48]

Canvassing was a process of several stages. During the first, candidates and their supporters visited members of the electorate, usually in their homes, to ascertain how each individual planned to vote. Lists of voters and their preferences were kept for future use. Canvassing parties also tried to persuade the undecided voter, often with favors, music, and other forms of solicitation. Since the ultimate act of voting was a public one, an agreement to vote in a particular way was tantamount to a pledge on the part of the elector. Many, however, remained uncommitted after a first, or even second solicitation; a well-organized campaign ensured that such voters were repeatedly visited until a decision was reached.[49] Finally, every candidate was responsible for transporting his voters to the polls; precise lists enabled this important last stage of canvassing to be carried out as efficiently as possible. Because Westminster was so large a borough, effective canvassing—persuading, identifying, and getting all your supporters to the hustings at Covent Garden, happy but sufficiently sober—was especially challenging.

It was in fact Georgiana's apparent affability with these voters of lower rank that provided much of the novelty of the campaign. "During her canvass," Horace Walpole wrote, "the Duchess made no scruple of visiting the humblest of the electors, dazzling and enchanting them by the fascination of her manner, the power of her beauty and influence of her high rank, and sometimes carrying off to the hustings the meanest mechanic in her own carriage."[50] Walpole was not the only one whose eyebrows were raised by this new campaign style. "If men find themselves abashed on being under the necessity of applying for votes among strangers and people of rude and unpolished manners," one commentator inquired, "what are we to expect from women?"[51] But the unabashed duchess was an innovative and energetic campaigner. It was not enough just to participate in large parties of dignified members of the quality: Georgiana and her fellow female canvassers left their carriages to chat with tradesmen, shopkeepers, and young mothers in their homes and shops.[52] Nor was it enough for the duchess to provide voters with transportation to the hustings: she invited them to ride with her in the ducal carriage.

It was this comfortable familiarity with the lower orders that horrified Pitt's supporters. "The ladies, throwing off all their femalities," the bishop of Llandaff wrote the duke of Rutland, indignantly, "have not blushed to pollute the simplicity of their minds by canvassing butchers and tailors."[53] Similarly, Lord Fife was reportedly appalled to discover that the duchess of Devonshire had canvassed his pastry cook,[54] while Lord Cornwallis was aghast at hearing that she "was in the most blackguard houses in Long Acre by 8 o'clock this morning."[55] "What contamination is there in the abode of a poor tradesman merely because he is poor?"[56] was the appropriate rejoinder on behalf of the Man of the People. But outraged propriety knew better.

Frank O'Gorman has pointed out that elections of this time were, among other things, rituals of inversion, in which candidates and their supporters asked favors of voters, who were normally somewhat lower in rank.[57] Of course this had to be done carefully, so that what might be a valve for the release of social tensions, or better yet, an "opportunity to put a human face upon the stern realities of hierarchy"[58] did not lapse into carnivalesque comedy or social subversion. When done properly, these rituals of inversion might actually reinforce the established hierarchy. Canvassing processions normally consisted of the local elite in full party colors, O'Gorman tells us, "Dukes, Lords, Ladies all conspiring together to maintain that imposing attitude."[59]

In most constituencies there was nothing troubling about this custom. In the counties, electors were likely to be country gentlemen and their tenantry. In the boroughs, the electorate usually comprised proud city fathers like those of St. Albans, members of town government, and leading tradesmen. But the more populous constituencies were difficult even for many aristocratic men. The earl of Carlisle's friend Lord Fitzwilliam once asked him for assistance on behalf of his son Lord Milton, who was contesting Yorkshire in the hard-fought election of 1807. "My dear Fitzwilliam," Carlisle is reported to have replied, "Whatever votes I can command you shall have; but I could not stoop to ask a favour of any plebeian."[60] Soliciting votes from a "plebeian" was thus tantamount to "stooping," according to Carlisle and like-minded aristocrats. It meant that one had lowered one's self in the eyes of inferiors. And if that was dangerous for a man, how much more so for a woman.

It is fairly clear from these accounts that, while all of Fox's female canvassers were criticized for "asking favours of plebeians," Georgiana was usually the only one singled out by name. Yet it was certainly not because a canvassing lady was in itself such a novelty, or because only Fox's campaign made use of female canvassers. We cannot therefore understand what was, and was not, unique about the duchess of Devonshire, or what was, and was not different, about the two competing groups of lady canvassers, without looking more closely at these women, both Pittite and Foxite, who crossed the streets of Westminster during the arduous spring of 1784. It is, after all, the relative absence of this larger group from the historical record that has made Georgiana seem so exceptional. Yet, as we saw with Lady Salisbury and Lady Spencer, politics was often as central to other women's lives as it was to that of the duchess of Devonshire. And so it was with the four additional women we will look at from the 1784 election: the duchess of Rutland and Mrs. Hobart, who canvassed for Sir Cecil Wray in Westminster; and Mrs. Crewe and Mrs. Bouverie, who supported Fox.

≺ IV ≻

Canvassing Ladies of 1784

The chief rival "both in politics and fashion" of the duchess of Devonshire during the 1784 campaign was Isabella, Duchess of Rutland. An avid supporter of Pitt, Isabella was often described as a "remarkably beautiful woman." She was only a year older than Georgiana, being 28 at the time of the great election. The daughter of the duke of Beaufort, Isabella had been married to the fourth duke of Rutland since 1775, and had given birth to five children in as many years immediately prior to the Westminster campaign. Despite earlier opposition, her husband had joined Pitt's government in February 1784, on the eve of the great contest, being rewarded for his newfound loyalty with the lord-lieutenancy of Ireland. The Rutlands immediately developed a reputation "as the handsomest couple in Ireland," who "led the fashions in the drawing rooms and in the clubs."[61] Returning to Ireland immediately after the Westminster election, the duchess suffered a miscarriage. "The life she leads is enough to kill her," Lady Clermont reported to Lady Spencer in July from Dublin. The Rutlands "*breakfast* out of town at 5 o'clock in the afternoon."[62] Nevertheless, this duchess escaped the notoriety that plagued Georgiana.

The "rival duchesses," as the press liked to portray them, had known each other since girlhood, and as married women they were near neighbors in Derbyshire. Unlike the duchess of Devonshire, however, the duchess of Rutland was a very conventional member of the *ton*, if grandly so. No one would have mistaken the two duchesses for friends. Indeed, Georgiana believed that the rumor that she was having an affair with Fox originated with the duchess of Rutland.[63]

The visibility of the duchess of Rutland and the politicization of society generated by the 1784 election can be seen by an episode which took place at the opera. "I had several good political fights," Georgiana reported eagerly to her mother. "Lady Sefton says this is a great Aria in the History of England—the Duchess of Rutland said d— Fox, upon which Col. St. Leger with great difficulty spirited up Lady Maria Waldegrave to say d— Pitt."[64] The duchess of Rutland—whose husband was said to have passed out thousands of pounds in "donations" to the borough's residents—canvassed Westminster that spring and again in the by-election of 1788.[65] Meanwhile she was negotiating privately over the political fate of Cambridge, offering "all my interest" for the County "if the General and Mr. Yorke will give up all their interest in the borough to me and my family."[66]

The duchess of Rutland benefited considerably from her participation in the 1784 election. The visibility of her services to Pitt left her well placed to manage the Rutland interest when her husband died in 1787 at the age of only 33, the victim, as Lady Clermont had nearly predicted, of his own excesses.[67] His heir, now the fifth duke, was only nine years old. The duchess, who had always thrived on a fast-paced lifestyle, now found herself in charge of one of the nation's largest political interests, managing elections and other political business in areas as widespread as Yorkshire, Leicestershire, and Cambridgeshire. Until the young duke came of age some twelve years later, most of the vast Rutland patronage was in the duchess's formidable hands.[68] In her widowhood, she even signed her letters as simply, "Rutland," with a great flourish.

As mother and legal guardian of the largest landowner in Leicestershire, the duchess of Rutland was expected to be a real, rather than merely a nominal, political force. She was asked, for instance, to "signify her decided wish" at the County contest of 1790, both to strengthen Pitt's support and to "secure the Rutland interest till the

Duke comes of age."[69] As head of the Rutland interest she also received and responded to the numerous "begging" letters which found their way to her. Her husband was barely cold in his grave when she received a request from one John Lambert "to procure me some satisfaction for the losses I sustained by my attachment to his Grace's interest in the last Westminster election. My zeal for his Grace's interest on that occasion has been allmost my ruin."[70]

When the duchess could meet such requests from the patronage in her own gift, she did so. Otherwise, when she thought it politically useful to do so, she passed them along to Pitt, with whom she was in constant communication. "As an election draws near," she peevishly wrote the prime minister in 1790, after receiving numerous requests from Scarborough, "they always expect more to be done." She wanted a post for the son of a member of the corporation which "would be very advantageous to My Interest," but only if it could be secured "before the Election."[71] By 1793, her legendary haughtiness had so offended the Scarborough corporation that they rejected her choice for Parliament.[72] Her interest remained, however, and in 1802 she sponsored the candidacy of one of her younger sons—who lost.

If the duchess of Rutland benefited from her support for Pitt in Westminster, her fellow canvasser, Mrs. Hobart, did not fare as well. Always portrayed in the political cartoons as incredibly fat and grossly unattractive, the unfortunate Mrs. Hobart was already a 45-year-old mother of eight at the time of the Westminster election. She was thus considerably older than most of her fellow—and rival—female canvassers. The cartoonists were still having fun at her expense in 1787, when Gillray portrayed her, her obesity exaggerated, pouring incense at the altar of Venus.[73]

Nevertheless, Albinia Hobart was very much a part of a tightly knit Tory nexus. Her eldest son, already an adult, was an aide-de-camp to the duke of Rutland in Ireland. One of her husband's sisters was married to the sexually-challenged Lord Castlereagh. The daughter of Lord Vere Bertie and a cousin of the Westminster candidate Sir Cecil Wray,[74] Albinia had been married in 1757 to George Hobart, who became third earl of Buckinghamshire in 1793 in succession to a half-brother, who left him the title but not the estate. Blickling, along with its extensive Norfolk acreage, went, instead, to a sister. One senses that this couple were as hapless as the Rutlands were dashing. Rumor had it that the Hobarts lacked the fortune to maintain the dignity of his earldom, and that Albinia resorted to keeping a public faro bank at her home, inviting the public "to contribute in a polite way to the establishment of this needy Countess."[75]

Whether or not that were true, Albinia Hobart indeed enjoyed gambling. She was also widely known for her interest in amateur theatricals, in which she often acted and danced. Since these were passions she shared with the fashionable members of the Whig aristocracy, she seems to have socialized with them. Yet even her friends found her somewhat preposterous. "Poor woman!" wrote the Foxite Mrs. Crewe in her journal after visiting Mrs. Hobart in Paris in December 1785. "Such sort of People, who seem born to divert the world, and yet live upon its indulgence, make me at Moments feel quite melancholy."[76]

As this excerpt suggests, Frances Anne Crewe, who canvassed for Fox in Westminster, had a discerning and sympathetic intelligence. Both of her parents were in fact published writers, and her own "Extracts from Mr. Burke's Table-Talk at Crewe Hall" were published after her death. All her life Mrs. Crewe was acquainted with the finest minds of her time. Born Frances Anne Greville in 1748, she was the daughter of Fulke Greville and Frances Macartney, a lifelong friend of Lady Spencer's. Fanny Greville's father was the friend and patron of Dr. Burney, while Mrs. Greville became godmother to his daughter Fanny. The two Fannies—only four years apart—grew up together, the one becoming a famous hostess, the other, an even more famous author. In 1766 Fanny Greville married John Crewe, of Crewe Hall in Cheshire, who represented the Whigs for that county from 1768 to 1802. It was he who introduced the 1782 bill for the disfranchisement of revenue officers, one of the first great successes in the war against "Old Corruption." From the time of her marriage Mrs. Crewe was a well-known hostess, in the country as well as at the Crewes' Hampstead villa. Fox, Sheridan, Burke, and Reynolds were her frequent guests and correspondents, as was George Canning of the rising generation. Through her mother, the duchess of Devonshire probably knew Mrs. Crewe much of her life; we know that as early as 1778 the duchess visited the Crewes and Mrs. Greville at Tunbridge while the duke was at camp at nearby Coxheath.[77]

Contemporaries regarded Mrs. Crewe as something more than a

great beauty, though she was clearly that as well. Fanny Burney later wrote that Mrs. Crewe was so beautiful that no woman could bear the comparison. "She uglified everything near her," she said. Nevertheless, Fanny Crewe somehow maintained a virtuous reputation despite the odds against it. Fox wrote that though "she loved high play and dissipation," Mrs. Crewe "never lost an atom of character, I mean female honor."[78] Charles Arbuthnot, who met her in 1790, was surprised to find that "instead of a fine lady, she is a comfortable kind of a creature, that has read a great deal and is amazingly well-informed."[79] Becoming a Portland Whig after the party split in the 1790s, Mrs. Crewe had ties to the Whigs that were primarily those of friendship and conviction, rather than family. Nevertheless in 1793 her younger brother married a daughter of the duke and duchess of Portland, a match that was more the consequence than the cause of the ties that cemented the Crewes to the grand Whiggery.

Along with her beauty and intellectual connections, Mrs. Crewe brought with her into the Whig camp her friend Mrs. Bouverie. Harriot Bouverie, also born in 1748, was the only daughter of Sir Everard Fawkener. Her pedigree too, was as interesting intellectually and culturally as it was socially. Sir Everard, who had begun life as a merchant, ended as the ambassador to the Porte. Along the way, he had befriended Voltaire in Paris: when the philosopher visited England several years later, Sir Everard was his host.

In 1764 Harriot Fawkener married Edward Bouverie, who in later years would be known as the boon companion of the prince of Wales. A younger son of Viscount Folkestone, Ned had inherited Delapré Abbey in Northampton from his mother, which brought him into the orbit of the Spencers. Invited to contest the county in opposition to them in 1784, Bouverie declined: he in fact sat for the borough as a Foxite from 1790 to 1810. These connections, and Harriot's intimacy with Mrs. Crewe—Reynolds painted them together in 1769—brought her into the heart of Whig society.[80] Indeed, three months before the Westminster campaign began, Harriot Bouverie's brother married Georgiana, "Jockey," Poyntz, Lady Spencer's niece and the duchess of Devonshire's first cousin.[81] Politics and friendship once again predated family ties.

"The beautiful Mrs. Bouverie" ultimately had eight children, one of whom was less than a year old at the time of the famous Westminster campaign. Like her colleagues, Mrs. Bouverie was known as an enthusiastic Foxite. Lord Glenbervie, who met her in 1793, said "She looks very like a lady to be such a democrat." Someone had reported to him earlier that Mrs. Bouverie spoke a rather "democratical" language even then, and that "she hoped to see the time when there would be no overgrown fortunes and when the poor would be in easy circumstances and the fine ladies lay down their coaches and walk the streets."[82]

We are now ready to draw a portrait of the canvassing lady. Whether Whig or nascent Tory, she was likely to have close family and personal connections with members of her political "tribe," with whom she shared deeply cherished convictions. Many women canvassed and engaged in political activity throughout their lives. Far from representing an aberration, the decision to canvass in Westminster was a fairly typical expression of a woman's political stance, and often part of a family's overall political strategy. Many canvassing ladies even seem to have been happily married, usually to men who shared their political predilections and ambitions. What is striking particularly about the Westminster contingent is that most, like Georgiana, were young mothers with small children or even infants at home. This suggests that political engagements at such times in one's life was by no means unusual: nevertheless, the duchess of Devonshire was the only one criticized for it.

The canvassing lady of 1784 was untroubled by notions of public and private, and unaware that historians of the future would exclude her from the political nation. She herself was in no doubt. The duchess of Rutland was personally possessive over "My interest," that is, her political claims in Scarborough.[83] Similarly, the duchess of Devonshire saw herself as having a direct relationship with, and responsiblity to, the nation. "When I think the Country may be sav'd," she wrote Fox in 1804, urging him to form a coalition government, "I should be *mauvais ami et mauvais Citoyenne* [sic] if I did not tell you my opinion."[84]

Yet the duchess of Devonshire saw herself as both inside the political nation and as a gendered political subject in a way that would probably have been foreign to many canvassing ladies of her time. One cannot imagine "Rutland" or Lady Salisbury, for instance, responding to Philip Francis's inquiry as Georgiana did in 1798. Francis wondered why people kept voting for Pitt even though everyone liked Fox better. "The confidence of men are with Pitt," Georgiana admitted.

They respect him, as often a wife does a husband—think him a very disagreeable fellow, but a good manager of their views and happiness; and now, tho' they think he has been going and going on too far, yet they still cling to their spouse, least the separation or divorce should bring on immediate ruin; for they have given up all their settlements, jointure and even Pin money into his hands . . . but their hearts are with Charles. He is not rich enough for an elopement with him; and the husband, by extreme jealousy and misrepresentation, has hurt him a little in their opinion; but still they love him in secret. He has a heart. Pitt has none . . . They feel themselves in a bad situation, and if a long trial at last engages the people to break with Pitt, it will be for no petty intrigue, but for the lover whose ability and Genius could save them . . . and whom they have so long felt to be their destiny.[85]

When comparing Fox and Pitt supporters other differences emerge. The issue in 1784 was not whether canvassing ladies were operating outside their allotted sphere. The duke of Devonshire's highly critical family, who had the previous year attacked Georgiana's breast-feeding as an unnecessary romantic affectation,[86] had no such qualms about her political activities. The worst thing Lord John Cavendish, her husband's uncle and the political leader of his family, could find to say about Georgiana's canvassing was that she perhaps displayed "too much vivacity."[87] Lord Spencer, as quoted earlier, wished his own wife would canvass. The duke of Portland's did. The discussion is really about how women of rank should conduct themselves in public, particularly in the troublesome presence of common folk. It was not the *fact* of the canvassing that seemed indecent, but the way it was done.

Standards of decency were being contested: standards of decency that conveyed political meaning in a particular political context. It was not so much what a woman did as how she did it that concerned the dowager Lady Spencer. As we have seen, even in the first months of widowhood she took charge of a political campaign. But when appearing "in publick," she advised her younger daughter, Harriet Lady Duncannon, in 1786, it was essential "to maintain a certain dignity that should belong to your station in life."[88] So the critique was at least as class-specific as it was attached to gender. And Foxite ladies apparently observed a different fashion in public behavior than did their opponents. "Though by no means devoid of attractiveness and charm," A. S. Turberville wrote some years ago, the Tory women "were not possessed of the altogether exceptional magnetism and brilliance, and vivacity of the Whig ladies; nor," he adds importantly, "were they so ready to unbend and to woo the populace by such bold methods of allurement."[89]

Once again the perceptive Mrs. Crewe comes to our assistance. "The Mechanical, or technical part of politeness," she observed in her journal in 1786, "is much less attended to in London than in Paris," where she was enjoying an extended stay. "I hate the Ceremony of formal visits," she noted. "If the most intimate Friends in London were all resolved to visit each other in the stiff way they do at Paris, there would very soon be no such thing as Friendship. It would be all form and nothing more." But on further reflection, and upon conversation with Miss Carter—possibly the bluestocking Elizabeth, a friend of Lady Spencer's—Mrs. Crewe realized the difference was as much a generational one as a national one. The formal manners she witnessed in Paris with such intense dislike "is exactly what it was in England thirty or forty years ago," and which many of the elderly or more conservative English, in her view, continued to practice.[90]

As with comportment, so too fashion itself, although here Mrs. Crewe was less sanguine about the beneficence of the change. "All the old Laws belonging to it are repealed, so that many a poor Body who has not much judgement or taste, Sins more innocently, and is laughed at for an affectation of her own,"[91] she wrote after yet another visit to the unfortunate Mrs. Hobart, who like Mrs. Crewe was lingering in Paris in 1786. In other words, although personal intimacy was enhanced through the relaxation of manners, spontaneity in fashion simply gave women enough rope to hang themselves. Even the usually self-confident Mrs. Crewe recognized the inherent dangers of too much latitude in dress.[92] The fashion for romantic simplicity, she thought, had overwhelmed the women of her circle. As she reflected ruefully in her journal, "the dress with us inclines all to the Arcadian. Surely last spring in London every woman seemed more like a Shepherdess out of her element than any other thing!"[93]

Obviously, this "Poetical," Arcadian style of dress suited the more informal style of manners—but was hard to carry off. Nor did it convey rank and grandeur in the way that more formal clothes and manners do. Mrs. Hobart apparently lacked the easy grace that it required, and that the duchess of Devonshire, the comfortably beautiful Mrs. Crewe, and the democratically beautiful Mrs. Bouverie all had. Nor had Mrs. Hobart the more traditional aristocratic hauteur of a Lady Salisbury or a duchess of Rutland. But that aristocratic hauteur would itself become unacceptable to increasing numbers of voters, like those at Scarborough. Yet the more relaxed, informal style, which was denominated "ease" when exemplified by a distinguished man, too often became translated as "easy," with all its unpleasant sexual connotations, when practiced by a woman.

That there were political meanings attached to fashion and manners did not escape the attention of contemporaries. Even as early as 1776, the pamphlet literature suggested that the duchess of Devonshire wore her famous feathers, not for aesthetic reasons, but for political ones. Lady Louisa Stuart was sure this was so. The queen was known to dislike tall feathers, Lady Louisa recalled, and the ladies of the Whig opposition were "glad to set her Majesty at defiance and express their disaffection by wearing ostrich plumes."[94]

Styles changed, but fashion continued to communicate political meanings. Lavinia, Lady Spencer—who, in her husband's words, lacked the spirit to canvass—hated the unstructured fashion which by 1793 had become predominant. "We are all so sensible of the benefit of mental liberty," she wrote her mother-in-law sarcastically, "that we think bodily liberty must be as delightful."[95] If this was a style detested by Conservative Evangelical women like Lavinia, one can well imagine that it suited her sister-in-law, the duchess of Devonshire. Indeed, Georgiana probably began the fashion in the first place.[96]

The notion of romantic, Arcadian simplicity recalls the anecdote about Georgiana losing her shoe in St. Albans. It is impossible to imagine the duchess of Rutland willingly canvassing barefooted—or claiming to—in quite the same manner, just as it is impossible to imagine Georgiana volunteering to help someone—but only if it can be done before an election. So the parties of canvassing women are by no means interchangeable. The well-known diarist Nathaniel Wraxall succinctly summed up the women of the two sides when he recalled that the haughty Lady Salisbury, the duchess's rival in both the St. Albans and the Westminster campaigns, never forgot her rank—and never allowed anyone else to. But Georgiana, he added, never remembered.[97] And it was this very indifference which made Georgiana so effective a campaigner and such a target for abuse in the great constituency of Westminster.

◄ V ►

Sex, Lies, and Stereotypes

It is only within this context that we can appreciate Georgiana's achievement. In a constituency where the voters were not gentlemen, and where a duchess—a beautiful, young one at that—apparently refused to adopt that "imposing attitude," social subversion might be the fearful result. From this point of view, it did not matter whether Georgiana had allowed herself to be kissed by a butcher: what mattered was that she had put herself in the power of lower-class men.

Butchers themselves played an important symbolic role in this campaign, embodying upper-class fears of the lower classes who, only a few years later, would be famously labeled the "swinish multitude." Pittite propaganda was filled with sneering references to the traditional rough music of "marrow bones and cleavers," the tools of a butcher's trade, which were said to follow in the duchess's wake.[98] The blood-stained figure of the butcher was used by the Wray campaign in an almost synecdochal way to represent the lower-class voters. Whether in verse or cartoon, Georgiana is always found in a butcher's embrace, which suggests its ultimately mythic purpose. Even the St. Albans story, therefore, may be apocryphal: she was said to be entering a butcher's shop when her shoe came undone.

Yet less threatening lower-class stereotypes were available. Foxite verse from the 1784 campaign usually portrayed the humble Westminster voter as a cobbler or tailor. "E'en cobblers she canvass'd, they would not refuse," began one such effort,

> But huzza'd for Fox and no wooden shoes.
> She canvass'd the tailors and ask'd for their votes,
> They all gave her plumpers and cried no turn coats.[99]

In a properly deferential and paternalistic society, the remote dignity of an upper-class woman was her protection. The duchess of Devonshire's offense was to cross the chasm between herself and butchers, and in so doing, reduce herself to being "no more than woman." Do away with the pretensions of rank, and all women are the same—and therefore, fair game. "On this scheme of things," Edmund Burke protested only a few years later in his outraged homage to Marie Antoinette, "a queen, is but a woman; a woman is but an animal; and an animal not of the highest order."[100] Following a similar line of reasoning, one of the nastier but more telling squibs for Wray in the 1784 campaign predicted that

> Beautiful ladies, in all future Elections, it is thought, will be provided by all Candidates to assist them in seducing the Electors. Girls will be brought from Armenia, and the Grecian Islands; Covent Garden with its environs too, will supply females for electioneering. In short, since it has become fashionable to seize the voters by this *handle*, there is no saying what may not be done.[101]

Thus gender became the issue of the day. This provided the Pittites with the opportunity to argue that women had no right to "interfere" in elections, a claim that was not made in any other election I have studied prior to 1784, nor was it made in St. Albans, where Lady Spencer found herself fighting Lady Salisbury for the representation of that ancient borough. But the claim was made by the campaign of Sir Cecil Wray. "The ladies who interest themselves so much in the cause of Elections are perhaps too ignorant to know that they meddle with what does not concern them,"[102] assured one of his broadsides, though he must have known better.

≺ VI ≻

Vindicating the Rights of Women

These attacks provoked appropriate responses from the Fox campaign, arguing that women did indeed have political rights. One of the major points made was that England had no Salic law[103] and had benefited from the wisdom of her female monarchs. Saying that a woman could wear the Crown but could not even canvass for a man was stuff and nonsense. One Foxite squib soberly praised the duchess of Devonshire for "exerting herself to the utmost in what she thinks right ... the cause of liberty and the public good."[104] Female canvassers were often praised for their courage, enthusiasm, and, especially, their patriotism, the quality that Georgiana came to personify. "By truth directed, shall my lay commend," wrote Frederick Dutton, clerk to the Fox Committee,

> The patriot heroine, and the faithful friend
> Who to avert her country's threatened fate,
> Deign'd to lay by her dignity and state.[105]

More typically, humor and satire were used to get the voters' attention. As in many elections, the format of highly stylized Biblical verse was used to present the electoral personae as powerful, abstract, but recognizeable, symbols. The duchess of Devonshire figured prominently in these efforts.

4. So it came to pass that there arose a fair and wise woman from the west; and she said, "I will prevail against the unfaithful, and will join in the cause of the just."
5. Then she ordered the steeds to her chariot, and girded herself with the armour of truth; and her face was bright as an angel, and her voice as a fine-toned cybal.
6. Then she went into the city, saying, "Hearken unto me, O ye patrons, our fathers left us a free people, let us break the shackles preparing for us, lest our children be bond slaves." And they blessed her, yea women with infants at their breast sang in her praise.[106]

There was also a wide variety of cartoons sponsored by Fox's campaign which praised the duchess and other female canvassers. Perhaps the most successful was Rowlandson's "Liberty and Fame introducing Female Patriotism to Britania," in which a demure and behatted woman, clearly identifiable as the duchess of Devonshire, represented female patriotism. In another cartoon, Georgiana embodies "Virtue" while her sister Harriet is in the even less likely guise of "Prudence." Other cartoons deal more explicitly with the circumstances of the Westminster Campaign. "Vox, Populi, Vox Dei," which was "Dedicated to the Ladies who so Conspicuously Exerted themselves in the Cause of Freedom," shows Fox, armed with the staff of Liberty, standing next to the duchess who holds a "Shield of Virtue" to protect her from the arrows of "Woman Hater." In "Apotheosis of the Dutchess," which celebrated Fox's victory after the election was over, Georgiana is depicted trampling on "Scandal" and "the Morning Post," while supported by "Truth and Virtue."[107]

Fox's campaign even seems to have recognized the dilemma faced by an upper-class woman: criticized for being frivolous, she was not allowed to function as a serious member of society. "Let it be known from this time forth," went one eloquent defense, satirizing all the elements of the Pittite attack on Georgiana,

That it shall be downright impudence in any woman of rank to have the condescension of speaking to any person of a lower condition.
That Ladies of quality have no right to entertain friendships, or if they

should be so indiscreet and unfashionable as to prefer one man to another, that it is absolute vulgarity in them to expose it to the world.

That Ladies of quality have no business with the affairs of the nation.

That Ladies ought never to come out of the nursery except to make a pudding for dinner; and that, if they have any spare time, it should be occupied in the stitching of chair covers.[108]

Ultimately, though, this was no laughing matter. The "rights of man" debate, which was in part, at least, both cause and consequence of the recently concluded American Revolution, created an intellectual context in which the rights of women might also be discussed. Donna Andrews has described the development of public debating societies which began to flourish in London during the 1770s, in which men and women, both separately and together, could argue the issues of the day. By 1780 there were 35 differently-named societies advertising debates in the London newspapers, attracting as many as 700 persons of a Saturday evening.[109] Political rights and proper gender relations were increasingly popular topics. In the 1780s alone there were eleven advertised debates which explicitly dealt with the question of political rights for women, including not only the right to vote, but also the right to hold public office and the right to take University degrees.[110] In the 1790s the ideas of Mary Wollstonecraft were much debated, the Westminster Forum devoting a full week in April 1797 to a discussion of her work,[111] shortly before Pitt outlawed the debating societies as subversive and seditious.

There was, then, a larger ideological context in which the 1784 campaign took place, a context in which women's rights were proclaimed. People who attended these public debates were well aware of the political activities of the duchess of Devonshire and other women in their constituency of Westminster. During the spring campaign itself the audience at Coachmakers' Hall took up the question "Is it consistent with decency for the female sex to interfere in elections?" a question that was overwhelmingly decided in the affirmative. Four years and another election later, the Westminster School of Eloquence took up the topic, noting that "As Several illustrious Females have the last two elections for Westminster taken a very active part on behalf of their favorite Candidate, it has been requested that the propriety of such conduct be submitted to a fair and candid discussion." As a newspaper reported the following day, "It was determined that the Fair Sex deserved praise rather than censure for their interference in Elections."[112]

Fox's campaign did not shrink from these conclusions or from its own contributions to the question of women's political rights. The day after the debate at the Coachmakers' Hall, for instance, a political squib appeared advertising that a decisive majority at Coachmakers' had voted in support of the efforts of canvassing ladies.[113] Indeed the Fox campaign believed that attacks on the duchess of Devonshire represented government attacks on all women.

Thanks to Fox's opponent in Westminster, the blundering Sir Cecil Wray, these connections were easily made. Not content with demanding the destruction of the Royal Chelsea Hospital as a waste of taxpayers' money, Sir Cecil also proposed a tax on maid-servants. One Foxite correspondent was quick to make the connection between this and the vitriol used against the Duchess. Has *"the Knight of the Hospital"* he asked rhetorically, "having first endeavored to oppress the lower order of women, thought it expedient to proceed with the same good-natured intention to the highest?"[114] One bit of Foxite propaganda presented a purported government "Secret Service Ledger," which included such expenses as £10 "for several paragraphs against women," a handsome £500 for "indecent engravings," and £100 for "abusing the female sex," the latter listed as "by order of Mr. P—," as well as a £20 fee to a news proprietor for "abuse of the D—ss."[115] Thus the Foxites accused the government itself of orchestrating this campaign against women. The charge is by no means a ridiculous one.

≺ VII ≻

Masculinity in Crisis

If Fox was the Danton of English politics, than surely the 24-year-old William Pitt was the Robespierre: the incorruptible he was called, even then. "In the flower of youth," recalled one memoirist, "he could not have exhibited more coldness, indifference, or apathy towards women."[116] Pitt's celebrated virginity was already reputed to be, not merely of the youthful, but rather of the perpetual, variety. The famously rakish Fox thought his young rival was ridiculous. Indeed, according to Wraxall, Pitt's apparent apathy toward women was a point "on which his enemies exhausted their wit, dwelling on Pitt's chastity with "malignant, though impotent satisfaction."[117] Thus, one of the frequent defenses generated from the Fox campaign, was not only that women had political rights, but that a real man would be happy to have his passion and his vote swayed by a lovely woman. "The hearts of Englishmen are not yet insensible to the attractive graces of beauty," exhorted one Foxite squib. "It is in vain that the unmanly runners of the immaculate youth revile the sex," argued another.[118] So Georgiana's charms were highlighted, if only to broadcast Pitt's indifference to them.

Consequently and ironically, then, the Fox campaign's emphasis on the beauty of his canvassers encouraged much of the gross abuse heaped upon them. With friends like this, Georgiana did not need enemies. It was Fox's committee, for instance, who put out notices early in the campaign advertising that "the beautiful Duchess of Devonshire is a constant visitor to the sport in Covent Garden." Another informed voters that "the lovely captivator has ensnared with a glance and carried her point by the majestic sweetness of her graces."[119] So the Foxite defenses were by no means limited to the issue of whether women were entitled to political rights. The debate was also about who was a real man.

And for this, too, there was a context. Fear of enfeebled masculinity was another prominent theme of the debates studied by Donna Andrews. In December 1786, for instance, the topic addressed at Coachmakers Hall was, "Which is the most exceptionable character, the Man-Milliner, the Libertine, or the Miser?" The overwhelming response was that the Man-Milliner was most exceptional. In April 1789, the debate topic was similar: "Which is more censurable, the effeminate Foppery of the men, or the masculine Boldness of the Women?"; effeminate Foppery was overwhelmingly agreed to be the more censurable vice. On three occasions in November 1791 alone the group at Coachmakers addressed questions of masculinity. Nor were they by any means the only London group to be concerned with modern masculinity. In 1790 the City Debates took on the question, "Which is the greater Deviation from real Manhood, the Effeminacy of a Man-Milliner, or the Brutality of the modern Boxer?" Even Pitt's bachelorhood was in fact a source of public anxiety. In 1795 the Westminster Forum asked of the young prime minister, leading the nation in an as yet unpopular war against the French, "Which is most likely to subdue the Obstinacy and tame the untoward Disposition of the British Minister—a Peace—a Reform—or a Marriage?"[120]

Where were these gender anxieties coming from? It is probably true that they are always present, but there are also factors specific to this period that we could point to. The question of women's rights was surely as unanswerable as it was intolerable. The loss of the American colonies might have given rise to the sort of belligerent masculinity that other nations have experienced after a particularly galling defeat. And at least according to Randolph Trumbach's account, by 1784 London would certainly have urbanized sufficiently to create a homosexual subculture vibrant enough to scandalize the heterosexual majority.[121] But for all this, we need not ignore the peculiar sexual personae of our major players.

Pitt's very real misogyny cannot be overlooked. His personal spleen was very much in evidence when he spoke to the House of Commons the day after Fox's victory was secured. Pitt denied that that election had been a true test of public opinion as it had been "eminently produced by the interference of female charms."[122] Political cartoons of the time illustrate the thoroughly masculine nature of the parades organized in his support, in contrast to those of his contemporaries. If women were not to be accepted as part of public opinion, then clearly they had no place in public spectacles. They were no more to be seen than heard.

It is, however, Pitt's career, despite the potential vulnerability of his celibacy, which is perhaps most in need of explanation. A shrewd politician, he certainly understood that a vigorous offense is the best defense. The point made was that a rake like Fox was defined by women, while the aloof and entirely independent Pitt had no need of them. Pitt kept his distance—Fox could not keep away. And so we get what the Fox campaign regarded as a choreographed attack upon women.

But there are other factors which I believe worked in Pitt's behalf. One was the growing popularity of George III. Despised as a despot and a tyrant only a few years earlier, by the mid-1780s the king was already remaking himself into Farmer George, a benign, loveable masculine figure of authority. Fox's East India Bill and the Fox-North coalition were public relations windfalls for the king. His large family and modest queen were real assets in this reconfiguration of his image. "His private virtues and domestic character drew a veil ... across the errors of his Government," Wraxall noted, "The father, and the husband, protected and sheltered the Prince."[123] Together, George III and Pitt were changing both the terms of political debate and the construction of modern masculinity.

It is perhaps most telling that it was the avidly heterosexual Fox who was increasingly portrayed as effeminate[124] by the cartoonists, transforming his plumpness into pulchritude. Beginning with a 1784 campaign cartoon, in which a single face is split in two—half Georgiana, half Fox—there were at least four cartoons in which Fox is portrayed as a woman.[125] As Gerald Newman has told us, "the fundamental issue" in the 1784 election was "the moral contrast between Pitt and Fox." Pitt succeeded, he argued, by portraying himself as "the embodiment of the English National Character." Fox's intellectualism, his enlightened internationalism, and his life of pleasure, would consign him to the moral and political outer darkness.[126] His dependence on glamorous females to win an election was precisely what was most wrong about Fox. As Phyllis Deutsch has recently pointed out, he was widely regarded as unfit for public office because he had been "unmanned by corrupt female influence." And by then the British public was connecting private behavior with its public consequences.[127] In short, by 1784, Fox's rakish, aristocratic amorality just seemed old-fashioned. Pitt's austere virtue, coupled with George III's paternal authority, was just the thing.

If Pitt and later Castlereagh were vulnerable to the charge that they were not manly enough, it is not only because politics demanded scrupulous obedience to prescribed sex roles, but because it specifically demanded manliness. The duchess of Devonshire, too, had a powerful sexual persona. She was especially vulnerable to attack because her beauty and highly gendered sense of self made her so womanly. This, coupled with her effectiveness with voters, made her especially threatening. One election notice insisted that if women had a right to participate in politics, their power over men would be complete. "Is it to be endured," this writer asked, "that they should not only triumph over us in figure and face, but that they should also be superior to us in accomplishments and sense?"[128]

That such superiority could not be endured was evident. Moreover, the duchess's success with voters of lower rank, in combination with her Foxite politics, made her truly dangerous. Her conduct revealed the surprising dangers that lurked within the ostensibly comfortable confines of deference. Her apparent unconsciousness of rank only had meaning *because* she was in reality, a duchess, and not Citoyenne Cavendish or "Mrs." Crewe. It was not simply the duchess's beauty, but her rank that supposedly dazzled the impressionable Westminster voter. Was she to be the Pied Piper of Covent Garden, leading butchers down the primrose path to democracy? One cartoon addressed this very fear, showing Fox entering the House of Commons on the shoulders of the duchess, followed by a cheering crowd of the ubiquitous butchers.[129] Political fears mixed with sexual ones to create a heady brew. If she forgot her place, would she persuade butchers to forget theirs? How could upper-class men protect the chastity of—that is, their property in—upper-class women if they could not keep them from roaming freely about the streets, mingling with men of the lower classes?

≺ VIII ≻

In Conclusion

The primary novelty that was introduced in the 1784 Westminster campaign was the friendly interaction between women of rank and voters of humble station. This created a host of class and sexual tensions, exacerbated by the success of the female canvassers. Simultaneously, the sexual personalities of Pitt and Fox brought issues of masculinity visibly to the fore. Even the defenders of female patriots offered highly gendered arguments. In their zeal to showcase Pitt's presumed inadequacies, they used female canvassers to sell "female charm," another novelty of the Westminster campaign, one made easier by the apparently exceptional beauty and relaxed deportment of Fox's contingent.

But for too long, the historical memory has focused on the mythical image of a duchess kissing butchers for votes. It may well be that, while Fox had the more effective canvassers, Pitt had the better cartoonists. Or perhaps lewd drawings simply linger longer in the memory than do decent ones. But as an indicator of popular political attitudes, cartoons are surely less reliable than the election results themselves. Political cartoonists, after all, were not simply talented representatives of the *vox populi*. They were hired political agents. James Sayers, for instance, was rewarded with a sinecure by

Pitt for the anti-Fox cartoons he produced in 1784, which, his victim complained, "had done him more mischief than the debates in Parliament or the works of the press." The diarist Wraxall concurred. "It is difficult to conceive the moral operation and wide diffusion of these caricatures through every part of the country," he noted.[130]

Political strategy definitely dictated the content of the caricatures. Fox could not retaliate in kind, once he had asserted that women had a right to participate in the political life of their nation, and that it was unmanly to launch *ad feminem* attacks on them for doing so. But partisan attacks on the duchess of Devonshire, far from being symptomatic of the Fox campaign's "inability" to legitimize and explain her endeavors, as Colley would have it, were quite the reverse. It was the duchess's success, not the lack of it, that frightened Wray and the Pittites. One squib gave the game away by actually begging Georgiana to change sides,

> Deluded by friendship, no more go astray,
> Thy Carlo give up, and assist honest Wray.[131]

It is not difficult now to see why the duchess of Devonshire was singled out for persecution in the partisan press. It was not necessary to attack all of Fox's canvassers, when the leader of the pack was such an easy target. Famous well before the 1784 election, Georgiana was already iconographically accessible to the public. A ridiculously long feather, a picture hat, a riding coat, and—for the more skilled cartoonists—a smile at once demure and coquettish immediately identified the duchess of Devonshire. She was as much a gift to cartoonists as was Fox himself, whose girth and heavy-browed swarthiness made him instantly recognizeable.

And while there may have been those sincerely troubled by the existence of a real woman so famous that she had become a symbol, Georgiana has also been a source of inspiration to women and men alike. In the opening pages of Lady Randolph Churchill's 1899 *Anglo-Saxon Review*, her friend Louise, the eighth duchess of Devonshire, recalled

Boswell's account of the Bard who brought to Dr. Johnson for his opinion an "Ode to the Warlike Genius of Britain." Said Johnson, "Here is an error Sir; you have made Genius feminine." "Palpably, Sir," cried the enthusiast; "I know it." But, in a lower tone, "It was to pay a compliment to the Duchess of Devonshire, with which her grace was pleased. She is walking across Coxheath in the military uniform, and I suppose her to be the genius of Britain."[132]

The 1784 Westminster campaign encapsulated so many anxieties about class and gender, and on so many levels, that they bubbled to the surface, capturing the attention of contemporaries and historians alike. At the most general level, we have a host of fears generated by the instability of gender roles and class definitions of the time, undoubtedly heightened by the recent success of the American Revolution. In 1784, discussions about "rights" were not mere abstractions: there were concrete issues of power at stake. Although neither Fox nor his female partisans had anticipated a campaign based on women's rights, the dialectic, once started, could hardly be stopped. That is, the complaint that women had no rights forced Fox's campaign to claim that they had. This is quite different from the usual tradition of landed women campaigning, as they had in St. Albans, on the basis of rank and interest.

But the specifics of the election also contributed to the significance of the campaign. The particular sexual personae of both Fox and Pitt cannot be overlooked in understanding why the campaign degenerated into lewdness. Nor can we disregard the unsavory atmosphere of Covent Garden, or the demographics of Westminster, whose lower-class voters came to be symbolized by the bloodstained figure of the butcher, empowered by an electoral process in which the rich sought the favor of the poor.

But ultimately we must come back to the engaging figure of the duchess herself. Politically active for the rest of her life, Georgiana, Duchess of Devonshire, remained a political force in the many far-flung constituencies where either Spencers or Cavendishes were traditionally influential. But her views remained her own. When the Whig party split in the 1790s, so did the families, Georgiana following Fox into the political wilderness of opposition, while Portland and her brother, the second Earl Spencer, joined Pitt's administration. During the Middlesex contest of 1802—the year she became a grandmother—she actively supported the radical candidate Sir Francis Burdett, whose adherents once again toasted the "healths of Charles Fox and the Duchess of Devonshire and other female canvassers."[133] For many aristocratic women like Georgiana, "ami and Citoyenne," politics indeed remained a subject that "one must think and feel about."[134]

British Women and Radical Politics in the Late Nonconformist Enlightenment, c. 1780–1830

KATHRYN GLEADLE

THE FALL OF THE BASTILLE in 1789 was greeted with ecstatic joy by middle-class dissenting women in Britain. They expressed their delight by dancing around trees of liberty, publicly singing the hastily-composed revolutionary songs, and participating in celebratory dinners. The tricolor badges, cockades, and ribbons sported by women and men alike were visible and public symbols used to signify their support for the revolutionary principles.[1] Two women, Mary Wollstonecraft and Helen Maria Williams, were so thrilled by events in France that they were to travel to Paris to witness the scenes for themselves.[2] In the coming years, as events in France began to turn sour, radical British women could be kept in an agony of suspense as they awaited news from the Continent. Catherine Buck, a young Suffolk woman, bewailed "the anxiety with wch [sic] I wait the arrival of every post[,] the tears I shed."[3] As government hostility toward the Revolution and British radicalism intensified, women of these circles were prepared to risk their personal security, their reputations, or their livelihoods for the sake of their political principles. Amelia Alderson, a leading force in the radical politics of Norwich, was apparently under government surveillance.[4] Eliza Fletcher of Edinburgh, with close friendships and connections across the radical dissenting networks, was widely rumored by her neighbors to carry a dagger under her cloak, and to behead her poultry with a small guillotine, in practice for revolution![5] In South Molton, Devonshire, a young dissenting schoolteacher, Eliza Gould, was forced by her community to choose between her radical politics and her job. She had little hesitation in choosing her principles.[6]

Given the intensity of political passions such as these, it is extraordinary to consider that the political activity of middle-class women during the period 1780–1830 has received scarcely any attention from historians.[7] Catherine Hall's assumption, that women were excluded from public spheres as the ideology of domesticity came to dominate middle-class cultures, has been almost universally accepted.[8] While the late Enlightenment is recognized as producing exceptional figures, such as Mary Wollstonecraft, the growing hold of domesticity has been thought to have restricted most women from political activity. Even women's involvement in extra-domestic activities such as philanthropy has tended to be seen as reflecting women's identification with the Evangelical emphasis upon womanly love and compassion.[9]

Yet, as many historians are now beginning to argue, the project of assigning simple, gendered meanings to the language of separate spheres is highly problematic.[10] These are insights which are only just beginning to be applied to analyses of middle-class women's political activities.[11] As Kathleen Wilson has recently demonstrated, the vibrant cultural and political activities of eighteenth-century provincial England could, despite their masculine ethos and ultimately exclusionary implications, open up some opportunities for women to engage in extra-parliamentary culture, and thus to construe themselves as civic actors.[12] Wilson's thesis is, of course, very much in keeping with recent developments in the historiography of the Enlightenment. Spurred on by the translation of Jürgen Habermas's influential works, historians are now particularly interested not so much in the "big names" of Enlightenment philosophy, but in its social context: the fluorescence of coffee houses, salons, debating societies, and the like; and the ways in which Enlightenment ideas were disseminated and debated.[13]

Historians are becoming increasingly aware of the gendered implications of this new public space.[14] And yet, scholarly debates over the impact of the Enlightenment upon the emergence of a feminist consciousness have been rather slow to reap the rewards of such an approach. Discussion, particularly of the British experience, has tended to focus upon the treatment of gender within Enlightenment discourses, without relating this to the specificities of social and cultural practice. Elizabeth Fox-Genovese, for example, has acknowledged the potential for liberating discourses on women to emerge from Enlightenment theories, but notes that those who pursued such paths were limited to "a few daring writers." She, among others, argues that the overall effect of the Enlightenment was to encourage the growth of the domestic ideal, as new concepts of virtue, combined with a persistent unease concerning female sexuality, came to construct the home as the sphere in which women could best fulfill their potential to themselves and society. In so doing, she asserts, "the male heirs of the Enlightenment repudiated the notion that women, like men, should enjoy political rights—should be citizens."[15] Such an analysis, which assumes that domesticity and political agency were necessarily incompatible, is representative of the historiography.

This chapter seeks to develop possible strategies for uncovering more precisely the gendered reception to Enlightenment ideas. It does this through an analysis of a specific intellectual constituency—British Nonconformity—during the years 1780–1830.[16] In particular, it focuses upon the rational dissenters—a community which played a significant role in the dissemination of late Enlightenment culture in Britain. It considers the ways in which the radical culture of the late Enlightenment could foster a spectrum of empowering possibilities for women. In so doing it analyzes the ways in which this culture facilitated a political conscience among radical dissenting women, while also conditioning the complexities of its expression.

≺ I ≻

The Position of Women within Rational Dissent

The self-perception of the rational dissenters was that they were a community which highly respected women. Certainly they were extremely interested in investigating and discussing the position of women. Their literature was steeped in the tenets of Enlightenment history, in particular the belief that one might test the progress of civilization by analyzing the position of women. Joseph Priestley, one of the key practitioners in the movement, was typical in following Montesquieu, Robertson, and Alexander in tracing the comparative well-being of women throughout the various stages of history—barbarism, feudalism, chivalry, and so on. Most were agreed that the spread of Christianity had been a critical moment for promoting the well-being of the female sex.[17] But within these schema, the analysis of women's contribution to and progressive treatment within society was predicated upon frequently conflicting assumptions. Particularly during the earlier years of this survey, historical treatments of women's position could be veined with that sexual objectification of women, against which Wollstonecraft was later to protest.[18] On the other hand, the more progressive anthropological analyses could point to the political rights which women enjoyed in certain North American tribes but which were denied to English women.[19] And yet, in most of these discussions, the redefinition of virtue to signify domestic values, so central to the Enlightenment project, remained predominant. As a consequence, women came under renewed scrutiny for their ability to educate children and to institute harmonious, moral home lives.[20]

Women's role within the home should certainly be located at the very heart of the rational dissenting ideology. But, as the following discussion will illustrate, this does not mean that the home was understood purely in terms of domestic or maternal duties, for the home too could function in terms of political space. Nor does it follow that women were not welcomed into other "public" forms of activity and expression. Still less does it imply that women were denied the opportunities for political expression and agency.

The rational dissenters owed their philosophical premise to Locke and Hartley. Following Lockean insights that the individual was born with a "blank sheet," and learned through experience and physiological association, they inclined toward an environmentalist view of individual capabilities and potential. Consequently, the rational dissenters placed a tremendous emphasis upon the role of education. Through their excellent academies, such as Daventry, Hoxton, and Warrington, the rational dissenters were able to make a significant contribution to the cultural life of late Georgian England. These academies pioneered new approaches to tertiary education with their emphases on modern languages, biblical criticism, and science; and they also gave enormous impetus to the fostering of informal, intellectual communities.[21]

The rational dissenters, and their successors the Unitarians, were widely famed for their equally pioneering approach to female education. The progressives among them might extend environmentalist philosophy so as to question the validity of "natural" gender differences; even those with more conservative estimations as to women's nature might argue, as did Priestley, that the exercise of one's intellectual faculties was essential to the development of moral faculties. Unitarian educators such as Lant Carpenter instituted excellent provision for girls at their schools, and individual families took female education very seriously, providing top-rate tutors for their daughters.[22] Nevertheless, there was a wide range of ideological and personal motivations which lay behind such an emphasis upon female education. For many, their desire to improve female education derived from an application to women of Lockean ideas concerning the rationality of the individual. Such a perspective tended to emphasize the benefits an education might bring to women. Wollstonecraft's wish to seek "a little peace and *independence*" was a recurring theme among the more radical young women of these circles.[23] For feminists such as the Unitarian Mary Hays, female education was essential; she wished to "rouse my sex from the state of mental degradation, and bondage, in which they have so long been held."[24] However, the Lockean heritage was highly problematic, many concluding from Locke the need for a gender-specific education, which would prepare girls for motherhood.[25] Moreover many dissenting families encouraged the intellectual cultivation of their daughters out of a desire to better equip them as intellectual companions to their future husbands.[26]

Within this wide spectrum of practice and belief, there was potential for women to attain high levels of female academic achievement (even if those who did so were typically represented defensively, as combining "manly wisdom and feminine gentleness").[27] If women could not study at the dissenting academies, then they could at least profit from the intellectual culture which such institutions fostered. Mary Hays, for example, gained much from the public meetings and lectures given by the Unitarian New College at Hackney.[28] One of the more radical women connected with these circles was Mary Robinson, who argued that women's intellectual powers merited the establishment of their own university, complete with scholarships for the less well-off.[29] However, most appeared to have considered that the home was the most appropriate site for advanced female studies. Eliza Fletcher and Susannah Taylor used their female networks to extend their teenage daughters' education, sending them for lengthy visits with the renowned educationist and political radical A. L. Barbauld. Under Barbauld's tutelage they received highly advanced intellectual instruction.[30] The culture of the rational dissenters may have been constructed upon the building blocks of Locke and Hartley, but it was often the women in the family (fuelled by the powerful ethos of female self-education which was typical of these circles) who studied their texts most assiduously.[31] Indeed, women were critical to the evolution of rational dissenting religious culture. Catherine Cappe, for example, enjoyed a nationwide reputation for her contribution to Unitarian theology through her meticulous and scholarly editing of the works of her late husband, Newcombe Cappe (Cappe and Mary Hughes were instrumental in the establishment of the Unitarian Christian Tract Society); while Elizabeth Rayner used her financial resources to assist in the publication of key Unitarian texts. Elizabeth Price capitalized on her intellect and good sense to become a leading advisory figure in the cause of rational dissent in Wales, where she was "eagerly sought for by rich and poor, churchmen and dissenters."[32]

This identification with the religion of rational dissent was in itself immediately politicizing. Under the Test and Corporations Acts, rational dissenters were (in theory) debarred from participating in key aspects of local and national political life.[33] Such discrimination hit at the very heart of the rational dissenting ideology, which championed the causes of religious toleration, the rights of man, and the freedom of expression. By the late 1770s, galvanized by the American fight for independence (which they strongly supported), rational dissenters had begun to mount a vociferous campaign to repeal the much hated acts.[34] Women were active in the propaganda campaign to secure the bill of repeal and were evidently extremely well informed as to its political fortunes. They intervened in the public debate by publishing a variety of literary genres on the subject, at carefully calculated moments. Commissioned by Joseph Johnson, Mary Wollstonecraft translated Jacques Necker's *De L'Importance des Opinions Religieuses* (1788), as part of the propaganda push in the run-up to the presentation of a new bill to Parliament.[35] "The Poem on the Bill," written by Helen Maria Williams (herself the product of provincial Dissenting circles and closely connected to key Unitarians), demonstrated clearly how the campaign to secure the rights of nonconformists drew into its net the wider ideological issue of the rights of man.[36]

It was A. L. Barbauld's influential pamphlet, *Address to the Opposers of the Repeal of the Corporation and Test Acts* (1790), however, which drew out most clearly the full implications of the rational dissenters' position. Written as a direct response to events in Parliament, Barbauld demanded the dissenters' "natural and inalienable right" to hold civic office. Her pamphlet made subversive swipes at the legitimacy of the established constitution and ended with a dramatic, revolutionary climax; which, given the developments occurring in France, was redolent with significance: "All the power and policy of man cannot continue a system long after its truth has ceased to be acknowledged . . . Whatever is loose must be shaken; whatever is not built on the broad basis of public utility must be thrown to the ground."[37]

While Barbauld consistently argued for the rights of dissenters to representation and civic office, she did not extend her philosophy to argue for the rights of women. Indeed, her poem "The Rights of Women" warned that a strident feminism might jeopardize women's existing status and damage gender relations.[38] Yet within the circles in which she moved, feminism was much debated. Mary Wollstonecraft (with whom she was friends) was intimate with the circles and coteries with which this chapter is concerned, being particularly associated with Richard Price, Joseph Johnson, and William Godwin.[39] Wollstonecraft, moreover, was but one of many progressive voices on women within this milieu. As Jane Rendall and Angela John emphasize in this volume, male support for feminist causes could form a key element in the make-up of progressive milieus. Thomas Beddoes, for example, the radical chemist and physician, was daring in his determination to give lectures on physiology to a female audience, was at pains to employ a female compositor to print his work, and believed wholeheartedly in the intellectual equality of women.[40] John Jebb, among others, was concerned with the legal subordination of women;[41] leading figures, notably the Unitarian minister William Shepherd, upheld the principle of female enfranchisement.[42]

Many of the rational dissenters' contacts in the wider radical community were similarly liberal—both Thomas Holcroft and John Gale Jones believed in the equality of the sexes.[43] Views such as these were not confined merely to the progressive metropolitan literati but also found a warm reception in many provincial circles.[44] As the flood of feminist works which followed Wollstonecraft's *Vindication on the Rights of Women* demonstrated, there was a widespread audience for progressive discussions on women's rights.[45] Yet *Vindication* remained but one possible application of Enlightenment theories. While the existence of feminist voices was undoubtedly enormously stimulating for debates on women within these circles, there was not an inevitable corollary between the ideology of rational dissent and a feminist view point. If the politically active women considered in this chapter did share Wollstonecraft's feminist critique, this was not an agenda to which they necessarily wished to give priority. After all, dissenting men as well as dissenting women were disenfranchised: it was the discrimination against their community as a whole which most women wished to redress. Women within the rational dissenting milieu appear to have embraced the opportunities for education, the emphasis upon individual rationality, and also the Enlightenment emphasis upon female domesticity to develop their own traditions of radical political expression, without necessarily embracing, or at any rate advertising, feminism.

≺ II ≻

Women in the Political Culture of Radical Nonconformity

The radical politics which underpinned rational dissent were evident from the highly politicized nature of dissenting ministers' sermons. As James E. Bradley has observed, "many Dissenting ministers in the provinces not only articulated radical ideology; these preachers helped popularize and legitimize political dissent." Dissenting ministers commonly encouraged the formation of political associations and urged congregations to sign petitions to Parliament—for example the peace petitions of 1775.[46] Clearly women's attendance at services conducted by radical dissenting ministers would have been an important source for their engagement with the political world and contemporary affairs. Nonconformist women debated sermons among themselves, corresponded on the issues they raised, and made specific arrangements to hear the sermons of distinguished figures such as Priestley.[47]

However, the highly developed cultural world of rational dissent provided a plethora of opportunities for female engagement with political and current affairs which extended far beyond the reach of the pulpit. The educational sophistication of the movement led to high levels of literary attainment, enabling its practitioners to lead a prominent role in the rapidly evolving print culture of the day. Rational dissenters proliferated as booksellers, publishers, and writers.[48] In London a vibrant community of male and female writers, actors, and playwrights was closely engaged with the sociable world of the radical intelligentsia, clustering around the radical Unitarian publisher Joseph Johnson. In the provinces the rational dissenters were responsible for some of the best provincial journalism of the day, to which women, as we shall see, often contributed.[49] There, as in the metropolis, the vibrant social and intellectual networks fostered by the dissenters encouraged a wide range of cultural activities (singing, debating, acting, literary composition) which were highly conducive to female involvement and brought women into direct contact with many of the influential thinkers of the day. In Chichester, for example, the Quaker poet Maria Hack was a respected member of a cultural circle which included fellow writers and Unitarian ministers.[50]

In addition to such informal cultural gatherings, at which women were evidently prominent, the rational dissenters consolidated their cultural prominence by establishing more formal institutions. Up and down the country they were responsible for a host of book clubs and debating societies, in addition to the highly esteemed Literary and Philosophical Societies—all bodies which were crucial for the dissemination of Enlightenment culture.[51] The interaction of women with this more formalized set of cultural activities was variable. Women appear to have been excluded from the membership of most formal political and cultural societies. Eliza Florance was clearly piqued at her exclusion from the Non-Con Club (a politically conscious Unitarian Society) of which her fiancé was a member; "[A]re you afraid," she teased, "like the freemasons, of their telling the world that you are but as other men, and have, in fact, no secrets worth knowing?"[52] However, in some cases, women were afforded greater access to some of these institutions than the official record books might suggest. The Literary and Philosophical Societies, for example, are presumed to have been exclusively male domains; yet Eliza Coltman of Leicester and her friend Mrs. Reid were very excited to become the first women in the city to participate in the Literary and Philosophical Society there, by attending a lectures series on the latest scientific developments in electricity and hydraulics.[53] Only further research will reveal how representative (or otherwise) such an incident may have been.

Most book clubs were open to women and indeed were often established by them.[54] Clubs such as these could provide a forum for women to project their own principles onto the larger community. A. L. Barbauld, a champion of political and religious toleration, persuaded her local book club to admit Jewish women.[55] As Donna Andrew has revealed, London debating societies of the period provided stimulating and often mixed-sex venues for the discussion of contemporary issues.[56] It would appear that in the provinces, bodies such as book clubs could provide a similar forum for radical political debate. In the little town of Royston a radical book club was established by two local Unitarian families. When Henry Crabb Robinson attended he found almost equal numbers of men and women, who had gathered together to discuss the philosophy of William Godwin.[57]

Among the most radical elements in political and dissenting culture, women were sometimes admitted to political societies and secret meetings. Rachel Lee, for example, the daughter of the radical Francis Dashwood (an early supporter of the Unitarian movement) was asked to attend a "meeting of the people" in London, by a supporter of "furious, jacobinical principles," who addressed Lee "by the epithet of citizen."[58] In Norwich, a hot-bed of rational dissent, women were given membership of certain radical political societies.[59] Women's engagement in political debate was not necessarily confined to the defined spaces of exceptional radical societies, however. Their confidence as political actors could lead women to claim a voice in amorphous public settings. Even single women traveling alone had the political self-assurance to engage in controversial debate. On his journey from Maidstone to Rochester, the radical activist John Gale Jones shared a coach with a young woman, an earnest democrat, who eagerly discussed politics and parliamentary reform with him.[60] When Thomas Hardy, recently acquitted of treason, was on a journey to Leicester, a lady passenger sprang to his defense when he was insulted by a gentleman on the coach.[61] At times, such self-assurance might erupt into more extraordinary behavior. In

Norwich in 1794, when a crowd of over 1,500 so-called "Jacobins" had assembled at the town hall to protest against the local Whig MP, William Windham, three radical middle-class women, Amelia Alderson, Annabella Plumptre, and Anne Plumptre, took the stage. With the Plumptres cheering her on, Amelia Alderson proceeded to make a long speech to the gathered crowd.[62]

≺ III ≻

The Politicization of the Domestic Site

For radical women such as these, the domestic setting was unlikely to be seen only as a politically-neutral sphere, reserved for the inculcation of spiritual and moral values. For a woman like Ann Jebb, an intimate friend of Anne Plumptre, the home was the center of radical activity. In 1784 Jebb was fully involved in the efforts of her husband, John, to create an association of the people in an attempt to keep the issue of constitutional reform alive. Consequently, their house functioned as an office, from which Ann Jebb penned her considerable correspondence attempting to galvanize reform efforts, as well as a meeting place for radical discussion.[63]

Women were also adept at creating their own cultural and political spaces within their domestic environment. One such context for women's political expression lay in the extensive correspondence networks, which were common to elite women of this period. Such networks could foster a vibrant community of letters, which might encourage female articulation of political beliefs and, at times, stimulate a nascent feminist consciousness. This was so of the rational dissenter Mary Scott, whose *Female Advocate* was published in 1774. This work (assumed by one Unitarian journal to have been directly inspired by the Enlightenment[64]) arose out of a long debate concerning women's intellectual position which had preoccupied Scott's correspondence network of politically-conscious Nonconformist provincial women in the southwest.[65] For women with cultural, social, and economic influence, the salon facilitated, as Gary Kelly has recently observed, a "social space at once public and domestic to develop Enlightenment culture."[66] In Norwich, the salon of the radical dissenter Susannah Taylor attracted not only the cream of the local intellectual elite—William Enfield, Amelia Alderson, and William Taylor—but also figures of national stature such as Henry Brougham, Robert Southey, and James Mackintosh. Despite her radical politics and intellectual repute, Taylor does not appear to have supported particularly progressive views on women's position. Certainly her habit of darning her children's stockings while holding forth with some of the best male intellects of the day encapsulated the combination of the domestic with the political, which was such a feature of these women's lives.[67]

Many women capitalized upon their intellectual confidence (fuelled as it was by the access they had to education, debating societies, lectures, and the like) by positioning themselves as mentors to young men. Thus, they could create their own sphere of influence. Lord Brougham always maintained that the Edinburgh radical Eliza Fletcher had been of "great use to him as a young man."[68] Similarly, the young Henry Crabb Robinson came to look on Catherine Buck as his "oracle." Catherine Buck was the eldest child of William and Sarah Buck, whose house in Bury St. Edmunds formed a salon for local radicals and nonconformists. Catherine and her closest friend, Sarah Jane Maling, thrived in this atmosphere; they were, Maling declared, a "glorious tribe of *intrepid thinkers*" who addressed each other as "citoyenne" and "citoyen." They read widely and were known for their skilled and fierce political debates, Sarah earning herself a nickname as "Tom Pain [sic] in petticoats." Crabb Robinson recalled that he was the disciple of these two young women, who introduced him to the principles of the French Revolution and to radical political thought.[69]

The efforts of women such as these to establish political and cultural purchase, from within their essentially domestic sites, was typical of their approach to the role of the home and domesticity. Their performance of domestic and familial tasks could function as an extension of their deeply held political views. Even the management of the household could signify political allegiances, particularly when it came to consumer decisions. Rosamund Beddoes, the sister of the radical physician Thomas Beddoes, in Shifnal, was delighted by Thomas Hardy's acquittal from the charge of treason, and ordered "two or three dozen pairs" of shoes from him, as an expression of her support.[70] Traditional female activities such as the provision of food could also assume political significance. One radical woman made clear her defiance of government policy by organizing a huge banquet for her local community on a fast day.[71] As J. E. Cookson has noted, for the rational dissenters, fast days were "an outlet for political sentiment over which the state had no control."[72]

Wider issues were also at stake, however. For practitioners of the Nonconformist Enlightenment, a renewed emphasis upon domestic virtues formed part of a wider political critique of the seemingly exploitative and self-seeking relationships of courtly society.[73] Even the most progressive predicted that women would remain at the center of the home.[74] But they sought new family models, in which relationships were dictated by reason and affection and in which politically-informed mothering could create the rational, egalitarian citizens of the future. This concept of "republican" motherhood has attracted a good deal of attention, encapsulating as it does Wollstonecraft's conviction that women could fulfill their duties as citizens through the performance of maternal duties.[75] Historical analyses of the "body" have, in this context, tended to view such developments negatively. They are seen to epitomize the equation of women with the natural, which was so prevalent in discourses of the Enlightenment.[76] However, for radical women, the family provided the site whereby the male body, criticized by contemporary feminists for its continual slide into sexual desire, might be sublimated within the new rational marriages.[77]

Moreover, the new models of motherhood were, for these women, a source of empowerment whereby they felt able to express and actively promote political ideals. George Dyer, a prominent Unitarian radical, wrote to Mary Hays of his delight in staying with his friends James Green, a radical MP, and his family. Green's wife, he noted, shared her husband's progressive "manners and principles." This "most agreeable of women" ensured that her children were not "trained up like boarding schoolmisses," (whom, Dyer notes, Hays had "so properly characterize[d] in *Emma Courtney*") but rather had taught them "the simplicity and generosity of republican manners."[78] Eliza Fletcher, the renowned Edinburgh radical, provides further insights into the ways in which women carved out their own political model of mothering. Fletcher was evidently determined to provide her children (and later her grandchildren) with a political education, often taking them to hustings during elections, where they stood for "several hours" to hear the candidates' speeches.[79] As this example indicates, political motherhood was not merely a question of inculcating appropriate manners and attitudes in the home environment, but could slip easily into the public world of electoral politics.

Further subtleties in the ways in which women sought to position and express themselves politically may be evidenced through their various understandings of their roles as "political wives." Retrospective memoirs of radical women often tended to foster the image of a sympathetic wife, dutifully supporting the politics of her husband. Such representations are frequently misleading, however. The elderly Eliza Fletcher, when looking back upon her life, tended to portray her own radicalism in terms of her sympathy for the principles of her late husband, Archibald, one of the foremost Scottish advocates of borough reform. Yet contemporaries perceived Eliza to be the true radical force in the family. In a parliamentary speech Lord Brougham praised Eliza's "inflexible principles and deep political feeling," which "further excited" her husband's zeal for political reform. Indeed, through salons, largesse, use of the radical network, and sheer force of personality Eliza Fletcher created her own political authority within Edinburgh, which was complementary to, but distinct from, that of her husband.[80]

The work of Ann Jebb was similarly portrayed by contemporaries in the context of her husband's radical activities. Widely known for her brilliant political acumen, she was passionately involved with contemporary radicalism—and as her obituary noted, "her zeal rose to the full level of her husband's."[81] The role of a supportive wife did not mean merely the provision of domestic succor and encouragement, however. For Ann Jebb it meant launching herself fully into the fray of fierce public debate. Her first polemical writings arose when John Jebb, as a young tutor at Cambridge, campaigned for the institution of annual examinations and protested over the necessity of subscribing to articles of faith. Such protests were a significant factor leading to the emergence of a distinctive Unitarian denomination. Ann Jebb's stinging articles in the public press attacking the establishment case in this key debate became widely cited. On Jebb's resignation from Cambridge they moved to London where they became involved with the first Unitarian church, Lindsey's Essex Street Chapel. Thereafter, as her contemporary biographer notes, Ann Jebb "took a leading part with him in the discussion of all the great constitutional questions." Indeed between 1780 and 1785, Ann

Jebb published widely on such topics as American Independence, Irish nationalism, annual parliaments, the right of universal suffrage, Fox's India Bill, and ship money.[82] The public association of Ann Jebb's work with that of her spouse appears to have spared her much of the vilification that met her contemporary Catherine Macaulay. Macaulay's political ideas and personal associations were very similar to those of Jebb, yet she entered into political debate fully in her own right—thus illustrating the subtle web of barriers and prejudices which *could* (but did not invariably) constrict female political involvement in even these liberated circles.[83]

≺ IV ≻

Female Political Writing and the Radical Responses to the French Revolution

As the case of Ann Jebb illustrates, the fact that women's political engagement was based to a great extent within the domestic environment did not prohibit them from making a considerable contribution to the canon of radical literature. Indeed, by the time the French Revolution broke onto the British political scene, literary and intellectual women discovered that it was *expected* of them that they would contribute to the political debate.[84] As A. L. Barbauld explained to her brother early in 1791, "I do not wonder at your asking whether I am answering Burke['s *Reflections on the Revolution in France*], for the question has been asked me even from Paris."[85] When Charlotte Smith published her pro-Revolutionary novel, *Desmond*, reviewers of all political shades took issue with her preface defending the appropriateness of women's political writing. They took it for granted that women might wish to write upon current affairs.[86]

However, historical treatment of the female radical response to the French Revolution has focused almost exclusively on the work of Mary Wollstonecraft. Edmund Burke's fierce denunciation, *Reflections on the Revolution in France* (1790), in which he criticized the influential radical dissenter Richard Price, sparked off a furious pamphlet war. Wollstonecraft's *Vindication of the Rights of Man* was the first of a number of replies to Burke to issue from Joseph Johnson's stable. Drawing closely upon the thought of the key dissenters with whom she was associated—Price, Priestley and James Burgh—Wollstonecraft called for the cultivation of true civic virtue and for the political rights of (male) citizens to be recognized. By positing herself as the voice of manly reason, she made a cutting attack upon the enervating luxury and vice of the governing class and upon the affected sensibility of Burke's work.[87]

For Wollstonecraft to have entered into the supposedly male domain of the political disquisition is often seen as an extraordinary, even revolutionary gesture.[88] However, while the length and tone of her piece were certainly ambitious, her writing should be placed within the context of a long-standing and vibrant tradition of female political writing. In any case, Wollstonecraft was not the only female radical to respond to Burke. Catherine Macaulay issued her own powerful disquisition against Burke, *Observations on the Reflections of the Rt. Hon Edmund Burke, on the Revolution in France* (1790). Macaulay (who had already engaged in a pamphlet battle with Burke twenty years previously[89]) objected, like Wollstonecraft, to Burke's recourse to flowery rhetoric at the expense of "cool investigation" and reason. She eloquently denounced the culture of chivalry which Burke appeared to represent and praised the French for awarding the rights of representation "on the basis of industry alone."[90] Less well known is that the fact that A. L. Barbauld also composed a reply to Burke. As was the case with much of her work, rather than opting for publication, she chose to circulate it among her extended intellectual circle, where it was enthusiastically received. One acquaintance waxed, "I hardly know anything in the English language superior in delicacy of irony, and strength of reasoning, to that truly eloquent performance."[91] While Barbauld's reply to Burke remained confined to a limited audience, her published pamphlet on the Test and Corporation Acts had already identified British radical causes with those of the French (in terms very similar to those used by Wollstonecraft) and urged France to "Be our model, as we have been yours."[92]

For radical female writers, treatment of the French Revolution could be incorporated quite naturally into their own tradition of writing on the themes of liberty. The contemporary Unitarian radical George Dyer noted that this was a subject in which women writers particularly excelled, citing Jebb, Wollstonecraft, Williams, Barbauld, Smith, and Macaulay to support his case.[93] Poetry, in particular, had become a popular medium for women's championing of liberty, freedom, and independence and their consequent attacks upon colonialism and tyranny.[94] At this point, themes such as anti-slavery that later came to be equated with philanthropic motives, were, in these circles, tightly allied to a radical ideological perspective which condemned the abuse of natural rights and argued for the equality of all. Horace Walpole, for example, was quick to detect that Barbauld's "Epistle to William Wilberforce" was politically motivated, marred (as he saw it) by its "measure of faction."[95] Following the Revolution, works such as H. M. Williams's "A Farewell for Two Years to England" and her *Letters Written in France* (1790), Mary Robinson's "On Liberty," and Charlotte Smith's *Desmond*[96] were testament to the ways in which the principles of the Revolution could be used to highlight the ubiquitous presence of tyranny and injustice in a variety of political and social guises.

Meanwhile, governmental fear of radical activity, combined with the turn of events in France, resulted in a massive propaganda campaign to disparage both the radicals and the Revolution. The work of Hannah More, in particular her *Village Politics* (1792) and later her *Cheap Repository Tracts*, is well known in this context.[97] But other women were also active in contributing to the propaganda war. Hester Thrale Piozzi expressed the view that "the more of these things go about the better; if one misses, another may hit." She therefore composed broadsheets and anti-revolutionary ballads to support the conservative cause.[98] Radical women made similar attempts to enter the propaganda war, employing a wide variety of genres. Mary Hays's "Thoughts on Civil Liberty," with its defense of the Revolution and her warning that the same fate might befall the British establishment, was penned for a comparatively select audience.[99] Barbauld, on the other hand, was more adventurous. In addition to her poetic works, such as her "On the Expected General Rising of the French Nation in 1792," which urged France to "Obey the laws thyself has made,/And rise the model of the world!," she wrote prose pieces such as *Civic Sermons to the People*, in which she addressed the working classes directly. The *Civic Sermons* set forth clearly and simply the principles of democratic government. It championed the cause of popular education and embraced its political implications: "You who are sober, industrious and thoughtful, you are worthy to consider the affairs of a community."[100] Barbauld's *Sins of Govern-*

ment, *Sins of the Nation*, a more moderate work politically, nevertheless went on to exploit the occasion of the fast day to protest against the government's declaration of war with France.[101]

Ann Jebb also threw herself wholeheartedly into the propaganda war with her two tracts, *Two Penny-Worth of Truth for a Penny* and *Two Penny-Worth More*. These were a direct response to William Jones's *One Penny-Worth of Truth* and *One Penny-Worth More*, which were among the most extreme of the counter-revolutionary tracts.[102] Jebb appropriated Jones's characters, Tom Jones and Brother John, to argue that the British people had been misled by egregious propaganda into demonizing dissenters and radicals as violent and seditious. All they wanted, she argued, was to "meet quietly in different parties, rejoice at the French revolution, wish for a reform of parliament, and of some other abuses which have been suffered to creep into our constitutions." Jebb's pamphlets probably did little to quell the fears of moderates, however, arguing as they did for overtly republican principles.[103]

As these examples indicate, during the early 1790s radical dissenting women were making a significant contribution to the political debate on the French Revolution. However, as another work dating from 1793, Laetitia M. Hawkins's *Letters on the Female Mind, Its Powers and Pursuits*, suggests, there were mounting anxieties as to the propriety or acceptability of such contributions. Hawkins's reactionary work argued that politics was not a suitable subject for the female mind and she dismissed even the concept of female patriotism (and the whole anti-slavery case too, for good measure). Hawkins revealed a tremendous fear as to the consequences of revolutionary principles. Pouncing upon the radical implications of those such as Hays, she scoffed at the possibility of democratic families. She drew the specter of an anarchic world, in which servants refused to obey mistresses, and children were left to fend for themselves.[104]

It is interesting that Hawkins chose Williams as the object for her attack. For Williams, far more than Hays, Smith, Barbauld, or Wollstonecraft, exploited traditional modes of femininity in the development of both her literary strategies and her analysis of the Revolution itself.[105] Indeed, Williams's work, with its heightened gender sensitivity and its mode of employing feminine discourses for political purposes, was symptomatic of the greater anxiety, even among progressives, as to women's participation in political life. This is evident at one level in the changing metaphors employed to describe political women. In the 1770s and 1780s Barbauld's political compositions were compared to the works of the general Tyrtaeus and to the "manly" Juvenal. Such comparisons were unlikely to be employed in the 1790s.[106] There was an uneasy attempt among dissenting radicals to envisage new *female* political role models, rather than merely equating women with masculine examples. It became common to compare radical women, such as Susannah Taylor and Eliza Fletcher, with Madame Roland (known for her conservative views on women's position).[107] This was a gradual and uneven process. *The Analytical Review*, for example, responded positively both to Macaulay's use of cool reason and to Williams's cultivated femininity. However, a greater sensitivity to the gendered implications of women utilizing "male" genres of political writing was beginning to emerge.[108]

In this context, some political radicals, such as Hays and her associates, appeared to be edging cautiously toward defining a particular political contribution for women. William Frend believed that Hays's first pamphlet had made a specifically feminine contribution to public debate: "So much candour and sound reasoning cloathed in insinuating language excite in us the hopes that the aid of the fair sex may in future be often called in to soften the animosity and fervour of disputation."[109] Hays herself, while railing against the contemporary subordination of women, maintained that their social position did make them disinterested observers of the political scene. She began to forge what we might term a "woman friendly" concept of politics, arguing that it was not necessary to possess an in-depth knowledge of the workings of the political world: "a benevolent mind cannot view with indifference its fellow-creatures sinking into deprivation and consequent misery. Plain general principles are obvious to everyone who stops to reflect."[110]

≺ V ≻

*Beyond the Revolution: Changing Directions
and Currents in Radical Female Political Expression*

Hays's words indicate the early stages of a cultural process in which women's involvement in the public sphere was to be ever more closely identified with philanthropic concerns. The new caution and self-consciousness which was beginning to creep into female political discourse was indicative of broader trends within the radical movement. The government repression made radical activity so difficult that most radicals found it impossible to sustain their political activities. As the revolution in France became more bloody and extreme, fears within Britain heightened and the political climate became increasingly oppressive. Anxiety about a copycat revolution in Britain and terror of invasion from France strengthened Evangelical calls for a reformation of manners, based on comforting certainties in which everyone knew her place. British public opinion increasingly identified revolutionary France with a wild and dangerous social order. Hordes of rioting women roving the Parisian streets; women asserting their rights to break free of traditional marriage vows—these specters haunted the public imagination. In this atmosphere the value put on the feminine woman, restoring peace and virtue by her loving dispensation within the home, became a powerful ideological crutch against the threat of supposedly anarchic revolutionists. Hence, by the late 1790s, female political involvement was viewed with increasing hostility.[111] The publication of Godwin's memoirs of Mary Wollstonecraft in 1798, revealing her sexual transgressions, could not have come at a worse time. The public's suspicions concerning the wider agenda of French-loving radicals was confirmed.[112] The vilification of Wollstonecraft which followed had a rapid domino effect throughout the radical community, as many erstwhile supporters of Wollstonecraft now strove to establish their own respectability or distance themselves from her ideas.[113]

Historical assumptions concerning the disastrously reactionary impact of the French Revolution upon both feminism in particular and discourses on women in general do at one level appear then to be substantiated. As the effects of the war began to take hold of British society and culture, it is noticeable that many radical women began to find alternative, less politically threatening ideological outlets. Some turned to Quakerism, where female expression was valued, but less politically directed. Others found in Romanticism an appealing recognition of their needs for individualism and self-expression.[114]

However, there has been a tendency to caricature such developments, with little attention given to their precise nature, in all their complexities. It would be wrong, for example, to assume that there was a neat and tidy shift—from women as potential political actors in the eighteenth century, to confined domesticity in the early nineteenth. During the first two decades of the new century, radical Unitarian and dissenting women continued to play a public role in elections and to make unique contributions to political writing, as well as maintaining their lively presence in the informal activities of extra-parliamentary political culture. Amelia Alderson Opie, among others, remained undaunted by the new climate. Now married to the painter John Opie, she may have professed herself to be a wife of the "old school," but this did not stop her from expressing her political views passionately in public. In 1803 she lengthened a visit to Norwich in order to participate directly in the election, in an attempt to unseat William Windham. As her angry and embarrassed (but not, it would seem, shocked) husband remonstrated, "I am very sorry to find this cursed election lasting so long, and I wish you would not appear so prominent in it... What business had you to get mounted up somewhere so conspicuously?"[115] Women such as Susannah Taylor, Eliza Fletcher, and Maria Edgeworth also continued to follow elections closely, attending hustings and political meetings.[116]

Meanwhile the war with France remained a problematic factor, often splintering the radical dissenting community. Barbauld, as her "Song for the London Volunteers" evinces, came to believe (in common with many other radicals) that in the face of Napoleon's imperialist ambitions, duty now lay in preparing to defend the country against attack.[117] Other women, such as Catherine Cappe, appear to have been more concerned with pressing their critique of the "war system," seeing British involvement in continental affairs as part of an invidious culture perpetrated by an oligarchic and power-greedy government.[118] Yet others, including Sarah Jane Maling and Anne Plumptre, presented another perspective, by their continuing admiration for Napoleon. Hence, in 1810, Plumptre published her *Narrative of a Residence in France*, giving her the opportunity to rehearse arguments that had already disgusted many of the metropolitan literati; namely, her insistence "the country would be all the happier if Buonaparte were to effect a landing and overturn the Government. He would destroy the Church and the aristocracy, and his government would be better than the one we have."[119] This was a view with which Catherine Hutton also had some sympathy.[120] The expression of political sentiments such as these suggests the need for further research into the role of women in both the peace and the loyalist movements, if we are to arrive at a fuller understanding of women's political engagement during these years.[121]

One trend does appear to be discernible in women's evolving political engagement: that is the emergence of a new kind of female political consciousness—a departure which may be explained by the rise of the philanthropic movement. Traditionally, the rise of philanthropic activity among women has been related to the growth of Evangelicalism, which urged that such work was particularly suited for women's loving and solicitous natures. Philanthropy accorded with the conservative politics of the Evangelical movement, which hoped to revitalize paternalistic structures, with an eye to pacifying a restive and increasingly politicized working class.[122] However, for dissenting women, the influence of Evangelicalism in encouraging charitable work may have been a less significant factor than developments within Unitarianism itself. Following the bitter riots against the rational dissenters and suspected Jacobins during the late 1790s, most rank and file Unitarians were concerned with establishing their respectability and trustworthiness to their neighbors. In any case, the Unitarian movement, which had been so critical as a seedbed for political dissent, had now lost the older generation of politically motivated leaders, such as Price and Priestley. As the movement looked inward to its reorganization and consolidation, there was a discernible trend to "reconstruct" itself as a less subversive force in British society. Many Unitarians now showed a marked preference for engagement with broader humanitarian issues, such as peace and anti-slavery.[123]

This was a development in which women could fully participate. As we have seen, the blurring of the boundaries between philanthropy and politics had already begun to engage progressive women in the 1790s. The years which followed saw women's involvement in philanthropic activities reach a new peak. As Peter Mandler demonstrates in chapter 4, this involvement was equally true of aristocratic women. However, the philanthropic activities of rational radical dissenters indicate the subtle and divergent meanings which philanthropy might hold for contemporaries during this first upturn in charitable activity. For radical women, philanthropic activity could signify the fulfillment of, not religious, but, in Catherine Cappe's words, "civic duties."[124] Eliza Fletcher caused a considerable stir in Edinburgh in the late 1790s when she and a group of likeminded female friends formed a female benefit society—apparently the first institution of its kind to be seen in Scotland. The local authorities were vehemently opposed to any such scheme being established by ladies of "democratic principles." The fact that these women were proposing to take a leading role in the management of a public institution was "considered so novel and extraordinary a proceeding as ought not to be countenanced."[125] It was not immediately obvious to contemporaries that such female action was the natural extension of their womanly duties; rather it was understood to be one more example of the dangerous, democratic tendencies harbored by Fletcher and her associates.

The greater awareness of social problems, which involvement in philanthropic activity occasioned, appears to have had an impact upon many radical women's political ideas, producing a remarkably holistic vision of both politics and social policies. The most striking illustration of this departure issued from the pen of Rachel Lee. Lee (who has hitherto been completely overlooked by historians) came from a Unitarian background and had mixed in extreme Jacobin circles in London during the 1790s. In 1808 she published her *Essay on Government* under the pseudonym "Philopatria."[126] This *Essay* rehearsed clearly and simply the political philosophy of the radical dissenters. It insisted that the basis of government should be to ensure the common good and argued for the rights of the people to oppose any measures which might violate these principles. Lee mounted stinging attacks upon the institution of slavery and boldly advocated ideas for which radicals had been castigated in the aftermath of the French Revolution. She upheld "levelling" ideas of social equality and envisaged democratic modes of family life, in which children would be trained to use their reason to enable them fearlessly to question the principles they encountered. She urged for full rights to be bestowed upon illegitimate children and argued in favor of the need for divorce. Lee argued that supposedly "seditionary" societies were necessary to defend the rights of the people and she fiercely attacked the state's use of spies and agents provocateurs. The *Essay* ranged from subjects as diverse as schools, servants, and marriage to war, taxation, duelling, dress, judges, oath taking, and funerals. For Lee envisaged a radical refashioning of society whereby everything that furthered its rationalization and the equality of its citizens should be effected by government. This included a visionary understanding of the role of local government, urging that government should assume responsibility for roads, street cleaning, graveyards, and the like as part of its duty to provide for the "*happiness of individuals.*"[127]

This encompassing approach to government was not clearly grasped by even the *Essay*'s sympathetic reviewers, who attempted to cast it in the mold of more traditional genres, such as educational works on political philosophy.[128] The work is much better understood if it is placed in the context of an evolving female political consciousness; a consciousness which was increasingly influenced by women's philanthropic activity. Writing in 1807 for the *Athenaeum*, A. L. Barbauld had also urged for the rights of secret combination, insisting that such action "can never be prevented, because it is founded on interest of the many, and the moral sense of all." Barbauld's work, in common with that of Lee, urged that all men should be made citizens and contribute to the framing of the country's laws. Barbauld, recognizing, as did Lee, the necessity of reforming the environment, talked of the need to "Destroy dirt and misery" and secure "comfort, and cleanliness, and decent apparel." Yet Barbauld was inherently more conservative than Lee and envisaged that social distinctions should be lessened, but not extinguished. Barbauld, significantly, looked to philanthropy and not to government to procure many of the advances she saw as necessary if the country was to be peopled by virtuous citizens.[129]

For many radical women, then, philanthropy could function as one of the ways in which they expressed their political sentiments. It might provide them with the opportunity to alleviate the worst social consequences of the political system they opposed and enable them to contribute to the emergence of a more just and humane society. These issues are well illustrated in the life and work of Elizabeth Heyrick, who following the death of her husband in 1797 became a Quaker and embarked upon a career of extraordinary activism. The historiographical tendency to focus on women's philanthropy rather than on their politics has meant that Heyrick is principally known for her anti-slavery campaigning and not for her composition of political pamphlets. Yet for Heyrick, politics and philanthropy were closely interwoven. Thus in her *Appeal to the Electors of the United Kingdom, on the Choice of a New Parliament* (1826) she urged her audience to vote for candidates who would promote a "universal philanthropy"—that is those who supported such causes as anti-slavery, anti-corn laws, and anti-blood sports. Her sympathy for the sufferings of the impoverished local framework knitters, moreover, brought her to assist them not only through acts of philanthropy, but also in her published pamphlets, of which she wrote over twenty.

Heyrick's political pamphlets inveighed against the ruling classes for their callous disregard for the welfare of the poor and railed against the inhumanity of the political economy preached by the local manufacturers. She argued that charity was insufficient to remedy the problems of low wages, calling for political intervention to secure a minimum wage, a maximum working week, and trade protection. Despite the paternalism which tinged her work, she evoked the language of natural rights, claiming that "The Rights of Man—the Rights of Woman—the Rights of Brutes—have been boldly advanced but the Rights of the Poor still remain unadvocated." Heyrick attacked new pieces of government legislation such as the Vagrancy Laws of 1824 and protested against the state's heavy handed repression of popular discontent. Like Barbauld and Lee, she was bitterly opposed to the combination laws and she lent her support to local strikes. In common with other radical dissenting women, she followed the electoral process closely, discussing in print the significance of local election results.[130]

There has been little attempt to relate Heyrick's work to the broad tradition of female political writing, which formed part of the culture of the Nonconformist Enlightenment into which she was born. Heyrick was the daughter of a radical, Unitarian couple, John and Elizabeth Coltman of Leicester. John Coltman had played a leading role in local Dissenting and political issues as well as in the cultural life of the city. Elizabeth Coltman, the daughter of an ardent republican, had enjoyed a minor literary career before her marriage.[131] This background gave Heyrick access to a dynamic network of women who supported, influenced, and criticized her work, as well as providing links with wider radical communities. In her anti-slavery work, Heyrick worked closely with an intimate friend, Susanna Watts, who published material on the anti-slavery cause in her own right and was editor of the *Humming Bird* (1824-25).[132] In her animal welfare work, for example in her campaigns against bull-baiting, Heyrick worked alongside her sister, Mary Ann Coltman. Coltman, in common with another prominent Leicester radical, Richard Phillips (for whose publication she wrote), was a strict vegetarian. Her more militant animal rights philosophy was no doubt a critical influence upon Heyrick's politicization of animal welfare issues, as is evident from her pamphlet *Cursory Remarks on the Evil Tendency of Unrestrained Cruelty*.[133]

Mary Ann Coltman and Elizabeth Heyrick enjoyed friendships and correspondence with like-minded Nonconformist and Unitarian women in Birmingham and the provinces. Before her marriage, Heyrick was part of the correspondence network of politically-engaged, provincial intellectual women centered in Salisbury, which included the Nonconformist poet Anne Steele, Anna Seward, and Mary Scott (author of the *Female Advocate*).[134] Coltman was particularly close to Catherine Hutton of Birmingham, with whom she discussed Heyrick's pamphlets. Hutton, a contributor to *La Belle Assemblée* (the publication on which the important contemporary feminist Mary Leman Grimstone cut her teeth) was the daughter of William Hutton, a distinguished intellectual figure in Birmingham and an intimate of Joseph Priestley. In addition, Heyrick was in close contact with women from Quaker circles who were themselves engaged actively in the "public sphere"—Elizabeth Fry and the female minister Mary Capper, for example.[135] Clearly the activism of such women did not derive from their positioning as helpmates and assistants to political male relatives, but was built upon alternative, politically-conscious female networks. Whether such female networks were more typical of the post-1800 period, with the older generation of women engaging more directly with radical culture in itself, only further research will demonstrate.

The political writing of women such as Heyrick, Lee, and Barbauld represented the crest of a wave in which radically-minded provincial women continued to see themselves as closely involved and implicated in the political process throughout this period. This is evident in the response which feminist-minded MPs elicited from the females in their constituencies. For example, during the 1832 election, the radical Unitarian reformer Matthew Davenport Hill took pains to ensure that places were provided for women during his election addresses in Hull and on one enthusiastic occasion went so far as to proclaim his belief in the equality and rights of the sexes. Hill was elected; and, when he was unseated two years later, the ladies of Hull presented an epergne to him on which was inscribed the interest they felt for his re-election "to perpetuate their admiration of his faithful services, commanding talents, and incorruptible patriotism."[136]

◄ VI ►

Conclusion: Reassessing the Chronologies and Modes of Women's Political Expression

The Nonconformist Enlightenment was, then, a period of rich cultural activity in which women played a considerable role. Within this tradition, the ideology and culture of rational dissent provided a particularly politicizing milieu for women. By the early 1830s, stimulated by the growing ferment of co-operative ideologies, a new alignment of progressive reformers, the "radical unitarians," began to revive debate upon the position of women within society. The radical unitarians, who originally coalesced around the radical ministry of the Unitarian preacher William Johnson Fox at South Place Chapel in Finsbury in the early 1830s, drew heavily upon the Unitarian traditions with which many of their acolytes were closely associated. In articulating what they hoped was a humanitarian creed, designed to solve the ills of the emerging industrial society, the radical unitarians promoted the ideals of rationality and equality. Yet they also insisted upon a Christianized version of early socialism which privileged the importance of love and sharing within social relations. By the late 1840s, the fluid coteries of radical unitarianism had begun to extend and adapt their message as they found a voice in the more popular reforming journals of the day, such as the *Howitt's Journal, Douglas Jerrold's Weekly Newspaper,* and *Eliza Cook's Journal.*

Within radical unitarianism, the feminist tendencies which had been implicit in elements of the earlier rational dissenting ideology were explored to the full. An ambitious feminist agenda, which found much inspiration from contemporary communitarian philosophies, evolved, in which the principle of women's rights became central to wider social and political programs.[137] Nevertheless, middle-class women's direct participation in reforming politics continued to be a highly problematized and complex phenomenon. As radical women became involved in a new generation of causes (such as co-operation, animal rights, anti-corn law movement, Jewish civil rights, anti-slavery, Chartism, and European nationalism) they adopted a variety of roles—as patrons, secretaries, writers, fundraisers, and administrators—as they wrestled to reconcile deeply-held political convictions with their varying perceptions as to woman's position and nature.[138]

The revival of claims for female enfranchisement which began to mount in rational dissenting quarters during these years should also be placed in the context of the changing position of Unitarianism. The legalization of the Unitarians' doctrinal position, combined with the repeal of the Test and Corporations Act in 1828 and the widening of the franchise in 1832, may well have fractured the identity of dissenting women. Whereas before they had perceived themselves to labor under the same legal discrimination as their menfolk, this was no longer the case. It was now the legal position of women, and not that of the dissenters as a whole, which loomed as a stark and anomalous grievance. As Jane Rendall makes clear in chapter 5, these rich traditions of dissent, including those of Unitarianism and radical unitarianism, were an important element in the make-up of liberal and radical networks in the later campaigns for female suffrage.

When the work of the radical unitarians of the 1830s and 1840s is placed alongside the earlier practice of female political involvement and political writing which this chapter has observed, the need to construct a whole new chronology of middle-class women's political activity and feminist consciousness becomes apparent. Female political engagement was not suddenly born out of a mid-Victorian reaction to the imposition of "separate spheres." Middle-class radical women had for decades been vitally involved in politics and political activity. Radical female political activity (out of which a feminist conviction could often, but did not necessarily, arise) had begun to coalesce in the late 1770s, as a consequence of the growing radicalism of rational dissent. Between the onset of the Terror in France and the 1832 Reform Act, radical female political engagement does appear to have entered a phase of greater quiescence. This was a temporary dip in female involvement and not, as customarily assumed, an archetypal snapshot of female containment.[139] Moreover, it was during these years that we can discern a marked shift in emphasis as women began to confront the social problems which their involvement in philanthropy underlined.[140] By the 1830s, spurred on by the energy and vision of the early socialist movement, there was a recrudescence of female political agitation and feminist activity, which, via the radical unitarians, led to the women's rights campaigns of the 1850s and 1860s.

In addition to emphasizing the egregious neglect of female political consciousness in the historiography of late eighteenth- and early nineteenth-century women, this chapter has also sought to re-evaluate the meanings of the home and domesticity to radical women. As we have seen, conventional analyses concerning the growth of the domestic sphere during the Enlightenment, which supposedly sapped women's potential to function as political actors, utterly fail to take into account the way in which the domestic might itself be construed as political space. The home was the site of salons, informal discussion groups, political correspondences, ideologically motivated consumer choices, politically-inspired child-rearing methods, and so on, all of which were crucial to the emergence of specific radical political cultures. The chapter thus points to the weaknesses inherent in any analysis which constructs women's identities as wives and mothers, and their involvement in charitable and associative life, in monovalent narratives (either, as Enlightenment historians have tended to do, as wholly antithetical to political identities;[141] or, as historians of the nineteenth century have implied, with recourse to a single ideology—that of Evangelicalism[142]). Such readings fail to capture the constellation of ideas on women which the Enlightenment engendered and blot out the complex, nuanced ways in which women may have understood and expressed their lives and their political convictions.

≪ 4 ≫

From Almack's to Willis's: Aristocratic Women and Politics, 1815–1867

PETER MANDLER

WHAT CAN THE STORY of aristocratic women tell us more generally about the history of women in the public sphere? The answer may be, not very much. A recent burst of literature has argued forcibly that the public privileges enjoyed by aristocratic women, especially in the eighteenth but also through much of the nineteenth century, were privileges of their class rather than of their gender. The essentially familial or dynastic nature of aristocratic society meant that wives and daughters shared integrally in all aspects of aristocratic power—in the management of estates, in the disposal of patronage, in the exercise of political influence, even in party organization and government. It follows from this argument that the public roles of aristocratic women had more in common with the roles of men of their own class than with the roles of women of other classes. It also follows that the privileges of aristocratic women rose and fell with the privileges of aristocratic men, declining under successive democratic assaults in the nineteenth century.

This chapter examines the political functions of aristocratic women over the crucial half century between, roughly, the Battle of Waterloo and the Second Reform Act. It begins by surveying the persistence of traditional aristocratic privileges in this period, drawing attention to those functions in which aristocratic women evidently played a prominent role, sharing the power and prerogatives of men of their class. But it then goes on to suggest that, as those traditional aristocratic privileges came under democratic or meritocratic pressure, it was aristocratic women who were among the first to break from them. Subordinated within these traditional structures, perhaps less wedded to them and better able to detect their weaknesses than were aristocratic men, aristocratic women developed their own critique of a "privilege" which, as women, they did not always share with men. In making this critique and in fashioning for themselves alternative public roles, it will be suggested, aristocratic women joined with middle-class women and made a signal contribution to the construction of new, liberal forms of political subjectivity in the early nineteenth century.

These liberal forms of subjectivity—the new norms of the self-governing, rational individual, replacing the more tribal and familial norms of pre-modern political subjectivity—have hitherto been interpreted as largely the province of the middle class, and of the middle-class male at that, the public, masculine side of the famous "separate spheres" allegedly demarcated in the early nineteenth century. Acknowledging the distinctive contribution of aristocratic women to the redefinition of the public sphere in the nineteenth century may help, therefore, not only to restore a gender dimension to the study of the British aristocracy; it may also help us to understand better these liberal forms of political subjectivity, not so clearly middle-class or male as they are sometimes portrayed.

≺ I ≻

Aristocratic Power in the Early Nineteenth Century

In many ways, aristocratic women were in a position of extraordinary political privilege at the beginning of the nineteenth century, in relation both to other women and to most men. Their traditional roles in the organization of aristocratic society—as the transmitters of wealth by dowry or inheritance, as the bearers and rearers of heirs, as the guardians of minor peers—were probably at a peak in this period. The tremendous wealth and power then vested in great agricultural estates meant that considerable social and legal pressure was brought to bear on the task of keeping estates together and passing them down in an unbroken line of succession, a task in which the active participation of wives, mothers, and heiresses was essential. A substantial minority were landowners in their own right; up to ten percent of all landowners were women who had succeeded in default of a male heir. Others were equipped with pin money, jointures, and constructive trusts that gave married women of the landowning classes powers to control their own property that were not available to lesser women.[1] The rise of companionate and romantic marriages, prevalent earlier in aristocratic than in lower-rank circles, meant that there was more communication and collaboration on all matters, great and small, between aristocratic husbands and wives.[2]

At the same time, aristocratic political power was also at its zenith. Monarchical power was in terminal decline and democratic politics were hardly evident; aristocratic control of the Commons in addition to the Lords was thus consolidated at a point when Parliament's business and responsibilities were extending at an unprecedented rate. Outside Parliament, the aristocratic grip upon local government, the Church, the legal system, and the bureaucracy had not yet been loosened by the attack on "Old Corruption" mounted after 1815.

The combination of women's enhanced importance in the aristocratic family and the aristocracy's enhanced powers of political control over society at large gave aristocratic women a wide array of potential political functions. Those who were landowners in their own right evidently had no difficulty in disposing of political and clerical patronage and influencing the course of parliamentary elections as if they were men, though they could not vote in elections or sit in either House.[3] Women who were not themselves landowners also had access in varying degrees to the political and clerical patronage of their fathers, brothers, sons, husbands, or lovers.[4] So long as aristocratic men put themselves forward in large numbers as candidates for the House of Commons, aristocratic women appeared alongside them on the hustings and in the canvass, as well as behind the scenes, soliciting votes and influence by letter and in person.[5]

The vicious attacks aimed at Georgiana, Duchess of Devonshire, for her canvassing in the 1784 Westminster election had more to do with the peculiar circumstances of that election and that lady than with female canvassing in general, which by no means ceased after that date.[6] At another Westminster election 35 years later Lady Caroline Lamb carried on in much the same way, "going into taverns and dancing and drinking with the electors" and then "[taking] all the greasy voters in her carriage to the hustings." "People have no idea to what an extent women influence the elections in England," commented Princess Lieven on her performance.[7] Even after the Victorian franchise extensions, with the accompanying development of party organization, canvassing by aristocratic women remained common, even compulsory (as candidates were expected to supply a female "ornament"), right up until the 1883 Corrupt and Illegal Practices Act which, by stamping out venality, actually put a premium on the unpaid labor of female relatives.[8]

Less publicly, in an age when politics was largely conducted in private, women on terms of intimacy with powerful men could also exercise—in the salon, the dining room, or the bedroom—considerable influence over public life. The duke of Wellington was said to be guided at different points by Mrs. Arbuthnot, Princess Lieven, Lady Shelley, Lady Jersey, Lady Burghersh, and Lady Salisbury. George IV was supposed to have been influenced in favor of the Catholics by his lover Lady Conyngham. Among Whigs Lady Holland was described as "the only really undisputed monarchy in Europe."[9] Disraeli was launched on his public career by Ladies Londonderry and Jersey. As Kim Reynolds has recently argued, an entirely new species (albeit a rare one), the political hostess, emerged in the mid-Victorian period as a means of providing the more extensive entertaining and networking facilities needed in a period of greater parliamentary activity but before party organization had developed sufficiently. For Reynolds, the political hostess represented the culmination of "a long line of politically-active aristocratic women ... the end of [a] tradition" that was eclipsed only toward the end of the nineteenth century by the advent of mass party politics.[10] Others have suggested more broadly that the institutions of High Society were developed from the 1820s to filter and acculturate an increasingly mobile and diverse political elite, with aristocratic women playing a crucial gatekeeping role, not only to help build political networks but also to police standards of social and moral conduct until they were so well diffused and so widely accepted that gatekeepers were no longer required.[11]

The difficult question to answer about these functions is to what extent women were exercising them as surrogates for aristocratic men and to what extent as accepted actors in their own right. The variety of roles that women exercised may testify more to the ramified power of the landed elite as a whole in a complex society, as well as to certain conventions about the titular responsibilities of women inside that elite, rather than to any explicit disregard of gender distinctions, much less approval of women's role. Most of the recent literature surveying women's participation in the "public" functions of the aristocracy has assumed that that role was consensual, viewed similarly by aristocratic men and women, and relatively static over time.[12] Reynolds employs the anthropologists' concept of the "incorporated wife," whose role was subordinate but integral to a common aristocratic project. The class solidarity of the aristocracy is held to have bridged any conceivable gender divisions; indeed, Reynolds suggests that aristocratic women were *more* likely to cling to class privileges than men because they had more to lose by exposure to a masculinized "outside" world.[13]

In what follows, however, we will consider evidence of gender differences and tensions within aristocratic culture that limited aristocratic women's ability to participate in the public life of their class. Beneath the surface of familial solidarity, there are signs of conflict between men and women over women's public role. These ever-present tensions may well have made women more alert to the growing precariousness of aristocratic political power. They may have induced aristocratic women to seek alternative public roles being opened up contemporaneously by women of other ranks. In this event, it will be suggested, aristocratic women might have had less rather than more motive than their men to protect the distinctive privileges of their class, and more motive to explore a re-definition of politics that would give women of all classes an enhanced role, even at the cost of a reduced role for aristocratic men *qua* aristocrats.

≺ II ≻

Aristocratic Women under Pressure

The eighteenth may have been England's "aristocratic century," but aristocratic women were placed in a different relationship to that hegemony than aristocratic men: the Georgian public sphere was gendered, just as was the Victorian public sphere. Contemporaries noted, as have historians since, that compared to the French aristocracy the British gave a decidedly constrained public role to its women.[14] Michele Cohen has argued that the British idea of "politeness" that emerged after 1688 granted women a function as conveyancers of language and social skills to young men, but that in conscious contrast to the French experience this function was limited to domestic or quasi-domestic settings and not extended to the more clearly public space of the salon. Furthermore, again in explicit contrast to the French, it was expected that adult male Britons should be fully free of the feminine influences that had some utility in childhood.[15] In the course of the eighteenth century a very masculinized culture of political virtue was built up, based upon a classical education (increasingly, away from home), the male arts of the public meeting and public oratory, and the tight fraternities of the two houses of Parliament. It was in fact its masculine character that was held to make aristocratic political behavior in Britain so pure and incorruptible and thus so needless of reform: it was one of the elite's chief bulwarks against political change. Radical intimations that the British aristocracy was Frenchified, feminized, ill-suited for government, could thus be rebutted: on the contrary, the British aristocracy was *British*, masculine, a natural governing class; and its robust health after 1790 the proof of the pudding.[16]

Thus while aristocratic women were free to come out in public in support of their men, particularly in ritual occasions such as electoral canvasses and the hustings, they were peculiarly restricted in their ability to play any independent role—possibly more restricted than women in inferior stations. Contractarian thinking may have lightly influenced the judges who made the law of property, and more profoundly influenced the middling classes, allowing ebullitions of feminism at the end of the eighteenth century, but it made little impact at all upon the centers of political power.[17] Aristocratic women were not supposed to address public meetings nor even put their name to published writing. Lady Louisa Stuart regretted the vogue, new in the 1830s, for ladies to publish novels under their own name: "I cannot get over my old, perhaps aristocratic prejudices, which make it a loss of caste." She recalled the case of Lady Hood who was told in 1815 that the plebeians would have no objection to her turning authoress, but that the consequence would be "no more salaams to the Begum." "Do you know I was on the very point of publishing a book?," Lady Hood confided to her second husband. He replied, "I am sure I would never have married you, if you had."[18]

Women were excluded not only from sitting in Parliament but also from witnessing its deliberations. In order to spy on debates in the Commons, it was necessary to squeeze into the dreaded "ventilator," a squalid space in the roof of the chamber which provided audio without video, an exhilarating but also a humiliating experience.[19] Conditions were not much better in the Lords: only a few daredevils "skulked behind the throne, or were hid in [Black Rod's] box." It was only around 1830 that these conditions changed for the better: aristocratic women first forced themselves into the Lords in large numbers for the debates on Catholic Emancipation and especially on the Reform Bill; and special galleries were provided for them in the reconstruction of the houses of Parliament after the fire of 1834.[20]

Indeed, the masculine nature of public life *before* 1830 was such that it could pose problems for relations between aristocratic men and aristocratic women. For the tendency within the aristocratic family from the middle of the eighteenth century onward toward greater informality and emotional interaction—the tendency toward companionate and romantic modes of marital relations—did not, as Judith Lewis has pointed out, always integrate well with the more formal aspects of the elite's public role.[21] It is possible, even likely, that aristocratic men and women grew more intimate in private while retaining their social distance in public. Certainly outside observers in the early nineteenth century commented on the bizarre *hauteur* with which aristocratic men and women treated each other in public settings. Looking backward from 1862, Captain Gronow marvelled how "female society amongst the upper classes was most notoriously neglected" by the Regency male: "How could it be otherwise, when husbands spent their days in the hunting-field, or were entirely occupied with politics, and always away from home during the day; whilst the dinner-party, commencing at seven or eight, frequently did not break up before one in the morning." Though Gronow admired the proud, aloof ladies of Regency society, he recognized the sacrifices their divided selves entailed: "strong temptation, overwhelming passion, self-sacrifice, remorse: often the blighted heart and early grave—things almost unknown in these days of flirtation and frivolity."[22]

The private influence that intelligent women sought was no doubt an earnest attempt to bridge this public-private chasm, but it is striking how unwelcome even the men who succumbed professed to find it. This may have been due in part to men's guilt when, having failed to achieve their desires by "honorable" means "man-to-man," they had to resort to back channels. Princess Lieven liked to brag of her political influence among her women friends but was viciously denigrated by the men to whom she was supposedly so close.[23] Lady Conyngham's female friends played up her influence on the king but her son insisted that "she never talks to the King ... upon politics at all."[24] Lord Holland took a dim view of Lady Holland's ambitions as a *salonnière*. "You have the advantage," he once wrote to his friend Lord Granville, "of a wife who makes no mischief and with more talents than all the Ladies who meddle with politicks, never squabbles about them."[25]

More perceptive men understood the difficulty in which their equivocal position put aristocratic women. "[I]t is a very good habitual state of mind for a woman not to concern herself at all about politics, except when they force themselves on her attention," wrote W. H. Lyttelton to his wife Lady Sarah in October 1819, "and I think I am to blame in having said so much to you on the subject, and still more so, perhaps, in having allowed them to engross so much of my own attention at times when I was not called upon to act at all in respect of such matters."[26] Political women, too, recognized the awkwardness of their position. The most famous female wirepuller of the early nineteenth century, Lady Cowper (later Lady Palmerston), recommended to her brother that he *not* marry the likes of her, steering him instead toward a Miss Jones, "very young and probably may be formed to anything, has a good temper and has been very regularly, strictly and religiously brought up."[27] As if confirming her hunch, Lady Cowper's daughter-in-law reflected much later, "I am sure neither party like political women, and Ladies Salisbury, Jersey, Palmerston and Co. have never been thought the better of for the line they took."[28]

The two-faced way in which aristocratic men spoke of women's political influence in the Regency is perhaps best exemplified by the case of Almack's, the celebrated social club run in the Regency period by seven so-called "Lady Patronesses," chief among them Lady Cowper, Lady Jersey, and Princess Lieven. Almack's assemblies, held in rooms in King Street, St. James's, were at the height of fashion and exclusiveness between 1814 and 1830. So desperate were men and women alike to get tickets that the lady patronesses who controlled the supply were spoken of as virtual despots, and the fact that several of the patronesses were close to leading politicians gave this charge of despotism further spin. And yet it is possible to see the mystique of Almack's as another means of blurring over (rather than bridging) the gulf between aristocratic women's private claims upon their men and their near-total exclusion from political life. It was convenient for men to opine that Almack was the ladies' Parliament, to concede facetiously that Parliament had to avoid sitting on Almack's evenings, that the patronesses directly controlled 23 votes in the House of Commons, that, as one novel of 1828 put it, "the fate of nations, the interests of commerce, and the weal of the constitution depend on their exertions." Conversely, the lady patronesses collaborated in the play-acting. Legislation was enacted; for instance, the 1819 order "to prevent the admission of Gentlemen in *Trousers.*" Mock superiority was asserted on the occasion, much discussed, when the duke of Wellington was turned away for tardiness.[29] While feigning anger, men clearly got a lot of secret pleasure out of such charades, as perhaps did the patronesses, collaborating but also wreaking what little revenges were open to them. Almack's was no cockpit of power, but rather a theater in which was played out a sophisticated melodrama of powerlessness, and it sums up the tense relations of gender and power prevailing in the early nineteenth-century aristocracy.

≺ III ≻

Reshaping the Public Sphere: Religion, Education, Philanthropy

These conditions of growing intimacy in the private sphere and yet continuing exclusion from the public were not tolerable to all women and were increasingly intolerable to many. If nothing else, women's pride as aristocrats was touched. And they may also have come gradually to see the elite masculinity of politics as a liability for the whole of their class; that is, whereas the new sentimentality of domestic life was something the aristocracy shared with wider segments of society, the splendid, aloof, brittle patrician style of high politics appeared more and more isolated and vulnerable. This is why women of the landed classes were peculiarly susceptible to new moral, religious, and philanthropic currents sweeping through society in the early nineteenth century and why their evangelicalism was applied not only to their social inferiors but also to their male peers. It was a means of breaking down the private-public distinctions that bedevilled their own lives while at the same time opening their men to a new definition of the public, one that was in fact better suited to the changing conditions of the nineteenth century.

Because evangelicalism has traditionally been thought of as a "middle-class" value system (a tradition reinforced by the prestige of Davidoff and Hall's *Family Fortunes*[30]), we tend to forget that it began and in many respects continued as a movement for the reform of upper-class mores.[31] Its heartland was the Church of England; its social ideal, owing much to the book of Ruth, was rural, traditional, hierarchical; and some of its earliest and most fervent exponents were women from the landed classes. Hannah More is the prime example. It has been said of Hannah More, in fact, that her evangelicalism stemmed directly from her disappointment at the failure of the bluestocking circle to make female learning respectable in high society.[32] In reaction she turned to a different kind of reformation, but with the elite still firmly in mind. Her gospel was widely and eagerly taken up by women of the landed classes as a way of bringing together private values and public functions, and extending the ambit of the domestic sphere. More's *Coelebs in Search of a Wife*, published in 1809, was the trigger for a wave of philanthropic work by women of all classes, but by the gentry and aristocracy above all.[33] It was Countess Spencer who was responsible for introducing Hannah More to Sarah Trimmer, the other great woman evangelical of the day (one with better middle-class credentials), and it was Countess Spencer, too, who by establishing Sarah Trimmer's daughter as the governess in Devonshire House started a fashion at the very height of society for training girls in religious and philanthropic as well as social duties (one of her pupils was the Lady Granville that Lord Holland praised for not meddling in politics).[34]

Of course it may well be felt that the shift from bluestocking to evangelical was a descent of catastrophic proportions, a total exclusion from public life rather than an extension of opportunity. But it is possible to see this transition differently. Yes, More called for women to abjure politics—but hers was also a critique of the way politics then worked and its long-term effect was to change the way politics worked, in fact the way politics was defined. It may be argued that the evangelical movement caused aristocratic women to recoil from involvement in politics narrowly construed, but it can hardly be argued that evangelicalism induced its adepts to withdraw from the public sphere: on the contrary, it put them far more visibly within it.

Personal religion gave many women of the landed classes a public mission which they pursued in spheres hitherto denied them.[35] From *Coelebs* onward, for instance, respectable women began to appear frequently in print under their own names, thus triggering Lady Louisa Stuart's complaint about fashionable authorship. The most popular form was the Society novel with the moral message, combining the exclusive world that aristocratic women knew best with the ideology they shared with their inferiors. As Muriel Jaeger pointed out a generation ago (disapprovingly), there is a clear progression in three generations from Georgiana, Duchess of Devonshire's equable and anonymous novel *The Sylph* (1779), to her niece Caroline Lamb's wild and emotional *Glenarvon* (1816), to her granddaughter Lady Georgiana Fullerton's *Ellen Middleton* (1844), "gloomy, maudlin and pious, ending in a general redemption and the heroine's triumphant death-bed," but the only one of the three to appear under the author's name and also the most widely popular and influential.[36]

Though aristocratic women made no leaps forward in formal education until later in the century, the new religious and moral sensibility gave them pretext and motive for much self-education on a range of topics that went far beyond Scripture. French, German, and Italian as well as English were acquired to gain access to the poetry thought necessary for the moral cultivation of the self; art and history taught moral lessons; theology and political economy were central to the philanthropic project.[37] In old age, Wellington's confidante Lady Shelley complained of how far this tendency had gone: "Every young lady now feels herself competent to argue about divinity and political economy better than many clergymen; and not being afraid to walk where angels fear to tread, these young persons make the Sacred Mysteries a gabble for the tea-table."[38]

The religious point of view not only gave aristocratic women more to think and write about; it gave them a great deal more to do. Like all leisured women of their day, aristocratic women took part in endless philanthropic activity, sitting on committees, organizing events, and, eventually, speaking in public. As Frank Prochaska has shown, women progressively took over existing charities—as contributors and as organizers—and began for the first time to organize charities on their own; and aristocratic women were in the vanguard of this movement. Charity bazaars, or fancy fairs, were pioneered by aristocratic women in the early 1830s under the patronage of Queen Adelaide, raising up to twenty five thousand pounds each for hospitals, schools, missions, and church-building.[39] Philanthropic work also became a key part of aristocratic women's local responsibilities and for this reason they could claim with justice to have more face-to-face contact with estate dependants than had their brothers away at boarding school or their husbands who kept a longer London Season.[40]

Not all women—not, perhaps, even a majority—embraced personal religion, even in its full flood after 1830. For some it must have indeed appeared too self-effacing, and risked putting them, at least at first, at a greater distance from their husbands. But if the spirit of evangelicalism was not universally appealing, the sphere of activism it offered could be exploited more widely. Philanthropic work, it is important to stress, was *not* seen as busy work or a pious retreat from public life. It is striking how the most extrovert personalities ambitious for a public role, often also the most scornful of religion per se, were also those most involved in the charitable world. Lady Jersey, one of the Almack's patronesses who had made a doomed attempt to wield political power in the 1820s and 1830s, was a pioneering philanthropist who opened a servants' training school at Middleton Stoney.[41] The duchess of Sutherland, who succeeded her as "Queen of London Society," also had thwarted political ambitions, though of a Whig rather than Tory variety. For a time she tried to live vicariously through her husband, but he proved even less of a political animal than she.[42] In one curious incident, at the North Staffordshire election of 1847, she tried to act for her husband in his absence, throwing the family influence behind a relative, Lord Brackley, who turned out embarrassingly to be allied with the Tories. Despite her subsequent attempts to make amends, she was rebuked sharply by Whig party leaders in public and in private.[43] Her status as a duchess hardly exempted her from the casual prejudices against women in politics: "these are the sort of mistakes made by women," concluded the duke of Bedford, "who act from impulse, and do not see the consequences of their actions."[44] Whereas a *bourgeoise* might have subsided peaceably under such pressure, however, a duchess's pride was not so easily quenched and the range of alternatives open to her was wider. So she channelled these energies into enterprises such as the women's petition against slavery of 1853, a campaign to relieve the Spitalfields silk weavers, and further adventures in local philanthropy (which included the foundation of another servants' training school on one of her estates).[45]

Lady Noel Byron, the poet's estranged wife, was interested in politics but could find no way to express herself in this sphere, so she turned to local estate matters and by the early 1830s was running several model schools on advanced continental lines, schools which directly influenced the work of James Kay-Shuttleworth and the development of State education.[46] Henrietta, wife of the second Lord Stanley of Alderley, with strong political opinions of her own, was bitterly disappointed to be stranded on the family estate in Cheshire while her husband dallied in town. She, too, turned her hand to local educational matters (day schools and Sunday schools), then broadened her interests to include "ventilation & emigration & such like philanthropic pursuits," and "the amelioration of the working classes." After her husband's death, she increasingly turned to public enterprises, becoming a founder of Girton College, Cambridge; the Girls' Public Day-School Company; the Medical College for Women; and, late in life, the Women's Liberal Unionist Association.[47] None of these women was naturally subservient, but on the contrary found philanthropy provided an ideal theater for the play of personal ambition. Such opportunities simply had not existed on the same scale for previous generations.

It could be argued, of course, that these opportunities opened up only because a separate, subordinate, not genuinely public sphere had been demarcated for them.[48] Yet, as historians of "bourgeois" feminism have often pointed out, it was a pretty capacious sphere and one which eventually opened up the public space for modern feminism, a point which could equally well be applied to aristocratic women.[49] Florence Nightingale (herself connected to a landed family, though an unorthodox one) leaned heavily on her titled friends for the support of her nurses' and midwives' training schemes.[50] The first higher-education institution for women, Queen's College, Harley Street, owed its start to the patronage of the Hon. Amelia Murray, a maid of honour at Victoria's court; Lady Stanley of Alderley was another of its early patrons.[51] Aristocrats were leaders in the women's departments set up by the Social Science Association from its founding in 1857. Even Jessie Boucherett, founder of the Society for Promoting the Employment of Women, was a squire's daughter.[52]

Beyond this, it is clear that—perhaps in contrast to their more *bourgeois* sisters—aristocratic women did not see piety, morality, and philanthropy as their work alone. Just as aristocratic women expected men to reciprocate in the sentimentality of the newly domesticated family, so they put pressure on men to remoralize themselves in private and in public. Early nineteenth-century private correspondence is cluttered with appeals from women to men to take communion, to devote themselves more faithfully to moral duties on their estates, and in general to reform their manners in public as well as in private. This tension is particularly evident in sections of the aristocracy, such as the Grand Whiggery, where godlessness had become most prevalent and personal religion was a novelty imported by the women. Lord Robert Grosvenor, for instance, readily credited his mother with his conversion from the young wastrel of the 1820s to the leading evangelical politician of the mid-Victorian period: "you have ever been to me the faithful monitress . . . it is to your instructions, and repeated injunctions, to look but to one means of guidance, direction, assistance, protection and consolation, that I owe the little good which under the blessing of Divine Providence I am able to effect."[53]

Less successful, if equally persistent, were the duchess of Devonshire's grandchildren, the Howard sisters Caroline, Georgiana, and Blanche, who had a powerful religious influence on their husbands and children but failed to convert their mother Lady Carlisle or, the biggest fish of all, their uncle the bachelor duke of Devonshire. In a concerted campaign of 1837, when Devonshire's breach with his latest mistress seemed to offer an opening, the nieces noted with glee signs of emotion in church and a general air of gloom and introspection, all thought to be tokens of repentance. For a time Devonshire eluded their grasp by decamping to the Mediterranean for a cruise with his gardener Joseph Paxton. On his return, however, he did seem to be impressed by the piously intimate marriage between his heir Lord Burlington and his favorite among the Howard sisters, Blanche. But on Blanche's sudden death in 1840, the jig was up. "I must either seek distractions in other countries," he wrote to Burlington, "or surround myself with new interests and objects to become attached to at home"—a sinister hint. He begged Burlington to come and live with him at Devonshire House to avert disaster. Burlington, with his own duties and griefs to attend to, curtly refused, and Devonshire reverted to his old ways. But if the sixth duke was lost, the seventh duke was not, and when Burlington succeeded to the title in 1855 he added considerably to the reputation of the mid-Victorian aristocracy for stolid respectability.[54]

These campaigns to moralize the aristocratic male had much private import—women wanted to save their men's souls, to curb their philandering, to get them to spend more time at home—but it is not far-fetched to see public import in them as well. The long-term political and social predominance of the aristocracy required a de-emphasis on gradations of status and birth, which were patently offensive and not long defensible, and a shift to new grounds for hierarchy, based on service to the nation, personal worthiness, and good conduct as judged on a universally-acceptable barometer. The public display of exclusive political skills by men of great landed property—the old basis of political subjectivity at the top—was not a recipe for popularity; but the public display of philanthropy, personal piety, and morality—a new definition of public service, a new liberal subjectivity for the public sphere—might yet be. This new liberal subjectivity was *not* always defined solely in terms of rationality, a male trait; morality, if anything a female trait, was just as important an element. As the burgeoning literature on the earliest "origins of modern feminism" suggests, the shift toward a liberal subjectivity—a political subjectivity based on individual rights and responsibilities rather than tradition and birthright—was a shift to which women could and did contribute. Within the aristocracy, women were in the vanguard of this movement, and to the extent that they were successful in shifting the image of their class, they also contributed directly to the political longevity of aristocratic power in Britain.

Their embrace of this new liberal subjectivity may also have given them substantially more power, more freedom to intervene on public questions, than they had had under the old order. Aristocratic women's exploitation of their privileged position in the landowning community had had its limits and had always been vulnerable to cynicism or outright hostility, among not only outsiders but aristocratic men as well. The power exerted at Almack's had been chimerical and at the same time the subject of ridicule. But when after the early 1830s Almack's went on a decline, it was replaced—literally as well as figuratively—by a public space in which aristocratic women both had more real power and were less likely to draw criticism, being in advance of rather than behind public opinion. For the hall in St. James's where Almack's met, known as Willis's Rooms, became in the early Victorian decades the best-known venue for charitable meetings, benefit dinners, bazaars, concerts, and lectures. Kemble, Thackeray, and Dickens performed there. So did many philanthropic ladies, until, that is, their events grew too large for the space and had to spill over into the Albert Hall or Regent's Park.[55] The point is that the distance between Almack's and Willis's is not so great as has been supposed, and it is certainly not a descent from authority to powerlessness.

≺ 5 ≻

John Stuart Mill, Liberal Politics, and the Movements for Women's Suffrage, 1865-1873

JANE RENDALL

IN 1868 PRISCILLA MCLAREN wrote to John Stuart Mill to offer him consolation for the loss of his Westminster seat and, at the same time, to express the gratitude of the women's movement for his achievements. In his response Mill agreed that his making of women's suffrage a parliamentary question was now "a thing accomplished" and, handsomely, "the most important public service" he had been able to render during his years in the Commons from 1865 to 1868. He thought the cause now had enough supporters in the House of Commons to carry on the contest, if only "the intelligent women of the country" would give them support.[1] He was to echo these words in his *Autobiography* a year later. Even the hostile observer Leslie Goldwin Smith, who in 1874 aggressively denounced the very idea of female suffrage, awarded Mill paternity as "the real father of the whole movement."[2]

The extent and the consequences of Mill's role in the women's suffrage movement were the subject of much contemporary discussion and have attracted subsequent historical controversy. Many women active in the early women's suffrage movement fully acknowledged the extent of their debt to Mill. On the publication of the *Subjection of Women* in 1869, Barbara Bodichon expressed her feelings:

> I feel a great deal more than I can say about it. It is almost painful to be so dumb & to feel not able in any way even to reply what even to me personally Mr Mill has done of good. Then it is a great subject of rejoicing, to feel that the book is written & Mr Mill is on our side for ever & ever.[3]

Kate Amberley wrote to Helen Taylor, Mill's stepdaughter, "I cannot tell you what pleasure Mr Mill's book has given me."[4] Elizabeth

Garrett Anderson expressed her "heartfelt sympathy & gratitude" for its tone, "aggressive against slavery rather than apologetic for freedom."[5] Even cooler voices heard after Mill's death expressed some gratitude. Lydia Becker responded tartly to Goldwin Smith that "women who felt the love of liberty" did not need a philosopher to prove it to them, though they had needed a political leader capable of promoting the cause in the House of Commons. Mill's work had been to Becker "an essential element" in making the issue practicable.[6] In 1978 Brian Harrison wrote that the Mills and the Fawcetts, between them, "laid the intellectual foundations of the cause of women's suffrage."[7]

But in two key articles by Barbara Caine and Ann Robson, also published in the 1970s, a rather different perspective emerged.[8] While Mill's stature and commitment was acknowledged, both wrote also of the damage he inflicted upon the women's suffrage movement. Throughout the 1850s and early 1860s he had ignored women activists. From 1867 onward he and Helen Taylor succeeded in dividing the energies of the movement, and in driving out the original London committee for women's suffrage, behaving in what Caine calls an "arbitrary, underhand and dictatorial fashion" toward the majority of able women in the movement. Mill's correspondence on this subject with George Croom Robertson includes very precise instructions for the manipulation of the committee of the London Society for Women's Suffrage, from which women like Caroline Biggs and Millicent Fawcett were to be excluded.[9]

More recently, Ann Robson has focused specifically on Mill's parliamentary role in the years 1865 to 1868 and has concluded that Mill had indeed succeeded as he himself suggested, in placing women's suffrage on the parliamentary agenda without subjecting it to an undue degree of ridicule.[10] His name and stature gave him an immense advantage, even though the record of his activities might seem a little thin. His speeches were well judged, conciliatory, and moderate. His tactical sense—in selecting his moment, in deferring to Gladstone wherever necessary, and in alluding to Disraeli's self-proclaimed support for the measure in principle—had its effect. His amendment to the Reform Bill in 1867 was defeated by 73 votes to 196, but—however paltry that vote may appear to us—it was the minority who cheered 73 unexpected votes (81 including pairs and tellers), representing to Mill and to those who watched "a great triumph."[11] I have found Robson's account of John Stuart Mill's tactical skills as a parliamentarian convincing if unexpected and it is not my intention to differ from her in this. But my argument in this chapter is simply that there is much more to the story.

The *Englishwoman's Review* estimated, probably on the basis of Lydia Becker's calculations, that the Commons elected in November 1868 contained 90 known friends to the cause.[12] In 1869, Jacob Bright introduced an amendment to the Municipal Franchise Bill which permitted women ratepayers to vote; the amendment passed unopposed as the redressing of an anomaly. On May 4, 1870, Jacob Bright's Women's Disabilities Removal Bill passed its second reading in the House of Commons by a majority of 33 votes. Though defeated in committee a week later, by 220 to 94, the bill had been supported by a total of 148 MPs in the two divisions, considerably exceeding expectations. Such results cannot be understood entirely in terms of Mill's inspiration and early leadership, or the power of his arguments alone. Lydia Becker had written of Mill's success as "an essential element in the conditions which have resulted in the present aspect of the question." Mill's work was essential, but is also an insufficient explanation of the whole picture. These parliamentary divisions suggest a complex political history of support for women's suffrage in the years between 1866 and 1874, inside and outside the House of Commons. In Becker's terms, there are other essential elements, which still remain to be recovered.[13]

Of course, the weight of powerful and continuing political opposition to women's suffrage in Britain, until 1928 and beyond, should not be underestimated. Yet the assumption that the women's suffrage movement developed slowly and progressively, from small beginnings in 1866 to final success in 1928, may have distorted a rather different, not necessarily linear, and much more complex history.[14] To understand the conditions of the vote of 1870, we have to look not only at the alliance between the individuals and organizations of the women's movement, and the reputation, intellectual appeal, and tactical skills of John Stuart Mill, but also at the broader social and political contours of support suggested by that vote. Twentieth-century assumptions about an absolute and gendered division between political and private worlds have created a gulf in the historiography, between political history and the history of the women's movement. That gulf can be overcome only through examining the source materials of both worlds.

The relationship between John Stuart Mill and the women's movement has to be placed within the different and pre-existing networks of support and interest among women and men, which responded to Mill's leadership and to some extent challenged it on the issue of women's suffrage. The history of such networks can partly be related to the complex legacy of that radical culture of the late Enlightenment, of which Kathryn Gleadle has written in chapter 3 of this work, whether through the circles of the politically active intelligentsia which succeeded to rational dissent, or in the framing of approaches to social science. Equally, the growth of new forms of liberalism, especially among the civic elites of mid nineteenth-century Britain, encouraged a degree of political understanding and consciousness among a small minority of middle-class women. Within these circles, in the years before 1866, there was support for political engagement by women, an engagement which was still limited in degree and which did not assume an opposition between domestic and political interests. Like the practice of the Anti-Corn Law League and the Social Science Association, it strove rather to identify those interests. In such settings it became possible to conceive, and claim, a role for women as full political citizens, though women and men did not necessarily do so in the same terms. The scale and initial success of that claim, here measured simply through the parliamentary divisions of 1867 and 1870, can help to clarify the socio-political history of this aspect of the women's movement, a history which went far beyond the alliance and paternal patronage of John Stuart Mill.

≺ I ≻

John Stuart Mill and the Movement for Women's Suffrage: "The Real Father of the Whole Movement"?[15]

In the first years of the women's movement in Britain, middle-class women had come together to forge their own periodicals and pressure groups, and from the mid-1850s to the mid-1860s the question of enfranchisement was not high on the agenda.[16] In 1858 two young

Unitarian women, Bessie Rayner Parkes and Barbara Bodichon, from politically radical middle-class families, established the *English Woman's Journal*, and, in Langham Place, a center for women's activities. They attracted other women from a variety of backgrounds, including the clergyman's daughter Emily Davies and, from the landed gentry, Jessie Boucherett. The *Journal* was committed to a better standard of education for middle-class girls, the opening of a wide variety of occupations to women, and the idea of a "sanitary mission" for middle-class women in the homes of the poor. The origins of the women's suffrage movement have usually been located in the year following the election of John Stuart Mill to the House of Commons in 1865. Parkes and Bodichon had campaigned for him in his Westminster constituency and with Helen Taylor drew up a petition to the House of Commons which Mill presented in June 1866.

Mill's *Subjection of Women* was published in 1869, though it was drafted from 1860, after the death of his wife Harriet Taylor in 1858. It drew upon their joint work of a lifetime. He deliberately delayed publication until, he felt, his parliamentary work had prepared the public. Nevertheless even in much earlier writing the outline of his arguments was already apparent. Recent analysis of the work has focused on Mill's approach to women's citizenship, rooted in individual self-development and cultivation of individual faculties, in all their variety and diversity; on Mill's broad acceptance of a sexual division of labor; and on the asexual concept of the "marriage of true minds."[17] It has not however always identified that framework which Mill shared with a much wider public, his historical approach to the condition of women. Mill placed his analysis within an evolutionary history of civilization in which in the earliest stages women were to be found in that state of slavery, which, dependent on the rule of force, characterized a wide section of society. Though the slavery of men was gradually abolished with advancing civilization, the condition of women, while to some degree moderated, retained its original taint, "an almost solitary exception to the general character of their laws and customs."[18]

Mill's first published comments on this subject appeared as early as 1826, four years before his meeting with Harriet Taylor, in a review of work on medieval French history for the *Westminster Review*. In this he showed himself familiar with the writing on the history of women of John Millar, the Scottish Enlightenment historian, to whom he then referred as "the greatest of philosophical enquirers on the civilization of past ages." This review was located precisely within that Enlightenment historical heritage which traced the evolution of women's condition from the slavery of early savage societies to the limited improvements made in the modern commercial West. Mill wrote then to counter the arguments of the works under review, which betrayed admiration for an age of chivalry, that "If it could be proved that women, in the middle ages, were well treated, it would be so decisive a proof of an advanced stage of civilization, as it would require much evidence to rebut." Here, he adopted what had become Enlightenment commonplaces, in observing that "Good treatment of women . . . is one of the surest marks of high civilization."[19]

This approach did not, however, exclude perceptions of sexual difference, and could indeed encourage them. Such an historical framework could have didactic and prescriptive purposes, if used to encourage the appropriate moralized and domestic framework for a modernizing society, as in eighteenth-century Scotland. Yet it could also offer a political impetus, in the challenge which it presented to those who saw progress in the relations between the sexes as lagging far behind a more general pattern of improvement. That political impetus was already present in Mill's unpublished essay "On Marriage" of 1832. It was to be sharpened during the years first of his friendship with and then marriage to Harriet Taylor, from the 1830s to the 1850s. It found practical application in their joint newspaper articles on the nature of domestic violence and tyranny:

The barbarities of which history is full, and which in barbarous countries flourish as rankly as ever, very few persons in a civilized country now suffer from political authorities—millions are liable to them from domestic ones.[20]

As Ann and John Robson have pointed out, Harriet Taylor and Mill criticized what we would term sexist language, and accepted an associationist psychology suggesting the malleability of human nature. Yet they also explored the notion of "completing counterparts," that is the possibility of complementary natures and talents, in, for instance, the roles of the Artist and the Scientist. The latter theme is particularly relevant to Mill's often contradictory perceptions of the nature of women, and of the condition of marriage.[21] In the *Principles of Political Economy* (1849), he wrote, though very briefly, of the condition of laboring women.[22] Joint unpublished notes of the late 1840s, in Mill's hand but amended by Taylor, suggest that in those years he was already reflecting on the claim for women's suffrage, placed within the framework of the history of progress, and the educational advantages of citizenship, for married as for unmarried women. Taylor's article "The Enfranchisement of Women" of 1851 gave a radical signal of their thinking.[23] And in his *Considerations on Representative Government* (1861), Mill indicated that his case for "universal, but graduated suffrage" took no account of sex "as entirely irrelevant to political rights, as difference in height, or in the colour of the hair."[24]

The women who established the *English Woman's Journal*, Bessie Parkes and Barbara Leigh Smith, had followed such publications avidly. In 1849 they read together the *Principles of Political Economy* by "beautiful lucid Mill" as Parkes called him. Smith then wished that Mill had gone further to write on the law of marriage, and even something rather different, "a Moral Philosophy, a treatise on the Duties of men to one another in their various relations."[25] They were to remain nervous of a claim which was for rights rather than duties. Parkes, as editor of the *English Woman's Journal*, declared at the outset in 1858 her nervousness of contentious issues such as "divorce & the suffrage."[26] Her review of Mill's work in 1860 stressed that women interested in questions of employment should be familiar with his opinions and examined especially his *Logic* and *Principles of Political Economy*. She drew attention to his stress on the progressive development of human society, and to his discussion of the advantages of co-operation, which such development made possible; for "the more human creatures cast behind them the savage theory that might makes right, which may be termed the political economy of wild beasts, the more possible become the independent labors of the gentler sex."[27] Yet others in her circle were less cautious on the question of suffrage, and by 1862 an abstract of Harriet Taylor's article was ready for publication in the *Journal* though Emily Davies, then the editor, wished to hold over this "startling manifesto" for the right moment, which did not come until 1864. Even then the article was not reprinted in full, probably because of what Davies perceived as the "bitterness" of Taylor's language.[28]

In May 1865 Emily Davies recorded her first sighting of John Stuart Mill at the Social Science meeting held in Sheffield, comparing his appearance to that of Frederick Denison Maurice:

His outward shell does not to my mind express what he is & in that respect he is very unlike Mr Maurice, who sat near him at the same meeting ... I hope in future that Mr Mill's outward form will be more expressive of the many-sided soul. It may be that being very shy, he does not *choose* to express anything but what he cannot help, namely refinement. *That* cannot be concealed. It was very beautiful to see the varying expression of Mr Maurice's face while Mr Mill was speaking.[29]

In July 1865 Bodichon (formerly Smith), Davies, and Parkes actively supported John Stuart Mill's successful election campaign, in which he committed himself to support women's suffrage on equal terms with men.[30] This provision of course implicitly excluded married women, though in private campaigners were committed to their enfranchisement also. In November of that year the newly formed Kensington Ladies Debating Society, which had arisen from the Langham Place circle, discussed the question: "Is the extension of the parliamentary suffrage to women desirable and if so under what conditions?" Five women, including Barbara Leigh Smith Bodichon and Helen Taylor, wrote papers for it.[31] It is clear that the idea of a committee to work toward the suffrage for women had already been mooted. As Emily Davies wrote on November 10, "some people are inclined to begin a subdued kind of agitation for the franchise."[32]

On May 9, 1866, Barbara Bodichon sought the guidance of Helen Taylor and John Stuart Mill, and on June 7 Mill presented the first petition on the subject in this session. In the next twelve months, between August 1866 and the passing of the Conservative Reform Bill, the first women's suffrage committee was organized in London. Yet sharp differences among the women and men involved, and more especially between the Mill-Taylor axis and the Langham Place women, were already apparent, both in terms of organizational strategy and in principle. Emily Davies was wary of too close an association with the politics of Mill:

The newspapers have got into a way of treating the question as an individual crotchet of Mr Mill's. That secures to us all the support that his name can bring. What we must show is that it is not a personal crotchet of anybody's. If Mr Mill had made it his *first* concern, it would have been a different case. As it is, we get mixed up in the public mind with Jamaica and the Reform league, which does us no good.[33]

By October 1866 a committee drawing on both Langham Place and associates of John Stuart Mill was formed, but it never achieved a working harmony. Nine months later it had ceased to exist, and Emily Davies and other women associated with the *English Woman's Journal* had left, though they continued to give support in principle, and to comment through the *Journal*'s successor, the *Englishwoman's Review*. The new committee, formed in July 1867, was known as the London National Society for Women's Suffrage. It was dominated by Mill, Helen Taylor, and their associate Clementia Taylor, and, without the active commitment of the most experienced women suffrage campaigners in London, proved to be administratively entirely ineffective in the demanding needs of organizing a national campaign.[34]

Nevertheless, Mill's ideal of citizenship undoubtedly helped to shape the ideals of suffragists, especially those in his immediate circle in the last years of his life. Education and cultivation were to these liberals the key to citizenship.[35] To Julia Wedgwood, describing the narrowness and lack of opportunity of the life of the middle-class woman, female suffrage and citizenship itself were claimed rather from a need to take up duties and responsibilities than any desire to demand rights, "more for what it would make us than for what it would give us."[36]

Equally, many agreed with Mill that not all members of a society were ready for such citizenship. Influenced by Mill's distrust of democracy, they noted the ways in which he proposed to limit its effects, such as the test of literacy and numeracy for voters he had proposed in his *Considerations on Representative Government* (1861). They also, like Millicent Fawcett, admired the proposal for proportional representation put forward by Thomas Hare, which was intended to ensure the representation of minorities, and in particular the election of "men of talent and character," clearly men like Mill and his friends.[37] Qualifications based on education and character would not exclude the married woman, ideally benefiting from Mill's ideal of companionship in marriage.

Those sympathetic to Mill tended to disassociate themselves from the language of philanthropy and "woman's mission," associating it as Millicent Fawcett did with the "spurious philanthropy" of charity.[38] Julia Wedgwood, writing of women who might mistakenly encourage pauperism out of an overly feminized and sentimentally

Christian compassion, spoke of a woman's perception of political economy as belonging "to a secular male world, with which she has nothing to do." Citizenship should bring a sense of responsibility to replace the easy pleasures of charity, an involvement in the national life, and an understanding of laws of political economy which might through "beneficent discipline" end the "rot of pauperism." The incomprehension of the poor shown by the legislators of the House of Commons could be very obviously remedied by the special qualifications which women might bring to such work, once informed by a sense of responsibility and by "intellectual training."[39] Finally, suffragists also shared Mill's consciousness of participating in a progressive movement of civilization, to be differentiated from other parts of the world, yet also requiring a further impetus for women's condition to be properly a part of that advance.

John Stuart Mill brought to the cause of women's suffrage an attractive intellectual influence and reputation, an unexpectedly effective parliamentary voice, and a willingness to court ridicule in its name. Yet the power of his name and personal commitment have tended to obscure developments already at work within some liberal and radical circles by the 1860s, and evident to an extent in the support he received in the House of Commons in 1867.

When on May 20, 1867, Mill put his amendment to the Conservative Reform Bill that "person" be substituted for "man" in clause 4, dealing with the occupation qualification for voters in the counties, his motion attracted 73 votes against an opposition of 196. He was supported by his closest disciples in the Commons, Henry Fawcett and Viscount Amberley. Other supporters from the Victorian intelligentsia were the Christian Socialist Thomas Hughes and the radicals George Otto Trevelyan, Laurence Oliphant, and Duncan McLaren. A striking, though not the largest, group of supporters in this vote were the advanced liberal and radical MPs from the major industrial cities, of whom I have identified 19, including Edward Baines from Leeds, Isaac Holden of Bradford, M. T. Bass of Burton and Derby, W. H. Leatham of Wakefield, John Platt and J. T. Hibbert of Oldham, and George Hadfield of Sheffield. They also included radical unitarians Peter Taylor of Leicester, Joseph Cowen of Newcastle, and James Stansfeld from Halifax. The O'Donoghue, nephew of Daniel O'Connell, was a supporter and a Reform League activist. The radical leader John Bright and Henry Labouchere both voted for

Mill's amendment, though not for later women's suffrage bills. Other supporters included the gentry radical Peter Locke King and the Liberal administrator George Shaw-Lefevre. Although the amendment related only to England and Wales, 13 supporters held Irish seats and 5 were from Scottish seats. The largest single group of voters, however, 35, were from the backbenches of the Liberal party, with 12 Conservatives also voting in support, including Robert Peel's elderly brother Jonathan and the young John Edward Gorst.[40] Benjamin Disraeli told Mill that though in favor of female suffrage, he could not vote for the amendment "on account of his colleagues, but that he was working for it within the Cabinet."[41] Although the degree of support for the amendment may appear limited, it surprised and pleased many, though the *Englishwoman's Review* had hoped for more.[42] The national and local press covered the debate seriously, with even those opposed, like *The Times*, giving it full coverage, and other papers like the *Leeds Mercury* under Edward Baines offering supportive argument.[43]

This response to Mill's amendment cannot be explained simply by the relationship, both admiring and unhappy, established between the campaigners of the women's movement and Mill's personal commitment and powerful name. The connections between the various liberal and radical alliances of 1866–67, which made possible the election of the Liberal government of 1868–74, and the women's suffrage movement have been too little studied.[44] Of course not all supporters, women or men, came from radical or reforming backgrounds. The backgrounds of Emily Faithfull, the daughter of a country parson, and of Jessie Boucherett, from the Lincolnshire gentry, did not necessarily predispose them to the cause. The Conservative Recorder of London Russell Gurney was to prove an important stalwart to the cause in the House of Commons. Kate Stanley married Viscount Amberley, the son of Earl Russell, from one of the great Whig aristocratic families, and as Viscountess Amberley was humiliated at the dining table of Downing Street for her feminist politics.[45] Yet, overall, the movement for women's enfranchisement drew most extensively upon overlapping networks of radical and liberal opinion. Though Mill's synthesis of ideas in his *Subjection of Women* was given considerable importance by his reputation and personal commitment, those ideas were already widespread within some liberal and radical circles by the 1860s.

≺ II ≻

Liberal Coalitions: Women, Men, and the Case for Women's Suffrage

In this period the term liberal—or Liberal—was extraordinarily elastic. As Jonathan Parry has written, the Liberal party between the 1850s and 1880s was a coalition incorporating "an astonishing range of classes and groups, from aristocrats to artisans, industrial magnates to labour activists, and zealous Anglican high churchmen to nonconformists and aggressive freethinkers."[46] They were supported by merchants and shopkeepers of the northern and midland cities, Dissenting chapels and trade unions, the "literary, legal and academic intelligentsia," and Anglican aristocrats and country gentlemen. The particular form which the alliance took in the mid to late 1860s was to prove temporarily sympathetic to the case for women's suffrage.

The liberal coalitions of the third quarter of the nineteenth century have been the focus of much recent historiography, though relatively little attention has been paid to the gendered nature of that liberalism, and to the ways in which women as well as men were participants. Recent work is nevertheless suggestive on this issue, in that it tends to discard notions of a liberalism shaped by a stereotyped and dogmatic individualism. It indicates rather that certain positions within radicalism and liberalism overlapped with and in some respects went beyond the ideas of John Stuart Mill. So Parry has identified as the major components of a whig-liberal creed that increasing acceptance of a code of law, which marked out a steadily growing and character-forming citizenry within a genuinely British polity, extending its values to its empire.[47] Eugenio Biagini and Alastair Reid have explored the significance of the recovery of a progressive popular liberalism, and its connections to an academic and socially-oriented intelligentsia, while also stressing that such a politics had meaning only within the collective identities of localities.[48]

Some elements within the Liberal party were unsympathetic to the case for women's suffrage. The liberalism of William Gladstone, with its Peelite and conservative antecedents, was to influence the much less sympathetic atmosphere of the 1870s and 1880s. The trade unionist leadership of the Reform League was unreceptive to the arguments, as were positivist intellectuals like Frederick Harrison and E. S. Beesly.[49] Yet within radical unitarianism, Manchester radical liberalism, Christian socialism, and academic liberalism, and among a small group of Whig-liberal administrators, there was a significant degree of support for the women's suffrage cause. Such groupings were themselves, of course, by no means unanimous on the issue. They were also, briefly, drawn together between 1864 and 1868 in other causes, in unity against the Test Acts, in support of the North in the American Civil War, and in the campaign for household franchise. Though women and men from such backgrounds acknowledged the importance of Mill's intervention on the issue of women's suffrage, their own politics were by no means necessarily governed by it.

Kathryn Gleadle's recent work has very clearly demonstrated that in the 1830s and 1840s, from that middle-class dissenting group most associated with political radicalism and social unorthodoxy, the Unitarians, had come a small minority committed to enlightenment, education, and democracy, who had consistently argued for women's suffrage. They were already familiar with those historical narratives of the condition of women on which Mill had drawn.[50] By the 1840s young lawyers like William Shaen and James Stansfeld, and Unitarians close to Owenism like Catherine and Goodwyn Barmby had already identified women's enfranchisement as an essential element in that political transformation of society which they hoped to see. Radicals like George Dawson of Birmingham and W. J. Linton echoed them, and the issue was not peripheral but central, an uneasy point of tension, in the relations between radical unitarianism and the Chartist movement. Unitarians argued as Mill was to do that it was not, as Chartists suggested, the drudgery of hard labor for women which constituted slavery, but the effects of longstanding patriarchal oppression and its shaping of the submissive—or slavish—character of women. Linton, for instance, wrote in 1839 of "the false position in which women have ever been placed, and in which they still linger by reason of those remains of barbarism which yet give to physical force the advantage over all kinds and degrees of moral and spiritual power."[51] This historical framework was not distinctively Mill's but one familiar to many and especially to circles of dissenters, many of them educated in Scottish universities, by the early nineteenth century.

Gleadle notes that within this world, one which grew out of a male radical politics within which feminism was one element of a larger ideological commitment, men were dominant, although women played an important part through their writing and their organizational support. The force of that radical unitarianism, which had drawn so much energy from William Johnson Fox and the South Place Chapel, was clearly on the decline by the 1850s, though it was an important element within the nationalist politics of radicalism in the years after Chartism. Margot Finn has identified a middle-class radical culture of the 1850s, strongly "centred on family life, private houses, Nonconformist chapels and liberal salons."[52] Among such centers were the radical unitarian households, Joseph Cowen, Junior's, Stella House in Newcastle; Peter and Clementia Taylor's Aubrey House in London; and the home of William Ashurst at Muswell Hill, all of which entertained Mazzini, Kossuth, and Louis Blanc. All had been, since the 1840s, also centers of support for women's rights and enfranchisement, and were to remain so in the 1860s; it is perhaps important to note here the unity between familial and social life, and the political cultures of such households.

The commitment of radical unitarian men was to be an important element in the support of the women's suffrage movement of the 1860s. Gleadle's work has enabled us to place the interests of John Stuart Mill and Harriet Taylor in their wider framework, shared by a number of others. Many of the radical unitarian members of the Friends of Italy, founded in 1851—George Dawson, Francis Newman, James Stansfeld, Joseph Cowen, Junior, Peter Taylor, Samuel Courtauld, W. E. Adams—were among those to lend their support and patronage in a variety of ways to the cause of women's suffrage fifteen years later.[53] In 1858 Samuel Courtauld helped Parkes and Bodichon to start the *English Woman's Journal*, which had W. J. Fox as its auditor.[54] James Stansfeld was a stalwart of the women's suffrage cause and more generally a parliamentary spokesman on behalf of the women's movement for many years. Any local study of the first years of the provincial movement rapidly reveals also the role of key Unitarian and radical Dissenting ministers, like the Unitarians Henry Crosskey of Birmingham, Estlin Carpenter of Bristol, and Saul A. Steinthal of Manchester, just as it does the importance of their chapels and halls as meeting places. The ex-Owenite Goodwyn Barmby, now the Rev. Goodwyn Barmby, became an activist in the Yorkshire women's suffrage movement.[55]

But Gleadle's work also clearly indicates the significance of radical unitarian influences upon the women of the early movement. Barbara Leigh Smith and Bessie Parkes both moved within these radical unitarian circles. They too met Kossuth and heard Mazzini, and modelled their literary efforts on those of this radical intelligentsia.[56] Clementia Taylor played a central if not entirely successful role in the formation of the first and second London Committees for Women's Suffrage. The Ashurst family provided many of the early women activists, including Caroline Ashurst Biggs, whom Mill sought to exclude from his London committee in 1871, and who later as editor of the *Englishwoman's Review* gave prominence to the cause of peace and internationalism.[57] The Mazzinian vision of a new social and economic framework was one which continued to inform both the *Englishwoman's Review* and the *Woman's Suffrage Journal*.[58]

However, radical unitarianism, though profoundly influential, was not the only route by which women and men came to participate in the movement for women's suffrage. It has to be placed as one—very significant—partner in a series of alliances constructed between those who in the 1860s linked liberal and radical aims. Those who voted for Mill's amendment of 1867 included a significant group of advanced liberal and radical MPs from the major industrial cities of northern England and the midlands. Their votes reflected a degree of support from the more radical sections of the nonconformist and urban provincial leadership, united not only by the campaign against slavery, but by the Anti-Corn Law League, by the common interests of nonconformity, and by sympathy with a nationalist politics. Supporters of the amendment also included leading manufacturers and merchants for whom the tenets of Manchester political economy were a part of their world. Some, though by no means all, were Unitarians. In 1868, it was to be Lydia Becker of Manchester who firmly swept the leadership of the women's suffrage movement out of the hands of an ineffective London committee, and who after an initial correspondence virtually severed relationships with Helen Taylor and John Stuart Mill. The liberalism of the Manchester school, whose influence spread far beyond Manchester, gave critical encouragement to the women's suffrage movement.

Such a liberalism had in the past drawn upon that wider involvement of women in different forms of pressure group politics, first and most clearly identified with the anti-slavery movement.[59] In the 1840s George Wilson and Richard Cobden, the political organizers of the Anti-Corn Law League, chose to draw upon the organizational power and influence of women. That mobilization can be attributed to the legitimating power of the sentimental concept of "woman's mission." But it can also be interpreted as a recognition of the capacities of women to understand and participate in the arguments of political economy. Women also took the initiative, petitioning and organizing, sometimes in association with their religious congregations; the arguments of the League, like those of earlier sugar boycotts, tended to politicize the role of women within the domestic economy. In the development of the bazaar, women also identified an imaginative mode of fundraising in which they might collaborate, and even take a lead, on behalf of the League. Such participation was controversial, and its extent could depend on individual factors, such as women's own family commitments and the distance at which they lived. Nevertheless the League had provided an approach to "women's issues" and a view of female citizenship, linked to their domestic position, which allowed women some political space.[60] The same ambivalence toward widening roles might be found within the peace movement of the 1850s, among those women who participated in Elihu Burritt's Olive Leaf Circles, backing peace rather than intervention.[61]

The Cobdenite radicalism of Manchester maintained a powerful political and electoral machine (the "'Newall's Buildings' clique," in the words of opponents) from the 1840s to the 1860s, dominating Manchester politics and those of a number of neighboring towns. It was strongly linked to local dissenting communities, including key Unitarian and Independent chapels, and to Quakerism. By the end of the 1850s, it has been argued, the relatively weak survivors of Chartist radicalism in Manchester were increasingly subsumed within a broader Cobdenite consensus. That consensus also rested on an electorate which had steadily expanded; by 1860 Manchester was benefiting from a relatively efficient and automatic system of voter registration.[62]

Leaders of the Manchester school continued to pursue their earlier commitments to peace, retrenchment, and reform throughout the 1850s and early 1860s, though they linked them to noninterventionist support for European nationalisms, moderate extension of the franchise, and the politics of temperance. In the 1860s Wilson still ran a powerful Liberal political machine in Manchester, backed by Alexander Ireland, editor of the *Manchester Examiner and Times*, which expressed a lively Liberal populism with wide-ranging appeal to reformers and radicals. Two organizations which brought together important elements of liberal opinion in the early 1860s were created through Cobdenite initiatives. One was the Union and Emancipation Society, founded in 1863, which united many shades of opinion on behalf of the North in the American Civil War, including former Chartists like Ernest Jones and Edward Hoosen. Its most prominent officers included Thomas Bayley Potter, MP for Rochdale, and Jacob Bright, brother of John Bright.[63] The foundation of the National Reform Union in the spring of 1864 brought together, under Cobdenite leadership, existing middle-class reform organizations, former Chartists, and local manhood suffrage campaigners in Lancashire and the north.[64] In these organizations Manchester politicians took the lead, though they also united radical unitarians and others discussed below, including some academic liberals and Christian socialists.

This background is also one of relevance to the early history of the women's suffrage movement. It can be traced in the responses of women activists to the League and allied movements, and their sympathies for a populist, anti-aristocratic politics. Elizabeth Pease, from a leading Quaker family in Darlington and deeply involved in the anti-slavery movement, admired the anti-aristocratic politics of the League, and women's involvement in it, as well as actively supporting the Chartist movement and Sturge's attempt to bring the League and Chartism together in the Complete Suffrage Union.[65] Elizabeth Wolstenholme recalled her childhood emotion at the processions of the Anti-Corn Law League.[66] Bessie Parkes in 1847 had also identified with "the people who have just learned their power by the victory of the Anti-Corn Law League."[67] She and Barbara Leigh Smith had attended the Birley lectures of the Peace Society, and followed dissenting battles against Anglican claims to monopoly in education.[68] The politics of political economy had both interested and divided the women of the *English Woman's Journal*.[69]

Although a Manchester committee may have existed as early as October 1865, the first meeting recorded by the first historian of the movement, Helen Blackburn, was held on January 11, 1867, with six members. Jacob Bright took the chair and its members included the Unitarian minister Saul Steinthal and Elizabeth Wolstenholme and Elizabeth Gloyn, both very active in work for women's education. In February they were joined by Lydia Becker, who became its secretary; and by Richard Pankhurst, already a member of the National Reform Union.[70] In the next few months the committee recruited the Rochdale MP Thomas Bayley Potter and ex-Chartists Ernest Jones and Edward Hoosen. Other women members included Josephine Butler and Mary Hume-Rothery.[71] Max Kyllmann, friend and correspondent of Mill, was the treasurer, and R. D. Rusden, the secretary of the National Reform Union, was a constant source of support.[72]

And in the by-election in Manchester in November 1867, Jacob Bright was the candidate of a United Liberal Party which united moderate and advanced Liberals with manhood suffrage campaigners. This candidature was significant for the women's suffrage movement for a number of reasons, as significant in many ways as Mill's at Westminster. First, Jacob Bright, like Mill, had indicated his support for women's suffrage in his electoral campaign, and, on the hustings, a woman called Lily Maxwell actually cast a parliamentary vote for Bright.[73] Lily Maxwell's vote was of course fortuitous, a clerical error, a lucky gift opportunistically and enthusiastically exploited by Becker and by Bright. But by October 1868 the Manchester branch of the National Society for Women's Suffrage was describing Lily Maxwell's vote as the event which "removed women's suffrage from the region of theoretical possibilities to that of actual occurrences."[74]

Second, Jacob Bright's enlistment marked not only his own adherence but that of his extensive family. His brother John Bright had voted for Mill's amendment, just as he had signalled his support, in principle if not immediately, for the cause some nine years earlier, though by 1871 he had clearly changed his mind.[75] But Jacob Bright was to be a major figure in the movement. His wife Ursula, from the wealthy Liverpool Mellor family, was a leader not only of the women's suffrage movement, but also of the campaigns to reform the law on married women's property, and against the Contagious Diseases Acts. Jacob Bright's two sisters, Margaret Bright Lucas and Priscilla Bright McLaren, helped to provide much of the leadership of the new suffrage societies founded in Edinburgh, Bristol, and Bath, linked as they were also to the Priestman, Clark, and Estlin families.[76] They built upon the networks of the Society of Friends and brought with them experience and commitment generated in the anti-slavery, abolitionist, and peace movements in which women like Mary Estlin had co-operated with radical unitarians. They also built transatlantic links with supporters of William Lloyd Garrison in the United States. Their commitment, as Sandra Holton has demonstrated, maintained a radical edge to the suffrage question. The Brights, with Becker, were at odds with Mill from the London split of 1867. They were later to challenge the London society for national leadership by forming the new Central Committee of the National Women's Suffrage Society in 1871, and they were referred to by Mill as an "obnoxious set," with "common vulgar motives and tactics."[77]

Third, Bright's candidature marked the beginning of an extensive and complex relationship between the politics of women's suffrage and that of provincial radical liberalism, which drew sustenance not only from Manchester political economy but from campaigning Dissent and an increasingly organized temperance movement. It is clear that many Manchester reformers were committed to women's suffrage. In February 1868, well before the publication of the *Subjection of Women* but drawing on very similar language, Alexander Ireland wrote in his editorial in the *Manchester Examiner and Times* of arguments against women's suffrage as "not distinguishable in principle from those which have held rule for ages in the mountains of Circassia, in the slave markets of Constantinople, and in the plantations of the southern states of America." The paper called for "the development of feminine character in its social and political relations" and argued that "it is desirable that wives and mothers should know what citizenship means."[78] In the pages of the same paper, Mary Hume-Rothery, a committee member of the Manchester society, called for universal adult suffrage.[79] In February of 1868 a meeting of the National Reform Union gave an extremely sympathetic hearing to a call for the vote for all qualified women by committee members Alice Wilson and Jacob Bright, though the Chair ruled that the rules of the association could not be altered without notice. Jacob Bright believed that a more forceful response might have succeeded in winning the Union over.[80]

Lydia Becker followed the vote of Lily Maxwell by an energetic campaign to have all women who paid rates enrolled on the parliamentary register for the election of 1868.[81] That campaign has to be placed in the context of Manchester radical liberalism. In calling for women to be enfranchised on the same terms as men, it drew upon the long-established rhetoric of the "independent" man, calling attention to the respectability, industry, and political interests of women householders. Implicitly, though not explicitly, it excluded married women, disfranchised by their inability to own property and by the legal principle of coverture. The campaign was launched in a major meeting in the Free-Trade Hall in Manchester on April 14, 1868. This meeting was chaired by the Liberal mayor of Salford, the industrialist Henry Pochin, with reform leaders, including Jacob Bright, Thomas Bayley Potter, Benjamin Whitworth, and R. D. Rusden, on the platform, as well as leading women members. The meeting was widely reported and judged a great success, as was that in Birmingham on May 8.[82] In the movement to register women voters, Becker liaised closely with representatives of the Liberal Registration Societies, though recognizing that Conservative candidates too could potentially benefit from the registration of women voters. There is much to suggest that the methods used by the society drew upon the canvassing practices of the political parties, although Lydia Becker warned the London committee against approaching Liberal Party agents, given the need to be above party.[83]

In the chaos of the registration courts in the aftermath of the Reform Act, that aspiration appears to have been slipping since the battle did take on something of a party character. The claimants themselves could not be represented by counsel. In Manchester the case for 5,750 female claimants was put forward by counsel instructed by the Liberals and opposed by the representative of the Conservative Association, who claimed to be there "more to watch than to oppose." In Birmingham on the revision of the list for North Warwickshire, the Liberal representative suggested that something like four thousand women were qualified to vote, though he was opposed directly by the agent of the Conservative Party. In Edinburgh the veteran Elizabeth Pease, now the widowed Elizabeth Pease Nichol and a committee member of the Edinburgh Society for Women's Suffrage, fought the battle for a vote on behalf of women householders, defended by John McLaren, son of the Liberal politician Duncan

McLaren.[84] Similar battles, on which further research is needed, took place elsewhere.[85]

The three Liberal Manchester candidates, allied as United Liberals in 1868, the Palmerstonian Sir Thomas Bazley, the radical-Liberal Jacob Bright, and Ernest Jones the ex-Chartist, were all supporters of women's suffrage, though in different degrees; however the Conservative Manchester employer Hugh Birley, who defeated Ernest Jones, was also to support women's suffrage in 1870. Elsewhere, the extent of the support given to women's suffrage by local Liberal leaders remains to be explored. In her campaigning tours of 1869, especially though not exclusively in industrial northern towns, Becker was to draw upon their support and that of dissenting ministers, at meetings in Mechanics Institutes, town halls, and dissenting chapels. In Newcastle she spoke to "a respectable and attentive audience of both sexes" supported by Joseph Cowen, Senior, his son, and two local Unitarian ministers, who helped to form the new Newcastle Committee of the National Society for Women's Suffrage. In Leeds, with the backing of Edward Baines and the *Leeds Mercury*, she found a good audience, "many of whom were working people."[86]

Local Liberal leaders—often with strong dissenting links—participated in varying degrees in that rapprochement with advanced radical politics which briefly characterized Manchester liberalism in 1867–68, and which aided the emergence of an active and campaigning women's suffrage movement. But the tactical concessions made by women campaigners who took their place on such platforms based on the goal of household suffrage were in future to limit and to divide them.

Another group associated with the women's suffrage movement came from academic liberalism and the intellectual world of London. The campaign to improve the education of women from the mid-1850s had attracted as patrons a substantial input from academics, especially those from Oxford, Cambridge, and Edinburgh. Henry Sidgwick, George Butler, Frederick Myers, and James Stuart were all active in the university extension movement and in the North of England Council for Promoting the Higher Education of Women, formed in 1867. These interests can be placed within a broader political context. In the Universities of Oxford and Cambridge, the campaign against the Tests Act (which restricted University posts to

Anglicans) and support for the North in the American Civil War brought such liberals much closer to a campaigning nonconformity. By 1865 Oxford and Manchester, and especially Manchester Unitarians, were in dialogue over the repeal of the Tests Acts. As Jacob Bright remarked in this context: "If Oxford and Cambridge stretch out the hand for help to Manchester, I do not believe that Manchester will turn a deaf ear."[87]

In Christopher Harvie's otherwise excellent study, *The Lights of Liberalism*, he has suggested that "by and large, throughout their careers, the academics were resolute opponents of women's suffrage," with Fawcett, Edward Caird, and Henry Sidgwick the only exceptions.[88] This assertion is not confirmed by the sources of the women's suffrage movement in the period I am dealing with, although many academic liberals, especially those influenced by positivism, were of course indifferent or opposed. In the petitioning campaigns of 1867, designed to demonstrate support for Mill's amendment and presented between March and April, Emily Davies focused her attention particularly on Oxford and Cambridge colleges. The petition organized by the London Committee succeeded in securing the signatures of 26 college fellows and 5 professors, that by Manchester 43 fellows, and that by Edinburgh 8 professors. Even Goldwin Smith was an early signatory.[89]

A focus on the group whom Harvie designates as academic liberals in this period suggests certain more specific links. There were indeed some connections to the authors of the *Essays on Reform*. Josephine Butler edited a collection of essays, which was, according to Emily Davies, originally conceived as one of a number of parallel works to that volume. It was first suggested in 1867 by Albert Rutson, editor of the *Essays on Reform* and a friend of Josephine Butler's husband, George Butler. Josephine Butler wrote to potential contributors of the persuasion exercised by the publisher Alexander Macmillan, and of her own preference for a mixture of male and female contributors.[90] The first suggested list of contributors included Rutson himself, George Butler, James Bryce, Leonard Courtney, and Frederick Myers, as well as Julia Wedgwood, Barbara Bodichon, and Adelaide Manning, with Emily Davies as editor.[91]

The final collection, published as *Woman's Work and Woman's Culture* two years later, looked very different but did contain two essays by contributors to the *Essays on Reform*, Charles Pearson and

John Boyd Kinnear, both of whom regularly attended meetings of the London National Society for Women's Suffrage after 1869. Their interests included the reform of the married women's property legislation as well as women's suffrage. Their essays placed their concerns directly within that historical framework which was already commonplace within the women's movement. Pearson wrote in his essay of "the legal relations of husband and wife [as] . . . a relic of primitive times."[92] Boyd Kinnear, whose wife was an active committee member of the London Suffrage Society, dealt in his essay with both women's work and their participation in politics, as with "the surviving barbarism of our laws." He argued that in these areas there were no duties which women should not undertake, even if not identically, including "the highest public duties" and "those matters which seem furthest removed from the domestic life."[93] In her introduction to this volume, which appeared just after the *Subjection of Women*, Butler noted the similarity in their approaches, but pointed out that each of these essays had been written before Mill's work had appeared, and indeed pursued some of his themes in more detail. The books were frequently reviewed together.

Other regular attenders at such meetings among the reform essayists included Lord Houghton, Thorold Rogers, Bernard Cracroft, George Brodrick, and Frank Hill. Some were evidently drawn in by Mill, as was Richard Monckton Milnes, Lord Houghton.[94] Auberon Herbert and his wife, Lady Florence May, had close links with Mill and Helen Taylor.[95] Others drew on different connections, with Albert Rutson a source of continuing advice to the Manchester circle through his friendship with the Butlers. Lydia Becker approached him for advice in May 1868 on ways of persuading London overseers to register voters.[96]

In Edinburgh too it is clear that a small group of academic liberals, led by David Masson but including the MPs Lyon Playfair and David Wedderburn, were in alliance with Duncan McLaren to organize the major women's suffrage meetings which attracted large crowds in the early 1870s. Masson, formerly professor at University College London, and editor of *Macmillan's Magazine* from 1859 to 1868, became professor of rhetoric and English literature in Edinburgh in 1865. He was there a consistent and dynamic supporter of women's education and women's suffrage.[97] In Glasgow Edward Caird, professor of moral philosophy, was also strongly committed.[98]

Some academic liberals clearly owed their inspiration to Mill. He and Helen Taylor carried with them, on the committee of the London National Society and in the press, an active group of academic supporters, sometimes, like Thomas Hare, and John Elliot Cairnes of Queens College Galway, with wives and daughters similarly active in the movement. But Mill was not their only inspiration. The political economist Thomas Cliffe Leslie was a committed supporter of the movement, and correspondent of both John Stuart Mill and Lydia Becker, from its beginning.[99] G. M. Trevelyan recalled his father, George Otto Trevelyan, who voted for Mill's amendment in 1867, as indebted more to Bright than to Mill for the origins of his radicalism; he was also connected by marriage to the Philips family, long-established Manchester Cobdenites.[100] The wider group of radicals and liberals which met in the Century Club from 1866 included a number of supporters for women's suffrage—like Charles Pearson—whose inspiration may be associated as much with the politics of Christian socialism and with a historical and comparative outlook on the condition of women as with Mill's concept of citizenship.

Academic liberals were contributors to and editors of the progressive journalism of the period, the journals in which members of the women's suffrage movement staked their claims. The editor of the *Daily News* and reform essayist Frank Hill was, with his wife, regularly in attendance at women's suffrage meetings. The *Fortnightly Review*, published from 1865 and edited by John Morley, was widely recognized as the most influential journal among self-styled progressive thinkers in the 1860s and 1870s; Morley in these years attended women's suffrage meetings, and also translated the Marquis de Condorcet's pamphlet on women's citizenship to demonstrate his support.[101] Both the *Contemporary Review*, whose editor the dean of Canterbury was a consistent supporter of women's suffrage, and *Macmillan's Magazine*, edited by Alexander Macmillan, a friend of the Fawcetts, were normally sympathetic also.[102]

There were other routes toward the cause of women's suffrage. Although their numbers were small, Christian Socialists had a disproportionate influence, as well as an involvement in other radical groupings; they had played a leading part in the movement for women's education and also joined the Union and Emancipation Society and the fight against the University Test Acts. As has been seen, Emily Davies contrasted, very directly, the inspiration of F. D. Maurice with that of Mill. Maurice's influence was felt not only by Davies and her brother, but also by Millicent Fawcett and many others.[103] Charles Kingsley, Thomas Hughes, and Llewellyn Davies were all signatories to the petition presented for women's enfranchisement in 1867, and all attended women's suffrage meetings in the late 1860s and early 1870s. Kingsley and Maurice both published in support of the cause.[104]

Christian Socialists supported women's suffrage for the same reasons that they were committed to the education of middle-class and working women and encouraged women's "sanitary mission." They shared a conception of the different and complementary natures of women and men, and of the "purity and earnestness" and moral powers, which women might bring to the political process.[105] Maurice had been a defender of improving women's education since the 1820s, and in his *Lectures to Ladies* on the founding of Queen's College wrote:

The more pains we take to call forth and employ the faculties which belong characteristically to each sex, the less it will be intruding upon the province which, not the conventions of the world, but the will of God has assigned to the other.[106]

Maurice's philosophy of marriage and family stressed the complementarity of women and men in the divine order, as individuals to be brought to share God's work. Yet while defending their "domestic duties," he also believed them to be "crippled" in performing those duties if denied the rights of citizenship. Women's suffrage had to be seen "as a positive strength to the moral life of England."[107]

Charles Kingsley had written, also for his audiences at Queen's College, of the distinctive vocation of women and of "the chivalrous belief of our old forefathers among their Saxon forests, that something Divine dwelt in the counsels of woman." He had urged women though to recognize that inspiration could best be followed "not by renouncing their sex, but by fulfilling it . . . by claiming woman's divine vocation, as the priestess of purity, of beauty, and of love."[108] It was in that spirit that he appealed to the women of the Ladies National Association for the Diffusion of Sanitary Knowledge to exercise their chivalric instincts in the saving of future generations.[109] Bessie Parkes saw the *English Woman's Journal* as potentially the official voice of the Association with its hopes for a "social and sanitary crusade" in every town and parish.[110]

In 1869, when Kingsley welcomed Mill's *Subjection of Women*, he did so acknowledging that there were those—and the implication is that they included himself—who had held similar views for many years. In many respects, however, Kingsley and the Mills differed greatly. Harriet Taylor Mill had in 1851 condemned the notion of women as a kind of "sentimental priesthood" and in 1869 Mill echoed her in writing scathingly of women's "addiction to philanthropy" and a "great and continually increasing mass of unenlightened and shortsighted benevolence."[111] Kingsley suggested however that the Reform Act of 1867 had indeed created a new peril for women:

it is no wonder if refined and educated women, in an age which is disposed to see in the possession of a vote the best means of self-defence, should ask for votes, for the defence, not merely of themselves but of their lowlier sisters, from the tyranny of men who are as yet—to the shame of the State—most of them altogether uneducated.

Kingsley was here in an unlikely alliance with Mill, in defending what the essential qualities of women, here middle-class women, could bring to the political order to combat the new majority. For Kingsley, "the State commits an injustice in debarring a woman from the rights of a citizen because she chooses over and above them, to perform the good works of a saint."

Even in 1869 Kingsley had expressed his doubts of "certain female clubbists in America."[112] These doubts surfaced again by 1870 when in correspondence with Clementia Taylor and John Stuart Mill he expressed his deep unhappiness at the involvement of women in the campaign against the Contagious Diseases Acts, and his continuing commitment to "woman as the teacher, the natural and therefore divine, guide, purifier, inspirer of the man."[113] Mill's diplomatic but possibly not entirely insincere response was to agree: "Cannot we associate the cause with quiet, upright and ladylike women as well as with vulgar, questionable, and pushing ones?"[114]

The language of the "sanitary mission," which also offered one definition of the "separate spheres" of women and men in public life, was steadily to increase in importance for women campaigners. In 1866, Barbara Leigh Smith had asked why women should not take an active interest in "all the social questions—education, public health, prison discipline, the poor laws and the rest—which occupy Parliament, and by bringing women into hearty cooperation with men, we gain the benefit not only of their work, but of their intelligent sympathy."[115] Christian Socialism was of course not the only impetus to such responsibilities for "social questions." These were also indebted to middle-class women's longstanding philanthropic interests, and to another important area of Liberal activism for both men and women, the Social Science Association, founded in 1858. Lawrence Goldman indicates how the Association represented the full range of those sections of the political nation that we associate with the mid-Victorian process of Liberal coalescence.[116] It brought together hardworking liberal MPs like G. J. Shaw-Lefevre, H. G. Liddell, and Henry Bruce; professional administrators like Edwin Chadwick and William Farr; co-operators; advanced employers; and Christian socialists and academic liberals. It was not of course in any way united in support for women's suffrage. Nevertheless in representing that generation which came to political maturity in that climate of the 1850s and 1860s it was something of an alternative parliament, sometimes satirized as a ladies' parliament. As Goldman demonstrates, a focus on the Social Science Association offers a rather different insight into the structure of mid-Victorian liberalism than does an entirely Gladstonian perspective; and perhaps the Association also demonstrates how measures for women's suffrage could divide that liberalism yet also win significant if temporary support.

For the women who became increasingly active in the Social Science Association, it was a welcome meeting place, within which they might themselves speak. It was also, as Eileen Yeo has suggested, a place of negotiation, where the relationship between social science and service could be defined through the interpretation of the sexual communion of labor, the complementary roles of women and men within the social sphere.[117] In the early years of the suffrage issue, each yearly meeting was an important occasion for debate and local influence. Barbara Leigh Smith's paper had inspired Lydia Becker in Manchester in 1866, and the interest of the Belfast suffragist Isabella Tod was equally first aroused at the Social Science meeting there in 1867.[118]

The secretary of the Association, George Hastings, had been one of the most active male supporters of the women's movement from the mid-1850s onward, and an adviser to the *English Woman's Journal* from the outset. John Westlake, subsequently secretary, had equally supported it from its origins, as had his wife and daughters. Some of its leading members were to prove powerful friends. In March 1867 a general petition with 3,559 signatures collected by the London committee was presented to the Commons by Henry Austin Bruce, a South Wales industrialist, landowner, and committed administrator. Two years later, when Jacob Bright introduced an amendment to the Municipal Franchise Act for England and Wales, the support of Bruce, now the "heaven-born Home Secretary" in Gladstone's ministry, whom Goldman describes as typifying the Association's mode of operation, was critical.[119] Bright stressed the conservative intention of his amendment, suggesting that the previous Act, of 1835, had been innovatory in its exclusion of women, an invasion of established right. Bruce rose to say:

... the hon. member had shown conclusively that this proposition was no novelty and that in every form of local government, except under the Municipal Corporations Act, females were allowed to vote. The clause introduced no anomaly, and he should give it his cordial support.[120]

To those who watched, surprised by Bright's success, it was a demonstration that "the tide of opinion in the House of Commons is beginning to turn."[121]

After 1869 women were granted the municipal franchise, though after 1872 it was clear that only single and widowed women could vote; they were given the right in 1870 to stand for school boards and after 1875 as Poor Law Guardians. In these settings middle-class women activists were to put into practice a view of citizenship which transcended sharp boundaries between domestic, social, and political responsibilities. Their vocabulary came to unite the powerful inheritance of political radicalism with discourses of philanthropy, Christian socialism, and social science. Yet the case for full citizenship was not to be accepted for another 60 years.

≺ III ≻

"Capable Citizens" or "A Nation of Amazons"?: Support for the Women's Suffrage Bill, May 1870

One index of the initial support which women's suffrage attracted has to be the first Women's Disabilities Bill,[122] introduced into the House of Commons in 1870, two years after Mill's defeat in his Westminster constituency at the general election of 1868. When Jacob Bright introduced its second reading on May 4, 1870, it was passed by 33 votes, with 124 in favor and 91 against. Of those in favor 93 were Liberals, including four members of the government, and 31 Conservatives; 52 Liberals and 39 Conservatives were against. Both parties were clearly split, but a preponderance of support came from the Liberal Party, as it did again when, a week later, the bill was defeated at its committee stage. Gladstone led a substantial majority of 220, 137 Liberals and 83 Conservatives, against 94 committed supporters, 60 Liberals and 34 Conservatives.

In all, 148 members supported the cause in these two divisions, sharing Lyon Playfair's view "that women are capable citizens must be admitted from our laws of property, and from their possession of the municipal franchise."[123] Only three, Fawcett, Dilke, and Herbert, can be regarded as close disciples of Mill. Twenty-six members could be considered advanced radicals, in the main also in favor of extension of the franchise, and with links to militant Dissent and, for some, the politics of temperance. Most represented major industrial cities. Among nonconformist representatives were Edward Miall, Alfred Illingworth, and Samuel Morley. Wilfred Lawson, Peter Rylands, and Jacob Bright represented the informal affiliation between the women's suffrage and temperance movements. Leeds and Manchester each gave their three votes for the bill, and Birmingham two. Twelve constituencies, including Bolton, Brighton, Bristol, Edinburgh, Oldham, and Sheffield, each cast both their two votes for the bill. Seven members sitting for Irish seats can best be described as nationalists or Home Rulers. In total 18 of these voters sat for Scottish seats and 21 for Irish seats. The close links between the politics of Dissent, both Nonconformist and Free Presbyterian, in England and Scotland, and Irish Liberal campaigns for disestablishment, may perhaps be reflected here. The link between women's suffrage, campaigning Dissent, and a dominant urban liberalism was present in Scotland and in Ireland as in England. It was seen in the powerful votes of Duncan McLaren, a representative of voluntaryist Dissent in Scotland, and brother-in-law of Jacob Bright; and of Sir John Gray, the supporter of Irish disestablishment, a powerful figure in Dublin Liberalism, and leader of the National Association of the 1850s.[124]

The majority of these votes, of course, came not from such radical dissenters, but from the 71 Liberals, 8 Liberal-Conservatives, and 32 Conservatives who supported Bright. Perhaps they were persuaded by the moderation of the measure and its continuity with municipal enfranchisement, which would have enfranchised women as householders and ratepayers only. They included the gentry radical Peter Locke King, active members of the Social Science Association like the Liberal William Cowper-Temple, and the academic and minister Lyon Playfair. There were few prominent Conservatives, though the stalwart Russell Gurney voted in support, as did Hugh Birley, MP for Manchester and a leading Manchester employer. One future prime minister, Henry Campbell-Bannerman, supported Bright in both divisions. Percy Wyndham, Conservative member for West Cumberland, had voted for Mill's amendment in 1867 and later defended his vote on the grounds of his support for the widows of tenant farmers in West Cumberland; he supported Bright at the committee stage.[125]

An examination of the 19 MPs who voted in all three divisions, for Mill's amendment in 1867 and twice for Bright's bill in 1870, shows, however, a clearer picture of commitment; among them are only one Conservative and one Liberal-Conservative.[126] The Conservative William Gore-Langton was with his wife, Lady Anna, an active supporter of the cause. The Liberal-Conservative H. G. Liddell was a prominent member of the Social Science Association. Henry Fawcett was the one of Mill's disciples able to give such continuing support. Eight of these 19 may be regarded as advanced Liberals. Three—Joseph Cowen, Senior; Stansfeld; and Taylor—had links with radical unitarianism and a commitment to the women's cause which stretched back to the 1840s. Five came from a campaigning, urban Liberalism, with links to voluntaryism, across the United Kingdom: Edward Baines of Leeds, Robert Dalguish of Glasgow, John Gray of Dublin, J. T. Hibbert of Oldham, and Duncan McLaren of Edinburgh. Two, the Cork journalist John Francis Maguire and William

Stacpoole, were committed to Home Rule for Ireland. The remaining six Liberals included the Manchester MP Sir Thomas Bazley; Sir Francis Goldsmid, campaigner for Jewish rights and, with his wife, actively involved in the women's suffrage movement; and Grosvenor Hodgkinson, author of the key amendment abolishing compounding in Disraeli's Reform Bill in 1867.

Mill himself reflected that such a defeat "cannot be fairly called a check" but marked "enormous progress."[127] But the key was of course to be the attitude of Gladstone's government. Henry Bruce, earlier supporter of Bright's amendment to the municipal franchise bill, had equivocated. As home secretary, he could not indicate approval for Bright's bill of 1870, though he made it clear that "neither personally nor as a member of the Government was he giving any opinion on his merits."[128] One week later, on the motion to go into committee, the Liberal Edward Pleydell Bouverie, a consistent and predictable opponent, pointed to "serious consequences to all our social and domestic relations" if enfranchisement brought "a nation of amazons" clamoring to enter the House of Commons. Much more significantly, William Gladstone himself expressed his surprise and disappointment that the measure had got so far.[129]

≺ IV ≻

Conclusion

What has been suggested here is that in the years immediately preceding Mill's amendment to the Reform Act of 1867, extra-parliamentary networks which were ready to respond existed even before Barbara Bodichon and Emily Davies approached Helen Taylor and John Stuart Mill. Jacob Bright made the case for the enfranchisement of women in May 1870:

Women are political, and they cannot fail to be so in the circumstances in which they are placed. They are born in a free country, where public meetings are held on every variety of subjects, those meetings being open to everybody; they are born in a country where we have a daily Press which is the ablest, the most interesting, and the cheapest which the world has ever known. We were told some time ago by the right hon. Gentleman the First Minister of the Crown, that eviction notices fell like snowflakes in some parts of Ireland. The daily papers fall like snowflakes in all our houses; and if we are not to make our women political, we must shut the doors against the Press. To tell me that women should not be political is to tell me that they should have no care for the future of their children, no interest in the greatness and progress of their country.[130]

His rhetoric suggested a concept of the "political" which integrated the public and the domestic, the interests of the mother and the nation, in a progressive country in which the values of a free press permeated the household as they did the public meeting, a country here differentiated from the condition of Ireland. Women's suffrage is in his speech located within the social and political context of a radical-liberal politics.

The relatively favorable reception given to women's suffrage in its first parliamentary hearings can in part be explained by its wider location in a period of expansion and development for both radical and liberal politics. Those who supported it were in the main predisposed by forms of politics in which the relationships between domestic and political themes had already been explored.

But the achievement of 1870 was not to be matched before 1897. The death of Mill in 1873 released some existing hostility. Writing from the United States in 1870 of the vote of that year as causing "a sensation here," Goldwin Smith had signalled to his friend Thorold Rogers, a supporter of the movement, his fears of reactionary consequences: "I am not sorry that they are beaten. Nine tenths of them would have voted Tory, and thus the Liberal majority in the country would have been to a great extent cancelled."[131] After Mill's death both Goldwin Smith and James Fitzjames Stephen indicated their fundamental hostility to the measure; in private, Smith wrote to James Bryce that "total emasculation in every sense would be the certain result of the changes."[132] When Smith launched his onslaught on the women's suffrage movement in *Macmillan's* in 1874, identifying Mill as the paternal inspiration of the movement, his misogyny was clear, and it divided his friends in academic circles.[133] A number, including Thorold Rogers, John Morley, and Albert Dicey, were later to shift ground to become opponents of women's suffrage.[134]

Another element lies in the divisiveness of the very goal of the movement, the granting of suffrage on equal terms, a provision which excluded, implicitly or explicitly, married women. Sandra Holton has traced the subsequent history of that radical-Liberal wing of the movement which following Jacob Bright and Elizabeth

Wolstenholme continued to proclaim the rights of married women. The weaknesses of a politics built upon the shifting and uncertain alliances of 1865–70 were rapidly exposed. The constraints and tactical concessions imposed upon women campaigners were to bring damaging splits from 1874 onward.

Above all, the changing conditions of Liberal politics did not favor women's suffrage. Declining Liberal strength in Lancashire did not aid those networks which had initially drawn such strength in 1867–70 from a Manchester Liberalism still rooted in the days of the Anti-Corn Law League. Perhaps the growing closeness between some elements in advanced radicalism and the new trade unionism, absent from the discussion above, saw some reduction of interest in the issue of women's suffrage.[135] As Martin Pugh has pointed out also, the defeat of 1874 reminded Liberals of the limits of their own support and led them to focus their attention on the weaknesses of the electoral system as it affected men. The positivist view of women as too likely to be an anti-progressive force gained ground among many Liberals, who came to share the views of Goldwin Smith; among them was William Randall Cremer, once a supporter, who by 1886 believed that "giving the suffrage to women would have a reactionary effect and prevent progress for many years to come."[136]

In 1897, a Women's Suffrage Bill again passed its second reading in the House of Commons.[137] Although in the last 30 years of the century, suffragists did achieve "the building up of suffragism among politicians of the centre," they did so throughout decades of dispiriting parliamentary defeat and the active mobilization of the case against women's suffrage.[138] There is much which still remains to be recovered of the first 30 years of the campaign for women's suffrage. That recovery has to site the movement firmly within late Victorian political, social, and familial lives, and across assumed divisions between private and public worlds, as between local and parliamentary politics. Only by doing so can we understand why, in June 1868, it seemed to Priscilla McLaren that "really this woman's question in its various aspects is, along with the Irish Church, the question of the time."[139] To one of the liberal coalitions of the late 1860s, it appeared briefly, that the time of women's suffrage had indeed come; that hope was rapidly to be disappointed.

≪ 6 ≫

Contesting the Male Polity: The Suffragettes and the Politics of Disruption in Edwardian Britain

JON LAWRENCE

IN 1908, WHEN THE suffragette campaign of political disruption was at its height, the distinguished American political scientist A. L. Lowell observed that the English displayed few signs of wishing to purge disorder from public politics. On the contrary, he suggested, "Englishmen regard an ordinary political meeting as a demonstration, rather than a place for serious discussion, and as such they think it fair game for counter demonstration. This view does not seem to be a mere survival from the roughness of the old hustings, since it shows no marked signs of dying out. Nor is the practice of breaking up meetings condemned by average public opinion, for if it were, a little determined action on the part of the police ... would quickly put an end to it."[1]

Unfortunately historians of English popular politics have generally overlooked Lowell's comments and have mistakenly argued that the late nineteenth century witnessed the "taming" of popular involvement in the political process.[2] We are told that electoral disturbances declined sharply after 1880 as society became less tolerant of public displays of license and disorder,[3] and that in any case disturbances carried little political significance since they simply reflected either a spontaneous "love of disorder,"[4] or the malign influence of the free drink and cash distributed by party agents.[5] As I argue elsewhere, by underestimating the widespread tolerance of robust forms of "street politics" and electioneering, historians have obscured many of the ambiguities at the heart of the relationship between leaders and led in the late nineteenth- and early twentieth-century British polity.[6] Crucially, they have also misrepresented the context in which from 1905 the activists of the Women's Social and

Political Union (WSPU) sought to carry their "Votes for Women" campaign into the enemy camp by disrupting meetings addressed by Liberal cabinet ministers.[7] Politicians might claim, in the excitement of a chaotic meeting, that suffragette disruption was overthrowing the cherished traditions of British political life, but we should be wary of taking them at their word. In fact from the outset, the WSPU campaign of disruption was shaped by a creative interaction with established political customs. This is not to argue, however, either that the WSPU simply *imitated* essentially male customs, or that its efforts at "appropriation" were necessarily successful.

≺ I ≻

Street Politics in a Male Polity

Before examining the suffragette campaign in detail, however, it will be useful to say a little more about the male politics of disruption so familiar to Lowell and his Edwardian contemporaries. Given the determination to expunge violence from other aspects of public life, it is clearly surprising that political violence was still so widely tolerated.[8] As Lowell observed, the explanation appears to lie with contemporary perceptions of the political meeting as a distinct type of public space in which normal codes of behavior need not necessarily apply. Because it was still generally accepted that political legitimacy rested, at least in part, in the acclaim of the open public meeting, parties frequently competed with each other to occupy symbolic public space at times of political excitement such as elections or foreign crises. In many constituencies pitched battles would be fought over the right to hold meetings in front of the town hall or in the main square, while indoor meetings would frequently be stormed and the platform overturned.[9] "Ticketing" might be used to prevent disruption (since then the audience could be confined to known sympathizers), but this strategy frequently exposed a party to the charge that it was too unpopular to hold a genuine open meeting.[10] The alternative was to rely on a plentiful supply of burly stewards, and on the fighting instincts of one's supporters, to ensure that opponents felt obliged to absent themselves from the meeting.

Thus, force was central to the dynamics of the English political meeting during the era of (partial) male democracy between 1867 and 1914—so too were notions of "manliness" and male "honor."[11] Politicians were frequently celebrated for their bravery (or "pluck") in the face of hostile crowds. "True" manliness, it was argued, lay not in the seething crowd (which was generally portrayed as "unmanly" and even child-like), but in the moral and physical strength of the lone male politician. "Manliness" here meant forbearance and self-control, but it also meant control of one's body and physical "presence." Stories abound of "mobs" quelled by fearless male (usually upper class) "heroes," and, when force of character was not sufficient, of vulgar "roughs" taught a lesson by a well-deserved "thrashing."[12] In practice, of course, street politics did not always work out so agreeably for would-be manly heroes—despite the great class inequalities in height which meant that upper-class politicians would often quite literally have towered above the vast majority of their working-class audience.[13] At Southwark in 1900, a Tory candidate's son sustained serious injuries after using force to eject a persistent heckler because the man's friends refused to recognize the politician's notions of a "fair fight."[14] Equally, there were many male politicians who fell far short of the ideals of the "manly hero"— whether from weakness of character or of body.[15] For such men public meetings often proved tortuous affairs—especially, one suspects, in the wake of the Wilde trials of 1895, when "effeminate" manners became more suspect than ever in popular culture (in this respect the politics of male deportment remains sadly neglected).[16]

The undercurrents of violence at political meetings tended to make them powerfully male environments despite the fact that women were rarely formally excluded. Not only was the idea of "manly assertion" central to the whole notion of how one controlled a large public meeting, but, as I have suggested, the successful prosecution of a meeting often hinged on the organization, and if needs be on the use, of male physical force. This was underlined by the fact that women were often confined to specific, supposedly safer, sections of the hall, such as the platform itself, the gallery, and the front rows nearest the press. The main body of the meeting, on the other hand, frequently became a bear-pit of partisan masculinity.[17] Moreover, women rarely spoke at set-piece political meetings—even from the platform—unless they were speaking on behalf of an absent or incapacitated male relative.

Thus, while public political space was not formally segregated along gender lines, men and women did not possess that space equally. The presence of women at a meeting was often encouraged as a symbol of respectability—politicians arguing that "ladies" need have no fears of being outraged at *their* meetings. Indeed, it was not unknown for the presence of women to be used as an excuse for ticketing—so that women became the pretext for excluding one's opponents, and thus for absenting oneself from the politics of force.[18] Women were not, therefore, mere "ornaments" with which to decorate the platform, but nor were they full and equal participants in the meeting. Women's presence complicated the gender demarcation of late Victorian and Edwardian public politics, but it did not represent a gender revolution. On the contrary, men alone remained recognized as the full and active citizens for whom set-piece political meetings were staged. Whether from platform or floor, men alone were expected to have a decisive impact on shaping the conduct and outcome of the meeting. This partial inclusion of women was a contradiction, like many others in the male polity, which the suffragette campaign was mercilessly to expose and to exploit in the years after 1905.

As the preceding remarks should suggest, women's involvement in party politics (including what one might term "street politics") did not begin with the suffragettes' campaign of militancy in the mid 1900s. Quite the reverse—there was a long tradition of women's involvement in both "high" and "low" forms of political activity. As Judith Lewis reminds us, aristocratic women had frequently played a prominent part in canvassing and other forms of party propaganda. Often, it is true, they did so explicitly as the wives or daughters of powerful male politicians, but even then, ties of partisanship were frequently as important as ties of kinship.[19] At the same time plebeian women could also claim a long and honorable tradition of involvement in public politics. In the eighteenth century it was common for women to be active participants in food riots and other crowd phenomena; and in the early nineteenth century they played a similarly prominent role in radical protest.[20]

Perhaps understandably, the iconography of the Peterloo massacre moves women's contribution to the struggle for reform to the foreground, but this was more than just emotive propaganda.[21] Women were active in most facets of early nineteenth-century popular politics, from the campaign for universal suffrage and the Queen

Caroline affair, through early utopian socialisms, to the militant working-class opposition to the New Poor Law of 1834.[22] According to Anna Clark, the potential existed to build a vibrant, mixed-sex plebeian political culture in the early nineteenth century, but this was lost because from the 1830s male Radical leaders turned increasingly to the ideology of domestic respectability (and *pater familias*) as a defense against the harsh strictures of political economy, and against the charge that working-class men were unfit for the vote.[23] Radicalism, she argues, had compromised the legacy of Painite democracy and divided its potential constituency. Worse, from the 1840s the state began to demonstrate its willingness to make concessions to the ideal of plebeian "domesticity" without showing any inclination to bring working men within the polity. The logical conclusion of this process, it is suggested, was the limited male householder franchise eventually established in 1867—a franchise which excluded most single men, and all women, from the rights of citizenship.[24]

As an account of the brief flowering of "male democracy" in Britain, there is much to commend the Clark thesis, but we should not exaggerate the extent to which the public sphere became closed to female participation. Nor should we forget that by the later nineteenth century women's groups were developing rhetorical strategies which reclaimed "domesticity" as a source both of social status *and* of the claim to full political rights. In terms of "public space," women continued to assert a presence in many of the more theatrical forms of street politics—especially at the hustings (until their abolition in 1872), and in other, less structured, election rituals. On polling day, it was customary in many districts for women to demonstrate their partisanship by wearing party colors. Middle-class women usually confined themselves to displaying a prominent rosette or ribbon, but in the poorer districts of many towns journalists delighted in discovering women prepared to dress from head to foot in their party's color—though it was *usually* only the men who were prepared to paint their hands and face to match.[25] Women sometimes played a wholly independent role in election rituals, as at Wakefield in 1868, when a group of local mill-girls carried out a mock "chairing" involving a fellow (female) worker dressed in the colors of the Liberal candidate.[26] Similarly, women also featured prominently in the politics of the street-corner—often forming a sizeable proportion of the crowd drawn by the soap-box politician (who, incidentally, frequently chose to speak from the back of a lorry to give a degree of elevation and enhanced personal safety). Indeed when politicians took to the streets they frequently complained that they drew audiences dominated by women and children. They also complained that women could be merciless in their persecution of an unpopular or unwelcome speaker.[27]

Despite the long tradition of women's involvement in all forms of public politics, there seems little doubt that from the early 1880s this involvement became increasingly formalized. A crucial factor here was undoubtedly the growing demand for volunteer workers within party politics. With the electorate greatly increased by the reforms of 1867 and 1884, and with open voting abolished by the Secret Ballot Act of 1872, it was proving harder for party organizers to manage the electorate. Their problems were simply compounded when, in 1883, the Corrupt Practices Act made it imperative that the bulk of routine party work—such as canvassing, registration, and leafleting—should be undertaken by unpaid volunteers. This alone would have placed a premium on encouraging women's systematic involvement in party politics, but in addition there was also a growing sense that women propagandists could add a novel and alluring dimension to street corner (and village green) politics.

There are, therefore, strong grounds for arguing that women became more visible as public political figures in the late nineteenth century.[28] Fiery campaigners such as Lady Randolph Churchill became popular personalities in their own right,[29] while many women with less celebrated connections threw themselves into the demanding propaganda work of organizations such as the Tories' mixed-sex Primrose League, the single-sex Women's Liberal Federation and Women's Co-operative Guild, or the new, and supposedly egalitarian, socialist parties.[30] All of these organizations not only recognized women as full members, and hence, in an important sense, as citizens;[31] they also made extensive use of them as itinerant propagandists—relying on the female speaker to draw good, male-dominated crowds even in the most unpromising communities. Conservatives, in particular, felt considerable anxiety at the "unseemliness" of such developments, but for the most part their reservations were subordinated to the dictates of electoral competition.[32] It is perhaps surprising, therefore, that these developments appear to have had little impact on the gender dynamics of the set-piece public meeting. But then, as the suffragettes never tired of pointing out, women's involvement in party politics had also done little to change the gendered nature of the wider polity.[33]

From the outset, the rationale of the WSPU was to break women's dependence on party by organizing on strictly independent lines—as labor had begun to do a decade earlier.[34] As militant tactics developed in later years these too were stamped with strongly antiparty undertones—at least until the final phase of the campaign. For instance in 1908 one suffragette justified breaking her pledge not to disrupt a Liberal meeting by arguing that, after all, "[t]hey were dealing not with men but with politicians."[35] There seems little doubt that the suffragettes, like most campaigners for women's suffrage, always assumed that the transformation of politics must go hand-in-hand with the transformation of women's political status—but their understanding of *how* the polity should be changed was not immutable. As the campaign of militancy evolved, so the suffragettes' understanding both of the existing political system and of the impact of their own actions evolved with it. By focusing in detail on one aspect of the militant campaign, the disruption of political meetings, I hope to be able to draw wider conclusions about, firstly, the nature of the suffragette challenge to the Edwardian male polity, and, secondly, the forces sustaining the continued male dominance of public political space.

≺ II ≻

The Campaign of Disruption

Our understanding of suffragette militancy has become increasingly sophisticated in recent years. Long obsessed with the celebration or vilification of militancy as a political tactic, historians are now much more concerned to stress the diverse forms which militancy could take, the fluidity of membership between supposedly "militant" and "constitutional" organizations, and the militant movement's strong roots in the traditions of nineteenth-century popular Radicalism.[36] At the same time, there is a new desire to understand the forces that prompted and sustained militancy, the ethos that underpinned it, and the mythologies that it subsequently generated.[37] With the context of militancy thus redefined, it becomes possible to analyze militant *acts* in ways that are much more alive to their complex cultural meanings.[38] It is very much in this spirit that this chapter seeks to reinterpret the WSPU's appropriation and reworking of the politics of disruption between the mid 1900s and 1914.

As is well known, the tactic of intervening at cabinet ministers' meetings began in October 1905 when Christabel Pankhurst and Annie Kenney attended Sir Edward Grey's meeting at the Manchester Free Trade Hall.[39] From the outset, the tactic was for women to stand, either at the end of the meeting or during the minister's speech, and demand to know whether the government would introduce immediate legislation to enfranchise women on the same terms as men. The story of the Manchester meeting, and the subsequent arrest of Kenney and Pankhurst, is well known, but it is nonetheless worth stressing that this was not a full-blown attempt at political disruption (however much Christabel Pankhurst may have been determined that the night would end in her arrest).[40] On the contrary, the two women appear to have obeyed the normal rules of political meetings—waiting until the chairman asked for questions before pressing Grey on "votes for women." They did not heckle or interrupt, their rebellion lay elsewhere—in their determination to force a "women's issue" into the arena of (male) party politics, in their refusal to relent when Grey declined to answer, in their decision to unfurl a "Votes for Women" banner to underscore their message, and, of course, in being women "who dared to intrude ... into a man's meeting."[41] Intrude, that is, not by their presence, which as we have seen was unremarkable, but by their insistence on being treated as full participants in the theater of public politics.

According to Teresa Billington-Greig, the WSPU changed tactics during the 1906 general election. At first members continued to wait until question time to demand "votes for women," but this quickly gave way to an "interruption policy" which favored heckling and other organized forms of disturbance during the main part of the meeting.[42] Billington-Greig offers little explanation of this escalation, but the Pankhursts always insisted that it was the inevitable consequence of ministers' refusal to answer women when they "played by the rules" and waited until the close of a meeting.[43] Frederick Pethick-Lawrence offered a similar explanation when looking back on the evolution of the WSPU's heckling policy—though he laid greater emphasis on the worse violence done to women when they waited until the close of a meeting.[44]

It is not easy to offer a concise summary of WSPU disruption tactics; they were too varied. Questioning, heckling, and outright disruption were all pursued from time to time as the circumstances allowed. Moreover, although in 1914 Emmeline Pankhurst claimed that the WSPU had never sought to *break up* political meetings, in practice this was often the avowed purpose of suffragette interventions.[45] Thus, Mary Gawthorpe's determined and successful harassment of Samuel Evans at mid-Glamorgan in October 1906 was widely celebrated in suffrage circles because Evans had recently talked out a women's suffrage bill.[46] Similarly, defending the WSPU's tactics of political disruption in 1907, Christabel Pankhurst bluntly argued that "[i]f Mr Asquith would not let her vote, she was not prepared to let him talk."[47] Even the popular suffragette tactic of serial interruption—with each woman waiting her turn to shout a question—could be seen as an attempt to halt a meeting by provoking pandemonium among its volatile audience. This was certainly how Helena Swanwick interpreted the tactic, and it was undoubtedly its practical consequence at many meetings.[48] On the other hand, it is clear that stopping a meeting was rarely the *principal* objective of suffragette disrupters (except in unusual circumstances such as the mid-Glamorgan campaign); much more important was that the disruption should pose an attention-grabbing and unambiguous challenge to male political authority. Jane Marcus has described disruption as a tactic intended "to split asunder patriarchal cultural hegemony by interrupting men's discourse with each other."[49] The argument is a good one, although, as will be seen, the intention was not always realized in practice. The communication of the WSPU's powerful message often suffered from the dissonance introduced by engagement with the messy world of popular or "street" politics.

This is not to deny that the suffragette strategy of organized disruption posed a fundamental challenge, both to male authority and to the existing gender dynamics of public politics.[50] But it is to suggest that there were tensions at the heart of WSPU tactics which meant that the precise nature of that challenge was not always so clear. For one thing, disruption tended to be viewed simultaneously both as the appropriation of male rights and customs by women, *and* as a strategy designed to expose the brutality and misogyny at the heart of the existing male polity.[51] Often, it is true, this tension was overcome by stressing that women's struggle for their rights relied on purely symbolic forms of disruption and violence—whereas men had used brutality to win the vote (just as they now used it to deny the vote to women).[52] It is not difficult, however, to find examples of suffragettes arguing that women must deploy the *same* methods of struggle as men in order to share men's political rights—if only because men would understand no other language. Even the Pankhursts frequently argued that women were justified in *mimicking* male tactics such as heckling, disruption, and violence against property. Moreover, in so doing they displayed great familiarity both with popular histories of the great nineteenth-century reform struggles, and with the customs surrounding disruption at public meetings.[53] For instance, at their own meetings there are many examples of WSPU speakers refusing to give way in the face of tumultuous opposition until they had spoken (unheard) for an hour. Their reason was simple: in many districts custom dictated that a meeting had not been "broken up" if it lasted more than an hour.[54] Similarly, WSPU activists knew the political significance of unfurling hostile "colors" at a party meeting—successfully raising the party flag at an opponent's meeting represented one of the great symbolic triumphs of traditional party warfare.[55] Hence the suffragettes' determined efforts to smuggle "Votes for Women" banners into Liberal meetings in order to display them from prominent positions such as the balcony or a private box. Hence, also, the fact that crowds often reacted more violently toward the woman banner-holder than toward the woman interrupter.[56]

It should be noted, however, that in one important respect the suffragette campaign of disruption differed markedly from the customs of (male) party politics. In normal party "warfare," the politics of disruption were essentially a local matter—that is to say they represented a contest over "legitimacy" played out on a local scale, where both sides sought to defend their own meetings and overturn those of their opponents. For the suffragettes the politics of disruption had a very different purpose—their goal was not local "legitimacy," but national publicity, and in consequence they targeted a type of meeting ordinarily left unmolested in party conflict—the set-piece, ticketed meetings addressed by high-profile party leaders.[57]

It was these meetings that tended to attract representatives of the national press, and therefore it was these meetings that the suffragettes had to disrupt if they wanted to secure good "copy" (positive or otherwise) in the morning press.[58] Billington-Greig's famous argument that women should have continued to question rather than interrupt ministers appears to recognize the distinctiveness of these set-piece meetings since it is couched in the langauge of "custom." She, at least, seems to have recognized that these meetings were *not* like the type of open-door election meeting where heckling was expected.[59] One consequence of the suffragettes' approach was that they placed themselves doubly at odds with political custom—not only were they disrupting the "wrong" meetings, but they were doing so for the "wrong" reasons—namely to win national publicity, not demonstrate local popularity (in *both* respects the protesters' sex appeared to have little bearing on their "crime"). It became all too easy to turn one of the oldest tropes of party politics against the suffragettes—to allege that they were "hooligan" outsiders who knew nothing of local custom and tradition. The fact that very often, either from necessity or from choice, all the protesting women *were* outsiders clearly did not help here.[60] From the propagandist's perspective, however, the fundamental problem was that opponents could discredit the women's cause without focusing on their sex— their sin was not to "intrude . . . into a man's meeting," but to intrude into a locals' meeting.[61] An extreme example of this was the tendency of Liberal organizers in north Wales to allow admittance only to women who spoke Welsh, thereby underlining the "outsider" status of the would-be protester.[62] It was not impossible for itinerant suffrage campaigners to overcome this disadvantage, but to do so they had to work very hard to build alliances with sections of the local community—as Gawthorpe apparently did with the Glamorgan miners in 1906.[63]

≺ III ≻

The Politics of Violence

Interestingly, in the first phase of the campaign Teresa Billington-Greig argued more vociferously than most that women's political powerlessness made "violence imperative." She also argued that women should learn lessons from the fact that men had secured political liberty only through conflict.[64] Later, wholly detached from the movement, she attacked such positions with equal vociferousness—rejecting the idea that women should treat "the men who use violence as a precedent," and arguing that "violence is the weapon of the mob."[65] Disillusioned by the weakness of the break-away Women's Freedom League (WFL) she had helped to found in 1907, and by the "superficial" militancy of the WSPU, Billington-Greig went further. She argued that from the outset, militancy had been "conceived in the same spirit that is found manifesting itself in ordinary party warfare; it was planned to hit the enemy and to make a good political beginning for the movement; it was on the level of the ordinary, double-dealing party move."[66] Here was the most stinging indictment of those who sought to appropriate the traditional weapons of male party politics to female ends. The irony was, however, that by the time Billington-Greig was writing (1911) few suffragettes harbored any illusions about the suitability of using men's weapons for winning women's battles. By then, the argument had shifted decisively toward the view that incursions into male political territory could have only one purpose: to expose the rotten core of the existing (male) polity.

There can be no doubt that the women who disrupted meetings were frequently subjected to considerable violence both by party stewards and by members of the audience. As Elizabeth Robins and others made clear early in the campaign, this violence was often overtly sexual.[67] Lloyd George's address to the Women's Liberal Federation at the Albert Hall in December 1908 provided perhaps the most notorious case of such abuse. Though its reporter originally made light of the violence used by stewards, even *The Times* subsequently published frank allegations of assaults on the women protesters. In one letter, a man who had been at the meeting (and who claimed not to support women's suffrage) insisted that stewards had used "extreme violence" against the women, and that when two Liberal women sitting near him cried "Shame!" at the shocking scenes they were "immediately attacked by a man in the row behind them, who urged more violence and said that the brutes deserved all they got."[68]

Understandably, there was great admiration for women who were prepared to face angry political crowds in this way. Like male politicians, suffragette speakers were often celebrated for their fearlessness—or "pluck"—and there are many accounts of hostile crowds quelled by the sheer determination and strength of character of a suffragette speaker.[69] Moreover, it seems clear that these qualities were often as admired by non-aligned men as they were by the propagandists of the WSPU. The Pankhursts proved a great attraction at many by-elections, and their meetings were usually packed by crowds so keen to see the infamous leaders in action that they were intolerant of any disorder which might spoil the show.[70] Emmeline Pethick-Lawrence recalls how at the Peckham by-election of March 1908, Christabel Pankhurst, "a girl standing on an improvized platform, the centre of a crowd of men," was able to win the crowd with her wit and perseverance. So much so that a persistent heckler was apparently driven off amidst cries of "We've come to 'ear 'er—not you, see!"[71]

In essence the suffragettes became part of the "sport" of politics for many men—at its worst this meant that the women's own meetings became "legitimate" targets for disruption, but it also meant that sometimes men took up their cause simply for the pleasure to be had from seeing a prominent politician worsted.[72] A famous example of this was Miss Molony's one-woman crusade against Churchill at the Dundee by-election in 1908, when she found enough sympathizers among the working men at open-air meetings to prevent Liberal party stewards from silencing her. Even Churchill was forced to concede that "we all admire her pluck," while *The Times* made much of her self-control—that quality most admired in the "manly" politician—describing her as "[not] the least excited. She was perfectly cool, collected, and in the best of good humour."[73] Churchill was convinced that Molony had won the crowd by exploiting the fact that she was "a young and pretty woman."[74] This may be so; many commentators, both hostile and supportive, made similar observations about Christabel Pankhurst's ability to control a crowd. One should not, however, overlook the fact that both women were also skillful exponents of the theatricality of street politics.[75] At Dundee, Molony's coup had been to turn up at Churchill's meetings brandishing a large railway-porter's bell, which she threatened to ring continuously until he issued an apology for allegedly insulting the WFL about its role in the recent Peckham by-election. The bell proved a great "stunt," quickly becoming as popular with the crowd as Molony herself—good looks alone, one suspects, would have been much less effective.[76]

The apparent ability of Molony and the Pankhursts to command a crowd raises many interesting questions. The suffragettes may not have pioneered the female platform, which possessed a much longer pedigree; but they did throw themselves into the rough and tumble of street politics with unusual abandon.[77] In Victorian literature women such as Margaret Hale in *North and South* had faced the angry "mob" confident that their sex and their moral certainty would quell the urge to violence (though in fact it was only horror that her sex and her purity had *not* protected Margaret from the violence of "savage lads" that ultimately pacified the rioters).[78]

For self-proclaimed female rebels such as the suffragettes it was even harder to mobilize the ideals of chivalry and morality as a defense against male violence. As Sandra Holton and Martha Vicinus have both noted, one response to this problem was for suffragette protesters to make a habit of dressing in fine and ostentatiously "feminine" attire.[79] There were a number of reasons for this. The social taboos surrounding middle-class womanhood remained powerful, and fine clothes gave suffragettes some hope that, just as lady "visitors" might boldly venture into the deprived urban slums, so they might enter the maelstrom of street politics and emerge unscathed.[80] Another factor was that by emphasizing their "femininity" through dress, suffragette women were able to challenge the expectations of critics who suggested that only "unsexed freaks" would be interested in the vote (the emphasis on Mrs. Pankhurst's maternal qualities and that on Christabel Pankhurst's beauty and poise were variants on this strategy).[81] Here "femininity" was generally presented as a universal, rather than a class ideal—an important refinement of the symbolism of dress since many suffrage militants, such as Teresa Billington-Greig, Mary Gawthorpe, Annie Kenney, Mary Leigh, or Hannah Mitchell, came from humble backgrounds.[82] These women could never pass themselves off as Edwardian "ladies," but they could project an appeal to the supposed male ideals of chivalry and honorable conduct.[83]

Both the WSPU and the WFL were acutely conscious of the problems class brought to the women's movement. In particular, they knew that if women traded on the power and privilege of class, they risked more than just alienating members from poorer backgrounds.

They also risked confirming the allegations of those Liberal and Labour politicians who claimed that the movement's real goal was "votes for ladies," rather than votes for *all* women. In this respect, the famous case of the imprisonment and brutal force-feeding of Lady Constance Lytton proved to be a propaganda coup for the suffragette movement. Having previously been released from prison rather than force fed on the grounds of ill-health, Lady Lytton determined to expose the class prejudice and barbarism of the prison system by disguising herself as a working woman, Jane Warton, when she was next arrested for suffragette activity. The story of "Jane's" barbaric treatment in prison became a *cause célèbre* which turned the tables on the suffragettes' supposedly radical and class-conscious critics. Not only did it expose the class-based and inhumane character of the "judicial" system over which the Liberals presided, it also presented a suffragette woman renouncing the privilege of birth—at appalling personal cost—in order to demonstrate the universal nature of the struggle for women's rights.[84]

As the story of Constance Lytton illustrates, the suffragette cause needed noble, self-sacrificing female martyrs at least as much as it needed those "womanly" heroes, such as the Pankhursts and Molony, who were able to tame the "mob" by force of character and presence. Indeed, suffragette propaganda was dominated by women who lived out Emmeline Pankhurst's dictum "to use no violence, but rather to offer ourselves to the violence of others."[85] Thus Sylvia Pankhurst recalls seeing Annie Kenney disrupting an Asquith meeting at Sheffield in 1906 and thinking to herself, "[s]he is no longer asking a question; she is only giving the signal which will bring this violence upon her!"[86] The violence done to women at such meetings undoubtedly had great political significance. At a time when many anti-suffragists were arguing that men's superior physical strength justified their monopoly of the parliamentary franchise, and that politics depended (in the last instance) on the ability of the majority to coerce the minority, it allowed suffragists to reveal such doctrines shorn of their intellectual veneer.[87]

Much time was spent within the suffrage movement exposing the logical fallacies at the heart of attempts to equate the franchise with physical force. The whole course of civilization and "progress," it was argued, had been characterized by the gradual triumph of brain power over brute force, and political life could not be exempted. One suffragist even quipped that if the "antis" were right then the navvy and the coal hewer, rather than wealthy landowners, would hold plural votes.[88] The brutality against women at political meetings opened up a different line of argument, since it suggested that men fell so far short of their own standards of "manliness" and chivalry that they could no longer be trusted with political power. Thus, having denounced the "disgraceful and savage way" in which women were treated at a Shoreditch Liberal meeting, one WFL activist concluded that such incidents demonstrated the danger of "leaving political power exclusively in the hands of a sex the majority of whose members are manifestly unfit for it."[89]

By adopting the politics of disruption, women knowingly exposed themselves to the full violence and brutality of the male polity—but they also exposed that violence and brutality in a starker light than ever before. They took solace from the belief that the violence done to women demonstrated the desperate need for the polity to be "feminized" as soon as possible. At the same time, by celebrating suffragette triumphs in the face of hostile crowds, and by focusing on the "chivalrous" and "manly" minority at meetings who demanded "fair play" for women, they held out the prospect of a different politics—a reformed (or "feminized") politics that their own campaign could help to bring about. The claim was a bold one, but it too was not without contradictions. For one thing, the suffragettes' emphasis on "feminizing" politics was by no means new. On the contrary, since at least the 1860s campaigners for the female suffrage had argued that extending the vote to women would help to temper the excesses of "male democracy."[90] The suffragettes inherited this rhetorical tradition, but their political tactics were not always easily reconciled with the tradition's essentialist logic about the calming influence of woman. True, suffrage militants sought to appeal to conventional notions of "femininity" and womanly "control," but they also sought to mimic unruly male behavior partly to win attention to their cause, and partly to highlight the full extent of female subjugation under the existing system. Embracing the politics of disruption was just one example of this approach, but it was one that nicely captured many of the ambiguities of suffragette tactics.

IV

The Problem with Men

As the preceding discussion of feminine dress codes has suggested, there was a strand within the militant movement which always hoped that the spectacle of women's suffering would ignite the "chivalrous" instincts of the great majority of men and thus make them see the justice of the women's claim.[91] In 1906 Teresa Billington-Greig argued that by stimulating "bigotry" and "abuse" on the part of the minority of men who were "bitterly and violently conscious" of their sex interests, militancy would shake the majority of decent men out of their complacency toward women's rights.[92] It was a theme frequently reworked both in suffragette journalism and in later memoirs.[93] Again, there were often strong class overtones, as in the letter to *The Times* from a Russian suffragist complaining that so few Englishmen seemed sufficiently to understand the demands of "manly honour" to stop "young ruffians" from disrupting women's meetings. The writer rejoiced in the actions of one man "deserving that name" who had apparently ensured that a group of "hooligans" had "had a good thrashing" for victimizing women speakers.[94]

In contrast, others, especially those with strong socialist leanings, sought to *invert* class stereotypes about "gentlemanly" behavior, reinforcing, in the process, their own radical credentials. Writing of a serious incident at Maidstone, Charlotte Despard stressed how "so-called respectable persons" in the crowd had done nothing to help when they were attacked, whereas a few men whom "the soft classes would call rough" had intervened to prevent her and her companions from suffering more serious injury.[95] Mary Richardson inverted racial stereotypes in her account of being rescued from a vicious mob by "a huge, coloured man" who then admonished the "so-called 'gentlemen'" for their disgraceful behavior.[96] Clearly the women's militant campaign destabilized more than just gender identities in Edwardian Britain—though this is perhaps less than surprising given the particularly dense intertwining of identities based on race, gender, and class at this time. It was no surprise that outraged men spoke in the name of "Britishers" or "gentlemen" when they denounced the mistreatment of women—nor that the suffragettes wished to demonstrate how far most men fell below the ideals supposedly synonymous with these identities.[97]

Besides the "chivalrous" strangers, there were also many men who played a more formal part in the women's suffrage cause.[98] In particular, it is clear that many local suffragette groups maintained strong links with male supporters in the Independent Labour Party (ILP) long after their national leaders had broken with the party in early 1907.[99] Hannah Mitchell writes of how ILP sympathizers in the northwest, recalling their own difficulties with the "hooligan element" during the 1890s, would form a bodyguard to make sure that suffragettes could hold open-air meetings uninterrupted. She also suggests that the same men would often infiltrate Liberal party meetings to prevent female disrupters from being thrown out by the stewards.[100] In the most extreme cases it is clear that male supporters were used, not simply to protect women from attack,[101] but to ensure that they were able to break up a Liberal meeting without the cabinet minister gaining a hearing.[102] It was problematic enough (if understandable) that women often relied on organized male strength to carry out their protests, but in the latter cases women again appeared actively to connive in the ritualized brutality of male public politics.

It is clear from the *men's* accounts of such incidents that they took great satisfaction in turning the tables on the women's would-be tormentors. The Men's League for Women's Suffrage (MLWS) offered the following account of the rout of Leeds University students who had tried to break up a women's suffrage demonstration: "[the students arrived] to find that a large proportion of the demonstrators were men, who promptly fell upon them and drove them back up side streets and put them to headlong rout. So active was the pursuit that some of the women intervened to prevent catastrophes."[103] Women militants may well have shared this sense of glee at seeing "the enemy" vanquished, but in many cases they were also conscious that such displays of male bravado complicated, perhaps even undermined, a central theme of the women's campaign—the need to transform the male polity. Christabel Pankhurst was particularly alive to such issues. She might praise the men who suffered brutal treatment for raising the "votes for women" cry at meetings closed to women, but she had no doubts that men were temperamentally inclined to violence, as women were not, and that consequently they could not be relied upon to observe the suffragette policy of non-violence (against the person).[104] Members of the WFL displayed similar unease about the implications of aggressive forms of male support. Describing how young men from the MLWS had been "savagely attacked" at a Liberal meeting in the East End, one WFL activist commented, "we hardly dare to thank them, as we have a terrible suspicion that they enjoy a fight, and we do not want to encourage the idea that votes for women can only be gained by broken heads for men."[105]

Besides threatening to perpetuate, rather than challenge, existing forms of "masculinist" public politics, men's involvement in suffrage militancy helped complicate the dynamics of gender politics in other ways. For one thing, it underlined the fact that male political privileges were being undermined "from within"—by men themselves—rather than simply attacked "from without" by disgruntled women. Moreover, the fact that men were prepared to go to such extraordinary lengths to repudiate their monopoly rights—often at great personal cost—made their apostasy all the more visible and shocking to many champions of the status quo.[106]

A further complication was that male suffragists tended, if anything, to be treated with even more brutality than their female counterparts when they tried to deploy the politics of disruption at Liberal party meetings.[107] Like extreme reactions to the display of suffragette banners, this violence against men suggests that there was more to male hostility than simply anger at the temerity of women for invading "male political space." We must not ignore the fact that men were no more tolerated than were women when they embraced the suffrage cause at political meetings. One explanation might be that, as the women's agents—which they manifestly were in most cases—they were seen either as "honorary" women, or perhaps even as "unsexed" (unmanly) men.[108] Another, more prosaic explanation, is that by engaging in the politics of disruption the suffragettes had locked themselves, their allies, and their cause into the world of partisan street politics—a world where the recourse to physical force was routine, and struggles over local "legitimacy" were of far greater import than abstract claims to chivalry and sex equality. We should, therefore, be wary of assuming that gender can explain everything when studying women's impact on public politics—such a monocausal approach would be profoundly unhelpful.

≺ V ≻
Rethinking Disruption, Reforming Male Politics

There can be little doubt that the disruption of political meetings became less important as a suffragette tactic after the first "truce" of 1910. Indeed there are some grounds for suggesting that the watershed came earlier—during the winter of 1908–1909—as activists reflected on the grim scenes played out at the Albert Hall when Lloyd George had addressed the Women's Liberal Federation. Revulsion at this violence was not the only factor of course—after all the strategy had in part been intended to provoke just such a reaction from the self-appointed guardians of male rights.[109] Christabel Pankhurst was always clear that the logic of escalation was built into the militant campaign, and not simply because there would always be a need for a new "sensation."[110] Responding to criticism of women who had thrown slates from a roof in protest at being barred from Asquith's Bingley Hall rally in 1909, she insisted that "every time they [the Government] took from them a milder weapon, they would arm themselves with a stronger one."[111] Moreover, one must recognize both that militancy took many forms besides the disruption of meetings, and that militancy was in any case never the whole movement. Within a year of Grey's Free Trade Hall meeting the suffragettes, in a dramatic break with the traditions of public politics, had extended the campaign against cabinet ministers into their private lives, and they had also organized their first mass lobby of Parliament. No less importantly, they had launched a massive propaganda campaign which blurred the distinction between militant and non-militant activity. Speaking at street meetings, selling literature, and opposing Government candidates at by-elections all took great courage for many women although, technically, these acts were neither illegal nor, by the mid-1900s, especially radical forms of female political activity.[112]

As Christabel Pankhurst's comments on the Bingley Hall meeting suggest, one reason for the declining emphasis on disruption was simply the thoroughness of Liberal counter-measures. By refusing to accept the constraints customarily placed on women at set-piece meetings, the suffragettes had highlighted the unequal way in which men and women were allowed to possess public political space. Just as importantly, their radical actions had prompted a response from party organizers which made the gender demarcations surrounding public meetings much more explicit. Thus, just as protests at the houses of Parliament led to the banning of women from the Ladies Gallery and a prohibition on demonstrations in the vicinity of Parliament, so the women's appropriation of the politics of disruption led party leaders to circumscribe women's involvement in political meetings. Many suffragette accounts insist that the mere sound of a woman's voice at an Edwardian public meeting was enough to provoke chaos in an audience: Evelyn Sharp tells of a woman mistakenly thrown out of a meeting when she asked only for a window to be opened.[113] And while the story itself may be apocryphal, there seems little reason to doubt that political meetings became environments that were more, rather than less, male-dominated during the years of suffragette disruption.

The most draconian counter-measure was, of course, simply to ban *all* women from attending a meeting. This tactic never became universal, perhaps because it seemed to signal a symbolic defeat of male power, but it was increasingly adopted at large, set-piece gatherings such as Asquith's Bingley Hall meeting.[114] Recourse to a blanket ban on women reflected, more than anything else, the ease with which the suffragettes proved capable of getting round customary ticketing arrangements (tickets could often be obtained through sympathizers, and forgery was an option).[115] Indeed, if women *were* allowed entry, ticketing often became far stricter than normal—elaborate proofs of identity were demanded, women were obliged to give individual assurances that they would not disrupt the proceedings, or, worst of all, they were only admitted if men vouched for their good conduct.[116] Inside the meeting it became common strictly to segregate men and women—partly so that the suffragettes could swiftly be identified, but mainly so that they could be separated from male supporters who might frustrate the stewards' efforts at ejection.[117] Finally, when men began to disrupt meetings on behalf of the silenced women, many Liberal organizers gave up any pretense of holding open meetings, and used ticketing not simply to bar women (and their known male sympathizers), but to restrict entry solely to the party faithful.[118] Well-versed in the elaborate codes surrounding political meetings, the suffragettes accused their opponents of being afraid to face the criticism of a genuine public meeting. The restrictive measures do not, however, seem to have been much resented outside suffragette circles (though it should be stressed that ticketing was by no means unusual for big set-piece meetings such as the ones commonly targeted by the WSPU).[119] Worse for the suffragettes was that even their "indignation meetings" were becoming difficult to mount as the police became increasingly determined to stop demonstrations outside cabinet ministers' meetings.[120] By the late 1900s, therefore, the options for effective militancy within the world of partisan "street politics" were becoming distinctly limited.

But, if Liberal counter-measures and the "logic of escalation" played their part in the declining importance of disruption as a militant tactic, so too did revulsion at the high personal cost involved for women activists. Suffragette autobiographies, in particular, tend to view the brutality shown toward women at the Albert Hall meeting in 1908, outside Parliament on "Black Friday" in 1910, and at Llanystumdwy in 1912 as turning points in the militant campaign.[121] Sylvia Pankhurst describes the first use of systematic window breaking in 1909 as "a protest against the violence done to women"—its rationale, she notes, was "let it be the windows of the Government, not the bodies of women which shall be broken."[122] Emmeline Pethick-Lawrence expresses similar sentiments, noting that the new policy—designed primarily to secure swift arrest—marked a shift away from purely symbolic forms of militancy that eschewed any form of violence.[123] Christabel Pankhurst suggests that the new policy was largely determined from below—even before "Black Friday," she recalls, "our women were beginning to revolt against the one-sided violence which they experienced." Afterward, having seen the ruthlessness with which Liberal stewards were prepared to use violence against them, women across the movement agreed that "property, rather than their persons, might henceforth pay the price of votes for women."[124] The break was not, of course, so clear cut in practice—hence the appalling assaults on women critics of Lloyd George at Llanystumdwy in 1912.[125] Indeed, the movement continued to make great capital out of the symbolism of female martyrdom, though it was increasingly the tortured bodies of force-fed suffragette prisoners that dominated its propaganda, rather than the hapless female heckler. The political symbolism of force-feeding was simply so much more powerful (and unambiguous) than anything thrown up by the politics of disruption. Here the violence against women was carried out directly by agents of the Government, rather than being the free-lance work of its zealous male supporters.[126]

In the long run, the militants' attempts to appropriate the politics of disruption did much to strengthen their determination to reform not just the franchise and the culture of Westminster, but popular politics as a whole. The franchise had long been seen as a means of changing wider social and political culture—hence the early links between suffragists and the "social purity" movement, and the widespread determination, among "militants" and "constitutionalists" alike, to end double standards in sexual morality.[127] But, as we have seen, the militants' involvement in the politics of disruption brought complications which threatened to undermine their reformist political project. During the early years of the militant campaign a powerful tension existed between, on the one hand, the wish to mimic men's volatile forms of political protest, and on the other, the wish to condemn the brutal and irrational polity created by male unruliness. Only slowly did the militants become convinced that their primary goal must be to transform, not imitate, English political traditions of disruption and violence. Christabel Pankhurst might subsequently claim that the WSPU "would never have interrupters turned out," but, as we have seen, one does not find the same absolutist rejection of normal party methods in the contemporary suffragette press.[128] Indeed, in November 1908, just before the infamous Albert Hall meeting, *Votes for Women* carried a report of a meeting in Birmingham where, besides using ticketing to keep out unruly students, the WSPU relied on stewards organized by Keir Hardie to eject those troublemakers who still managed to gain entry.[129]

One must also recognize that opposition to the politics of disruption was certainly not confined to the women's movement, and that in this respect the suffragette emphasis on the "feminization" of the polity was misleading, if understandable. Many mainstream politicians from all parties had long wished to purge popular politics of its disorderly and violent traditions. For decades, local Conservative parties had complained that the Liberal party machine (or Caucus) was used to organize intimidation and disruption at election time.[130] During the South African War of 1899–1902, when "Jingo" fervor made it almost impossible to hold meetings critical of government policy, the Liberals were equally forceful in their complaints about disorder.[131] So too were many labor leaders who argued that the workers would only begin to make good use of their votes when the old customs of party politics had been overturned in favor of a more "rational" political culture.[132]

The suffragette campaign gave these sentiments a new edge, not least because, as we have seen, the WSPU took the politics of disruption into the one arena where historically they had been least important: the great set-piece meetings of party leaders called to outline important questions of state policy. When Lord Robert Cecil introduced his Public Meetings Bill in December 1908, immediately after the Albert Hall meeting, there can be little doubt that his principal concern was to prevent the disruption of these set-piece meetings, which he considered essential to the smooth progress of constitutional politics. That said, and despite the timing of the measure, the suffragette campaign did not feature prominently in the subsequent parliamentary discussion of Cecil's bill. On the contrary, the debate developed into a contest between reformers and traditionalists over the desirability of transforming the character of public meetings *as a whole*. Lib-Lab politicians such as Fred Maddison, H. H. Vivian, and John Ward proved particularly forceful in their condemnation of Britain's disorderly political traditions, while a diverse (and rather small) band of libertarians and pugilists was still prepared to speak up for the old ways (with London labor veterans Will Thorne and Will Crooks prominent among them).[133] The bill itself, though passed easily, had little impact either on the suffragette campaign, or on conduct at public meetings (partly because it gave the police no powers of arrest).[134] It did, however, demonstrate an increasingly widespread determination to expunge force from British political life.

Despite these comments, however, there can be little doubt that in the years immediately before the First World War, the women militants were prominent advocates of the need to transform British political life.[135] When George Lansbury resigned his seat at Bow and Bromley in 1912 to fight a by-election on the women's suffrage issue, his campaign encapsulated the idea that admitting women to the polity must go hand-in-hand with a wider transformation of the political system—including the overthrow of party machines and the "taming" of street politics.[136] No less than Lansbury himself, the

WSPU saw the contest as marking the beginning of a new style in British politics. Indeed, according to Sylvia Pankhurst the most uplifting aspect of Lansbury's campaign was that "[t]here are no fierce, jostling crowds of men and youths frantically waving party colours and booing and howling down their opponents' speeches. There is no mud and stone-throwing, none of the heat and violence that are so common; yet there are more meetings, and larger meetings than at other elections."[137]

Here Pankhurst outlined a vision of democracy transformed that was shared by many across the political spectrum. It was a vision which in many ways anticipated the altered political culture of inter-war Britain, where violence had ceased to form an accepted part of mainstream party politics (which is not to say that violence itself had disappeared, only that it had been pushed to the margins of "respectable" political life).[138] It seems reasonable to argue that the pre-war women's campaign played its part in this transformation, though other factors were perhaps of even greater importance. Not the least of these was the war itself, since it raised profound fears about a "brutalized" masculinity, and about the use of violence by extremist parties of right and left.[139] Even so, it seems clear, firstly, that post-war politicians were very conscious that they faced a new and alien political constituency after the (partial) enfranchisement of women in 1918, and, secondly, that their perceptions of the political instincts of this new constituency were strongly influenced by the pre-war women's movement and its long-running critique of the traditions of the old male polity.

Women's part in curtailing the politics of disruption in Britain must not be overlooked. Nor, as this chapter has sought to demonstrate, should we overlook the ambiguities and contradictions which ran through the militant campaign to "feminize" the male polity. The tensions between imitating and undermining the customs of male party politics were resolved only slowly. Indeed, some might argue that in the case of the politics of disruption resolution could never prove wholly satisfactory. The suffragette engagement with the politics of disruption highlights an important aspect of militancy that has not always received adequate attention: namely the great difficulty of conveying unambiguous political meanings within the context of popular, or "street," politics. Politics is always beset by problems of reception, but these problems proved especially acute for the suffragettes—partly because there *was* something shocking and new about female militancy, but mainly because a dense web of exisiting cultural meanings traversed the field of popular politics. Put simply, almost any action or utterance in this field was bound to carry unintended and uncontrollable meanings with popular audiences. And so it proved when the suffragettes sought to reconstruct the politics of disruption as a weapon in the battle for female enfranchisement.

≺ 7 ≻

The Privilege of Power: Suffrage Women and the Issue of Men's Support

ANGELA V. JOHN

PRO-SUFFRAGE MEN COULD represent both a blessing and a hindrance for suffrage women. Both moderate suffragists and militant suffragettes could see that, accustomed to the privilege of power, men did not always find it easy to relinquish control or to recognize that they needed to become auxiliaries rather than instigators of policies or campaigns and react rather than dictate or seek to shape and control tactics. As Jon Lawrence[1] has demonstrated, these men fitted into a tradition of disrupting political meetings and were bolstered by decades of struggles for the extension of male voting rights. Many of them carefully drew on the past, establishing themselves as the rightful heirs of John Stuart Mill, thus reinforcing a teleological, linear view of the movement which, as Jane Rendall shows,[2] hides as much as it reveals. Such a reading of the past and present conveniently envisaged the winning of the vote as the final goal, signifying closure rather than conceiving this vote as a vital initial impetus to more fundamental and necessary changes in the very meanings and practice of gender relations.

This chapter will explore some of the ways in which women suffrage supporters handled the men's involvement in their movement. Firstly it will examine how men organized and articulated their support, considering how this could at times signal a reappropriation of control by those who were already privileged citizens. The focus will be on male supporters advocating votes for women on the same terms as men via suffrage societies. It will not, therefore, be highlighting the equally important issues of how unenfranchised men perceived suffrage; neither will it be concentrating on the views of groups such as the Peoples' Suffrage Federation and the hefty proportion of working class socialist men wary of priorities which appeared to privilege gender over class, who instead subscribed to adult suffrage.[3] It will, however, suggest something of what the ideas and activities of the male support societies might reveal about the shifting meanings of manhood and masculinity at a historical moment when the idealization of womanhood was being crucially and specifically challenged.

The latter part of the chapter will look at men and women working together for women's suffrage through the United Suffragists (US), a mixed-sex society formed just before the outbreak of war but continuing to function until February 1918, when limited women's suffrage was achieved. This society has until very recently been strangely neglected by historians, yet it played a pivotal role in the protracted negotiations leading to that vital initial, albeit partial, victory.[4] It provides a valuable means of viewing gender relations in the context of war, the pursuit of electoral power, and the ending of privilege.

Such a focus also helps to challenge the traditional representation of the chronology of women's suffrage. This, as Cheryl Law[5] has observed, tends to reduce women's suffrage to a few key years before the First World War, depicting it as "an isolated political pantomime characterized by eccentric middle class women, unrepresentative of their sex, propelling their cause with a flash onto the historical stage before disappearing into satisfied anonymity." As Jane Rendall[6] and Pat Thane[7] demonstrate, historians are now much more conscious of the earlier roots of the movement, the networks and feminist, party political, and religious alliances which helped make Edwardian suffrage and militancy possible, just as they are also beginning to recognize that 1918 marked the start of another important stage in the history of the women's movement and one which should not simply be judged by short-term results. Refocusing the parameters of the suffrage struggle may help us move away from the labels of "First Wave" and "Second Wave" feminism which not only somehow suggest that feminism is a fashion but also can camouflage the continuities, developments, and complexities of adapting needs and demands to shifting political circumstances.

≺ I ≻

*Contesting Control: Men's Societies,
Women's Reactions, 1907–14*

Men's support for women's suffrage assumed a variety of forms and did not begin in the Edwardian years. Moreover, although the female Pankhursts have dominated the historiography of early twentieth century women's suffrage, one male member of that family was publicly advocating the cause several decades earlier. Emmeline Pankhurst's husband, the barrister Dr. Richard Marsden Pankhurst, had drafted the pioneer Women's Suffrage Bill of 1870. Nineteen years later he spoke at the first meeting of the Women's Franchise League, founded by Elizabeth Wolstoneholme Elmy, Harriet McIlquham, and Alice Scatcherd to advocate single and married women's right to vote in parliamentary and other elections. As Sandra Holton has argued, this society helped develop the "intransigence and assertiveness" which was to become so familiar in later suffrage politics.[8]

Victorian men's advocacy of women's enfranchisement was also evident in another, albeit much smaller, consitutional forum. The Isle of Man effectively challenged its very name by extending the franchise to female property owners as early as 1881. Upholding the old radical principle of "No taxation without representation," Richard Sherwood successfully argued for the deletion of the word "male" from the bill being debated by the House of Keys. Consequently seven hundred women became voters, all those in his district voting for Sherwood.[9]

And when it came to men's own suffrage organizations, the pro-suffrage men predated the better known "Antis." In 1897, the year that saw the creation of Mrs. Fawcett's National Union of Women's Suffrage Societies (NUWSS), the Male Electors' League for Women's Suffrage was formed. The title is significant because it drew attention to the fact that here were privileged men, used to being given responsibility. These men came together with the express purpose, according to their membership form, of advocating the "abolition of sex distinction in the allotment and exercise of the Parliamentary franchise."[10] And in 1903, the year that the Women's Social and Political Union (WSPU) was founded, these same men presented a women's suffrage petition to the House of Commons.

The largest and most influential of the men's support groups was, however, the Men's League for Women's Suffrage (MLWS), founded in London in March 1907 by Herbert Jacobs, a middle-aged Jewish barrister and international chess player. Jacobs also became its chairman.[11] The specific aim of the MLWS was to promote women's enfranchisement on the same terms as men's. It proclaimed itself as constitutional in its approach, independent, non-party, and non-political, though during its seven-year existence there were times when, as circumstances altered in relation to suffrage bills, so it became slightly emboldened in its policies. For example, discontent with the Liberal government's prevarication over the compromise Conciliation Bill (drafted by a cross-party committee headed by the MLWS's president Lord Lytton) prompted the society to adopt a more oppositional stance. Between the autumn of 1910 and the summer of 1911 it declared itself opposed to all government parliamentary candidates except those sitting Liberal members who had already proved themselves effective on the Conciliation Committee.

The MLWS was composed of men who already possessed the vote. Indeed, they carefully justified their significance in the suffrage cause by stressing that, unlike the women, they were working for others, with no axe to grind. Yet claiming to be personally disinterested could backfire since this could be seen as divesting women's suffrage of its symbolic significance and importance for the longer-term transformation of gender relations.

The members of the MLWS drew on history and on abstract concepts such as natural justice to legitimate the claims of women's suffrage and validate their own role in what they tended to depict as a struggle essentially concerned with the evolution of democratic rights. Many were disappointed Liberals, though their ranks also encompassed Tories (as in the case of their president) and Socialists, and unlike their parliamentary counterparts, there were some who did not see themselves as party political. Although they stressed their inclusivity, there clearly were some tensions prompted by party membership. For example, a number of pro-suffrage Welshmen found themselves torn between their support for the women and their loyalty to the chancellor Lloyd George whom many women branded as a traitor, particularly after his "torpedoing" of the Conciliation Bill in 1911.[12]

Being a "somewhat grey-haired" group,[13] a significant number of

MLWS members had been crucially shaped by the tenets of Victorian liberalism and had also been active in early suffrage campaigns. Jacobs emphasized his credentials by stressing that he had been deeply influenced in his youth by the writings of John Stuart Mill. He had known Jacob Bright, who had helped introduce the first women's suffrage bill in 1870; in the following decade Jacobs had sat on the committee of the Central Suffrage Society.

To date, close on one thousand members of the MLWS have been identified. Although the MLWS was a progressive pressure group, a significant proportion of the first three hundred members enjoyed respectable posts in commerce and finance. More predictably, one tenth of these pioneer members were lawyers, perhaps reflecting Jacob's influence as a specialist in banking law. Jacobs was temporarily replaced in 1911 by Cecil Chapman, a more radical chairman but also a barrister, though highly unusual in being a pro-suffrage metropolitan stipendiary magistrate.[14] Jane Rendall has suggested that, inspired by a variety of motives, academic liberals appear to have played a significant role in the support for women's suffrage in the 1860s and early 1870s.[15]

This influence appears to have persisted, with writers and clergy as well as academics being very well represented in the MLWS. Indeed, many would have been part of the intelligentsia, priding themselves on being progressive men of the new century, attuned to the key worthy demands of the day. Not surprisingly, given their occupations, their aid was chiefly in the form of speeches and articles. They established numerous branches in England, from Bournemouth to Bridlington, and Welsh and Scottish branches in for example Pontypridd and Edinburgh. Some individual leagues emerged, such as the Manchester Men's League. They provided a model for leagues abroad. Within a few years eleven others were established, including leagues in the United States, Hungary, and France. They were affiliated to a Men's International Alliance for Woman Suffrage, which held its first conference in London in 1912 hosted by three of the key British men's societies: the MLWS, the newly-formed Men's Federation for Women's Suffrage, and the Men's Political Union for Women's Enfranchisement (MPU).

In many respects the MLWS can be seen as roughly approximating to a male version of the NUWSS. Similarly the MPU can be characterized as a fraternal version of Mrs. Pankhurst's WSPU—or rather, this is how the MPU liked to see itself. It even adopted the WSPU colors of purple, white, and green. Much smaller than the MLWS, it nevertheless also boasted a number of active branches, from Bristol to Glasgow. It was founded in 1910 by men impatient with the cautious, incrementalist approach of the MLWS, and its members tended to be younger though still in the main aspiring, if not yet fully-fledged professionals. It made its voice heard by activism. Smaller groups whose titles suggested something of their disposition included the Men's Liberal Society for the Parliamentary Enfranchisement of Women and the Men's Society for Women's Rights. The latter did range more widely than suffrage alone and sought, for example, to combat the sexual abuse of women and children.

Men were also active within the NUWSS. They were officers as well as playing prominent roles in special interest women's suffrage groups such as the Jewish League for Women's Suffrage (Jacobs was one of its vice presidents) and the London Graduates' Union. Over five hundred clergymen were members of the Church League for Women's Suffrage (CLWS), co-founded by Gertrude Hinscliff and the Rev. Claude Hinscliff. This society sought to influence the suffrage cause by educating people about the need for women to vote. Male domination of mixed societies led to some unease. Indeed some Anglican women, tired of the "male-centredness and timid policies" of the CLWS, formed the Suffragist Churchwoman's Protest Committee in 1912.[16] This advocated more direct action, such as church boycotts of hostile clergy.

In what other ways did women suffragists respond to these men who were affiliated to societies promoting female voting rights, and how helpful was these men's support? In examining how they responded we need to bear in mind the fact that the all-male women's suffrage societies amounted to men's clubs for those who saw themselves as the more progressive of their sex. Recent examinations of late-Victorian masculinity have stressed the formative role of the public school in validating masculine identity.[17] Many, perhaps the majority of the MLWS, would themselves have attended public schools and many went on to all-male university colleges before graduating into another form of total institution and male sodality via their profession, be it in barristers' chambers, as members of the clergy, or even in the armed forces. The men's societies contained more than a sprinkling of army and naval men. This was complemented in social terms by the homosocial environment of the gentleman's club, another significant constituent of middle-class masculinity. Societies such as the MLWS perpetuated such an ambience.

Of course women's suffrage also fostered commensality. The former suffragette Rachel Ferguson even drew upon the privileged male institutions to explain the sense of belonging which women encountered through membership of suffrage societies. This amounted to "Our Eton and Oxford, our regiment, our ship, our cricket match."[18] Yet women were forging their own traditions of solidarity, which, even allowing for the hierarchy imposed by the Pankhursts in the WSPU, had markedly gendered meanings, articulation, and reactions.

For many of the male supporters, women's suffrage was one more public cause to be espoused.[19] Their suffrage society could even be perceived as a refuge from both work and domesticity. And, of course, the association of individual men with women's suffrage was no guarantee of their wider commitment to gender equality. Indeed, examining the private lives of some of these men can be quite revealing. The second Earl Russell was a vice president of the MLWS and spoke at their first major demonstration, held at the Queen's Hall, London, in December 1907. One of Russell's three wives was a suffragist; he introduced divorce bills in the House of Lords; and he founded the Society for Promoting Reform in the Marriage and Divorce Laws of England. Yet his public espousal of radical reforms camouflaged an aggressive personal hostility toward women which emerged in his own marital conflicts and persisted throughout his adult life.[20]

For most women who joined suffrage societies, the experience became central to their definition of themselves, a means of recasting their lives and values. Some had been campaigning for women's rights for many years. Others had never before seen themselves as political beings. Most women would have empathized with the comments of Lady Rhondda that women's suffrage came "Like a draught of fresh air into our padded, stifled lives. It gave us release of energy, it gave us that sense of being of some use in the scheme of things, without which no human being can live at peace. It made us feel that we were part of life, not just outside watching it all."[21]

Some male supporters did articulate an awareness of the latitude they possessed by virtue of their gender and class. This latitude included for example a freedom to misbehave and an undisputed possession of public space. On June 18, 1910, a few hundred members of the MLWS joined the largest women's suffrage demonstration yet seen in London.[22] Organized by the WSPU in the wake of the successful first reading of the Conciliation Bill, it attracted many suffrage societies but was officially spurned by the NUWSS. Between ten and fifteen thousand marched in a procession two miles long from the Embankment to the Albert Hall. Sporting their black and gold badges, the MLWS members were led by Jacobs. Their new banner was held aloft by their secretary, J. Malcolm Mitchell, and its designer, the artist and playwright Laurence Housman. One of the contingent, the socialist writer Joseph Clayton, showed in his report of the event for MLWS members that he was aware of the gendered perceptions of the spectators. He noted his and his fellow members' possession of public space was viewed differently from that of the women marchers: "nobody bade us to go home to our golf clubs, or assured us that man's place was in the office or bar parlour."[23]

Dr. C. V. Drysdale, who, along with his father, was a founder member of the MLWS and was an honorary secretary for a couple of years as well as supporting the Men's Committee for Justice to Women, was also alive to the gendered control of public space. A few weeks after the MLWS was founded, he discovered that London University was discriminating against women by not permitting either its female academics or its women graduands to wear academic dress or participate in the procession at the university's ceremony in Westminster Abbey.[24] Instead the women were consigned to seats which kept them out of the limelight. Drysdale refused to participate in the ceremony, protested, and wrote to the press. He succeeded in restoring the women to an equal position with the men.

Such support could be invaluable. The propaganda and organizational work of the men's societies also helped bring together relatively disparate suffrage groups through large rallies and demonstrations. Men's support was significant because socially, professionally, and politically they could exert pressure whether through their membership in gentlemen's clubs, or in businesses or professional associations, or on councils or numerous committees. These men were either influential per se or had access to those whose opinions and votes could make a vital difference. A pamphlet by the WSPU organizer Mary Gawthorpe called "Votes For Men" emphasized the value of influential male supporters: "We want men voters who sympathise to bring pressure to bear on government through their members."[25] Some MLWS members were, became, or sought to be MPs.

Their support could involve some sacrifice. When the surgeon Sir Victor Horsley stood as Liberal candidate for the Harborough Division of Leicester, the agent pointed out in no uncertain terms that the constituency, which contained a large number of agricultural workers, was not in favor of women's suffrage.[26] Knowing that Sir Victor was one of a minority of pro-suffrage medical men, he warned him to avoid the subject in his local addresses. Yet Sir Victor's views received wider publicity in the press. He roundly condemned the Cat and Mouse Act in a speech at London's Queen's Hall in July 1913 and his statements on forcible feeding prompted the home secretary to complain to the Royal College of Surgeons. In November the executive committee of the Harborough Liberals decided that, since Sir Victor seemed to regard women's suffrage as the paramount issue in politics and, in their view, endorsed militancy, they could no longer support his candidature.

In the spring of 1912, during an increasingly volatile phase of women's suffrage militancy, Elizabeth Robins, the Ibsenite actress and writer turned suffragette (and a member of the WSPU executive), addressed a vast audience of suffragettes in London's Albert Hall. She asked them, "What other body of women can boast men friends ready to give up their personal ambition, ready to sacrifice money, peace of mind, ready to risk life and limb?"[27] She was not the only suffragette to applaud the men's share. Autobiographies and histories by, for example, Annie Kenney, Mary Richardson, and Sylvia Pankhurst, acknowledged their contribution.[28] Emmeline Pethick-Lawrence stressed that "Many men did not hesitate openly to ally themselves with us and to fight what to them was a particularly difficult battle: there were men who suffered financial loss, men who went to prison, men who drew upon themselves the vengeance of the police or who risked life and limb when they challenged the brutality of Liberal stewards."[29]

Yet the issue was complicated. Retrospective accounts of women's suffrage have to be treated with caution. At the time, despite her own husband's experience of prison, Emmeline Pethick-Lawrence had herself commented that "Men in prison only embarrass us";[30] and as Laura Mayhall[31] has noted, former suffragettes writing in the inter-war period tended to recall their formative years of suffrage militancy in distinctive ways which drew upon a language similar to that used to describe war heroes.

Moreover, Jon Lawrence[32] has shown how, by joining in the politics of disruption, supporters of women's suffrage could, in addition to exposing brutality and violence, appear to be perpetuating it. Male supporters who combated the "hooligans" who interrupted meetings were not necessarily advancing the cause or helping to keep the peace and might well have their own agenda. In his autobiography Fenner Brockway presented his position as part of a male bodyguard protecting women trying to present a petition to Parliament as a just retaliation for the humiliation he had felt aged twenty when the Pankhursts had spurned his services as a journalist.[33] H. W. Nevinson, who was well known as the champion of the underdog and especially renowned as a war correspondent, enhanced his reputation with male supporters when he floored a steward who had attempted to manhandle a woman for interrupting a speech by Lloyd George.[34] Yet although such actions seem to have been relished by the men, not least because their opponents taunted them as emasculated weaklings, the women were well aware that protection was not what really advanced the cause.

Many women suffragists were equivocal about male supporters' motives and behavior. They appreciated the importance of endorsement from key male figures in demanding political representation, especially after Asquith (a noted opponent of women's suffrage) became prime minister in 1908. They were only too well aware that they were dependent on an elite group of men in government and in Parliament. Yet, ironically, this knowledge was part of the problem. The male supporters were highly conscious of their own importance. As one Congregationalist minister put it: "They knew the women would never have the privilege of the vote unless the men commenced to agitate in their support."[35] Whether resorting to older concepts of chivalry or presenting himself as the progressive New Man of the new century, the pro-suffrage male must at times have appeared patronizing and smug to the women suffragists despite the support he offered.

Some men found it hard to resist the temptation to preach what they believed to be best for women. Not always alive to an appreciation that women needed to do things in their own way, they tended to revert to historical precedent to demonstrate what needed to be done. Thus one of the writers who sought to advise Elizabeth Robins on what women should or should not do to gain the vote assured her that window breaking was "stupid and mistaken," not comparable in any way with heroic radical protest like the Swing Riots of the early 1830s. Such men failed to listen to or appreciate the meanings of window breaking for suffragettes like Robins who believed that such symbolic acts represented the natural and correct concomitant to the violence which emanated from the authorities.[36]

An inquiry into the opinions on suffrage of men and women prominent in public life was published in 1911. It had sought assessments of the relative value of militancy and of its likelihood of imminent success, and suggestions for alternative methods. The views of 10 women and 51 men were printed. There was a notable gendered difference in the tone of the responses. Although a small number of men, like Sir Victor Horsley's colleague and friend Charles Mansell Moullin, provided considered responses, there were many more men, both supporters as well as opponents of women's suffrage, whose replies were flippant. Thus W. T. Stead suggested that the most powerful argument in its favor was "That women are believed to possess immortal souls" and his recommendation for an alternative to militant tactics was "The method of going baldheaded for the candidate who supports the cause and against the candidate who opposes it."[37] Some avowedly pro-suffrage men carefully distanced themselves from what one dubbed the "childish outrages" of militancy. As definitions of militancy had to be adapted over time, so too did the tendency to infantalize or caricature those who were, however loosely, associated with it.[38] Men also sought to reinforce the importance of women winning respect by emphasizing their femininity while reiterating the conventional representation of themselves as rational and reasonable, seeking to "secure an appeal from the logic of force to the force of logic."[39]

Escalating militancy did of course disturb many female as well as male supporters, though for men the transgressive nature of women's behavior put pressure on them to confront their own understandings of what constituted femininity. It thus began to raise uncomfortable questions about their own meanings of manliness and masculinity. It is no coincidence that the moment when men really articulated their unease about the suffragettes and when the women's patience with the male supporters began to wear thin, was precisely that point at which women assumed behavior which, although distinctive in its approach and intent, nevertheless appeared to be encroaching on what was traditionally seen as male territory. It thus destabilized concepts of acceptable female and male behavior and responses.

The major catalyst for deteriorating relations between the WSPU and male supporters appears to have been the crisis of November 1911. Prior to this crisis even Christabel Pankhurst could write "We are very proud of our men friends, who are fighting so bravely for us."[40] The Conciliation Bill of that year offered a measure of women's suffrage and passed its second reading, but in November Asquith unexpectedly announced that he would be introducing a manhood suffrage bill. This, suffrage supporters feared, would effectively scupper the chances of a Conciliation Bill. Although Asquith claimed that the new bill would be open to amendments for women's suffrage, the whole move was interpreted by many women as a retrograde step and gross insult. It not only triggered the renewal and escalation of militancy but also divided the suffrage movement internally over future tactics, fomenting suffragette suspicion of pro-suffrage men. There was real bitterness that the women's struggle had resulted in what Elizabeth Robins called "the hornets' nest"[41] of *manhood* suffrage and that now the chances for universal male suffrage looked like a certainty while women, who had been the prime agitators, were being offered at best only a possibility of enfranchisement.

The journalist H. N. Brailsford, who had worked long and hard as secretary of the Conciliation Committee and had taken over the editorship of the monthly newspaper of the MLWS, now became a scapegoat, derided for denouncing militancy and for showing faith in Lloyd George. Brailsford's friend H. W. Nevinson described the WSPU as "livid with rage and deaf to reason."[42] He correctly predicted that "a very unhappy time of disagreement and division is coming." To make matters worse, the WSPU bitterly resented the MLWS seizing the initiative by organizing a deputation to Asquith.

Many "fair weather" male supporters who had earlier muttered misgivings about militancy now became much more outspoken.

The WSPU's policy of opposing all government candidates at elections even if they supported women's suffrage had already antagonized a number of MLWS members. One of their prized younger supporters (later a member of the Conciliation Committee), the Liberal lawyer Walter Roch, had found himself a victim of this policy when he had stood for Pembrokeshire in the by-election of 1908.[43] He had been actively opposed by the WSPU but nevertheless got elected. In May 1912, influenced no doubt by Brailsford's position as editor of their paper, the MLWS decided to concentrate its electoral energy on contests where there was a prospect of returning a Labour Party MP and eliminating an "Anti."[44] This was in line with the new NUWSS policy which involved an electoral pact with the Labour Party through the Election Fighting Fund. At the beginning of the year the Labour Party conference had repudiated manhood suffrage and resolved that it would find unacceptable any measure of franchise reform that did not include women. Despite its original Independent Labour Party (ILP) credentials, the WSPU was now, in contrast, moving away from the Labour Party and by October 1912 was committed to opposing Labour at by-elections.

Sandra Holton[45] maintains that Christabel Pankhurst's increased determination to exclude men from the activities and deliberations of the WSPU should be seen as intrinsic to the specific definition sought for the suffragette and her methods. Her concept of militancy was increasingly predicated upon a female heroic and rhetoric of female rebellion which left no room for male intervention. There were two major casualties here: the MPU and the Pethick-Lawrences.

The MPU posed a different kind of threat to women's suffrage from the gentlemanly MLWS. For some members aggression was, as with the Chartists earlier, a case of adopting a language of menace intended to intimidate and ultimately prevent violence rather than actually provoke it. Yet this constantly meant walking a verbal tightrope with plenty of room for misunderstanding. Some of the MPU had graduated from the MLWS and they liked to suggest that they were different from the cautious, older society. Referring to Lloyd George's actions, Victor Duval boasted that "We in the Men's Political Union give a man one chance, but we do not give him two or three."[46] Nevinson found himself urging moderation from the chair but bravado and posturing seem to have been at the heart of many of the MPU's claims. Joseph Clayton muttered threats of getting together a party of men "to threaten to thrash McKenna"[47] (the home secretary) if forcible feeding were resumed, but it was the younger members who were more likely to take action. Nevertheless, the women's opposition to the MPU should not be exaggerated and only really developed as militancy intensified and Christabel Pankhurst sought to control it. It was also recognized that the somewhat impulsive attention-seekers (such as Hugh Franklin, newly graduated from Cambridge "pranks") were hardly representative of the bulk of respectable male supporters.

Moreover, a number of WSPU women applauded Franklin's bravery rather than condemning actions such as his attempted assault on Churchill at the end of 1910. For example, the WSPU organizer Bertha Brewster wrote "I think that all the women in the movement feel very grateful to the members of the MPU for the work they have done."[48] She even added that "it will be far easier and pleasanter now that men are taking their proper place in the struggle."

Yet in the changed atmosphere from the end of 1911 and Christabel Pankhurst's deliberate gendering of militancy, the MPU fell out of favor. Weakened by their own internal disagreements over tactics and Pankhurst's refusal to accept any help from or identification with their key figures, the society disbanded in mid-February 1914. It could, however, be argued that it was only the MPU that directly threatened the WSPU's conception of itself and its mission. The other men's societies soldiered on. A few such as the Liberal Men's Association for Women's Suffrage and the Northern Men's Federation came into being only in 1913. Indeed, the latter was led by a woman, Maud Arncliffe Sennett, who, according to Claire Eustance, from the start "determinedly placed herself at the center of decision-making processes."[49]

The WSPU, however, saw another threat closer to home. Although men could not actually be members of the Union, the power and financial influence of one man in particular had been immense. Frederick Pethick-Lawrence's position had always been anomalous and conditional, crucially shaped by three factors: his position as husband of Emmeline, his acumen as a lawyer, and his personal wealth which he had generously bestowed on the WSPU, most notably on the paper *Votes For Women*. Shortly before a fatal meeting in October 1912 at which the Pethick-Lawrences were ignominiously dismissed and the WSPU irrevocably split, Mrs. Pankhurst had written to Emmeline Pethick-Lawrence arguing that the authorities saw her wealthy husband as a potent weapon to use against the militant movement.[50] Yet behind this lay a determination to purge the Union and reshape it in a new form which was also untainted by male involvement.

In the light of the publicity sought and gained by the suffragettes it is, however, tempting to see their opposition and more specifically, Christabel Pankhurst's injunctions against male power and reappropriation of control, as dominant in the years before the war. Yet such a view needs to be set against other perspectives. The much larger body of constitutionalist women now moved much closer to the labor movement. At the local level NUWSS men and women had long worked together and NUWSS women also continued working with the MLWS, while Sylvia Pankhurst was organizing her own East London Federation working closely with men like Lansbury.[51] The Women's Freedom League (WFL) which had been formed after an earlier WSPU split in 1907, devised imaginative ways of organizing passive resistance, and men and women alike, in this and other societies, resisted paying taxes, boycotted the census, and generally tried to shame and embarrass the government into concessions.

There were other harmonious links between pro-suffrage men and women, more discernible at the local level. For example, although many ILPers were supporters of adult suffrage, the party was officially committed to equal suffrage. Research into the localities suggests greater convergence of support between men and women than the received national picture suggests. For example, in Liverpool a number of key women in the WSPU had ILP backgrounds and seem to have been part of political networks of activist women and men. Helen Jollie was a local WSPU organizer. In 1914 she invited a Mr. Fenn of the Fabian Society to speak to the WSPU on "Why I am a socialist." She was connected with the Edwardses. John Edwards spoke at a public meeting organized by the WFL on the labor movement and suffrage in 1912, opened the WSPU's new Liverpool offices the following year, and chaired or addressed numerous suffrage meetings and demonstrations held by the MLWS, NUWSS, WFL, and WSPU. He became president of the Liverpool branch of the US in 1916 and his Dutch wife (who translated John Stuart Mill into Dutch) was a member.[52]

Research into the familial dimensions of women's suffrage is suggesting how widespread were partnerships between suffrage supporters and this needs to be borne in mind when assessing relations between men and women supporters. There were even instances where suffrage activists attributed their involvement in the cause to their male partner's support. For example, Louise Mary Eates, secretary from 1906 to 1910 of the Kensington WSPU, one of the most active of the London Unions, readily acknowledged that her marriage to Dr. Eates was the decisive factor in making her a suffragette and it was apparently he who "made possible all her public activities."[53] And in the university town of Bangor in north Wales there co-existed branches of the NUWSS and MLWS with a number of members of the same families active across both organizations in the years leading up to the war.[54] The Oxford Women's Suffrage Society was led by a small group of women with active support from male relatives. The Magoliouth, Murray, and Rhys families provide examples of academic suffrage families who in some instances spanned several generations.[55] Not infrequently women had been active in local government, education, or nonconformist circles before moving into suffrage. Examining family connections and identifying networks of support for the women's movement from mid-century onward can prove useful in re-evaluating both women's and men's relationship to politics more generally, to gender politics, and to the "ownership" of the cause. Such an approach provides a corrective to seeing the subject solely through the prism of national organizations and the dichotomies and divisions they could engender.

It is also important to bear in mind the fact that what became known as the "Peth-Pank split" of October 1912 had wider repercussions on suffrage allegiances. Many erstwhile supporters of the WSPU now backed away from its increasingly autocratic stance. The Pethick-Lawrences had been popular figures and their newspaper had been extremely influential. Elizabeth Robins rapidly resigned from the executive of the WSPU and was one of many who deplored the shameful way the Pethick-Lawrences had been treated and the way that the cause was now controlled. Moreover, the fact that Christabel Pankhurst was now directing affairs from exile in Paris did not help. Nevinson's disillusionment with the WSPU resonates through his diaries at this time. He believed that by January 1913 the Pankhursts had lost their charisma and organizational ability, the "implicit confidence and faith" of many having evaporated since the split.[56] Henry Harben of the MPU, who, with his wife Agnes, was to be active in the US, also provided a critique of the pre-war WSPU.[57] In order to understand more clearly the issue of men's support and significance in the later years of the movement, we need to explore the efforts of those who moved in a somewhat different direction from the hard-line Pankhurstians, creating the mixed-sex US, which encompassed a wide range of supporters including, it should be noted, a number of key women and men who were disillusioned former members of the WSPU.

≺ II ≻

A Question of Balance: The United Suffragists 1914–18

Many chronologies of women's suffrage still finish with the outbreak of war in August 1914. Accounts that do consider wartime attitudes have broadened from the Pankhurst militancy to militarism line and there is also now recognition that a number of suffrage activists became pacifists.[58] Few, though, pay serious attention to the suffrage groups which persisted,[59] not just organizations like the NUWSS and WFL but also specialist societies like the CLWS, Catholic Women's Suffrage Society, and Forward Cymric Suffrage Union. Although the national MLWS folded in 1914, the Manchester Men's League carried on, as did the Northern Men's Federation and a North London rump left over from the militant MPU, while the formation of the United Suffragists presaged the start of a new attempt to get men and women working together for women's suffrage. Neglect of the US can be attributed to historiographical factors, notably the traditional focus on pre-war militancy and sex war, and the careful post-war shaping of suffragette memoirs. It is exacerbated by the way that historians have frequently tended to polarize the attitudes of suffrage activists. As Ian Fletcher has argued, many women and men initially attracted by militancy ultimately supported more moderate organizations.[60] Dichotomizing war and peace and associating suffrage activity with the disturbance of peace but not with the extraordinary conditions of war obscures still further the work of the US, which began in peacetime and developed during the war.

The basis for the new society was laid as early as December 3, 1913, when Nevinson and a few others who had been associated with the MPU or WSPU gathered at the home of the ex-gunner H. J. Gillespie (who had been a member of both the MLWS and MPU) to discuss the idea of a "new men and women's Union."[61] They met frequently over the ensuing weeks. By January 9, 1914, they had formed a committee, with Nevinson in the chair.

Their first meeting was held a week later. Gillespie was to be the treasurer, Barbara Gould the secretary. She was the daughter of the noted scientist Hertha Ayrton, who became a vice president and donated the first sum (£100) to the funds. Her half-sister was Edith Zangwill, whose husband the author Israel Zangwill was an old MLWS stalwart and a vice president of the US. Gould's husband, the journalist and poet Gerald Gould, was another US founder. Among the vice presidents and committee members could be found further husband and wife teams such as the Websters and Baillie Weavers. When women got the vote in 1918, Gertrude Colmore (Mrs. Baillie Weaver) commented that her husband Harold was "affected almost to tears."[62] He, like the cricketers G. L. Jessop and A. J. Webbe who also became vice presidents, had been in the MLWS. The impressive array of vice presidents also included Professor Caroline Spurgeon.

Nevinson, who had been a founder member of both the MLWS and the MPU, was joined by other former MPU officials on the committee, including the dockers' leader (and later MP for Stepney) John Scurr. The US claimed to be the first women's suffrage society in which men and women sat together in equal numbers on the committee (six men, six women).[63] In a neat reversal of the claims of equal suffragists to the vote, Nevinson declared that the US "turned all its guns on the Government and admitted men on equal terms with women."[64] The most energetic of the women members was the former WSPU activist (twice imprisoned), journalist, and novelist, Evelyn Sharp.[65] The US published her witty suffrage sketches *Rebel Women*. In 1917 Sharp's refusal to pay taxes led to the distraint of all her furniture including her precious typewriter.

The diaries and letters of the key US figures show not only that many of them were already acquainted as part of a radical London intelligentsia but also that the friendships which they developed in these years lasted for the rest of their lives. Their society's name was carefully chosen: gender neutral, it suggested cohesion and could be usefully incorporated into a slogan with the acronym "Join US." Press announcements were released in the first week of February

1914. The US prided itself on its openness: anyone could join the society. Indeed, its very inclusiveness posed a few problems.

Emmeline Pethick-Lawrence, who had initially expressed some reservations about the wisdom of such a society, did come into its fold, along with her husband. She joined the committee though there were some anxious moments in the autumn when she resigned but was then persuaded to change her mind. In a keynote speech in July at a well-publicized Kingsway Hall meeting she had announced that she and her husband were handing over their paper *Votes For Women* to become an organ of the US.[66] This was fortunate for the finances and future of the society. Rather less welcome was the tone of her speech in which, still extremely bitter about the expulsion from the WSPU, she dwelt on the breach with the Pankhursts. She emphasized that the US was an intermediate party, "occupying a position between the revolutionary section and the party of peaceful persuasion." While this suggested that the US occupied distinctive ground of its own, considerable concern was expressed by the committee about the implications of her words. They believed that boundaries should not be erected and that the society must remain open, even to extreme militants. The treasurer and secretary promptly exercised some damage limitation by writing to the press stressing that the US was emphatically not against militants: their only opposition was to intolerance and the government refusal to grant women's suffrage.

It was not the first time that the US needed to reassure supporters of its openness. It had already rebuked one vice president for breaking its tough rule of never criticizing any suffragist body. The diplomat, traveler, and writer Sir Harry Johnston had contributed an article to the *Westminster Gazette* which provoked considerable editorial comment.[67] He had commented that he had reached the reluctant conclusion that he should cease subscribing any money or support to women's suffrage until "outrages on persons or property cease." Referring to "bands of petroleuses, Dahomean amazons" and "stupid martyrs," he sought a superwoman who might, for the cause of women, threaten to "throttle or to fustigate all who departed from the principle that physical force was no real remedy in the redress of grievances."

Nevinson wrote to Sir Harry stressing the need to distinguish between attacks on persons and property and other protests and rebuking him for such a public outburst in defiance of the beliefs of the US.[68] In the *Westminster Gazette*, Eleanor Acland of the Liberal Women's Suffrage Union responded by warning readers about accepting advice on withdrawing support which had actually come from that arch-opponent of women's suffrage, Lord Curzon.[69] She ridiculed Sir Harry's invocation of the very violence he professed to deplore and noted his lack of attention to the "quiet strength of suffragists." Rather than denouncing men for trying to control the movement, she carefully focused her attention on those men who were working actively with women and praised them: "The one thing which most avails to keep the majority of Suffragists sane and hopeful, and therefore peaceable, is the growth of a band of men (both among statesmen and among the rank and file of the democracy) determined and faithful, and not to be cowed over by militant outrages into deserting a just cause."

The first point in the US constitution was a statement of belief that men and women "can usefully co-operate on equal terms."[70] The ostracism practiced by Christabel Pankhurst toward the MPU in particular had thus resulted not in men withdrawing from involvement or becoming even more aggressive. Rather, after internal divisions and a careful distancing of at least some of the MPU committee from Hugh Franklin's incendiary activities, they had regrouped in a new, more moderate form along with other male sympathizers and women activists keen on a constructive alliance. Krista Cowman[71] argues that with socialists like Scurr and Lansbury on its committee and through its involvement with various branches of trade unions via meetings the US signaled a realignment of militancy, reverting to the less problematic and more passive expressions of militant protest. It could also be said that this was where its members had wished to remain all along. After the WSPU split Elizabeth Robins had written that the Union was now "passing into another phase" but that she and "a legion are where we were."[72] Although she personally now focused on her fiction rather than suffrage activism, in many respects the US appears to have represented that "legion."

Accepting that women's suffrage was "the foremost political issue of the day," the US explained that its methods included putting pressure on the government, conducting electoral campaigns, "working in harmony with all existing suffrage associations," and correcting what it euphemistically called "journalistic inexactitudes."[73] Finally, in a statement which more than any other betrayed how in tone and temperament it differed from previous suffrage societies, and demonstrating the influence of Evelyn Sharp on its thinking, it besought members to keep in mind "the important truth that a merry heart goes all the way, and that a spirit of comradeship, good temper, and sense of humor has always characterized the women's fight for freedom."[74] Perhaps this reflected wishful thinking rather than exactitude, but its last words carefully reminded all just whose fight it really was.

Much has been written about the impact of the First World War on the construction of gender relations and systems. Historians of gender have questioned some of the problems of conceiving war in terms of remasculinization with its inherent gendered assumptions and definitions of what constitutes the experience of war.[75] The effect of war on the diurnal suffrage struggle cannot be overemphasized. As Nevinson wrote only two months after the conflict began, "the war has disjointed and reversed all interests."[76] Inevitably it had personal repercussions on the US, including the removal of some key male players. For example, Gillespie the suffragist now resumed soldiery as Major Gillespie. His experiences at Ypres and Cambrai left him "collapsed in brain and nerve" by early 1918.[77] Nevinson continued to work for the society whenever possible. Indeed, many of the leading articles for *Votes For Women*, particularly in the latter part of the war, were now penned by him.[78] As a war correspondent he found some unexpected links between suffrage and combat: in Salonika he was delighted to find the sister of the leader of the WFL running a hospital; he also found there a group of Scottish nurses "All suffragists and excellent."[79] At the Dardanelles he encountered the plucky Lieutenant Cather, former MPU activist.[80]

Nevinson delighted audiences at home with stirring stories of his exploits. They raised vital funds for the US even though the press chose to minimize the suffrage aspect of such occasions. One talk on Gallipoli raised over seven hundred pounds for their coffers.[81] In the month after war had been declared the US committee had considered closing their office and ending the paper due to financial problems, but in 1915 they managed to double their funds. Yet it was never easy. Some left on account of the society's refusal to undertake relief work. Beatrice Harraden, for one, objected to the unpatriotic tone of some *Votes For Women* articles, and the pacifism of its editor Evelyn Sharp was in stark contrast to the views of some readers. This led to some tension which was not easily reconcilable.[82] In his 1937 autobiography, Lawrence Housman noted the pacifist tendencies of the US and the suspicion this caused among some erstwhile supporters. Such wariness apparently passed into the historical representation of the women's suffrage movement in the inter-war period with its perception of militancy as service to the nation.[83]

Nevertheless, at the time the US survived remarkably well. They opened a women's club in Southwark, south London, largely attended by working-class mothers whose husbands were away fighting.[84] Attempts to make it appear more like a real club than a philanthropic institute[85] were not wholly successful but it did at least prove to be the one US creation which survived the disbanding of the society, changing its name in 1918 to the Woman Citizen's Club.[86] The US also protested against police supervision over soldiers' wives and objected to the court martialling of prostitutes in Cardiff who broke their curfew.[87] When the conscription of women was debated they stressed that only a free Parliament which represented women properly could be entitled to make such a decision.[88] By the end of 1915 the US had twenty branches and, as Cowman[89] points out, in many districts sustained a higher level of activity than the suffrage societies which undertook relief work.

They managed to win over a number of key former WSPU activists and organizers, such as Mary Neal and Mary Richardson, while the tolerant, humane tone which concerned some resulted also in valuable new recruits like Lawrence Housman from the MLWS. He had long been sensitive to gender issues and joined the US committee. Yet the society's frequent appeal to keep the suffrage flag flying is reminiscent of the rump of the Chartists who, in the changing political and economic climate post-1848, had urged supporters to "keep the old flag flying."[90] In 1914–18, with conflict and carnage on an unprecedented scale, suffrage was hardly high on most people's list of priorities. There were also some internal divisions, yet not, it would seem, primarily along gender lines. For example, in June 1915 Charles Grey and Bertha Brewster, in what Nevinson called their "wrecking mood,"[91] proposed a union with the WFL, Forward Cymric Suffrage Union, and other smaller societies to create one central organization. Although this was defeated, the committee resolved to work more closely with other societies in future.

In March 1916 the US adopted a new constitution and brought out the paper monthly instead of weekly. During this year the suffrage agenda also began to change. The older arguments against adult as opposed to equal suffrage were no longer relevant. The war had effectively disenfranchised many serving overseas who no longer satisfied the residency qualifications for voting. The need for registration reform raised wider possibilities of franchise reform. Evelyn Sharp mooted the possibility of adult suffrage at a stormy committee meeting in April.[92] By the summer, when a conference of sympathetic MPs and US and NUWSS representatives was held, there existed, according to Nevinson, a "feeling for Adult Suffrage almost without exception."[93]

During these months there was much discussion and negotiation between the various suffrage groups. The US found Mrs. Fawcett and her followers too inclined to be conciliatory and patient: "so used to waiting they can do nothing else."[94] In the autumn the National Council for Adult Suffrage was formed with Nevinson as chairman.[95] It was based in the US headquarters in Chancery Lane. The US representatives were not always in agreement with the somewhat obdurate Sylvia Pankhurst and her Workers' Suffrage Federation. Nevinson, who had earlier been much more supportive of this member of the Pankhurst family, now noted that "in spite of her excellence" she, like all her family, was "too suspicious and too determined that nothing shall succeed without her control."[96] Yet she and the others representing the labor movement were understandably concerned about establishing the voting rights of working women.

Following the US's suggestion, a speakers' conference composed of 32 MPs was convened. Pro-suffrage men were slightly in the majority and it included veteran supporters in the Commons such as W. H. Dickinson. In 1917 it ruled that the Special Register Bill could not include new voters. Its recommendations amounted to what the US dubbed "revolution by compromise."[97] These recommendations were broadly incorporated into the Representation of the People Bill which finally, after some delay, became law on February 6, 1918, four years to the day after *Votes For Women* had announced the formation of the US. Women over 30 fulfilling householder or other criteria were, for the first time, to be able to vote in national elections. By the time the Royal Assent was announced in Parliament even Mrs. Fawcett had gone home. Somewhat symbolically, only three campaigners were left there to celebrate: the US secretary Bertha Brewster, and the stalwarts Evelyn Sharp and H. W. Nevinson.[98]

Six million women were now able to vote (and five million women voters were added to the local government electorate). The US decided to disband. Their work was not completed: three million women below 30 remained voteless, as did a not inconsiderable number of older women such as professional women living in furnished lodgings. Gender discrimination remained rife.[99] Wives over 30 living in furnished rooms could not vote whereas husbands in such situations could. The British wife of an alien was not enfranchised, the British husband of an alien could vote. Not until July 1928 was there universal suffrage.

Yet it was hardly surprising that the women and men who had been United Suffragists felt they had something to celebrate after such a tough struggle for legislative change. Dr. Louisa Garrett Anderson commented that Christabel Pankhurst, clamoring for perpetual war, still seemed fresh and vital compared to the "overworked and exhausted people" who had worked for the US.[100] Nevinson and Sharp were honored with dinners and presentations for their sustained commitment to women's suffrage.[101] When the US held a celebration at the Caxton Hall, scene of so many suffrage speeches, they neatly fused the militant and military by the request on their invitation cards for guests to "Please wear decorations (prison or otherwise)."[102]

≺ III ≻

Conclusion

Women were not unappreciative of the part men had played in their cause, provided these men recognized whose cause it was and who must call the tune. Men's support for women's suffrage, which manifested itself in a host of ways, has clearly been underestimated in the past by historians. Their organized contribution was both varied and sustained, though how it was perceived and evaluated by women suffragists depended on timing, tact, and their societies' tactics. But it was also vitally affected by the women's own personal perspectives and by the men's understandings of what the vote signified.

In the early years their support could be helpful, not just within Parliament but in the way that their societies and most notably the MLWS helped to harness different groups of supporters of both genders in large rallies and meetings. This was followed by a period of tension, particularly after November 1911 when militancy escalated and, for differing reasons, WSPU and male supporters increasingly kept their distance from each other, a tendency exacerbated by Christabel Pankhurst's own vision of the way forward and by differences developing about who should be in control.

Nevertheless, what was being promulgated at a national level was not always reflected more locally. Further research on the relations between the NUWSS and male supporters at the local level would be useful and add to the new perspectives being suggested by focusing on familial links. And whatever the tensions before 1914, it is also the case that by the beginning of this year and before war forced new priorities, there were those who wanted to develop the potential for women and men working together to control the cause. Looking back in 1926, Evelyn Sharp acknowledged that the US had been "largely instrumental in keeping alive the suffrage movement between 1914 and 1918."[103]

Although the historical spotlight has been overwhelmingly fixed on Edwardian women's suffrage and the heightened militancy of the few years following, the US offered, as Cowman has observed, something which was lacking in those earlier years, for it was a society which "could unite disparate activists together in a concentrated campaign for the franchise."[104] It also helped shape a concept of the political woman concerned about women's fortunes generally, which helps make more explicable the feminist politics of the 1920s. In historical analysis such politics have tended to be contrasted solely with pre-war suffrage militancy. And while some former US members would dedicate themselves to equalitarian feminist politics in the 1920s, it is also interesting to note that a not inconsiderable number became committed to international and labor causes. For example, Nevinson and Sharp became involved in relief work in post-war Germany while Frederick Pethick-Lawrence and Barbara Gould put their faith in representing the Labour Party in Parliament.

Founded in peace but largely existing in the difficult conditions of wartime, when the meanings of masculinity and militancy were necessarily transformed, the United Suffragists had provided an unprecedented opportunity for women and men to work together in some harmony, challenging power and privilege. Moreover it prompted lifelong friendships and networks of support. Its motto had been "Usque Ad Finem" and it had played a crucial role in at last producing a result for women even though, ironically, that victory of February 1918 spelled adult suffrage for men and only a limited vote for women. Nevertheless, the end in the sense of universal female suffrage *was* now firmly in sight even though, as Pat Thane[105] shows, the full effect of change has to be judged in the long term.

≺ 8 ≻

What Difference Did the Vote Make?

PAT THANE

As PREVIOUS CHAPTERS have described, in 1918 the British parliamentary franchise was extended to women aged 30 years and over who were occupiers, or wives of occupiers, of land or premises of not less than five pounds annual value. It was also extended to women of 30 and over who held university degrees. The local government franchise, which since 1869 had included all women aged 21 or above who held property on which they were liable to pay local taxes ("rates")—mainly unmarried or widowed women—was extended to include the wives of male electors.

A conventional narrative has developed about the outcome of this partial concession of the vote to women in 1918: the previously active and united movement became splintered, divided, less publicly and dramatically effective; the impact of women as voters on politics and policy was slight, except possibly to reinforce conservative and Conservative Party values, including traditional values of domesticity; there was a backlash against the small shift in gender relations so far achieved. After women obtained the vote on equal terms with men in 1928, women's political involvement declined still further, reinforced by powerful and effective social pressure upon women to give primacy to their domestic roles. The Second World War brought only short-term and ambiguous gains for women, followed speedily by a reimposition of domestic values. Traditional gender roles were not seriously challenged again until the late 1960s, but even then with only limited and short-term effects.[1]

This narrative is not wholly mistaken, but it is far from being a complete representation of a complex set of processes. Just as other contributions to this volume argue for new understandings of women's political roles in earlier periods, this chapter argues that we need a more complex understanding of the twentieth century, which recent research is beginning to make possible. A large part of the problem historians have encountered in interpreting events after 1918 relates to expectations. How soon could women have expected to overthrow thousands of years of male predominance in the political culture? Too much writing on this theme assumes that because there were not dramatic changes in gender roles shortly after the partial attainment of the vote, therefore there were no significant changes. There is a danger of measuring the impact of the vote by impossible standards; of expecting change to be unrealistically rapid; and of underestimating, by applying the values of later generations, shifts which were more significant in the context of the 1920s and 1930s than they appear with hindsight. Martin Pugh has pointed out that the middle classes did not dominate British politics for many decades after they obtained the vote in 1832, or working men for almost 50 years after some of them gained the vote in 1867. "If these precedents are a real guide," he suggested in 1992, "we may be on the verge of a take-off by women in the 1990s."[2] And indeed the general election of May 1997 brought an unprecedented number of women into the House of Commons and into ministerial office, as a result of a commitment to greater gender equality on the part of influential sections of the victorious Labour Party. Following the election one-third of Labour parliamentary seats were held by women, compared with a little over one-seventh in the previous Parliament; the proportion of Conservative seats held by women barely changed. We need to think in terms of long- as well as short-term outcomes. However, the resistance to the policy of promoting female candidates suggests the resilience of opposition to women in political life even at the beginning of a new millennium.

But presence in Parliament is only one possible measure of women's roles in British political culture. Others have measured these primarily by the achievement of legislation which directly promotes gender equality.[3] This, surely, is also inadequate. Women can play a role in other areas of politics, and if equality with men is their aim, they should surely do so. The search for a more satisfactory picture can best start by asking what the suffragists themselves expected to follow from the vote.

≺ I ≻
What Did the Suffrage Campaigners Expect?

It is often argued that suffrage campaigners themselves had high expectations of the extent of social and economic as well as of statutory change that gaining the vote would bring about, and were disappointed by what followed. Maybe this was true of some, but many influential suffragists were shrewd enough politically and had enough experience of the extent of opposition to their cause to be less optimistic, to expect the struggle to continue and change to be slow. The militant suffragist Viscountess Rhondda commented in 1921 that, in gaining the vote, women "had passed the first great toll-bar on the road which leads to equality," but "it is a far cry yet to the end of the road."[4] Her biographer suggests that "while welcoming the [1918 Representation of the People Act] she was neither naive enough nor complacent enough to expect that such a limited measure would break down the still significant barriers to full emancipation."[5] In 1920 Lady Rhondda founded and edited the weekly journal *Time and Tide*, which was produced wholly by women and gave broad coverage to political and cultural issues, most of them not directly concerned with gender equality, in order to promote such equality both by demonstrating the capacities of women and by informing and educating newly enfranchised women. It also gave prominence to the issues of central importance to feminists until women obtained the vote on equal terms with men in 1928. Thereafter Lady Rhondda felt free to shift the emphasis to what she defined as "the real task of feminism," to "wipe out the overemphasis on sex that is the fruit of the age-long subjection of women. The individual must stand out without trappings as a human being."[6] In the 1930s the journal employed and published a balance of men and women and became one of Britain's most influential reviews of politics, the arts, and social questions. Despite Lady Rhondda's own increasing conservatism, *Time and Tide* continued to be a strong advocate of all forms of social equality, including gender equality.

Lady Rhondda appears in the historiography as a leading standard bearer of egalitarian "old" feminism, self-consciously promoting what is seen as the predominant commitment of the pre-1914 suffrage campaigners to complete equality between the sexes. Eleanor

Rathbone, on the other hand, is represented as a leader of welfare-oriented "new" feminism.[7] This recognized that women and men had some different needs and that, at least in the short run, women needed support in their roles as mothers. Some see "new" gradually replacing "old" feminism in the inter-war years, though in reality the distinction between them was by no means clear cut. Rathbone also recognized the struggle ahead. She believed that if women were to take advantage of their new political rights, new methods were needed, for women were no longer seeking "a big, elemental . . . simple reform," such as enfranchisement, but the "difficult re-adjustments of a complicated . . . antiquated structure of case law and statute law," which required sober and tricky negotiation.[8]

From another perspective again, Sylvia Pankhurst, from the family that had led militant suffragism before the First World War, had moved far to the left of her mother and sisters during the war. Unlike them, she was strongly committed to equal adult suffrage: the granting of the vote to all males and females at age 21. She was deeply disappointed that this was not achieved in 1918, that "masculine timidity entrenched itself against the dangers of majority rule."[9] Indeed recognition that there were more women than men in Britain over the age of 21 had strongly influenced the framing of the Representation of the People Act.[10] Reflecting in 1931, she believed that, nevertheless, "a breach in the sex barrier had been made" in 1918, but that its occurrence while a terrible war continued explained the sober response:

The pageantry and rejoicing, the flaming ardour, which in pre-war days would have greeted the victory, were absent when it came. The sorrows of the world conflict precluded jubilations . . .

The Suffrage movement, which lived through the vast holocaust of peaceful life, was a more intelligent and informed movement than that which, gallant as it was, had fought the desperate, pre-war fight. Gone was the mirage of a society regenerated by enfranchised womanhood as by a magic wand. Men and women had been drawn closer together by the suffering and sacrifice of the War. Awed and humbled by the great catastrophe and by the huge economic problems it had thrown into naked prominence, the women of the Suffrage movement had learned that social regeneration is a long and mighty work. The profound divergences of opinion on war and peace had been shown to know no sex.[11]

Sylvia Pankhurst's notably sober assessment calls in question not only the belief that suffrage campaigners expected the franchise to deliver instant transformation of gender roles but also the argument, based upon a limited range of literary sources, that the "Great" War so undermined masculine confidence that it bred a backlash against women's aspirations for change;[12] she believed, rather, that the war had drawn men and women closer together. It is questionable whether the concept of "backlash" is appropriate for the interpretation of this period, when it is not clear that the hostility to women's aspirations, which had long existed, was greater or more effective or had different sources than at previous times.

When sections of the press commented slightingly on the small number of women candidates in the general election of 1922, the Women's Freedom League (WFL) retorted that since men had been involved in the political process since 1265 and women for only four years, 33 female candidates was not an inconsiderable achievement, especially in view of the extent of opposition in political parties to women as candidates.[13] WFL was a radical group, which before the war had split from the Pankhursts' Women's Social and Political Union (WSPU) because it wished to campaign for broader social and economic change than for the vote in itself. It had about five thousand members in the 1920s and was very active.[14] WFL also had few illusions about how easy the way forward would be. After the vote was extended to all women in the same terms as men in 1928 its journal stated: "For sixty-one years women have striven to win an equal footing with men; it is only an equal footing they have gained, not equal political power."[15]

Prominent suffragists appear to have greeted the partial success of their cause with sober realism, but not to have given up the fight for further advance. The belief that women generally ceased to campaign after 1918 is often derived from a comparison of the sobriety of their politics after the war with pre-war suffragette militancy. Of course a substantial and indispensable component of the pre-war campaign, embodied especially in the National Union of Women's Suffrage Societies (NUWSS), was peaceable and constitutional.[16] The most prominent figure in the NUWSS, Millicent Garrett Fawcett, wrote of her reaction in November 1919 in the final chapter of her memoir *The Women's Victory—and After*, "The Difference the Vote Has Made." She challenged those who argued that it would make no difference:

If the vote makes no difference, why have our race all over the world attached such enormous importance to it? . . . the possession of the franchise is the very foundation stone of political freedom. Our fifty years struggle for the women's vote was not actuated by our setting any extraordinary value on the mere power of making a mark on a voting paper once in every three or four years. We did not, except as a symbol of free citizenship value it as a thing good in itself . . . but for the sake of the equal laws, the enlarged opportunities, the improved status of women which we knew it involved. We worked for it with ardour and passion because it was the stuff of the conscience with us that it would benefit not women only, but the whole community . . . it was the cause of men, women and children.[17]

Garrett Fawcett described how, immediately the extension of the franchise was decided, the council of NUWSS decided to extend its aims. The council retained the old single objective, "to obtain the parliamentary franchise for women on the same terms as it is or may be granted to men," but added two more: "to obtain all other such reforms, economic, legislative and social, as are necessary to secure a real equality of liberties, status and opportunities between men and women," and "to assist women to realize their responsibility as voters."

In assessing the impact of the vote it is also important not to abstract the experience of women in politics from the wider political context. The quieter public engagement of women activists in the 1920s compared with the drama of the pre-war campaign of the suffragettes is commonly interpreted as a change specific to women's politics;[18] yet, as Jon Lawrence argues persuasively, this preference for sobriety was a general feature of British politics at this time in which women shared. Contemporaries commented, with surprise, that there were so few "scenes" in post-war elections. *The Times* described the "almost cloistral calm" that prevailed in London on the day of the October 1924 election, but denied that this was due to lack of interest among women or men: "There is still a belief abroad that Eatanswill is characteristic of our election scenes and it is hard to convince the foreigner that voting does not necessarily mean more bloodshed and that British phlegm does not necessarily mean apathy."[19] Perhaps, as Sylvia Pankhurst suggested, this calm response to politics was a reaction to the violence of the war. Rathbone thought that on the part of women it was a response to a new political situation which required changed tactics. She answered critics who complained that the passion had gone out of the movement after 1918, and that she and her associates had become too cautious, by saying:

We knew when it was necessary to compromise. There is a school of reformers which despises compromise ... we acquired by experience a certain flair which told us when a charge of dynamite would come in useful and when it was better to rely on the methods of a skilled engineer.[20]

The violence of a strand of pre-war suffragism had been bred by frustration at the intransigence of resistance to the reasonable claim of women for the vote. Partial attainment of the vote led to calmer forms of political pressure, though not, as we shall see, to the cessation of demonstrations by women. Nor did violence wholly disappear from British public discourse about gender roles; rather it survived longer among anti-feminists than among feminists. In 1921 Cambridge, "that perverse university," as the suffragist and Cambridge mathematics graduate Ray Strachey described it,[21] refused to follow the example set by Oxford in the previous year, and other British universities long before, and voted against admitting women to full membership of the university as students and faculty. A gang of male undergraduates at Cambridge celebrated their victory by smashing up the bronze gates of Newnham, one of the two women's colleges at Cambridge. A reason for the low expectations of suffragists of the outcome of the extension of the franchise was their awareness of the continuing strength of hostility to women's claims.

≺ II ≻

Women as Voters

How did women use their vote when they acquired it? It has been claimed that "once the vote was gained it became clear that large numbers of women really had little interest in it."[22] There is no evidence to support this claim. Rather, contemporaries commented on how eager women were to vote. Ray Strachey, a leading member of the NUWSS and a close friend and colleague of Millicent Garrett Fawcett, wrote in 1928 that in the preceding decade feminists "had regarded the vote not as an end in itself, but as an instrument for securing other reforms; and now they proceed to use it."[23] Strachey herself stood unsuccessfully for Parliament as an Independent, in 1918 and 1922; became political adviser to the first woman MP, the Conservative Lady Violet Astor; and was active in a range of causes until her early death in 1940.

Certainly the percentage turnout of eligible electors in normal elections after women obtained the vote was not unduly low.[24] The first general election after the Representation of the People Act, that of December 1918, followed too soon on the change in the law and after the war (which had ended only one month previously) to be a reasonable test of the effects of the franchise changes for women and for men (for this was also the first occasion on which all adult men, from age 21, had been enabled to vote; previously about 40 percent of males were disfranchised). Many who had newly gained the right to vote were not yet on the voting register by the time of the election. The turnout was only 58.9 percent in 1918 compared with an average of 73.5 percent in the seven ensuing elections.

The next general election, in 1922, was a more realistic test of the effects of the change in the franchise. On the day following the election, *The Times*, which had no obvious commitment to the cause of women, commented:

The greatest surprise which those in charge of the polling booths had yesterday was the number of women who appeared to vote immediately after the booths were opened.

In 1918, wrote the reporter, women had been uncertain and diffident, "many of those who did vote were accompanied by men and their views were probably influenced by them." But,

Yesterday the contrary was the case . . . canvassers found themselves questioned alertly and adroitly on matters not usually considered women's questions. Foreign policy was a strong point in moving women in constituencies.

Women's questions as such played a small part in this election; women in many constituencies attended meetings especially called for them when they were held in private houses, but it may be doubted whether any candidate, woman or man, polled a large vote purely on his or her stand on these matters . . . in every constituency it was the big issues that counted and men's questions were undoubtedly also women's questions.

So far from married women voting as their husbands told them to, it was quite evident that where there was influence, it was not necessarily wielded by the man . . . the percentage of women electors who voted may be taken as possibly greater than that of men and their vote must have influenced if it did not secure the election of the majority of candidates.[25]

The Times similarly commented following the next election, of December 1923, that women had polled heavily,[26] and that it believed that the Conservatives lost partly on the "dear food" issue, especially with the women:

> At the last election the Labour Party was very disappointed at the fact that it did not poll more than about 35–40 per cent of the women's vote, but on this occasion the proportion seems to have been much higher.[27]

On the next polling day, October 30, 1924, which brought an end to the first, short-lived Labour government,

> The women in most of the London constituencies seemed to be mustering in great force in the earlier hours and in widely separated constituencies there was no doubt that they were far more interested than last year in the election. St Marylebone, in Battersea and at Bromley there were more women voters than there have been since they obtained the franchise.[28]

After 1928, when all women obtained the right to vote at age 21 on the same terms as men, women made up 53 percent of the electorate. Women voted on equal terms with men for the first time in May 1929, the election which brought the Labour Party into government for the second time. Before polling there was extensive press comment on "the sphinx of the election," "the enigma presented by the new woman voter."[29] There were predictions from some parts of the country that "there may be a great deal of indifference to political questions among the newly enfranchised women."[30] In Greater London it was reported that "there has been a remarkable absence of rowdyism" and that

> Women form the majority of the electorate in all save one or two constituencies and in many places they largely preponderate. This is one of the factors which all the parties have kept very steadily in view. So far as meetings are any guide, the women, including the new voters, have displayed quite as much interest as the men and they have shown great willingness to render voluntary assistance as canvassers and so forth.[31]

In the Midlands there was a "lack of excitement" about the election, but there were well attended meetings:

> Women only are wearing party favours and women have carried on most of the canvassing ... There is no doubt in the minds of any organiser that the electors—and particularly the women—are taking the election seriously ... Women are expected to poll heavily but no-one can form any opinion of how the woman's vote was going.[32]

The Times reporter in Scotland commented:

> The greatest riddle of the election is still the vote of the newly enfranchised young women. Nothing has arisen to entitle any party to expect a monopoly

of favour from this source or to disturb the conjecture that the vote of the women will be distributed among the three parties in measurable proportion to that of men.[33]

When the poll was completed,

> There was every sign in many constituencies that [the new woman voter] had risen admirably to the occasion. Though stories were told of her nervous uncertainty about polling procedures, general observation suggested that she had no need to ask her way, but displayed the coolness attributed to the modern generation.

Women were said to have polled well all over London, and

> in South Kensington where women largely outnumber men, no time was lost in going to the polling stations. The chances seemed that the division would poll a larger proportion of the register than had been its custom.[34]

The local press in the northern port city of Liverpool reported that women had polled in large numbers and that their votes appeared to have favored Labour.[35]

Nevertheless, the belief that women do not vote with the same frequency as men has become a conventional wisdom of British political science,[36] despite a striking absence of supporting evidence. No statistical surveys exist for the inter-war years. Studies for the later twentieth century (1960s to 1990s) support the journalistic observations of the 1920s that there were no significant differences in the tendency of males and females to vote in national elections.[37]

The comment of *The Times* in 1922 that women's voting preferences did not appear to be dictated by their close male relatives was a response to a commonplace assertion at the time, repeated in the historiography and more insistently in works of political science, that women largely followed the political preferences of men who were close to them. There is considerable biographical evidence that women as often led as followed the politics of their partner, or that couples were drawn together by a shared political preference.[38] The 1993 annual British Household Survey (of a nationally representative sample of British households) found that Labour-supporting women were more effective in persuading their families to follow their voting preferences than were Labour-supporting men. It would be unwise to generalize these findings to all political parties throughout the twentieth century, but, together with other evidence, they suggest that we should hesitate before assuming that female voters at any time simply stood by their man.

Newspaper comment on inter-war elections suggests that "women" were not immovably wedded to a single party but shifted their allegiance according to their assessment of salient political issues. In this women do not seem to differ from male voters. The electorate as a whole appears to have been volatile in the uncertain conditions of the 1920s and 1930s. Nevertheless it has become another axiom of British political sociology that women since 1918 have been more inclined than men to support the Conservative Party.[39] This has been put forward as one explanation for the success of the Conservative Party in remaining in office for most of the period since 1918. As one group of female political scientists has put it: "had there been no women's franchise . . . Labour would have been continuously in office between 1945 and 1979."[40] If this is so, of course, it suggests that women's votes have made a difference to British politics, if an unwelcome one in the eyes of many commentators. But David Jarvis suggests that this assumption also is insecurely based. It has been derived from statistical calculations which are riddled with unexamined technical problems.[41] A more careful analysis of all Liverpool parliamentary elections between 1924 and 1935 and of voting turnouts in all of the English parliamentary divisions in May 1929, which takes account of socio-economic variations among constituencies, suggests that class was a more important influence upon voting than gender. The evidence does not support a stronger conclusion than that women's voting behavior in this period "remains an open question."[42] The voting preferences of women and men have fluctuated throughout the twentieth century; and women, like men, do not vote as a bloc, undifferentiated by class, religion, or any other variable.[43] Nor is there any sign that women have been uninterested in voting.

≺ III ≻

Women and Political Parties

Nor have substantial numbers of women been averse to joining political parties, though this has always been a minority pursuit among both men and women. Women joined the Labour Party in significant numbers immediately on attaining the vote. By 1927 about 300,000 women were members. This was about half the individual membership of the party and in some constituencies the female proportion was higher still.[44] This proportion did not, however, give women as much power within the party as might appear. In accordance with the constitution of the Labour Party, the votes of individual members in the local branches were hugely outnumbered at the powerful annual party conference by the trade unions, each of which wielded a number of votes, in proportion to the size of their membership, whereas each party branch had just one vote.

Labour women could, however, make effective use of their numerical force in local politics, especially perhaps in areas with a strong tradition of women's public activity, possibly combined with paid employment, such as in parts of Lancashire,[45] though there is no study of women in local government after 1918 to compare with Patricia Hollis's work on the previous period.[46] One of the few local studies, by Michael Savage, describes how the textile town of Preston, Lancashire, was transformed from a Conservative to a Labour stronghold in the 1920s, when working women formed a strong women's section of the local party and persuaded an initially unsympathetic local party to adopt a program advocating improvements in education, maternity and child welfare, health care, housing, and the provision of such public amenities as baths and wash houses.[47] In Liverpool, women were made more welcome in the local party in the early 1920s, though they later met resistance from an increasingly powerful group of Roman Catholics in the party. Nevertheless Liverpool Labour women campaigned successfully for increased local provision of education, maternity and child welfare, baths, libraries, and recreation. The success owed much to the energy of Bessie Braddock, who was a city councillor throughout the 1930s and later a respected local MP, though she would never have described herself as a feminist.[48] In other areas, however, women met stronger resistance in local Labour Parties.[49]

There were about one million women in the Conservative Party in the 1920s.[50] The female membership of both parties appears to have declined a little during the 1930s.[51] Even the Liberal Party, which, in view of its leaders' lack of support for the suffrage movement before 1918, had done little to attract women, and which was weak and divided in the 1920s, attracted increasing numbers of women members, reaching about 100,000 by 1928.[52] Many women found Liberalism attractive philosophically and in terms of its broad policy commitments and believed that the ideas of the party of John Stuart Mill continued to be consistent with support for gender equality. A prize-winning essay by Mrs Penberthy of Exeter, "Why I am a Liberal," published in *Liberal Women's News* in 1925, expresses the blend of "equal rights," welfare, and other political issues which attracted women of no particular prominence or distinction into politics:

I am a Liberal because I wholeheartedly believe in Free Trade, in the League of Nations, in drastic Temperance Reform, Equal Suffrage, Religious Equality, Disestablishment, Revision of the Land Laws and Divorce laws and a host of kindred reforms which can only become possible when better housing obtains.[53]

The Labour Party constitution of 1918 provided a structure for the organization of women within the party. A permanent chief woman officer was appointed to preside over a network of women's sections of the party branches. She was assisted by regional women's sections officers. Women had four reserved places on the powerful national executive committee of the party, which was elected by the annual conference. Delegates of the women's sections met at an annual women's conference, but there was no obligation upon the annual party conference or the national executive committee to take account of their decisions. Women often felt that they had the appearance rather than the substance of power within the Labour Party and they had certainly to struggle, often unsuccessfully, to be heard. But they were not wholly ignored and the women's sections and the women's conference did provide environments in which women could develop their political ideas and their skills of organization in a manner which had not previously been possible.[54]

In 1918 the Conservative Party similarly reconstructed its machinery and sought to develop a mass organization in which women had a recognized place. Women were to have one third representation at all levels of party organization, presided over by a women's advisory committee at Conservative Central Office. The activities of the Conservative women are discussed by Jarvis.[55] Liberal women were organized in the, Asquithian, Women's National Liberal Federation (WNLF), which played an important part in organizing women and in campaigning for the party. However, having been estab-

TABLE 1
Women Candidates and MPs

	Conservative		Labour		*Liberal (Alliance)		Other		Total	
	Cands.	MPs	Cands.	MPs	Cands.	MPs	Cands.	MPs	Cands.	MPs
1918	1	–	4	–	4	–	8	1	17	1
1922	5	1	10	–	16	1	2	–	33	2
1923	7	3	14	3	12	2	1	–	34	8
1924	12	3	22	1	6	–	1	–	41	4
1929	10	3	30	9	25	1	4	1	69	14
1931	16	13	36	–	6	1	4	1	62	15
1935	19	6	35	1	11	1	2	1	67	9
1945	14	1	45	21	20	1	8	1	87	24
1950	28	6	42	14	45	1	11	–	126	21
1951	29	6	39	11	11	–	–	–	74	17
1955	32	10	43	14	12	–	2	–	89	24
1959	28	12	36	13	16	–	1	–	81	25
1964	24	11	33	18	25	–	8	–	90	29
1966	21	7	30	19	20	–	9	–	80	26
1970	26	15	29	10	23	–	21	1	99	26
1974	33	9	40	13	40	–	30	1	143	23
1974	30	7	50	18	49	–	32	2	161	27
1979	31	8	52	11	51	–	76	–	210	19
1983	40	13	78	10	(115)	–	87	–	280	23
1987	46	17	92	21	(106)	2	85	1	329	41
1992	59	20	138	37	144	2	227	1	568	60

SOURCE: David Butler and Gareth Butler, *British Political Facts, 1900–1994* (London, 1994, ©David Butler), 243. By permission of Macmillan Ltd.
*Including Social Democrat & Lib Democrat candidates

lished some decades before women gained the vote, the WNLF had no secure position in the constitution of the Liberal Party and experienced continual frustration at the unwillingness of the Party leaders to take account of the views of the council of the WNLF.

The women in all three major political parties in the inter-war years, and for long after, expressed frustration at the unresponsiveness to their views of their male-dominated parties, and at the difficulty experienced even by women with long records of party activity in achieving selection for winnable parliamentary or even local government seats.[56] Table 1 shows how few women stood for Parliament and the still smaller numbers who were successful between 1918 and 1992. The women's organizations of the political parties did, however, provide an opportunity for women to develop their political ideas and their organizational skills. All three aimed to educate women in the use of the vote. It is easy to caricature these organizations as subordinate to male-dominated parties, providing no more than domestic support to the real work of politics, providing the tea at meetings rather than the substance of policy making. Such comments underestimate the importance of sociability in political culture, in the building and sustaining of political parties; and they also underestimate the political impact of the women's presence in certain areas of policy, as we will see.

≺ IV ≻
Women and Non-Party Organizations

Apart from the large numbers of women who joined and were active in political parties, possibly larger numbers belonged to non-party political organizations that were dedicated to educating women in the use of their civil rights and that worked to achieve highly political goals of particular importance to women. These organizations were distinctive to the decades between the wars, when women first had the vote, though some were continuations of older associations in new forms and some survived long after the 1930s in new guises.

Even before the passing of the Representation of the People Act, suffrage societies began to organize to raise political awareness among women, to inform them about important political issues, to train them in procedures of campaigning, public speaking, committee work, and other essential skills of public life. Once women had the vote, they believed, it was important that they use it. In 1917 the National Union of Women Workers and the National Council of Women decided to form a network of Women's Citizens Associations (WCAs) throughout the country to provide this training. The first of these had been formed by Eleanor Rathbone in Liverpool in 1913. Membership was open to all women at age sixteen, so that political education could begin early in life. Women could join a WCA branch or a society which affiliated to it, as many local suffrage societies did. The role of WCAs was to "foster a sense of citizenship in women. Encourage the study of political, social and economic questions; secure the adequate representation of the interests and experience of women in the affairs of the community."[57]

The NUWSS moved smoothly from its major role in helping to

bring about the Representation of the People Act to that of putting it into practice. It published pamphlets guiding women through the complexity of getting themselves onto the voting register and of using the vote, such as: *And Shall I have the Parliamentary Vote?*, *Six Million Women Can Vote*, *The New Privilege of Citizenship*, and *How Women Can Use the Vote*. It changed its name to the National Union of Societies for Equal Citizenship (NUSEC), and in 1924 it merged with the WCAs. Both organizations were determinedly nonparty. This did not mean that they were necessarily wholly hostile to political parties. A substantial section of the pre-First World War women's movement—as of other sections of British society—was hostile to the party system, believing that party organization and discipline undermined the democratic process. When pre-war suffragists were asked what difference the vote would make, some of them replied: "the automatic disappearance of party government" and "the subordination of party considerations to principle."[58] In consequence many women ran for election as independents. Eleanor Rathbone was an independent member of Liverpool city council from 1910 until the mid 1930s and an independent MP from 1929 until her death in 1946. She held one of the anomalous university seats,[59] which regularly returned independents to Parliament. When the country was not at war it was almost impossible for an independent to be returned for a non-university constituency at any other time in the twentieth century.[60]

The relationship of women's non-party organizations with the political parties was a source of debate and tension. However, the WCAs and NUSEC were prepared to give support in elections and to work with party candidates, mainly female but also male, who were active in causes favored by the women's movement. They were anxious in principle to promote and to support women as candidates in national and local elections and they had to acknowledge that the political culture in some parts of the country was more receptive of independent candidates than it was in others. For example of the 13 women elected to Cambridge City Council between 1918 and 1930, 10 were independents. All of the 39 women elected to Manchester City Council between 1908 and 1939 were party representatives.[61] Of the 52 women elected to Liverpool City Council between the wars, 17 were not representatives of the three major parties. Four were independents, the remainder were scattered among a variety of causes including the Co-operative Party (4), the Communist Party (1), the Protestant Party (2), and "Anti-Waste" (1).[62] Many female local candidates had support from the NUSEC. As the parties recruited more women, and were often hostile to the non-party women's organizations,[63] the women's organizations had little to gain from withdrawal from electoral politics, and they recognized that beleaguered party women needed and appreciated support from women who shared many of their sympathies but were outside their party. There was frequent collaboration between party and non-party women at local level despite the disapproval of national party leaders.

A formal attempt to co-ordinate the activities of party and non-party women was made by the Consultative Committee of Women's Organizations (CCWO). This was initially formed by the NUWSS in 1916 to co-ordinate the demand for the vote and then to mobilize women voters. It became more active in 1921 when Lady Astor reorganized it to provide a link between members of parliaments and women's organizations. Forty-nine women's societies affiliated, including the NUSEC; the National Council of Women (NCW); the Six Point Group; and the Liberal and Conservative, but not the Labour, women. It had the support of a number of male MPs and campaigned against parliamentary candidates hostile to women's demands and for the supporters. It promoted networking, often at parties thrown by the wealthy Lady Astor, among women activists and politicians, seeking to draw women into the normal processes of political lobbying. It had some success in the 1920s but declined somewhat in the 1930s, as Lady Astor's concern to appease Nazism diverted her attention and lost her much support in women's associations.[64]

Alongside the women's organizations, such as NUSEC, which were primarily dedicated to encouraging women to use the vote, other women's organizations with either broader, or more specific, single-issue, objectives were also committed to the political education of the new female voters. The Women's Institutes (WIs) were founded in 1915 by suffragists, some of them former militants, to provide the large numbers of British countrywomen with opportunities for personal and political development, partly by providing them with a social space which was under their own control and independent of the traditional rural social hierarchy, in which the squire's wife was at the apex and the wife of the parish clergyman a little below. The democratically elected committees of the WIs aimed at initiating a shift in rural power relationships among women, while also providing experience of political organizing.

Equally importantly, they encouraged women to value their work and their skills, both in and outside the home, as men did, and to seek to improve their conditions of work in the home. They encouraged recognition of the value of women's products through sales of jams, chutneys, home-made garments, and other products at WI meetings and markets. These aims they held in common with the women of the Labour Party. The two organizations co-operated on campaigns to improve the quality of housing and to press their local authorities to take advantage of the inter-war housing legislation to build more and better houses. The WIs encouraged women to seek, as men were doing at the time, reduced hours of work and a wider range of leisure activities, encouraging sociability and activities such as drama and craft work and day trips. They also sought to provide country women with encouragement and training in using the vote and in campaigning for political changes of importance to them, such as improvement in the appalling state of rural housing, and access to piped water and electricity supplies—still absent from much of the countryside in the 1930s. The gradual spread of improvements in such essential facilities owed something to pressure from the WIs, though it is difficult to assess their precise input. It would be mistaken to over-rate the political or the cultural influence of the WIs, but they had an undeniable role in improving the living and working conditions of countrywomen and in increasing their sense of empowerment. They should not be overlooked within the large network of organizations seeking to encourage women to exert their civil rights.[65]

In 1932 the NUSEC established Townswomen's Guilds (TGs) as small town analogues of the WIs, in acknowledgment of the success of the WIs in providing a space for women previously excluded from the political culture. The TGs had an impressive 54,000 members by 1939.[66] A similar role of encouraging political awareness and political education among women, alongside other goals, was performed by women's trade unions, professional, confessional, and single-issue groups such as the National Union of Women Teachers, the Council of Women Civil Servants, the (Roman Catholic) St. Joan's

Social and Political Union, the Union of Jewish Women, the Women's Sanitary Improvement and Health Visitors' Union, the working-class Women's Co-operative Guild, and many others. At least 130 such organizations were active in the 1920s, almost certainly drawing into public life a larger number and a wider social range of women than ever before.[67] The impact of many of them is only beginning to be explored.[68]

For example, women challenged with a new vigor the established gender order in one of the key institutions of the English cultural hierarchy: the Church of England. The Church League for Women's Suffrage (CLWS) had been founded in 1909 as a democratic organization, including both men and women, initiated mostly by individuals with backgrounds in Christian Socialism. In 1919 it renamed itself the League of the Church Militant, protesting, convincingly, that the Church was "not half militant enough."[69] The League campaigned thereafter for greater representation of women within the Church and, particularly, for the ordination of women. The latter objective was not achieved until 1994. More immediately, in 1919, women were granted equal representation for the first time on the newly reorganized lay councils of the Church. The League carried on campaigning, especially among young women, for equal rights within the Church of England and on broader issues concerning women. Women were admitted more readily to the ministry of nonconformist religious institutions: by the Congregationalists in 1917 and by Baptists in 1926.[70]

The League was one of many organizations which both campaigned on single issues and also worked with others in support of causes in which the variety of women's associations felt a common interest, especially the campaign between 1918 and 1928 to equalize the franchise and the longer struggle against the marriage bar. In the 1930s women showed a distinct preference for membership in more specialized women's organizations over those whose rationale was gender equality. The membership of professional, confessional, and other organizations grew as that of the NUSEC (from 1932 the National Council for Equal Citizenship) declined. The number of societies affiliated to the NUSEC fell from 2,220 in 1920 to 48 in the later 1930s, while the membership of the TGs reached 54,000 in 1939.[71] This proliferation of women's organizations was not a splintering of the women's movement, rather it illustrates how women's organizations came to permeate public life in the decades after the vote was gained while continuing to co-operate on key issues.

In all three major political parties and in non-aligned organizations women worked hard to help women acquire the skills of political campaigning. This finding conflicts with assertions that since the political parties showed no strong inclination to support the issues on which many women felt strongly, women held aloof from the whole representative process.[72] It would indeed have been odd if women, having fought so hard for the vote on the grounds that it would benefit them, had immediately refused to use it on the grounds that it could not. Rather, many women argued that in a political system so dominated by political parties as the British, there was no alternative but to seek to influence the parties and to use the potential power of the vote to pressure them, fully aware of how difficult this would be. The argument that "the attainment of at least a measure of enfranchisement for women meant that legal and political rights ceased to be a dominating issue and were replaced by economic and cultural questions"[73] oversimplifies the perceptions of many new voters and of the leaders of women's associations. By the end of the 1920s many, including the leadership of the NUSEC, had come to realize, if they had not before, that a focus simply upon parliamentary lobbying and legislation by a small minority of women and their male supporters could not achieve gender equality—or at least, would not achieve it soon. Rather, there was a need for cultural change, drawing more women and men into awareness of the need for transformation, or at least modification, of gender roles and into awareness of their own power to effect change. This was the role of organizations such as the WIs and TGs. But at the same time it was not forgotten that much remained to be fought for that could only be achieved by legislative change: the divorce law and other aspects of family and property law, for one example. Making a reality of civil rights, putting them to use, remained as challenging as gaining them in the eyes of many women at the time.

But women found it difficult to reach positions of overt power from which they could promote these causes. We have seen (Table 1) how slowly they acquired access to parliamentary seats. When they were successful the House of Commons was inhospitable to women. Even Lady Astor was taken aback by the hostility she experienced.

TABLE 2
Women in Local Government

	1914	1923	1930	1937	% of total
County Councils	7	68	138	242	5
City & Boro' Councils	19	213	439	599	5
London Boroughs	22	116	289	253	15.8
Urban District Councils	11	104	308	225*	4.5
Rural District Councils	200	353		334*	4.6
Total	259	754	1174	1653	5.4
Board of Guardians	1536	2323	–	–	

SOURCE: Martin Pugh, *Women and the Women's Movement in Britain, 1918–1950* (Macmillan Pree Ltd., 1992), 57. By permission of Palgrave.
*Returns incomplete. If women had been represented in the same proportion as on bodies for which returns were made there would have been an additional 684, giving a total of 2346.

She later admitted: "If I'd known how much men would hate it, I would never have dared to do it." Local government, which was still of great importance especially concerning social policy questions in the inter-war years, was only slightly more receptive (see Table 2). There is, however, as the above account suggests, another level on which women's role in the political culture needs to be assessed: as members of interest groups lobbying, often successfully, for legislative change.

≺ V ≻

Women and Public Policy

The years immediately following 1918 saw a strikingly rapid flow of legislation for which women's associations had exerted organized pressure and which favorably affected women's lives. Millicent Garrett Fawcett judged that between 1902 and 1914 "only two really important Acts bearing especially upon the welfare and status of women had been passed—namely the Midwives Act, 1902, and the group of Acts dating from 1907 to 1914 dealing with the qualification of women as candidates in local elections";[74] but she stated that in the year following "the passing of the Reform Act of 1918 at least seven important measures effecting large improvements in the status of women have rapidly gone through all their stages in both Houses of Parliament."[75] Among these measures was the rapidly approved and largely unopposed legislation of November 1918, put into effect three weeks before the election, which enabled women to be elected to Parliament. Even suffragists were surprised that this came so soon and without a struggle, the more so because women were allowed to sit in Parliament before they could vote, at age 21.

Fawcett also included in her triumphal list the doubling, also in 1918, of the sum fathers could be obliged to pay toward the maintenance of an illegitimate child (from five shillings to ten shillings a week); and in the same year the Midwives Amending Act which improved midwife training, followed by measures to improve nurse training.[76] These improved both the professional status of women and the quality of care available to them. Curiously Fawcett did not include the Maternity and Child Welfare Act, 1918, which facilitated improvement in the care available to women—before, during, and after childbirth—and to their children. This was the outcome of campaigns by women, especially of the Women's Co-operative Guild (WCG), before and during the war. Further campaigning by women, at local government level especially, ensured the implementation of a measure which, like much social legislation, was permissive—that is, local authorities had discretion as to its implementation.[77] Improvement of the conditions of childbirth and childrearing were important preoccupations throughout the inter-war years, especially of organizations with a substantial working-class membership, such as WCG and the women's sections of the Labour Party. These included a desire to make birth control information easily available to women. Voluntary organizations opened birth control centers throughout the 1920s, but they were relatively few and scattered and generally required payment. Women and men campaigned that local authority health and welfare clinics should be enabled to give free advice. Governments were reluctant to take up an issue which was highly controversial in Britain, but in 1930 the Labour government granted permission for local authority centers to give advice to married women for whom pregnancy would be detrimental to health. This qualification was widely ignored and later modified. The response to this new dispensation was regionally variable and difficult to assess, but the decline of the national campaign gives substance to suggestions that many local medical officers and health visitors felt free to give birth control advice.[78]

Fawcett did include in her list of victories for women the Sex

Disqualification (Removal) Act, 1919, which in principle abolished disqualification by sex or marriage for entry to the professions and universities and the exercise of any public function (such as jury service or appointment to the magistracy). She regretted that this act was less comprehensive than the Women's Emancipation Bill put forward by the Labour Party, which had passed all stages in the House of Commons but was opposed by the government and rejected in the House of Lords, because, she believed, credibly enough, it included an equal franchise clause. In practice considerable obstacles remained in the path of women seeking to enter such professions as law and medicine or the higher levels of the civil service; they were the object of persistent campaigning by women through the 1920s, 1930s, and 1940s.[79] Nevertheless in 1920 two hundred women, including Fawcett herself, were appointed magistrates, presiding over the lowest but most active level of the judicial system. As well as admitting women to an influential area of public life, this change brought to an end the situation in which, throughout time, women involved in legal processes, such as those concerning marital or family matters or cases of physical or sexual assault, were facing courtrooms wholly composed of men. This was an experience against which organizations such as the NCW (founded in 1895) had long campaigned. There were 1,600 female magistrates in England and Wales by 1927, out of a total of 25,000.

Fawcett noted also improvements in the inheritance rights of women under Scottish law (which was distinct from that of England and Wales); and the Industrial Courts Act, 1919, which, due to an amendment put forward by the Labour Party, allowed women to sit in these newly established courts of arbitration on such matters as pay and conditions in the workplace. Fawcett also, with good reason, claimed as a victory the inclusion in the charter of the newly formed League of Nations of a clause enabling women to be eligible for all appointments in connection with the League. This inclusion followed a deputation from representatives of suffragists of the allied nations and the USA. Women indeed became active and effective within the League, especially on industrial and social questions. As Fawcett put it, by 1920, "The walls of our Jericho have not fallen at the first blast of our trumpet, but we have made great progress."[80]

The progress appeared to continue. In 1919 the NUSEC decided to focus upon a limited number of objectives at one time, for "we had learned that the field was so vast that success was jeopardised if we scattered our energies over the whole of it."[81] The NUSEC chose as its immediate objectives, equal pay for equal work; reform of the divorce law and laws dealing with prostitution and the establishment of "an equal moral standard"; pensions for civilian widows (they had been granted to war widows for the first time during the First World War); equal rights of guardianship of children; the opening of the legal profession to women. By 1926 there had been decisive movement on all of these, with the exception of equal pay.

The Deceased Brother's Widow's Marriage Act, 1921, enabled a woman to marry her deceased husband's brother, removing the oddity that this had previously been prohibited, while men had the right to marry a deceased wife's sister. This change was supported by the Women's Freedom League and the WNLF. It was a measure which promoted gender equality and also one of many of the period designed to stabilize family life, in this case by enabling a brother to support the family of a dead sibling.[82]

An important cause for a range of women's associations in the inter-war years was "the equal moral standard," essentially the protection of women and children against sexual and physical exploitation and abuse, within and outside marriage. Their campaigns contributed to the passing of the Criminal Law Amendment Act, 1922, which raised the age of consent in cases of indecent assault from thirteen to sixteen to match the age of consent for sexual intercourse; and it extended from six to nine months the period during which proceedings could be taken in cases of criminal assault. An anomaly remained that the age at which marriage was permissible (with parental consent) was still as low as twelve for females—though consummation was prohibited until age thirteen—and fourteen for males. This meant that a man could avoid conviction for unlawful intercourse by marrying the young woman concerned. In the 1920s about 24 girls each year were married before the age of sixteen, most of them pregnant. In 1929 the law was changed, raising the age at which marriage was permitted to sixteen for both sexes. This legal change owed much to the work of NUSEC, the St. Joan's Social and Political Union, and the YWCA.[83]

In 1922 the level of maintenance allowed to a woman and her children under a separation order was increased, giving further support to women needing to escape from intolerable marriages. Further legislation in 1925 extended the grounds on which either partner could obtain a separation to include cruelty and habitual drunkenness and abolished the requirement that the wife must leave the marital home before applying for a separation order. The NUSEC believed that separation, with adequate financial safeguards, was "the women's issue par excellence," because economic dependence upon men made women vulnerable to abuse. These legislative changes were supported by a diverse set of women's associations including the Catholic Women's Suffrage Society (CWSS, which shortly thereafter became the St. Joan's Social and Political Union), the Conservative Women's Reform Association, the Labour-supporting women's group of the Fabian Society, the Standing Joint Committee of Industrial Women's Organizations, and the WCG, the WFL, and the Union of Jewish Women.[84]

The Infanticide Act, 1922, removed another grievance highlighted by the women's organizations by eliminating the charge of murder for a woman guilty of killing her child where it was shown that she was suffering from the effects of her confinement. Also the long process of equalizing property rights went a step further in the Law of Property Act, 1922, which enabled a husband and wife equally to inherit each other's property and granted them equal rights to inherit the property of intestate children. The New English Law of Property, 1926, allowed both married and single women to hold and dispose of their property, real and personal, on the same terms as men. Further legislation in 1935 empowered a married woman to dispose by will of her property as though she were single; and, taking gender equality a logical step further, abolished the husband's liability for his wife's debts.

The Matrimonial Causes Act, 1923, relieved wives of the necessity to prove desertion, cruelty, or other faults in addition to adultery as grounds for divorce, thus bringing gender equality in the divorce courts closer. Divorce was a divisive issue, denominational associations affiliated to the NUSEC such as the CWSS being opposed to it. Nevertheless this was an instance in which the NUSEC was "unequivocally successful in the implementation of its policy,"[85] having played an important role in drafting and promoting the legislation. Further legislation in 1937 and 1950 extended the grounds for divorce. Women supported equal divorce legislation not only to enable women, and men, to escape from miserable marriages, but also in order to encourage higher expectations of, and behavior within, an institution which had encountered widespread criticism since the later nineteenth century. Similarly, the Bastardy Act, 1923, sought to promote stable family life and to remove a painful anomaly by enabling children to be recognized as legitimate on the subsequent marriage of their parents. It sought also to improve procedures to enable unmarried mothers to claim maintenance from the fathers of their children. The National Council for the Unmarried Mother and her Child had been founded in 1918 primarily to promote such changes, with the support of prominent women's organizations. Similarly the Adoption Act, 1926, which introduced the principle that a court must satisfy itself with the circumstances of an adoption, sought to protect adopted children who were often "illegitimate." The Intoxicating Liquors (Sales to Young Persons under 18) Act, 1923, was a further outcome of the campaign of many women's groups for the protection of young people.

In 1924 women acquired equal guardianship rights over infants following the breakup of a marriage. In the following year widows and orphans pensions were introduced. By 1933 pensions were granted to 725,000 women and 340,000 children, for the first time enabling these exceptionally poor people to escape from the Poor Law. This was an important campaigning issue for the NUSEC and other groups and was seen as the first step toward the objective of family allowances, granting unconditional payments to the poorest mothers. Family allowances, which had been Eleanor Rathbone's special cause, were introduced in 1945.[86]

Legislation was occasionally a cause of conflict. Legislation specifically protecting women in the workplace had long been a source of dissension. Some feminists argued that such legislation when applied only to women restricted their work opportunities; and that all workers, male and female, deserved protection from hazardous conditions. Others, especially female trade unionists, recognized the strict gender division of labor and believed that the working conditions of many women were so poor, and that women were so little supported by trade unions, that any legal protection was to be welcomed. Conflict broke out over the Factory Act of 1927 and led to the resignation of a number of members of the council of the NUSEC.[87]

Women's organizations played an active part in bringing about this succession of legislative changes. The NUSEC sent a questionnaire to all candidates in the general election of 1922, soliciting views on the issues it was committed to. These included equal franchise, equal pay and opportunities, equal guardianship of children, the equal moral standard, protection and maintenance of illegitimate children, the appointment of women police, admission of women to the House of Lords, improved separation and maintenance arrangements, admission of women to juries, widows pensions, the granting of full degree status to women at Cambridge University,[88] and proportional representation. Only on proportional representation was there no change by the later 1950s. The principle of equal pay was accepted in the public service in 1954, though not in the private sector until 1970. Women were admitted to the House of Lords as life peers when this new category was introduced in 1958, though not until 1963 were female holders of hereditary peerages admitted to membership of the House of Lords.

At the 1922 general election the WFL also distributed a questionnaire to candidates. This questionnaire gave priority to the franchise, admission of women to the House of Lords, gender equality in pay and opportunities, legal status and training, and relief for the unemployed (which NUSEC also supported).[89] Most women's organizations agreed on a cluster of objectives, though they differed in the salience given to individual items. They agreed on issues of welfare and income maintenance, mainly affecting poorer women and including housing, education, maternal and child health and welfare, widows pensions, family allowances and equal pay; on legal matters concerning property and taxation, which mainly concerned better off women; on wider access to employment, pay, and promotion for women at all levels; on issues around marriage and divorce and rights over children; and on the protection of women and children from sexual and physical abuse.

There was not the clear division historians once perceived between "old" "equal rights" feminists fighting for full gender equality and "new" "welfare" feminists concerned with more limited social improvements in women's lives. These goals could be held simultaneously and were complementary. For example, the active campaign by WCAs for the appointment of policewomen was as much a product of the fight for an equal moral standard as a product of the fight for wider employment opportunities for women. Victims of abuse were thought more likely to report their problems to policewomen than to men and in a range of situations, for example when confined to police cells, vulnerable women and children were thought to need the protection of other women. Policewomen had first been appointed during the First World War and local police authorities were reluctant to continue the practice after the war. In 1939, 43 out of 183 police authorities employed policewomen, but only 174 of them in a total force of 65,000.

Women's organizations lobbied skillfully for many of the legal changes of the inter-war years. It can be argued that one reason why there were fewer flamboyant demonstrations than before the war was that women's groups had become "political insiders rather than outsiders,"[90] seeking to achieve their goals by lobbying and negotiating in the corridors of power, successfully enough not to require resort to violence. Demonstrations, however, still occurred when it was judged necessary to make a public display of the united strength of women. The main focus of demonstrations in the 1920s was the extension of the franchise, though they occurred also on other issues, for example against the "marriage bar," which excluded women from many occupations on marriage.[91]

Fifty women's groups supported a demonstration in London in 1923 for the equal franchise. There were three major rallies on the issue in 1924 and public campaigning continued until the franchise law was changed in 1928, accompanied by some revival of talk about the need for a return to suffragette militancy.[92] In a great march to Hyde Park in 1926 3,500 women walked, many of them in professional groups (as teachers, journalists, and others) to emphasize the contribution women were making to society. The march included groups of women too young to vote, such as the Guild of Girl Citizens; representatives of American suffrage societies; female parliamentary candidates; mayors and magistrates; and veteran suffragettes wearing their prison badges. Millicent Fawcett and Annie Besant, both aged 79, Charlotte Despard, leader of the WFL, aged 83 and still politically active, and Emmeline Pankhurst, a mere 70 years old and by now a parliamentary candidate for the Conservative Party, walked the whole route; the pioneer aviator and member of the Women's Engineering Society Mrs. Elliott-Lynn flew her plane above the marchers in salute. On fifteen platforms in Hyde Park the array of women's causes was promoted. Visually, also, the march was striking. The *Woman Teacher* reported:

One after another, each with its distinctive colours, the contingents swept across the park; green, white and gold; blue and silver; green and rose; blue, white and silver; red, white and green; purple, green and white . . . in one section the members wore pink dresses with wreathes of green leaves, or green dresses trimmed with roses; in another section a group of "Under-Thirties" very appropriately wore bright green dresses, the colour symbolical of spring and hope.[93]

This procession, like many others, "was a reminder of the underlying unity of the extraordinary network which the women's movement had created in less than fifty years."[94] But it also showed how the movement had changed, in the very variety of different interests it expressed. Another occasion for a public demonstration of the extent of support for the women's cause was the funeral of Emmeline Pankhurst in London in June 1928. She lived until the equal franchise was assured of parliamentary success. Representatives of the range of women's associations attended the service and thousands of people lined the streets.

At least as impressive as the public demonstrations was the quieter work behind the scenes of Whitehall. The NUSEC in particular took on the role of developing the expertise which enabled it to achieve some of its own legislative goals and to help other groups to do so. It believed that it could "act for the whole women's movement as a kind of Corps of Royal Engineers, engineering its Bills on already prepared territory and continually exploring and pushing forward into fresh areas."[95] Its objectives were democratically decided at its annual conferences. NUSEC activists, such as Eva Hubback[96] and Chrystal Macmillan, gained expertise in drafting bills, which were introduced in Parliament by sympathetic supporters, usually male. These techniques were credited with securing in particular the 1925 Summary Jurisdiction (Separation and Maintenance) Act and the 1929 Age of Marriage Act.

The NUSEC worked jointly with the National Council of Women and the Consultative Committee of Women's Organizations (to which 49 organizations were affiliated)[97] and a range of other organizations (including the YWCA) to achieve these legal changes. The NUSEC was too realistic politically to expect to achieve its complete objectives, believing rather in gradualism and in securing the best achievable installment of reform. It recognized the inevitability of compromise. It was criticized by *Time and Tide* for placing too much faith in minor legislative changes and came to recognize the limitations of its approach, important though the outcomes had been for women. Larger changes, it was decided, such as major reform of the divorce law, or the achievement of equal pay, required involvement and pressure from women on a larger scale: hence the formation of TGs, designed to politicize a wider range of women. Different objectives indeed required different tactics.

Another important, and effective, level of political activity was that of pressuring local authorities to implement national legislation, as described above in connection with maternal and child-welfare legislation. Women in party and non-party organizations were active in pressing for, among other things, implementation of the succession of Housing Acts of the inter-war years and the improvement of education. It can be argued that women voters played an important role in placing social welfare centrally onto the national political agenda, especially in forms responsive to the needs of poorer women.[98]

≺ VI ≻

A Negative Achievement?

Consequently it has been argued that the impact of the new women voters was limited and ambiguous, that they did not achieve all of their ambitions since much of the legislation outlined above was the outcome of compromise, and such achievement as can be detected came about only with the support of political groups with differing motives from theirs.[99] Compromise, however, as the NUSEC and other women's associations recognized, is the nature of politics and they were realistic enough to recognize that they would not sweep all before them. Once more, it is important not to judge by impossible standards. The Labour Party was incomparably stronger in the 1920s than before 1914 and more securely established in the political system than were the women's organizations, but it also fell far short of achieving its full goals and indeed such achievement is rare in parliamentary democracies.

Because most of the legislation was the outcome of compromise it is difficult to assess the precise impact of women as voters, demonstrators, and political organizers or to answer the counterfactual question: would British politics between the wars, or later, have been different if women had not obtained the vote? Certainly there had been legislation before 1918 which favored women, and women as political activists had helped to bring about these and also other changes affecting men as well as women. But, as Millicent Garrett Fawcett pointed out, there was strikingly more such legislation after 1918 than before. It would be surprising if this flow of legislation was unconnected with the fact that women had, and used, the vote.

Some commentators minimize the impact of the women on the grounds that some of the changes they claimed as victories, such as the 1923 Intoxicating Liquors Act and the 1926 Legitimacy Act, are not perceived as "feminist," in the sense that they did not promote gender equality.[100] There is no reason why women as voters, even those who identify as feminists, should concern themselves only with the promotion of gender equality. Feminists in the 1920s did, however, give high priority to these issues. They regarded legislation which promoted the equal moral standard and civilized, non-violent, and non-exploitative relations between the sexes as protective of women and designed to civilize those men who required it, and hence as contributing to gender equality.

It has rightly been pointed out that women's associations came closer to achieving their goals in the sphere of personal life and social welfare than in that of the labor market and economic activity. Less convincingly, changes in family and welfare law are described, not as advancing the cause of women, but rather as serving to reinforce traditional gender roles, being concerned primarily with women in their maternal and domestic capacities, expressions of the reimposition of domesticity rather than of progressive advance.[101] This is too simple a view of the legislation and of the motivation for it. Firstly, the roles which it aimed to influence were by no means traditional. Reforms of the procedures for divorce, separation, and maintenance were designed to support rather than to undermine marriage as an institution; but they were expected to do so by demonstrating to men that the sexual double standard was crumbling, by creating sanctions against abuse of wives, and by enabling women to escape from oppressive and unhappy marriages and to enter more satisfactory partnerships or to live independently, if by no means always prosperously, as had not been possible before.

Measures for which women campaigned which improved conditions of child care and childbirth, housing conditions, and health care began dramatically to improve the appalling conditions in which many thousands of women and men lived their lives in the 1920s, as they had throughout history. Women's groups advocated these partly as being good in themselves. Many women had wanted the vote precisely because they believed that women's influence in politics would bring about improvements in social conditions which male politicians had allowed to fester for far too long. Prominent feminists, such as Vera Brittain, believed that women played an important role in bringing about the major extensions of state welfare which followed the Second World War. The relative importance of this role is difficult to estimate, but if women voters and campaigners helped to bring modern welfare states into being it was no small achievement. While not ambiguously beneficent, the modern British welfare state has done a great deal more for women and for men than simply reinforce gender roles.

But welfare improvements were not always seen by their supporters just as goods in themselves; they also could be seen as essential preconditions for the mass of women to play a larger part in the world outside the home; they were designed to liberate women from entrapment in domesticity, not to constrain them within it. It was believed that if women became physically fitter and less burdened with the care of decrepit housing they would have more time for and would be better able to engage in other pursuits. This view was propounded especially vigorously by the women of the Labour Party. An editorial in their journal *Labour Woman* in September 1922 asserted:

As soon as married women organize themselves strongly and make use of their political power in local and national elections, so soon will they be able to make such improvement in housing and the care of homes as will reduce their labour and give them more fruitful leisure . . . They must raise themselves out of the overwork and drudgery of their lives and insist on conditions which give them opportunities for
FREEDOM
HEALTH
REASONABLE LEISURE
and USEFUL PUBLIC SERVICE.

This view was shared by other women's organizations. It was not an appeal for further imprisonment in domesticity.

Welfare goals were not perceived by their female advocates in isolation from other goals nor in terms of domesticity being women's all-consuming role. Rather they took as their starting point the assumption that a very high proportion of women were likely to marry (and it was assumed that they *would* marry rather than that they *should*) and have children and that they should do so in conditions which ensured that domesticity did not control their lives and which allowed them choices as to how to spend their non-domestic time. Improvements in women's domestic lives were to be complemented by wider access to employment and training and to equal pay with men for work of equal worth once they were in paid employment. The aim was to give women a genuine choice between work in and work out of the home. Again, this was well expressed by the leader of the Labour Party women:

The right of a married woman to earn outside the home must be insisted upon; and equally her right not to be forced to work outside the home through economic necessity if she wants to make home and children her work. (In the past outside employment for married women has meant the burden of two full-time jobs instead of one.)[102]

It was an approach to social policy and labor market policy which saw these two areas as complementary rather than opposed, and which was designed to liberate rather than to constrain women. It gained wide agreement among women's associations in the 1920s and 1930s.

There is no doubt that alongside those who strove to ease the domestic roles of women in inter-war Britain were those who wished to lock women into lives dominated by domesticity and childbearing, at this as at other times. But as at other times it is important not to read prescriptive polemic, of which there was much, as transparent description of the lives of many women, or to assume that women were passive receptors of contemporary domestic imagery conveyed by the spreading new media of communications, such as women's magazines and films. The polemics were perhaps all the more strident precisely because many women were not embracing domesticity as their sole role. There was during the 1920s and 1930s an active contest between those who wanted to impose domesticity firmly upon women—all previous attempts having been less than wholly successful—and those who wished to enable women to control domesticity to serve their own interests.

The outcome of the contest in the inter-war years was mixed: the marriage bar spread and excluded many married women from paid employment, mainly in public service and professions and some industries. But increasing numbers of women, including married women, were recorded as being in paid employment in the 1930s, though not at the higher levels: they were concentrated especially in the expanding factory areas and in "white blouse" occupations. Demands for equal pay were less successful in the short run than welfare demands, but the campaign continued through the Second World War, was successful in the public service by 1954,[103] and was actively taken up by women in the trade unions from the early 1960s, leading to the equal pay legislation of 1970—which has had mixed but not wholly negative results. There is a danger of underestimating the continuity between the campaigns and aspirations of the inter-war years and the poorly researched post-Second World War situation. The environment of the inter-war years, of heavy, sustained unemployment and government non-intervention in the economy, was not favorable for any group seeking improved conditions in the labor market. The full-employment era from 1945 to the early 1970s was somewhat more hospitable to demands for certain types of change, though the outcome was limited.

Also in the 1930s many women were diverted from the issues which had preoccupied them in the 1920s by concern with the increasingly threatening world situation.[104] They could be forgiven for believing that Nazism was a greater threat at this time than sex discrimination.

Additionally, a higher proportion of women, and men, was married by the 1930s than before the First World War, and more of them had children, which might seem confirmation that a domestic ideology was triumphant. But family life was changing. The birthrate fell to an historically low level in the early 1930s, to an average of around two children per family, born earlier in the mother's life than had previously been normal. At the same time, life expectancy rose. A smaller proportion of a woman's life was encompassed by child-rearing and childbearing. This took place against the frequent and sometimes hysterical expressions of concern by public figures about the danger to the nation posed by the dwindling birthrate. Women were wholly unresponsive to such pressure to have more children, indeed were hostile to and suspicious of it when their opinions were surveyed. They made such comments as "They only want more cannon-fodder for the next war."[105]

For these women and their husbands, having fewer children was the key to improved living standards, to escaping from the poverty and misery of the large families they had known when they were young. They did not simply absorb official ideology. Official publications in the 1940s recognized that women were not to be so easily manipulated. The Royal Commission on Population was set up in 1943, in response to concern about the declining birthrate; its 1948 report, written when the birthrate was rising but not to previous levels, commented:

> It is clear that women today are not prepared to accept, as most women in Victorian times accepted, a married life of continuous preoccupation with housework and care of children and that the more independent status and wider interests of women today, which are part of the ideals of the community as a whole, are not compatible with repeated and excessive childbearing . . . Concern over the trend of population has led to attempts in some countries e.g. Germany and Italy in recent times to narrow the range of women's interests and to "bring women back into the home." Such a policy not only runs against the democratic conception of individual freedom, but in Great Britain it would be a rebuking of the tide. It ignores the repercussions which the fall in the size of the family itself has had on the place of women in modern society . . . The modern woman is not only more conscious of the need for outside interests but has more freedom to engage them; and it would be harmful all round, to the women, the family and the community, to attempt any restriction of the contribution women can make to the cultural and economic life of the nation. It is true that there is often a real conflict between motherhood and a whole-time "career." Part of this conflict is inherent in the biological function of women, but part of it is artificial . . . we therefore welcome the removal of the marriage bar in such employments as teaching and the civil service and we think that a deliberate effort should be made to devise adjustments that would render it easier for women to combine motherhood and the care of the home with outside activities.[106]

That such comments could appear, apparently unchallenged, in an official document suggests that there had been some shifts in gender roles and in influential perceptions of them since the end of the First World War.

⋖ VII ⋗

Conclusion

There is reason to question the assumption that a reasserted ideology of domesticity was successfully imposed upon women in the 1930s and again, after a brief respite, after the Second World War, with, among other results, conservative effects upon their place in the political culture. More generally this chapter has sought to examine what difference votes for women made to the first generations of women to cast votes, and to British politics; and to challenge the view that the change was insignificant. After 1918 women sought to assert their citizenship within the profoundly inhospitable political culture to which they had been reluctantly admitted. What is surprising is not that so few but that so many voted, agitated, campaigned, and made some indentations in the political order. Fully to assess the changes brought about by full democratization of the British franchise would require equally detailed study of the roles of women in politics in the second half of the twentieth century, a study which is urgently needed, but for which there is no space here.

Clearly there was no revolution in gender roles between 1918 and 1939, or 1945, or 2000. Equally clearly the roles of men and women were not the same in the 1990s as in the 1920s and the differences helped to shape the political culture and political decisions. There was change in the ways in which women lived their lives, which enabled successive generations to imagine a wider range of possibilities and a greater sense of their capacity to control their own lives. The feminists of the 1960s, after all, were the daughters of the first generation of women to grow up knowing that they could control the size of their families, that they had the vote on equal terms with men, and that they had effective equality before the law.

≺ 9 ≻

"Behind Every Great Party": Women and Conservatism in Twentieth-Century Britain

DAVID JARVIS

IN THE 1990S THE British Conservative Party faced one of the most serious crises in its history. Not only did it suffer, in May 1997, its worst electoral defeat since 1906, but also its membership dwindled to an unrepresentative, gerontocratic rump and few of the ideological certainties that had sustained the Party in power for eighteen years seemed secure any longer.[1] In fact the Party was embarking on a period of introspection, in which protagonists of both left and right would seek to draw lessons from its past history.[2] Although historians are more skeptical than are politicians of the didactic quality of the past, it is inevitable that future academic discussions of twentieth-century Conservatism will seek to trace the causes of the 1997 election defeat back to earlier, apparently more successful periods. This process promises much. So catastrophic is the current plight of the Party that the standard tropes of traditional Conservative historiography must surely be exposed to a more searching scrutiny than ever before. *Post hoc ergo propter hoc* explanations of Conservative success, that emphasize the Party's overriding appetite for power and the strength of its organization and leadership, can scarcely accommodate its changed circumstances unscathed. If this has the effect of catalyzing a greater scholarly engagement with the nature of Conservative ideology and recognition of the volatility of the Party's electoral constituency, these will be long overdue advances.[3]

As yet, however, one of the most interesting symptoms of Tory malaise—the decline of female support for the Party—has attracted little academic attention.[4] In the 1990s, and for almost the first time in the twentieth century, the dynamics of sexual psephology appeared to be operating to the Party's detriment. Although, as I will argue, both the scale and the permanence of the so-called "gender gap" in post-war British elections have all too often been exaggerated, Conservative electoral support among women had never appeared so precarious. Not only did the gender gap close; the Labour Party also had a very clear opinion poll lead among women under 40, a fact consistent with a trend of several years' opinion polling.[5] This shift coincided with an apparent hemorrhaging of female support away from the Conservative Party's voluntary membership, again particularly among young women. I believe that these developments are important, not just in their own right as a new chapter in the history of female political involvement in Britain, but because the Conservative Party's relationship with women is symptomatic of a broader existential crisis.

That the Party's predicament in relation to women has attracted so little attention should however come as no surprise to students of Conservative history. Despite considerable evidence of their electoral and organizational importance, women occupy an ambiguous position in the historiography of the Conservative Party. Precious little space is devoted to women in the semi-official Longman's series, *A History of the Conservative Party*, for example;[6] and most recent general studies of Conservatism have little or nothing to say about women.[7] To some extent, of course, this neglect simply reflects the preoccupation of Conservative historians with the parliamentary party and the world of "high politics."[8] The overwhelming masculinity of this world was scarcely offset by the elevation of Margaret Thatcher to the Conservative leadership in 1975. Party institutions normally adapted only to the extent of treating Thatcher as an honorary man, a response typified by the decision of the all-male Carlton Club to grant her honorary membership.[9]

Even where women's presence has been more prominent, in the extra-parliamentary party, historians have told us little substantive about their role. The sheer weight of institutional history that so bedevils Conservative historiography has ensured that the scale and operational dynamics of women's organizations within the Party have been examined in some detail.[10] Tributes to the crucial importance of the "Conservative woman" have also become a trope of journalistic writing about extra-parliamentary Conservatism. According to Rupert Morris, writing in the early 1990s, for example:

The Tory constituency worker is omnicompetent... She has the chutzpah of a door-to-door salesman, recruiting people to the cause and collecting their subscriptions. She must be numerate, because raising funds is the name of the game. She must be able to cook, because preparing food is one of the best ways of saving money, making money and providing an essential service to the community. She must be socially adept, a leader, motivator and comforter. And she must be resolute in a crisis.[11]

Similar tributes, whether born of affected political correctness or affected gallantry, appear parenthetically in most scholarly literature, but there has been very little effort to quantify or analyze the importance of women's activity within the Party.[12] Such tributes have merely become the academic equivalent of the ubiquitous votes of thanks "to the ladies" at constituency association meetings over the last hundred years.[13] This is doubly problematic. In the first place, it condemns estimates of female influence within the Party to the task of quantifying the unquantifiable. Precisely because fundraising, sandwich-making, and envelope-filling are "priceless," we are doomed never to evaluate their worth. Secondly, it comes dangerously close to colluding with a gendered definition of the "real" essence of politics, with women's contribution reduced to that of an ancillary service.[14] The cumulative effect is to attribute to women's politics a role that is simultaneously critical but marginal.

Political scientists, it is true, have on the whole been more willing than historians to acknowledge the importance of female Conservatism, if only in relation to the "gender gap" in British post-war elections. This apparent discrepancy between male and female voting patterns has been recognized since the 1950s and has acquired the status of a "given" in political studies textbooks.[15] Recent discussions of the gender gap have improved our understanding of its precise dimensions and generational dynamics.[16] Only rarely however have academics moved on from cataloguing this phenomenon to trying to explain it.[17]

It is therefore striking just how little serious effort has been spent on attempting to quantify women's influence upon the Conservative Party.[18] Not that historians have been averse to casual speculation. At various times women have been credited with "humanizing" the Party, making it more "sacerdotal" in tone and injecting it with a new sense of moral purpose.[19] At best such judgments are insufficiently critical of Tory women's self-assessment, at worst they amount to little more than essentialist projections of female character into the political process.

Significantly, the most systematic discussion of women's influence on the Party has come from outside academe, in the form of a study of *The Iron Ladies* by the feminist journalist Bea Campbell.[20] Campbell sought to explain not just why the well-documented scale of female Conservative membership had made so little impact on party policy, but also, in the revealing words of her book's subtitle, "why women vote Tory." Her explanation of the former, that "Conservative women's politics ... are a tactical calculation of the limits of challenge," has been broadly endorsed by other studies.[21] Her analysis of female support for the Party, on the other hand, while in many ways very stimulating, has proved rather more controversial. Broadly speaking, Campbell argued that women were attracted to the Conservatives by a combination of ideological affinity and cultural accommodation, in comparison with the Labour Party. The implications of the ideological stereotypes analyzed in *The Iron Ladies* will be discussed in detail later, but it is arguable that Campbell's roots in the Communist Party led her to present an excessively misogynistic picture of Labour popular culture, which understates the variety of experience described for example in Pamela Graves's *Labour Women*.[22] Whether or not this is true, the dichotomy set up in *Iron Ladies* between the respective receptivity of Conservative and of Labour organizational structures to women is surely overstated. Between the wars, for example, the increasing presence of women within the Conservative Party stimulated considerable resentment and hostility from their male colleagues.[23]

To date, therefore, the impact of women's involvement with the British Conservative Party remains unclear. This is an important deficiency in our understanding not just of Conservatism, but also of women's political activity in Britain more generally. It leaves an explanatory vacuum that is all too readily filled with formulaic paradigms of "false consciousness," "the power behind the throne," and cultural accommodation. Instead of relying on these illusory intellectual comforts, we need to re-assert the instrumentalism of female support for the Conservative Party and to recognize the latter's historic ability to construct political identities of considerable salience to its female audience. This can be done only by tracing the historic development of the Party's relationship with women, at the level both of practice and of ideology.

This chapter is divided into three sections. Section I examines the Conservative Party's relationship with its female electoral support since 1918. Much of this has become the stuff of legend. A reluctant and anxious convert to the cause of female enfranchisement, the Conservative Party appears to have benefited from an almost continual advantage among women voters ever since. Like all legends, however, this story has tended to get progressively taller in the telling. This inherent tendency to exaggeration has been reinforced by an unhealthy collusion between propagandists of right and left. The former, predictably, have sought to affirm the innate conservatism of women. More surprisingly, the latter have often fatalistically endorsed this, simultaneously identifying a scapegoat for Labour's electoral problems and legitimating a subtle form of socialist misogyny. Thus Perry Anderson, for example, claimed in 1965 that "if women had voted the same way as men, the Labour Party would have been continuously in power since 1945."[24] Whether or not such claims can be empirically substantiated, they are more revealing about the jaundiced perception of their audience enjoyed by political activists than they are about the nature of female Conservatism. I will argue instead that both the Party's perception of its female constituency and its support among women voters have been far from static. In fluctuating between hope and despair toward the "woman's vote," Conservatives thus unconsciously proved more willing than have most academics to acknowledge both the contingent nature of their female support and the consequent need periodically to reconstruct this peculiarly effective sociological alliance.

Section II examines an aspect of politics where the Conservative benefit from women appears to be less open to debate: the scale of female membership of the Party. This has always been seen as one of the great successes of "popular Toryism," with an apparently seamless transition from the Primrose League Dames, through the indefatigable women's associations of the inter-war period, to the oft-derided "blue rinse" backbone of the post-1945 voluntary party. The Party's junior offshoot, the Young Conservatives (YCs), also had a high female membership.[25] Again, the picture is more complex than it first appears. While it would be ludicrous to deny the importance of women's voluntary work for the Party, it is important to read ritualistic eulogies of the "indispensable ladies" as a coded language that sought to mediate a complex and frequently tense power relationship. In general terms, it seems that women's clout within the Party was strongest when they could credibly claim to represent a discrete sectional interest group, despite understandable official willingness to accord them such a status formally. But even this can only suggest a partial explanation of the fluidity of female Conservative support and influence. To move beyond this, it is necessary to reconcile quantitative data with an aspect of Conservatism with which women are rarely associated—the Party's ideology.

The third section traces the impact that female enfranchisement and subsequent political activity had on Conservative thinking, and in particular on the Party's models of freedom. I will argue that this impact has been far more significant than is generally acknowledged. At a critical formative time in the Party's development after the First World War, the simultaneous arrival of a mass Labour Party and of a female electorate ensured that Conservative anti-socialism was consciously and explicitly gendered. Both the negative critique of socialist freedom, which stressed the fine line between liberty and license, and the positive alternative offered, in the form of a welfarist "caring capitalism," were partly dictated by, as well as targeted at, the new female audience. The paradigm of "woman" thus came to provide critical reinforcement of key elements of Party doctrine. Because she was so constrained by her biology, she refuted *a priori* socialist claims about human nature; in her role as the center of the family she represented a bulwark against the over-mighty state; and as an arbiter of morals she stood firm against irreligion and sexual excess. But this centrality in Party thought was the product of a specific set of historical circumstances. Over time, the decreasing threat of class politics led Conservatives to be less sensitive to the distinctiveness of gender roles. The Party thus shied away from addressing the specific salience of economic freedom to women, preferring instead to subsume their identity in an undifferentiated constituency of consumers. This growing "gender-blindness" is, I believe, at the root of the Party's current plight, as it has failed to adapt to dramatic changes in the employment and family circumstances of British women.[26]

< I >

Filling the Gender Gap

In many ways the Conservative Party's success in appealing to women voters since 1918 seemed to typify the paradoxical historical relationship between "the Tories" and "the people."[27] The capacity to attract support from a constituency regarded with such ambivalence appears a paradigm of the Party's progressive adaptation to democracy. Thus both the 1918 Representation of the People Act and the subsequent Equal Franchise Act of 1928 have assumed the status of climactic chapters in the uniquely Whiggish Tory history of democratization. While it is indeed important to see Conservative attitudes to female suffrage in the context of their broader concerns about mass politics, both the Party's acceptance of its new audience and its success in appealing to that audience should not be exaggerated.

Although the Conservative Party's attitude to franchise enlargement was never unequivocally hostile, nineteenth-century electoral reforms had generated considerable Tory disquiet, even when the "leap in the dark" had been taken by their own side, as in 1867.[28] As well as standard fears about declining intellectual and moral standards where electoral contests were fought under conditions of democracy, Conservatives also had particular fears about political allegiances becoming determined by social class.[29] The most famously pessimistic advocate of this "vulgar Marxist" electoral sociology was the Party's leader in the 1880s and 1890s, Lord Salisbury.[30] Almost in spite of himself, however, Salisbury proved enormously successful at the polls, and the twenty years following the much-feared Third Reform Act of 1884 saw an almost unbroken period of Conservative dominance. So salutary a lesson in the common sense of the British working class was this held to be, that senior party officials often referred to it at the end of the First World War, when seeking to reassure their anxious charges in advance of another dramatic expansion of the franchise. In many cases, these reassurances carried all the greater conviction for being delivered by those who had served their political apprenticeship in the 1880s.[31]

The Edwardian period, however, proved extremely traumatic for the Conservatives, and it is no coincidence that it has recently been the subject of considerable historical interest.[32] Not only did their electoral dominance come to a shattering halt in 1906, but also the Chamberlainite tariff reform campaign precipitated a protracted and acrimonious civil war within the Party. The demagogic tone of the "Peers versus People" electoral campaign of 1910 also finally seemed to be bearing out earlier dire warnings about the class polarization of politics. By 1914, the Conservatives had lost three general elections in a row, and many of their number had begun to fear for the Party's future.

In such an anxious period, it was almost inevitable that the female suffrage issue to some extent compounded Conservative woes by opening up another area of division within the Party.[33] Despite the fact that parliamentary votes for women had long been on the political agenda, and despite the legendary success of the Primrose League Dames, the Conservatives had good reason to fear a female electorate. As is now well documented, the fears and expectations attached to the new voters, by politicians of all persuasions, were many and varied.[34] Certainly fears about the parochialism, ignorance, and political subservience to their menfolk of female voters were by no means confined to the Conservatives. Other concerns were more specific. One of these was feminism, or perhaps more generally the atmosphere of "sex-antagonism."[35] Just as Austen Chamberlain famously failed to understand why anyone living in a Birmingham slum would not be a "red revolutionary," so some Conservatives doubted that women could resist the attractions of feminism.[36] More worrying still, the price to be paid for resisting feminism might prove to be too high, if the traditionally narrow perceived range of female concerns came to dictate the new political agenda. For tariff reformers, in particular, this was a serious threat, because if women voted purely on cost-of-living issues they would be uniquely susceptible to the "dear loaf" arguments of Liberal free traders. It is therefore hardly surprising that the editor of the *Conservative Agents' Journal*, W. L. Joel, felt the need to stiffen the resolve of his colleagues in 1920:

We should divest our minds of prejudice and accept the fact that sooner or later the masculine element will be a minority on the Register and in the associations, and that no fictitious safeguards will prevent the women having their own way if they want it . . . We should show the courage of men, and not be terrified by the bogey of female domination. It is not that sort of woman who links up with our party.[37]

The prospect of "votes for women," however, also had a rather less predictable effect. For the first, but by no means the last, time, some Conservatives began to identify women as the panacea to the Party's electoral problems. One of women's great redeeming virtues, after all, was that their relative isolation from heavily unionized manufacturing industry made them less likely to vote on crude "class lines." Not only were they therefore supposedly more amenable to Conservative appeals in their own right; they were also potentially a means of influencing their husbands away from socialism.[38]

This idea that women voters would offset the dangerously class-based implications of manhood suffrage lent them a new, if controversial, status in Conservative thinking. Even if some resented the idea of women voters as a sort of "seventh cavalry," rescuing the Party from the horrors of manhood suffrage, only the most obdurately anti-feminist Conservatives saw their new female audience as an undifferentiated mass. Three critical distinctions were deemed to determine the approachability of women: social class, age, and marital status. Most conspicuously, working-class women were feared at least as much because of their class as because of their gender. Higher rates of paid employment among working-class women also presented problems, and it was no coincidence that the real Conservative fear in 1928 was less the "flapper vote" than that of the so-called "factory girl." This link with employment rendered older, and particularly married, women less threatening. The residue of these attitudes can clearly be seen within the Party's appeal to women voters in the inter-war years. One of the most striking features of this appeal is how little of it recognized female employment as a major issue. To draw on the fictional stereotypes examined in some of my earlier work, Mrs. Maggs tended to appeal to Betty the maid's common sense by projecting forward to her future life as a wife and mother rather than to her own career aspirations.[39]

It is therefore understandable that Conservatives continued to have their doubts about "the women," at least until 1931, although it is important to recognize that this was just as true of their attitude to the electorate as a whole.[40] In both 1923 and 1929 women were widely blamed within the Party for election defeats. In 1929, more than half the constituency associations canvassed by Central Office about the causes of defeat identified "the new women voters" as a major reason.[41] Conversely, many senior Party figures identified women as crucial "stabilizing factors" when the Party enjoyed convincing election victories in 1924 and 1931.[42] In the absence of reliable data, the precise extent of Conservative support among women voters between the wars is impossible to define. Analysis is further complicated by the fact that the female electorate between 1918 and 1928, a period that saw four of the six inter-war elections, was limited by age and property qualifications. Thus apparently dramatic findings, such as John Turner's evidence of the correlation between anti-Labour voting and seats with high concentrations of female electors in 1918, are complicated by the fact that the seats with most female voters also tended to be the most middle-class seats.[43] Nonetheless, the weight of statistical and anecdotal evidence suggests that the Party did enjoy a lead among women voters.[44]

After 1945, Conservative ambivalence toward women voters persisted. Many believed that they were responsible for returning Labour to power in 1945.[45] Even in the 1950s, their supposed political reliability was often attributed to their seduction by Anthony Eden's good looks.[46] Conservative women were scarcely more positive about their less enlightened sisters. As a Women's National Advisory Committee (WNAC) working party report in 1957 acknowledged: "It was recognised that women electors tended to be influenced through their emotions. This made them particularly vulnerable, at times of elections, to the scare tactics of Socialist propaganda."[47] Again, this suspicion of female voters was very much part of a more general collective uncertainty about the Party's electoral support. As Ewen Green has recently shown, even the increasing electoral majorities of the 1950s failed to reassure Central Office analysts, who became ever more obsessed with opinion poll findings.[48] In fact, with the possible exception of the late 1940s, Conservative expectations of women as a discrete electoral constituency diminished after the war, as growing evidence of "embourgoisement" gradually undermined fears of class-based politics. Increasingly, women's status was scarcely more distinctive than its identification as the ultimate consumer vote.

After 1945, the psephological findings become somewhat clearer, although even then they are by no means conclusive. At its peak in the early 1950s, the gender gap stretched to seventeen points, but it has never been static. As Ina Zweiniger-Bargielowska points out, "In 1945 and 1966 a majority of women supported Labour, [and] since

1970 differences in male and female voting behaviour have narrowed."[49] The difficulty of interpreting this data is borne out, though, by the 1983 election, which according to one source saw the gender gap remain strong (at eight points) and according to another saw it decline to insignificance.[50] There is more agreement, however, about the closing of the gap in 1987 and its subsequent re-emergence in 1992, stronger than at any election since 1979. According to Lucy Peake, "although the press reported that it was 'Essex man' who had given the Conservatives their election victory [in 1992], the votes of women made a substantial contribution to Tory success."[51] As ever, the devil is in the detail. Pippa Norris, for example, showed after the 1992 election that the gender gap was reversed by generation. In other words, younger women favored Labour and older women the Conservatives.[52] The 1997 election bore out these trends very eloquently. Interestingly, the kind of women who in the 1990s apparently deserted the Party in droves—young, employed, and single—sounded a distorted echo of Conservative fears in the late 1920s.

One major question remains, of course. Are we any nearer to understanding women's electoral support for the Conservative Party? To some extent, the refinement of our understanding of the "what" has improved our understanding of the "why." The evident volatility and the social and generational variables inherent in the gender gap should now lay finally to rest tired essentialist arguments about the "innate" or natural conservatism of women. Attention is therefore increasingly turning to the substance of the Party's appeal to women, which turns out at times to have had surprisingly feminist, or perhaps quasi-feminist, overtones. Some intriguing questions remain, however. Why, for example, did the Conservative lead among women decrease under the leadership of Margaret Thatcher? Simplistic arguments about Thatcher's conspicuous anti-feminism or her alleged reluctance to "make an issue" out of gender will not suffice. There is ample evidence, for example, that female members of the Party (and even of other parties) identified strongly with Thatcher, whose views on women were after all more enlightened than those of her predecessor, who famously instigated her Cabinet career when appointing his obligatory "token woman."[53] A broader question is the extent to which changes in patterns of family life and paid employment for women have had an impact upon the Party and its capacity to present a salient appeal to the female electorate. Further light may be thrown on these issues by relating the demographics of psephology to those of Party membership.

≺ II ≻
"Let's Hear it for the Ladies": Female Membership of the Conservative Party

Most accounts of popular Toryism attach considerable importance to the development of the Party's internal institutions in the last third of the nineteenth century, and with good reason.[54] Despite the ambivalence of the Party leadership to the National Union, the club movement, and the Primrose League, these agencies had achieved a level of integration in working-class communities by 1900 that opponents found easier to ridicule than to emulate. In the form of the League, in particular, the Conservatives had also already achieved a large and very public female membership. This has led many historians to stress the ease with which the Party was able to accommodate female enfranchisement after 1918. According to Martin Pugh, for example, "In view of their extensive traditional role as allied forces of the Party in bodies such as the Primrose League and the Tariff Reform League it is not surprising that Conservative women adapted to th[e] post-war system with little friction."[55] Yet again, the reality is more complex: both the underlying strength of the Party's position and the relevance of the tactics it had adopted to early twentieth-century politics are far from clear.[56] Nor is the Party's much-vaunted organizational strength in the 1920s and 1930s, or again in the 1950s and 1960s, quite as compelling as it first appears. Although there were undoubtedly more women politically active within the Conservative Party than in any of its rivals until very recently, the nature and social composition of this support suggests a less-than-complete success in terms of female recruitment.

That Conservative experience of working with women politically before 1918 sugared the impending pill of full female citizenship is beyond doubt. However, I have questioned the idea that this mobilization of women, particularly in the Primrose League, prepared the Party for the parliamentary enfranchisement of women. Both the social status of the League Dames, and the fact that they remained in the last resort a means of getting an all-male electorate to the polls, limited their relevance to the post-war world, and party activists were well aware of this shortcoming.[57]

This is not to deny the importance of the League Dames. Although total membership figures were never broken down by gender, such evidence that does exist confirms the perception of contemporary critics that women constituted a major force in the organization. The number of League Dames, for example, grew steadily, from 1,381 in 1885 to over 48,000 in 1890 and over 80,000 in 1910, by which time their numbers all but matched the number of Knights.[58] The League's first historian, Janet Robb, also concluded that women were "probably the greatest organisers of habitations [branches]," citing for example the case of Lady Mary Henniker, who was credited with founding nineteen habitations in Suffolk alone.[59] These women were of course by definition of considerable social standing, and although there is evidence that women also formed a high proportion of the ordinary "associate" membership, it is the elite women who have been the focus of historians' interest. It is undoubtedly the case, for example, that their effectiveness as canvassers, particularly in rural areas, stemmed from their capacity to extend the influence customarily available to them as aristocratic "visitors" in working-class homes.[60] This elision of political work with active support for voluntary associations remains a feature of female Party membership to this day.

What is difficult to assess is the extent to which such high levels of female participation affected the Party as a whole. In this sense the League is in many ways central to the "power behind the throne" explanatory model. According to Lovenduski, Norris, and Burness,

The kind of power that it [the League] afforded women was a behind-the-scenes power, an influence that was usable only if the asymmetric power relations between men and women were tacitly acknowledged and the influence used with discretion. The women, therefore, were obliged to negotiate different degrees of resistance to their participation, to deal with men who might be supportive or hostile to their participation, and to play the political game according to rules which men had made.[61]

Such analysis is more problematic than it first appears. It is not clear whether it is saying anything more than that power relations are always negotiated, and it comes close to attributing substance to a rhetorical construct of female influence that sat comfortably with masculine power structures. More pointed is Linda Walker's observation that the League "never evolved beyond the self-imposed boundaries of women's informal, indirect persuasion in politics. The notion that women gained and retained influence not by their talents but by their charms, that they had 'ten times more influence and three times as much tongue as any man' was precisely the sort of cant that feminists were trying to shrug off, not sustain."[62] In fact, such tributes to Tory women, with only a mild change of tone, were to form the staple of constituency functions for most of the following century as well. These constructs of female influence "behind the scenes," or as "subversive comrades," accord too comfortably with male tactical flattery to be taken at face value, and as yet the detailed archival work on the Dames and their political contacts sufficient to substantiate them simply does not exist.

In the aftermath of war and the 1918 Representation of the People Act, many Conservatives, and particularly local activists, expressed considerable nostalgia for the lost world of their political apprenticeship.[63] Yet although the legends of Victorian and Edwardian popular Conservatism grew ever longer in the telling, enthusiasm for this mystical past normally stopped short of endorsing the organizational structures of the past. This reticence reflected a normally unstated recognition that the Conservative extra-parliamentary edifice had been crumbling even before the challenges of a mass socialist party and the enfranchisement of women. Such realism, combined with the growth of cinema as a rival form of social entertainment, ensured that the League declined quite rapidly during the 1920s, thriving only in areas such as Oxford where it became the de facto local Conservative women's organization.[64]

Attempts to secure a greater representation of women at constituency level after 1918 therefore centered on the main Conservative associations, which rapidly began to create separate women's sections. In purely numerical terms, the record of these organizations appears one of enormous success.[65] By the mid-1920s, their growing reputation in relation to fund raising and canvassing had overcome traditionalist hostility in most constituencies, and by 1924 the Women's Unionist Association had over four thousand branches. Women's membership of the Party reached a peak of one million in 1928, and, although it subsequently fell to 940,000 by 1934, it remained comfortably higher than that of the Labour women's sections.[66]

Attitudes to women's associations varied considerably, however, not least because of the initially uncertain relationship between the new organizations and their Edwardian equivalents. Party agents and Central Office officials were anxious to dispel such confusion by stressing that the 1918 act represented a complete watershed and that associations needed to reform their institutions to take account of women's new status as voters.[67] Women's associations also had to meet many of the same accusations of sectionalism within the Party as the trade unionist Labour committees, and their supporters often felt obliged to reassure male colleagues of their benevolent intent and lack of feminism.[68] It is important not to underestimate either the continuing hostility within the Party to women workers or the growing concern about the wider implications of increased female political activism.[69] Many agents, for example, complained bitterly about the independence of women's associations under their control, and resignations over the issue were not unknown.[70] It is also worth underlining the unsurprising fact that women rarely achieved senior elected office within the full constituency association bodies.[71]

Contrary to the implication of the existing historiography of the inter-war Party, it is doubtful whether the assimilation of women within its organizational structures was sufficiently comprehensive to legitimate its propagandist self-description as the "real women's party."[72] While Conservative women's associations may have thrived in relation to their Labour and Liberal counterparts, they achieved only limited success in terms of making local executive committees more representative of their new electorate. Both the tone of the Party's in-house literature for women supporters and the extensive family links between the male and female branches of most associations suggest there is good reason to doubt the social inclusivity of female membership. The fact that Party meetings for women were often timed during the day indicates that domestic chores and child care were deemed significant constraints on female attendance. Conservative women were also often marginalized, patronized, and ignored, and the frequent eulogies of their political work-rate from male colleagues did little more than provide a veneer of civilization to a primarily exploitative relationship. There remains the suspicion, therefore, that female support for the Party, rather than representing an innate feminine Conservatism, was the product of a specific and finite set of historical circumstances, dependent in particular on the continuation of traditional patterns of employment and family life. The Party's election defeat in 1945, at a time when such norms were more than ever before under threat, therefore represented a very worrying augury.

After the war, little seems to have changed in terms of general attitudes to women in the Party. Publicly, Conservative women denied they faced any barriers within the Party. A section of a 1958 guide to Party organization subtitled "Where 'We Women' Come In" was unequivocal: "There is no restriction or limiting factor in the organisation of women within the Conservative Party. They are accorded honour and opportunity. It would be a tragedy if the women themselves failed to see the width of the horizon before them and to shoulder the responsibilities involved."[73] Privately, however, the continuing hollowness of male tributes to their female colleagues in the Party was leading to considerable alienation. A working party on the state of women's organizations in the mid-1950s put the point bluntly:

Women's sections provided almost all the "social" activity required by all the other sections of the Party organisation. In practice this really meant "food and drink." Whilst this responsibility was gladly accepted and discharged, the extent and obvious nature of work done in this way gave rise to the cry "women do all the work." This sentiment was very harmful. When used by the women themselves, it bred complacency and prejudice; when used by men or YCs, it implied the worst kind of flattery bestowed with a lively sense of securing favours to come in the shape of tea and sandwiches, coffee and even hot dogs![74]

Where women did not provide the tea, they were often consigned to another traditional role—that of providing the "glamour." This was certainly one of their major roles in the Party's youth organizations, the Junior Imperial League and later the YCs. The numerical predominance of women in the YCs was regularly exploited as a tactic to entice young men into the organization. Much YC publicity literature prominently featured photogenic young women, and the organization's beauty contests were given a high profile. Male readers of the YC newspaper *Right Way*, for example, were left in no doubt about the advantages of membership. Underneath a photograph of "Miss Leap Year," the caption read: "If you'd like to meet the nicest girls, why not join the Young Conservatives?"[75] This emphasis on the possibilities of meeting the other sex is confirmed by the memoirs of ex-YCs such as Julian Critchley, who summed up the organization as "two hundred thousand nubile girls in search of ten thousand politically ambitious young men."[76]

If female participation in the Conservative Party in the 1950s remained limited by traditional gender roles and continuing social exclusivity, at least the sheer scale of female membership bolstered institutional complacency.[77] By the mid-1960s, however, many women activists were becoming increasingly concerned at the decline in membership, particularly among younger women.[78] Over the next two decades, these fears grew, and also became increasingly focused on the apparent absence of professional women in the Party. Attempts to rectify the problem at a practical level by "targeting" professional women proved less than successful. The "Highflyers" Conferences organized by Emma Nicholson in the mid-1980s made explicit an intention to recruit more female filofax users,[79] but such efforts tended to be undermined by the Party's unwillingness to risk alienating its more "traditional" female support. By the early 1990s, as the work of Seyd and Whiteley illustrates, the demographics of female Conservative membership bore out the most pessimistic prognostications: the average age of constituency activists was 62, and it seems that, in particular, a whole generation of younger women was lacking from the Party.[80]

It is therefore clear that women's active membership of the Conservative Party has been no more static or "reliable" than their votes. That their practical contribution to the Party at constituency level has been enormous is beyond question. In addition to their industry and skill, particularly at raising money, their links with nonpolitical and often charitable local organizations have done much to integrate the Party into community life. In order to achieve a more rounded assessment of this work, future research must proceed in two complementary directions. Firstly, we need a firmer basis on which to make comparisons with women's work for other political parties. Secondly, we need to concentrate more on trying to *understand* the loyalty and support the Party was able to command from women throughout the twentieth century. To do the latter, it is necessary to analyze the salience of the Conservative message to its female audience during this period, and it is to that task that I now want to turn.

≺ III ≻

*Fear of Freedom? Gender and
Conservative Ideology since 1900*

Given that Conservative historians have been reluctant to acknowledge that Conservatism is an ideology at all, it is scarcely surprising that the impact of gender in shaping any such ideology has only recently been aired.[81] The standard tropes of Conservative belief—freedom of the individual, the virtues of enterprise and, increasingly, access to the free market—have been generally presumed to relate to a non-gendered subject. Just as women in the Conservative Party have done the work without much reward of power, so too it is assumed that they can be ideologically co-opted without making any discernible impact. This will not wash. I will argue instead that Conservative ideology has been very sensitive to, indeed was originally predicated upon, idealized gender roles, and that the salience or otherwise of this discourse to the female electorate has played a crucial role in determining the Party's success with that audience.

There is evidence that even before women attained the parliamentary vote, the Conservative Party was adapting as much ideologically as it was institutionally to the increased level of female participation in politics. Just as working-men's clubs increasingly lost ground to the more "family-centered" Primrose League, so too the libertarian Conservative defense of "masculine" popular culture gave way in the language of popular Toryism to a celebration of the values of "home and hearth."[82] Such a contrast should not be exaggerated, not least because of the predominance of the Irish issue in late Edwardian politics, and in Primrose League literature in particular. It is nonetheless a significant change of direction, particularly in terms of the Conservative Party's critical ideological shift in the early twentieth century from the rhetoric of anti-radicalism to that of anti-socialism. Above all, it reinforced the Party's increasing identification with negative models of political freedom. Conservatism offered the individual and his or her family the right to live free from the dangers of false liberty: free from imperial unrest, free from atheism and free love, free above all from that ultimate euphemism for the evils of modernity, socialism itself.

This emphasis on the dangers of false freedoms was a critical element of the Conservative response to the political challenge presented by "liberationist" ideologies. In many ways, the Party's fears about the potential attraction of feminism to women voters mirrored their fears about working-class voters' susceptibility to socialism. The urgent need for the Party therefore became to distinguish "real" from "imagined" freedoms, if necessary by stressing the danger attached to liberty. Thus the ultimate form of liberty would be license: the price of liberation, sexual exploitation and degradation. The sorry fate of Soviet women, detailed in graphic accounts of the "nationalization of women" and "Scenes from a Russian divorce court," underlined the moral in countless Central Office publications.[83]

Conservative women themselves were enthusiastic vehicles for this message. The Party's emphasis on threats to domestic order, and on the moral well-being of children in particular, was reputed to "go down well on the doorstop" and certainly implied a leading role for women in the fight against socialism.[84] Women were also being idealized in three other important ways. The first, which has perhaps not been stressed enough, was the idea that women, particularly as mothers, were uniquely aware of the constraints of biological determinism. Nothing better encapsulated the inescapable realities of "human nature" than biological destiny, and it was precisely these that a priori socialist "logic" sought to deny.[85] It was therefore no coincidence that one of Baldwin's most famous rhetorical assaults on equality was directed at mothers.[86] The second was women's role as compassionate nurturers, whose innate sympathy for ameliorative social reform would guide their party down the road of caring capitalism. Just as important as this quality, however, was their ability not to care too much.[87] Here another Tory demon was conjured up, and one that has recently come back to haunt them: the descent into sentimentalization, a weakness that women were deemed to be peculiarly prone to.

For the ideal woman to appreciate the dangers of excessive compassion, she would need her third virtue: common sense. This gift, partly genetic and partly the product of women's direct engagement in the harsh economic realities of domestic management, would enable women to distinguish "imagined" from "real" freedoms. This distinction presented the Party with both opportunities and problems. No liberty could be more certain or definite than the freedom to feed and clothe one's family, and the very simplicity of this message could be presented as a virtue in itself, conforming as it did with the idea of female common sense and practical judgment. The purse-string parochialism that was believed to constrain women's political judgment could thus be elevated to a philosophical insight. On the other hand, this was dangerous ground on which to fight. Consumer freedom implied the Party's capacity to provide an acceptable standard of living, which the revival of protectionist controversies threw into question. In the longer term, to define freedom in this way was to tie the Party to a domestic conception of womanhood that scarcely engaged with the world of paid female employment. As was noted earlier, this weakness is evident from the almost total failure of the Party's inter-war propaganda to address the concerns of "women workers." Equally, when Conservatives sought to explain the Party's apparent popularity among women voters, it was to women's domestic role that they invariably turned their attention. According to Walter Elliot, for example, writing in 1927:

The women's vote is, and must be, cast mainly as a consumers' vote. They are producers indeed, but . . . women produce life, and men produce property, and this is the reason of their respective bias, each stressing the value of the effort which they can realise. The introduction of the women's suffrage has without doubt done much to reinforce the bias towards the consumer. It is said that as consumers, and therefore interested above all in stability, the women's vote has gone largely into the Conservative scale.[88]

As several historians have recently demonstrated, Conservative revival after the shock of 1945 was extremely rapid. It also coincided with a particularly sustained propaganda assault on women voters, centering on a libertarian critique of socialist rationing and "austerity."[89] Once again the illusory freedom of Labour's ethical socialism was juxtaposed with a more tangible liberation—from shortages and queues. All of this chimed perfectly with "classic" Conservative ideology, which seeks to distinguish, in Ian Gilmour's phrase, between "certain, definite liberties" and an "abstract condition of liberty."[90] Yet although, as Ina Zweiniger-Bargielowska has recently emphasized, the Party briefly championed several important feminist claims for equal treatment in employment in the early 1950s,[91] the changing status of women in society as a whole was generating serious disquiet in the ranks. Much of this undoubtedly related to a wider Conservative unease about the moral consequences of affluence. The drive to achieve the better living standards for which the

Macmillan governments of the 1950s were so keen to take credit was leading more and more mothers to seek paid employment, a development that many Tories blamed for the growth of juvenile delinquency.[92]

The perceived need to redefine acceptable social aspirations for women therefore led to much soul-searching. As Joan Barnes noted in her 1960 pamphlet "A Woman's Place," not only were married women increasingly reluctant to "stay at home," but the dictates of the market determined that their labor was increasingly necessary for British industry.[93] Reconciling these trends with the idealized nuclear family that had become so important to modern Conservative ideology posed severe problems. From this point on, Conservative theorizing about the compatibility of economic liberalism with "traditional" gender roles and moral values became ever more anxious. In the past, the free market economic rhetoric that had periodically informed Conservative attacks on "socialist" planning, as in the late 1940s, had sat comfortably with a domestic discourse of femininity in which women were identified with the right to shop. But as women formed an ever greater proportion of the paid work force, the increasingly libertarian character of the Party's economic policy made it ever more difficult to define an ideal identity for women.

Indicative of this concern is the time spent by a 1961 Conservative women's discussion group addressing the issue of "married women at work." By this stage, Conservative women were evidently fully reconciled to the critical role played by married women in the national labor force and to the implications for family life of earlier marriage and higher life expectancy. When it came to the acceptable contour of work for married women, however, a sense of considerable anxiety intruded:

The group did not look with disfavour on married women working provided that it did not mean the weakening of home and family ties and responsiblities, and in this context we all agreed that married women with children under school age should not go out to work especially if it meant their children being placed in day nurseries or creches. To discourage this, it was thought that day nurseries should make the full economic charge for caring for children of married women except in exceptional circumstances. It was thought reasonable that mothers of school age [children] should in many cases go out to work and in these days of better housing, household gadgets and easier shopping, it was quite possible for women to work and still keep their homes nice. In home making the character of a woman counts much more than the time available.[94]

From the mid-1960s onward, such fears became increasingly overlaid with those of moral decay. Again, this was seen as an object lesson of a longstanding Conservative message—the danger of too much freedom, particularly for women.[95] It would be wrong, however, to exaggerate the uniformity of the Party's response to changing sexual mores, as social conservatism vied with a minority support for moral libertarianism—a tension that became ever more explicit in the 1980s.[96] For those on the New Right who saw no contradiction between the "free economy and the strong state," however, Margaret Thatcher's fusion of economic liberalism with moral authoritarianism was a heady ideological brew.[97] Even the most un-Thatcherite of her colleagues, Sir Ian Gilmour, endorsed her elevation of "the family" to the status of a guarantor of freedom. According to Gilmour, the family was as effective a protection against the over-mighty state as private property, since the only possible alternative, state-funded baby farms, would never be acceptable.[98] More orthodox Cabinet ministers, meanwhile, regularly identified the 1960s as the source of contemporary social evils.[99]

Yet neither this rhetorical onslaught, nor John Major's later, ill-fated, "Back to Basics" campaign, succeeded in addressing two growing problems for the Party. The first, and perhaps most obvious, was that if the Party became overly identified with an intransigent sexual Puritanism it risked alienating considerable electoral support. Even within the Party's existing membership, no consensus existed on contentious moral issues such as abortion.[100] In the wider public, the demographics of family life made the electoral risks increasingly apparent. The less obvious, but probably more intractable, problem was that to idealize a model of family life so increasingly at odds with the reality of female employment and child-care patterns was seemingly to deny women the economic freedom and incentives given priority by Thatcherite language.[101] Unsurprisingly, few Conservatives were prepared to acknowledge this issue with the frankness of Ian Crowther, who, writing in the *Salisbury Review*, admitted that "Conservative freedom is not about freeing women from the home."[102] Yet such views accorded with the majority of the voluntary party. As late as 1992, academics surveying the attitudes of Conservative Party members found that more than half of those questioned agreed with the statement "When it comes to raising a family, a woman's place is in the home."[103] Many Conservative women have become increasingly concerned about this. Revealingly, Teresa Gorman complained:

I'm not a mad feminist; I'm a politician, and we're wasting the opportunity to attract women's votes. Sometimes the Tory Party behaves as if women ought to be at home. This is absurd—80 per cent of women with children go to work. We can't insult our potential customers by telling them their lifestyle is wrong.[104]

Gorman's anxieties currently seem well-founded. Conservative policy in recent years in relation to tax relief, divorce reform, and single mothers has been conspicuous for the ambivalence it has demonstrated toward the phenomenon of "working mothers." It scarcely helps in this respect that so few female Conservative MPs survived the 1997 election cull. In the past, the Conservative Party could at least boast token advances on other parties: more recently it has appeared absurdly male-dominated in comparison with the "New Labour" ranks.

These problems of policy and personnel were further exacerbated by the Party's apparent ambivalence toward certain trends in popular culture that "focus group" research has identified as being popular among women voters. A particular focus of this alienation in more traditionalist circles is on the Blairite rhetoric of inclusive politics and, worse, of "niceness" and compassion. According to Maurice Cowling, for example, it was "not Socialism but the dismantling of 'virtue' and exposure of the emptiness which lurks not very far below its surface that is the problem of the 1990s and the Conservative Party which is the best equipped to deal with it."[105] Other Tory commentators extended this critique to attack an alleged public mood of fake sentimentality.[106] The defining moment for the Party here was the public response to the death of Princess Diana. William Hague's attempts to point up the exploitation of the mourning period merely underlined the Party's discomfort with the "Di phenomenon." The discomfort was not merely because of the implied affront to monarchical legitimism, but also because of the broader cultural imperative of public emotion. This was of course not the first time that the Conservative Party collectively had been out of step with the Zeitgeist.[107] Nonetheless, that both in her lifetime and in her death Diana was an icon for so many young women proved profoundly troubling for a party whose ideal woman eschews "sentiment" for "common sense."

It appears therefore that, since the early years of female enfranchisement, the dynamics of sexual politics had come full circle. For years it was the left that labored under the self-imposed handicap of gender-blindness. Many socialists of both sexes maintained that to acknowledge the possibility of distinct male and female political constituencies was to divert attention from the class struggle, and thus to confuse the realities of oppression. Conservatives meanwhile happily catered to a constructed female audience, content in the knowledge that to do so was to reaffirm the diversity of human experience and the fallacies of alleged socialist regimentation. But as Conservatives saw their worst fears dissolve, and as class conflict and socialism became less compelling threats, so the Party lost its incentive to address the implications of sexual difference. As it did so, the latent contradictions of its thinking became ever more difficult to reconcile with the changing social experiences of women. In particular, the Party had yet to adapt its ideology to the changing shape and purpose of family life. The archetypal nuclear family combined small-scale altruism with organized individualism in a way that made it a perfect building block for theories of Conservative sociology, and it is understandable that modern Party ideologists were reluctant to accept its passing.[108] For the Party now to reconstruct itself as a party of government, however, the implications of both its economic and its social policy for its potential female "customers" would have to be subjected to serious scrutiny.

≺ IV ≻

Conclusion

The centrality of gender to the fortunes of twentieth-century Conservatism has been consistently underestimated. This is due at least in part to a conflation of "women" as a gender construct in Party ideology with the identity and experiences of Conservative women in practice. For many years, the social make-up of the voluntary party encouraged this elision within the Conservative psyche of the fatalistic, supportive, and practical heroine of Party literature with the real social horizons of women. In thanking "the ladies" for their uncomplaining catering and money raising, Tory men were unconsciously acknowledging psychological reassurance as much as practical help. As long as the bazaars continued to thrive and the sandwiches continued to be provided, nagging doubts about predicating so much of the Party's socio-political analysis on timebound gender roles could easily be brushed aside.

Such complacency became impossible to sustain. So great was the loss of female support for the Party, both at the ballot boxes and in the village halls, that only the most intransigent essentialist could attribute its earlier strength to women's "innate" conservatism. Almost the opposite appeared to be the case. Precisely because the Conservative Party felt compelled in the early decades of the twentieth century to reposition itself electorally and ideologically in the face of female enfranchisement, it developed a gendered discourse of anti-socialism and social conservatism that directly reflected the prevailing orthodoxy of sexual roles. However classbound and idealized the stereotypes of female character upon which this thinking rested, "women" assumed a critical importance in Conservative ideology as moral guardians, pillars of fiscal rectitude, and practical imperialists. Out of fear was born status.

Much of this ideology focused on the exposure of false freedoms, not least the illusory promises of feminism. *Real* personal freedom consisted of a secure family life, free of excessive intervention by outside agencies and pressure to augment the demands of domestic management with paid work outside the home. *Real* economic freedom, insofar as it was pitched directly at women, related to the capacity to save, to acquire consumer goods, and to manage a reliable domestic budget. But these were essentially negative models of freedom, in which existing freedoms would be protected and strengthened from the threats of political and economic insecurity. As Conservatism simultaneously became increasingly identified with a more confident, free market-orientated discourse of opportunity and hostile to the alleged "political correctness" of sexual politics, it imperceptibly sought to rebuild its ideology around a universalized, non-gendered, model citizen. The consequent failure to address the different implications of economic freedom for men and women was surely a critical component of the crisis of late twentieth-century free market Conservatism so devastatingly set out by John Gray.[109]

Contrary to some of the more self-flagellating left-wing analyses of Tory populism so common in the 1980s, it is therefore now eminently plausible to maintain that Conservatism has not come to terms with feminism or with the major changes to women's lives in the last 30 or 40 years. History suggests, however, that the Party's opponents would do well to avoid complacency. An uncertain, fearful Conservative Party, such as that of the 1920s or 1950s, is liable to be more dangerous than the triumphalist beast of the years following 1975. Now that "Worcester woman"[110] is seen in Smith Square more as a threat than as a trusty ally, the Party may belatedly acknowledge the need to renegotiate this critical and much misunderstood social alliance.

REFERENCE MATTER

Abbreviations

BL	British Library
Bod.L	Bodleian Library, Oxford
CAJ	*Conservative Agents Journal*
CCO	Conservative Central Office
CPA	Conservative Party Archives
CW	*Collected Works of John Stuart Mill*, gen. ed., John M. Robson, 33 vols. (Toronto, 1962–91)
EHR	*English Historical Review*
ERO	Essex Record Office
EWJ	*English Woman's Journal*
EWR	*Englishwoman's Review*
HJ	*Historical Journal*
JBS	*Journal of British Studies*
JIH	*Journal of Interdisciplinary History*
LRO	Lancaster Record Office
MCL	Manchester Central Library
MET	*Manchester Examiner and Times*
MR	*Monthly Repository*
MT	Mill-Taylor Papers, London School of Economics and Political Science
ORO	Oxford Record Office
PPG	Parkes Papers, Girton College
PRO	Public Record Office, London
TLS	*Times Literary Supplement*
WCRO	Warwick County Record Office
WSJ	*Women's Suffrage Journal*

Notes

INTRODUCTION

This collection is the product of two collaborative conferences on women and politics held at the Center for the History of Freedom, Washington University in St. Louis, in October 1997 and September 1998. I am personally indebted to all the contributors for their cheerful collective creativity, their gracious acceptance of my assertions of prerogative from the chair, and their detailed critical comments on this introduction. For any remaining economies with the truth, I hope they will forgive me. In addition, I should like to thank our commentators Professor Martha Vicinus, Professor Susan Kingsley Kent, and Professor Jean Peterson for their many judicious interventions and our host Professor Richard Davis for his considerable organizational efforts. Further suggestions, corrections, and criticisms have come from Michael Braddick, Martin Francis, Joanna Innes, and Susan Thorne. I must also thank the Lancashire Record Office for permission to quote from manuscripts in their archives. For critical readings and sharing my burdens, I remain deeply indebted to John Styles. But it must be admitted any remaining mistakes are my very own.

1. M. B. Kramnick, "Introduction" to M. Wollstonecraft, *Vindication of the Rights of Woman* (Harmondsworth, 1982), 64.

2. J. Rendall, *Equal or Different: Women's Politics, 1800–1914* (Oxford, 1987), 1.

3. See G. Eley, "Rethinking the Political: Social History and Political Culture in Eighteenth- and Nineteenth-Century Britain," *Archiv für Sozialgeschichte* 21 (1981): 427–57.

4. J. Habermas, *The Structural Transformation of the Public Sphere: An Inquiry into a Category of Bourgeois Society* (Cambridge, MA, 1989), 25.

5. K. McClelland, "Masculinity and the Representative Artisan in England, 1850–1900," in M. Roper and J. Tosh, eds., *Manful Assertions: Masculinity in Britain Since 1800* (London, 1991), 83. See also A. Clark, "Gender, Class and the Constitution: Franchise Reform in England, 1832–1928," in J. Vernon, ed., *Re-Reading the Constitution: New Narratives in the Political History of England's Long Nineteenth Century* (Cambridge, 1996); and A. Clark, *The Struggle for the Breeches: Gender and the Making of the British Working Class* (Berkeley, 1995).

6. J. Lawrence, "Class and Gender and the Making of Urban Toryism, 1880–1914," *EHR* 108 (1993): 630–52.

7. See, for example, B. Pimlott, *Hugh Dalton* (London, 1985); H. C. G. Matthew, *Gladstone, 1809–1874* (Oxford, 1986).

8. For a lucid introduction to the literature, see C. Midgley, "Empire," in J. Purvis, ed., *British Women* (London, 1995). See for example A. Burton, *At the Heart of the Empire: Indians and the Colonial Encounter in late-Victorian Britain* (Berkeley, 1998). Women's role in diplomacy is a neglected subject, but see K. Hickman, *Daughters of Brittania* (London, 1999).

9. S. Mendelson and P. Crawford, eds., *Women in Early Modern England* (Oxford, 1998), 428.

10. Ibid., 430.

11. Chap. 4 below.

12. Mendelson and Crawford, eds., *Women in Early Modern England*, 49.

13. Yet even after Mary's accession to the throne, a queen's legal claim to the throne once married remained a problematic issue. See the excellent discussion of queens in Mendelson and Crawford, eds., *Women in Early Modern England*, 352–65.

14. *The Lawes and Resolutions of Women's Rights* (London, 1632), quoted in R. Thompson, *Women in Stuart England and America: A Comparative Study* (London, 1974), 222.

15. The traditional qualification for being a magistrate was the possession of £100 a year rental income from freehold land. There was no absolute legal prohibition against women becoming magistrates—Lady Margaret, Countess of Richmond, mother of Henry VII had acted as a J.P. A court ruling at the Inner Temple in 1503 held that married and single women could serve. However in the early sixteenth century, the duchess of Northumberland wanted to take over her husband's office as Justice of the Peace when he died. The magistrates in confusion took the matter to the high court of judges, asking can this woman actually hold this office? And the answer, after some consideration was predictably, no. See B. H. Putnam, *The Early Treatises on the Practice of the Justices of the Peace in the Fifteenth and Sixteenth Centuries* (Oxford, 1924). Moreover, I have never seen a single woman's name on the commission of the peace for Lancashire and Yorkshire in the eighteenth century. Another stickler for inheritance, Lady Anne Clifford, acted as high sheriff for Westmoreland, held courts baron, and appointed men to benefices in the late seventeenth century, but there are no recorded occurrences of such service in the eighteenth century. Another inherited privilege was the lordship of a manor which sometimes carried the right to make election returns. Anne Lawrence finds only two examples of women exercising this right in the sixteenth century, Dame Elizabeth Copley in 1553 at Galton in Surrey and Dame Dorothy Packington in Aylesbury in 1572. See A. Laurence, *Women in England, 1500–1760: A Social History* (London, 1994), 240. Women could serve on a semi-official jury of matrons in infanticide trials, but here they exercised power over other women, never over men.

16. All rate-paying occupiers (including women) were allowed to attend the meetings of the vestry, which typically met once a month, under the chairmanship of the vicar or rector, according to B. Keith Lucas, *The Unreformed Local Government System* (London, 1980), 77. In the Kings Bench case of Olive vs Ingram of 1739 it was ruled that women might hold the office of church sexton and vote for that office. Women's defenders argued "there is no reason to say that women are not qualified to be sextons, since they are qualified to pay scot and lot, and all poor rates, and to maintain a sexton." However in 1788 the court found that they could hold the office only because it was "only a private office of trust, to take care of the church etc. and therefore a woman may serve on it." See Mendelson and Crawford, eds., *Women in Early Modern England*, 57–58; and H. L. Smith, "Women as Sextons and Electors: King's Bench and Precedents for Women's Citizenship," in H. L. Smith, ed., *Women Writers and the Early Modern British Political Tradition* (Cambridge, 1998), 324–42. In Derbyshire women were nominated though disqualified from service as overseers of the poor during the last two decades of the seventeenth century, but one Mrs. Isabel Eyre was allowed to serve in that capacity in 1712. See J. C. Cox, *Three Centuries of Derbyshire Annals* (London, 1890), 1:112, 2:137–38.

17. Women's unsuitability for local office was asserted here in the context of constables, but doubtless it has a wider application; see J. R. Kent, *Villages Constables, 1580–1642: A Social and Administrative Study* (Oxford, 1986), 58. On the qualifications of a justice, according to the standard authority Reverend Richard Burn, *The Justice of the Peace and Parish officer* (1755), see N. Landau, *The Justices of the Peace 1679–1760* (Berkeley, 1984), 339. The model seventeenth-century justice was "a paternal ruler governing his community in the interest of God and sovereign" (333). The estimates come via a personal communication from Joanna Innes. The evidence about Yorkshire is a personal communication from Anne Fitzgerald.

18. L. Davidoff and C. Hall, *Family Fortunes: Men and Women of the English Middle Class, 1780–1850* (London, 1987), 137. National figures for office holding are lacking before the 1851 census, according to which only 865 women in England and Wales held office in parish or church government as compared with 26,235 men. See P. Corfield, *Power and the Professions in Britain 1700–1850* (London, 1994), 34. However it seems most unlikely that this represents a massive reduction in female office holding compared with the eighteenth century and earlier.

19. Crawford and Mendelson, eds., *Women in Early Modern England*, 396; R. Fieldhouse, "Parliamentary Representation in the Borough of Richmond," *Yorkshire Archaeological and Topographical Journal* 44 (1972): 208; Karl von den Steinen, "The Discovery of Women in Eighteenth-century Political Life," in B. Kanner, ed., *The Women of England from Anglo-Saxon Times to the Present* (Hamden, CT, 1979), 240–41. However, it is possible that the occasional female householder managed to vote when decisions were made by show of hands, as they were occasionally in the seventeenth century. In fact, in contested elections decided by group vote, defeated can-

didates tried to invalidate the opposition's win, by saying that women had swelled the numbers. (Personal communication Mark Kishlansky.)

20. E. Chalus, "Women in English Political Life 1754–1790" (Oxford D. Phil. thesis, 1997).

21. Quoted in J. Cannon, *Parliamentary Reform, 1640–1832* (Cambridge, 1973), 96.

22. F. O'Gorman, *The Long Eighteenth Century: British Political and Social History 1688–1832* (London, 1997), 368–69.

23. L. Colley, "The Female Political Elite in Unreformed Britain" (unpub. paper delivered to the Eighteenth-Century Seminar, Institute of Historical Research, June 25, 1993); E. Chalus, "That Epidemical Madness: Women and Electoral Politics in the late Eighteenth Century," in E. Chalus and H. Barker, eds., *Gender in Eighteenth Century England: Roles, Representations and Responsibilities* (Harlow, 1997), 151–78; J. Lewis, *Sacred to Female Patriotism: Gender, Class, and Politics in Late Georgian Britain* (in progress).

24. L. Stone and J. Fawtier Stone, *An Open Elite? England 1540–1880* (Oxford, 1984), 118–19.

25. J. Cannon, *Aristocratic Century: The Peerage in Eighteenth Century England* (Cambridge, 1987), 137.

26. B. Harris, "Women and Politics in Early Tudor England," *HJ* 33 (1990): 259–81; L. Levy Peck, *Court Patronage and Corruption in Early Stuart England* (London, 1990); F. Harris, *A Passion for Government: The Life of Sarah, Duchess of Marlborough* (Oxford, 1991).

27. Chap. 1 below.

28. Ibid.

29. See Crawford and Mendelson, eds., *Women in Early Modern England*, 379; F. Harris, "The Electioneering of Sarah Duchess of Marlborough," *Parliamentary History* 2 (1983): 71–92.

30. Chap. 2 below.

31. L. Colley, *Britons: Forging the Nation 1707–1837* (New Haven, CT, 1992), 244.

32. A. Foreman, "A Politician's Politician: Georgiana, Duchess of Devonshire and the Whig Party," in Barker and Chalus, eds., *Gender*, 185.

33. Ibid.

34. The duchess of Portland urged "There are a great many votes that you can command and NO ONE else and now if you only stop at people's doors it will be quite sufficient, and really your presence is quite expected." Quoted in J. S. Lewis, "Political Behaviour of Elite Women in England 1774–1832," *Proceedings of the Consortium on Evolutionary Europe* 13 (1983): 248–49.

35. Chap. 2 below.

36. Ibid.

37. See "The Beaux Disaster" (1749).

38. Foreman, "A Politician's Politician," 187.

39. Foreman, *Georgiana*, 159.

40. J. Vernon, *Politics and the People: A Study in English Political Cul-*

ture, c. 1815–1867 (Cambridge, 1993), 39; C. Hall, "Private Persons versus Public Someones: Class, Gender and Politics in England 1780–1850," in her *White, Male and Middle Class* (London, 1992), 151–71.

41. Quoted in Cannon, *Parliamentary Reform*, 32. Jeremy Bentham advocated the secret ballot and the vote for women, criminals, lunatics, and bankrupts in 1818, though he drew the line at female MPs.

42. J. Styles, "Embezzlement, Industry and the Law in England, 1500–1800," in M. Berg, P. Hudson, and M. Sonenscher, eds., *Manufacture in Town and Country Before the Factory* (Cambridge, 1983), 192 and 195.

43. D. Beales, *From Castlereagh to Gladstone 1815–1885* (London, 1969), 110–17; O'Gorman, The *Long Eighteenth Century: British Political and Social History 1688–1831*, 368–71. Although O'Gorman believes the continuity case can be stretched too far: "The supremacy of the Landed interest, the operation of electoral influence and property all survived 1832. Yet the struggle for the Reform Act had been a politicizing experience . . . The reform door had been opened and, it would never again be in the power of politicians to close it" (371).

44. K. D. Reynolds, *Aristocratic Women and Political Society in Victorian Britain* (Oxford, 1998), 1–2, invoking J. Parry, *The Rise and Fall of Liberal Government in Victorian Britain* (New Haven, CT, 1993); and R. Price, "Historiography, Narrative and the Nineteenth Century," *JBS* 35 (Apr. 1996): 220–56.

45. Reynolds, *Aristocratic Women*, 2. She states that hers is emphatically not "a study of adaptation to change, but a study of women living in accordance with a set of precepts and understandings of their world, which would have been familiar, in broad outline at least, to aristocratic women for many centuries."

46. Ibid., 150–52.

47. Ibid., 220–21.

48. Ibid., 4.

49. P. Jupp, ed., "The Letter-Journal of George Canning, 1793–1795," *Camden Fourth Series* 41 (1991): 118 and 283–84.

50. Chalus, "Women and Electoral Politics," 153.

51. Chap. 4 below.

52. Foreman, *Georgiana*, 17; A. Vickery, *The Gentleman's Daughter: Women's Lives in Georgian England* (London, 1998), 20 and 137.

53. S. Drescher, *Capitalism and Antislavery: British Mobilisation in Comparative Perspective* (Basingstoke, 1986), 222; S. Richardson, "The Role of Women in Electoral Politics in Yorkshire During the 1830s," *Northern History* 32 (1996): 133–51. Exciting new research on the engagement of less privileged women in Victorian elections was reported by M. Cragoe, "Women in General Elections, 1832–1868," in K. Gleadle and S. Richardson, eds., *Women in British Politics, 1780–1860: The Power of the Petticoat* (Basingstoke, 2000). Cragoe found that the wives of electors were as actively canvassed as their husbands. There is nothing comparable for the earlier period.

54. Mendelson and Crawford, eds., *Women in Early Modern England*, 353.

55. J. Brewer, *Party, Ideology and Popular Politics at the Accession of George III* (Cambridge, 1976), 35.

56. K. Wilson, *The Sense of the People: Politics, Culture and Imperialism in England, 1715–1785* (Cambridge, 1995), 9 and 12.

57. L. Colley, "An Icon of Fashion," *TLS*, May 29, 1998.

58. P. Macdowell, *The Women of Grub Street: Press, Politics and Gender in the Literary Market Place, 1678–1730* (Oxford, 1998).

59. One example must suffice here. In the 1760s and 1770s, Elizabeth Shackleton, the wife of an east Lancashire woollen merchant, received "a Dish of Politicks every Post-Day" in the form of London newspapers. By this means, Mrs. Shackleton kept up with the business of Parliament, receiving Saturday's news by Tuesday morning. Mrs. Shackleton copied into her diary the contents of pamphlets on subjects such as the utility of labor-saving machinery or the qualifications of prospective local MPs and declared the pleasure she derived from evenings spent discoursing upon literature, history, and politics. She may not have gleaned her gossip from a coffee house, but she was certainly an attentive and discriminating member of that general public addressed by both the *Leeds Intelligencer* and the *St James' Chronicle*. For Mrs. Shackleton's political reading, see LRO, DDB/81/37 (1780), fols. 127–29. Her taste in print journalism can be deduced from occasional remarks in her correspondence and letter books. From at least 1764, she read the *London Chronicle*, but in 1766 she recommended the *Whitehall* over the *Chronicle* "as a political or rather a party Paper." After 1768, she took the *St James Chronicle* or the *British Evening Post* on a regular basis. (See LRO, DDB/72/213 and 193 [1766–1768], W. Ramsden, Charterhouse to E. Shackleton, Alkincoats). From 1772, she also took a Leeds paper although she did not specify whether it was the *Leeds Intelligencer* or the *Leeds Mercury*. However, it was the Whig *Leeds Mercury* which carried comment on her Rabies medicine.

60. LRO, DDB/81/11 (1770), fol. 48.

61. E. Kimber, *The Life and Adventures of Joe Thompson: A Narrative Founded on Fact* (Dublin, 1750), 2:7. For further discussion, see P. Borsay, *The English Urban Renaissance: Culture and Society in the Provincial Town, 1660–1770* (Oxford, 1989), 133–37; R. J. Morris, "Clubs, Societies and Associations," in F. M. L. Thompson, ed., *The Cambridge Social History of Britain, 1750–1950* (Cambridge, 1990); J. Money, *Experience and Identity: Birmingham and the West Midlands, 1760–1800* (Manchester, 1977), 98–152.

62. Wilson, *Sense of the People*, 72.

63. *The Times*, Oct. 29, 1788, quoted in D. Andrew, "London Debating Societies, 1776–1799," *London Record Society* 30 (1993): xi. On public rooms, see x. On the suppression of political debate, see D. Andrew, "Popular Culture and Public Debate: London 1780," *HJ* 39 (1996): 421, but see generally 405–23. Andrew finds that the societies of the 1770s concentrated on political and theological questions, with just a few topics of wider cultural concern. Morals, emotions, and matrimony became more popular

as debating topics later in the century, but the interest in religion and the state persisted.

64. Beverley Lemire notes that the wife of a middling Manchester family attended a conversation club in the 1770s: see id., *Fashion's Favorite: The Cotton Trade and the Consumer in Britain, 1660–1800* (Oxford, 1991), 110. Catherine Hall finds evidence of women's participation in debating societies in the Midlands, but sees this as a fleeting phenomenon: C. Hall, "The Early Formation of Victorian Domestic Ideology," in id., *White, Male And Middle Class: Explorations in Feminism and History* (Cambridge, 1992). In Bristol, ladies were known to prefer morning to evening lectures. In Bath, there was a house by the pump room where the ladies could read the news and enjoy "each other's conversation," a "female coffee-house" where they could withdraw after general assemblies, plus lectures on arts and sciences laid on to amuse the "People of Fashion": see O. Goldsmith, *The Life of Richard Nash Esq.* (London, 1762), 43, 45, and 46. Smollett's Lydia Melford said the young were not admitted to the ladies' coffee house at Bath, "inasmuch as the conversation turns on politics, scandal, philosophy, and other subjects above our capacity; but we are allowed to accompany them to booksellers shops, which are charming places of resort; where we read novels, plays, pamphlets and news-papers, for so small a subscription as a crown a quarter": T. Smollett, *The Expedition of Humphry Clinker* (1771; Oxford, 1984), 40.

65. For these and other examples, see Wilson, *Sense of the People*, 49–51.

66. Foreman, *Georgiana*, 93.

67. See M. B. Norton, *Liberty's Daughters: The Revolutionary Experience of American Women, 1750–1800* (Toronto, 1980), 157–63; Foreman, *Georgiana*, 149; C. Midgley, "Women Anti-Slavery Campaigners in Britain" (Ph.D. thesis, Univ. of Kent, 1989), chap. 2.

68. E. P. Thompson, "The Moral Economy of the English Crowd in the Eighteenth Century, *Past and Present* 50 (1971). However the extent of female involvement has been debated by J. Bohstead, "Gender, Household and Community Politics: Women in English Riots 1790–1810," *Past and Present* 120 (1988): 88, 91, arguing that between 1790 and 1810 women participated in less than half of the 156 documented riots, dominating only 22 percent. However, this too has been questioned.

69. On crowds, gender, and public space, see N. Rogers, *Crowds, Culture and Politics in Georgian Britain* (Oxford, 1998), 215–47.

70. Colley, *Britons*, 237–82.

71. For Anna Clark, however, the story is one of female loss, when radical men abandoned equality as an ideal and seized on domesticity instead in the 1830s. By pushing the claims of the respectable male breadwinner, radical men hoped to gain more money for their families, more power over their womenfolk, and more esteem in the eyes of those who argued them unfit for the vote: See A. Clark, *Struggle For the Breeches*. For other views, see the review by Jon Lawrence in *Victorian Studies*, 1996, 144–46; S. Alexander, "Women, Class and Sexual Difference in the 1830s and 1840s," *History*

Workshop Journal 18 (1984); D. Thompson, "Women and Radical Politics: a Lost Dimension," in J. Mitchell and A. Oakely, eds., *The Rights and Wrongs of Women* (London, 1976); B. Taylor, *Eve and the New Jerusalem: Socialism and Feminism in the Nineteenth Century* (London, 1983); J. Fulcher, "Gender, Politics and Class in the Early Nineteenth-Century English Reform Movement," *Historical Research* 67 (1994): 58–74.

72. Mendelson and Crawford, eds., *Women in Early Modern England*, 387.

73. D. Andrew, "Female Charity in an Age of Sentiment," in J. Brewer and S. Staves, eds., *Early Modern Conceptions of Property* (London, 1995), 275–300; D. Andrew, *Philanthropy and Police: London Charity in the Eighteenth Century* (Princeton, NJ, 1989).

74. North Yorkshire Record Office, ZBA 25/1. In York, a Mrs. Faith Gray and a Mrs. Catherine Cappe were instrumental in the establishment and superintendence of a Spinning School (1782), a Grey Coat School for Girls (1785), and a Female Friendly Society (1788); see E. Gray, *The Papers and Diaries of a York Family, 1764–1839* (London, 1927), 54, 60, and 67. The Carlisle Female Visiting Society was set up in 1803; members engaged to search out the abodes of the wretched and supply their inhabitants with comforts. An Infant Clothing Society was set up in the same town in 1811. Similarly, Workington had an Infant Clothing Society (1811), A Blanket Society (1819), and a Dorcas Society (1818), which distributed 600 garments a year "mostly wrought by the fair hands of the contributors to this excellent charity." See W. Parson and White, *History and Directory of the Counties of Cumberland and Westmoreland* (1829), 308–9. In Hawkshead, a Female Union Society was instituted in 1798: LRO, DP 384/8 Rule Book of Female Union Society. Whalley boasted a Sisterly Love Society active from at least 1818: LRO, DDX 680/2/3. A Female Sociable Society was active in Wadsworth from at least 1810: West Yorkshire County Record Office, Bradford, Tong Ms 6/6, Membership Certificate. A society was active in Leeds from at least 1801: West Yorkshire County Record Office, Leeds, Leeds Female Benefit Society, 6; and in Wakefield from 1805: West Yorkshire County Record Office, Wakefield, C 281/7/10, Rules of the Wakefield Female Benefit Society. Chester had a lying in charity founded in 1798: Chester City Record Office, DNA/1 Minutes of the Chester Benevolent Institution. Liverpool boasted a Ladies Charity for the Relief of Poor Women in Childbed (1796), The Female School of Industry (1818), The Friends' Female Charity School (1818), and The Ladies Branch of the Liverpool Auxiliary Society (1818). This was doubtless a wide-ranging movement. Certainly there were similar socities set up in Edinburgh and Glasgow in the 1790s. See chap. 3 below.

75. M. Hunt, *The Middling Sort: Commerce, Gender and the Family in England, 1680–1780* (Berkeley, 1996), 111.

76. In 1820, the 62-year-old Londoner Mrs. Anna Larpent was an officer and regular attendant at her local female friendly society which was held in the parish vestry, was involved in the administration of a local school, operated a soup kitchen for poor children, did some work-house and parish visit-

ing, and sewed simple items for "Mrs Porter's charity repository." While Mrs. Larpent had always been a devout, observant Christian, comparing the diaries she wrote in 1790, 1800, 1810 and 1820 indicates how many more formal "opportunities" she had "of being useful" in her last years. See Huntington Library, H.M., 31201, Anna Larpent's Diary, vol. 11, 1820–1821, fol. 2, facing fol. 4, facing fol. 7, facing fol. 13, fol. 45, facing fol. 51, fol. 71 and fol. 130.

77. F. K. Prochaska, "Philanthropy," in F. M. L. Thompson, ed., *The Cambridge Social History of Britain, 1750–1950* 3 (Cambridge, 1990): 386.

78. Chap. 4 below.

79. Ibid.

80. S. Drescher, *Capitalism and Antislavery: British Mobilization in Comparative Perspective* (Basingstoke, 1986), 85.

81. C. Midgeley, *Women Against Slavery: The British Campaigns, 1780–1870* (London, 1992), 155.

82. See especially A. Burton, *Burdens of History: British Feminists, Indian Women and Imperial Culture, 1865–1915* (Charlotte, NC, 1995); S. Thorne, *Congregational Missions and the Making of an Imperial Culture in Nineteenth Century England* (Stanford, 1999), chapter 4; S. S. Maughan, "Regions Beyond and the National Church: Domestic Support for the Foreign Missions of the Church of England in the High Imperial Age" (Ph.D. diss., Harvard, 1995); C. Hall, "Missionary Stories: Gender and Ethnicity in England in the 1830s and 1840s," in Lawrence Grossberg, Cary Nelson, and Paula Treichler, eds., *Cultural Studies* (New York, 1992), 240–70; and A. Twells, "'So Distant and Wild a Scene': Language, Domesticity, and Difference in Hannah Kilham's Writings from West Africa, 1822–1832," *Women's History Review* 4, 3 (1995): 301–18; C. Lloyd-Morgan, "From Temperance to Suffrage?," in A. V. John, ed., *Our Mother's Land: Chapters in Welsh Women's History, 1830–1939* (Cardiff, 1991), 135–58.

83. B. Caine, *English Feminism, 1780–1980* (Oxford, 1997), 53.

84. Chap. 3 below.

85. Ibid.

86. Ibid.

87. K. Gleadle, *The Early Feminists: Radical Unitarians and the Emergence of the Women's Rights Movement, 1831–51* (London, 1995).

88. See J. Rendall, "A Moral Engine? Feminism, Liberalism and the English Woman's Journal," in Rendall, ed., *Equal or Different*, 112–38.

89. S. Richardson, "Well-Neighboured Houses: The Political Networks of Elite Women," in Gleadle and Richardson, eds., *Women in British Politics*.

90. M. Finn, *After Chartism: Class and Nation in English Radical Politics, 1848–1874* (Cambridge, 1993), 160. See also M. O'Connor, *The Romance of Italy and the English Political Imagination* (New York, 1998).

91. In addition to their important collection, *Women in British Politics, 1780–1860*, Gleadle and Richardson have embarked on a collective research project on "Middle-Class Women and Politics in the Nineteenth Century" which promises to reshape our understanding of the political.

92. J. Rendall, "Citizenship, Culture and Civilization: The Languages of British Suffragists 1866–74," in C. Daley and M. Nolan, eds., *Suffrage and Beyond: International Feminist Perspectives* (Auckland, NZ, 1994), 127–50.

93. Chap. 5 below.

94. Ibid.

95. There is of course a wide literature on the campaigns of the Victorian women's movement: for a selection, see S. Kingsley Kent, *Sex and Suffrage in Britain, 1860–1914* (Princeton, NJ, 1987); P. Levine, *Feminist Lives in Victorian England: Private Roles and Public Commitment* (Oxford, 1990); O. Banks, *Faces of Feminism: A Study of Feminism as a Social Movement* (Oxford, 1981); C. Dyhouse, *Feminism and the Family in England, 1880–1939* (Oxford, 1987).

96. Chap. 5 below.

97. P. Hollis, "Women in Council: Separate Spheres, Public Space," in Rendall, ed., *Equal or Different*, 192–213. For a fuller discussion see Hollis's magisterial *Women in Public: The English Women's Movement, 1850–1900* (London, 1979).

98. Although the leadership and male membership of the Socialist Democratic Federation were still ambivalent and often contradictory in their attitudes to socialist women. See K. Hunt, *Equivocal Feminists* (Cambridge, 1996).

99. L. Walker, "Party Political Women: A Comparative Study of Liberal Women and the Primrose League, 1890–1914," in Rendall, ed., *Equal or Different*, 165–91; but see esp. 172–73.

100. M. Pugh, *State and Society: British Political & Social History 1870–1992* (London, 1994), 61.

101. S. Stanley Holton, "The Suffragist and the Average Woman," *Women's History Review* 1, no. 1 (1992): 14. See also Holton, "In Sorrowful Wrath: Suffrage Militancy and the Romantic Feminism of Emmeline Pankhurst," in H. L. Smith, ed., *British Feminism in the Twentieth Century* (Amherst, MA, 1990), 7–24, and id., *Feminism and Democracy: Women's Suffrage and Reform Politics in Britain, 1900–1918* (Cambridge, 1986). The contribution of working-class women was first revealed by J. Liddington and J. Norris, *One Hand Tied Behind Us: The Rise of the Women's Suffrage Movement* (London, 1978). To get a picture of the movement outside southeast England read L. Leneman, *A Guid Cause: The Women's Suffrage Movement in Scotland* (Aberdeen, 1984); R. Cullen Owens, *Smashing Times: A History of the Irish Women's Suffrage Movement 1889–1922* (Dublin, 1984); C. Murphy, *The Women's Suffrage Movement and Irish Society in the Early Twentieth Century* (Hemel Hempstead, 1989); K. Cook and N. Evans, "The Petty Antics of the Bell-ringing Boisterous Band: The Women's Suffrage Movement in Wales 1890–1918," in A. V. John, ed., *Our Mother's Land: Chapters in Welsh Women's History 1830–1939* (Cardiff, 1991), 159–89. On male sympathizers and activists, see A. V. John and C. Eustance, eds., *The Men's Share? Masculinities, Male Support and Women's Suffrage in Britain, 1890–1920* (London, 1997). For a range of new approaches, sample the essays

in M. Joannou and J. Purvis, eds., *The Women's Suffrage Movement: New Feminist Perspectives* (Manchester, 1998).

102. Chap. 6 below.

103. A. V. John and C. Eustance, "Shared Histories, Differing Identities," in John and Eustance, eds., *The Men's Share?*, 24.

104. A. V. John, "'Chwarae Teg'": Welsh Women's Support for Women's Suffrage," *The Welsh Political Archive Lecture, 1997* (Aberystwyth, 1998).

105. John and Eustance, "Shared Histories," 23.

106. C. Law, *Suffrage and Power: The Women's Movement 1918-1928* (London, 1997), 1-2.

107. Chap. 7 below.

108. The debate surrounding the admission of women to the House of Lords is an interesting subject in itself: see D. Sutherland, "The Admission of Women Peeresses to the House of Lords, 1900-1963" (thesis in progress, Cambridge University).

109. S. Kingsley Kent, *Gender and Power in Britain, 1640-1990* (London, 1999), 318. On the welfare state and gender roles, see S. Pedersen, *Family, Dependence and the Origins of the Welfare State: Britain and France, 1914-45* (Cambridge, 1993), 336-56; E. Wilson, *Only Halfway to Paradise: Women in Post-War Britain, 1945-1968* (London, 1980); J. Lewis, *Women in Britain Since 1945: Women, Family, Work and the State in the Post-War Years* (Oxford, 1992).

110. For the most sustained exposition of this thesis, see S. Kingsley Kent, *Making Peace. The Reconstruction of Gender in Interwar Britain* (Princeton, NJ, 1993).

111. S. Kingsley Kent, *Gender and Power*, 271.

112. H. L. Smith, "British Feminism in the 1920s," in H. L. Smith, ed., *British Feminism in the Twentieth Century* (Amherst, MA, 1990), 52, but see generally 47-65.

113. Quoted in chap. 8 below.

114. C. Law, *Suffrage and Power: The Women's Movement, 1918-1928* (London, 1999), 228, 226.

115. Ibid., 229.

116. Chap. 8 below. There is now a Ph.D. thesis going forward at the University of Greenwich on the first women magistrates.

117. M. Francis, "Labour and Gender," in D. Tanner, P. Thane, and N. Tiratsoo, eds., *The Labour Party: A Centenary History* (Cambridge, 2000), 191. For a more pessimistic reading, see S. Pedersen, "The Failure of Feminism in the Making of the British Welfare State," *Radical History Review* 43 (1989): 86-110. For more on women and the Labour Party, read P. Graves, *Labour Women: Women in British Working-Class Politics, 1918-1939* (Cambridge, 1994).

118. M. Savage, *The Dynamics of Working Class Politics: The Labour Movement in Preston* (Cambridge, 1987), passim.

119. Chap. 8 below.

120. Ibid.

121. I. Zweiniger-Bargielowska, "Explaining the Gender Gap: The Conservative Party and the Women's Vote, 1945–1964," in M. Francis and I. Zweiniger-Bargielowska, eds., *The Conservatives and British Society 1880–1990* (Cardiff, 1996), 194–223.

122. Chap. 9 below.

123. Ibid.

124. Ibid.

125. Ibid.

126. J. Lawrence, "Party Politics and the Politics of Gender in Modern Britain" (unpub. paper, January 1993). I am grateful to the author for letting me quote from this.

127. Chap. 9 below.

128. See D. Jarvis, "Mrs Maggs and Betty: The Conservative Appeal to Women Voters in the 1920s," *Twentieth-Century British History* 5 (1994): 144. For the prequel, see J. Lawrence, "Class and Gender and the Making of Urban Toryism, 1880–1914," *EHR* 108 (1993): 630–52.

129. I. Zweiniger-Bargielowska, "Rationing, Austerity and the Conservative Party Recovery After 1945," *HJ* 37 (1994): 173–97; and I. Zweiniger-Bargielowska, *Austerity* (Oxford, 2000).

130. M. Francis, "Set the People Free? Conservatives and the State, 1920–1960," in M. Francis and I. Zweiniger-Bargielowska, eds., *The Conservatives*, 73.

131. Chap. 9 below.

132. Midgley, *Women Against Slavery*, 20.

133. Chap. 3 below.

134. L. Colley, *Britons*, 280.

135. A. Vickery, "Golden Age to Separate Spheres? A Review of the Categories and Chronology of English Women's History," *HJ* 36, 2 (1993): 383–414.

136. See chaps. 2, 3, and 7 below. For more on the constitutive role of gender in political discourse, see Wilson, *Sense of the People*; Clark, *The Struggle for the Breeches*; A. Clark, "Gender, Class and Nation: Franchise Reform in the Long Nineteenth Century," in J. Vernon, ed., *Rereading the Constitution: New Narratives in the Political History of England's Long Nineteenth Century* (Cambridge, 1996), 230–53; K. McClelland, "Some Thoughts on Masculinity and the Representative Artisan in Britain, 1850–1880," *Gender and History* (1989); K. McClelland, "Rational and Respectable Men: Gender, the Working Class and Citizenship in Britian, 1850–1867," in L. Frader and S. Rose, eds., *Gender and the Reconstruction of Working Class History in Modern Europe* (Ithaca, NY, 1995); Lawrence, "Party Politics and the Politics of Gender"; Lawrence, "Class and Gender and the Making of Urban Toryism, 1880–1914"; Jarvis, "Mrs Maggs and Betty."

137. Both quoted in C. Silvester, *The Pimlico Companion to Parliament: A Literary Anthology* (London, 1997), 584, 588.

138. D. Jarvis, "The Conservative Party and the Politics of Gender, 1900–

1939," in M. Francis and I. Zweiniger-Bargielowska, eds., *The Conservatives*, 172–93.

139. Chap. 8 below.

140. This discussion leans heavily on M. Francis, "Labour and Gender," 215. But see also K. Ahmed, "Women Wave Bye Bye to Tony," *The Observer*, June 18, 2000.

CHAPTER I

I would like to thank Hannah Barker, Paul Langford, Roey Sweet, Stephen Taylor, and the other contributors to this volume for their advice and comments on earlier drafts of this chapter. Funding for the initial research was provided by the Social Studies and Humanities Research Council of Canada.

1. Lady Beauclerk to Newcastle [n.pl.], Jan. 31, 1759, BL, Add. MS 32,887, fols. 442–43.

2. Thomas Pelham-Holles (1693–1768) was created duke of Newcastle in 1715 by George I. He was one of the few eighteenth-century politicians who did not profit personally from his lifelong involvement in Whig politics. Instead, he encumbered his vast estates and overspent an enormous rent roll in the Whig cause.

3. Linda Levy Peck, *Court Patronage and Corruption in Early Stuart England* (London, 1990), 3.

4. Mary Bateson, "Clerical Preferment under Newcastle," *EHR* 7(1892): 685–96. She sets the tone of the article at the outset: "The growth of a healthy sentiment against the solicitation of personal favors will be noted by historians of the future as one of the pleasing features of the nineteenth century."

5. Lewis Namier, *The Structure of Politics at the Accession of George III*, 2d ed. (London, 1960). Harold Perkin corroborates Namier's work in *Origins of Modern English Society* (London, 1991). See also J. H. Plumb, *The Growth of Political Stability in England, 1675–1725* (London, 1967); also his *The First Four Georges* (London, 1987), 78.

6. See, for instance, Richard Middleton, "Newcastle and the Conduct of Patronage during the Seven Years' War," *British Journal Eighteenth-Century Studies* 7(1989): 175–86; James J. Sack, "The House of Lords and Parliamentary Patronage in Great Britain, 1802–1832," *HJ* 23(1980): 913–38; M. W. McCahill, "Peers, Patronage and the Industrial Revolution, 1760–1800," *JBS* 16 (1976): 84–107. The preponderance of contemporary work on patronage has focused on the early modern period: Linda Levy Peck, "Benefits, Brokers and Beneficiaries: The Culture of Exchange in Seventeenth-Century England," in B. Y. Kunze and D. D. Brautigam, eds., *Court, Country and Culture: Essays in Early Modern British History in Honor of Perez Zagorin* (Rochester, 1992), 109–27; also her *Court Patronage and Corruption in Early Stuart England*; Barbara J. Harris, "Women and Politics in Early Tudor England," *HJ* 33(1990): 259–81; Kevin Sharpe, "Faction at the Early Stuart Court," *History Today* 33(1983): 39–46; Simon Adams, "Faction, Clientage, and Party: English Politics, 1550–

1603," ibid. 32(1982): 33–39; David Starkey, "From Feud to Faction: English Politics Circa 1450–1550," ibid. 16–21.

7. J. M. Bourne, *Patronage and Society in Nineteenth-Century England* (London, 1986).

8. See, for instance, Jeremy Boissevain, *Friend of Friends: Networks, Manipulators and Coalitions* (Oxford, 1974); S. N. Eisenstadt, "Preface," in Verena Burkolter, *The Patronage System: Some Theoretical Remarks* (Basel, 1976), vii.

9. Luis Roniger, "The Comparative Study of Clientelism and the Changing Nature of Civil Society in the Contemporary World," in Luis Roniger and Ayse Günes-Ayata, eds., *Democracy, Clientelism, and Civil Society* (London, 1994), 3.

10. Boissevain, *Friend of Friends*, 154–63.

11. S. N. Eisenstadt and Luis Roniger, *Patrons, Clients and Friends: Interpersonal Relations and the Structure of Trust in Society* (Cambridge, 1984), 48.

12. Ayse Günes-Ayata, "Clientelism: Premodern, Modern, Postmodern," in Roniger and Günes-Ayata, eds., *Democracy, Clientelism, and Civil Society*, 24.

13. Ibid.

14. Ibid., 215.

15. For a more extensive examination of eighteenth-century women's participation in patronage as part of their wider political involvement, see my *Women in English Political Life, 1754–1790* (Oxford, forthcoming).

16. Harris, "Women and Politics in Early Tudor England"; Peck, "Benefits, Brokers and Beneficiaries," 109–27; also her *Court Patronage and Corruption*.

17. Peck, *Court Patronage and Corruption*, 48, 68.

18. Sharon Kettering, "The Patronage Power of Early Modern French Noblewomen," *HJ* 32(1989): 817–41; see her "Gift-Giving and Patronage in Early Modern France," *French History* 2(1988): 131–51; also her "The Historical Development of Political Clientelism," *JIH* 18(1988): 419–47; and her *Patrons, Brokers, and Clients in Seventeenth-Century France* (New York, 1986).

19. Lord Henry Beauclerk to William Pitt [n.pl., n.d.]; Lady Beauclerk to Hester Pitt, Somerset House [n.d., but Nov. 1754–Dec. 1761], PRO, 30/8/19 (Chatham Papers, 1st Ser.), fols. 6–7, 10–11. The Beauclerks appear to have been working together to secure Pitt's support and that of Lords Ligonier, Barrington, and Bute in an effort to get the king to change his mind.

20. Lady Beauclerk to Newcastle [n.pl.], Feb. 3 [1759], BL, Add. MS 32,887, fols. 489–90.

21. Lady Beauclerk to Newcastle [n.pl.], Feb. 20, 1759, BL, Add. MS 32,888, fol. 200.

22. Newcastle to Lady Beauclerk, Newcastle House, Feb. 21, 1759, ibid., fol. 208.

23. Lady Beauclerk to Newcastle [n.pl.], Mar. 20, 1759, BL, Add. MS 32,889, fol. 167.

24. The missing letter requesting the Lieutenancy of the Tower was probably written in October 1759, for one seeking William Pitt's support survives in the Chatham Papers: see Lady Beauclerk to Newcastle [n.pl.], Mar. 31, 1760, BL, Add. MS 32,904, fol. 135; Lord Henry Beauclerk to William Pitt [n.pl.], Oct. 13, 1759, PRO, 30/8/19, fols. 6–7.

25. Lady Beauclerk to Newcastle [n.pl.], Mar. 20, 1759, BL, Add. MS 32,889, fol. 167; Lady Beauclerk to Newcastle [n.pl.], Mar. 31, 1760; Lady Beauclerk's Memorial to George II [n.pl., n.d., but Mar.–Apr. 1760]; Lady Beauclerk to Newcastle [n.pl.], Apr. 14, 1760, BL, Add. MS 32,904, fols. 135, 137–38, 396–97.

26. Lady Beauclerk to Newcastle [n.pl.], Mar. 31, 1760, BL, Add. MS 32,904, fol. 135.

27. Newcastle to Lady Beauclerk, Newcastle House, Apr. 1, 1760, ibid., fol. 157. Newcastle did more than just reassure her, however. In a memorandum for the king, written on the same date, he mentions her by name (ibid., fol. 145).

28. See her subsequent letters: Apr. 15, 1760, BL, Add. MS 32,904, fols. 396–97; May 11, 1760, BL, Add. MS 32,906, fols. 54–55; June 10, 1760, BL, Add. MS 32,907, fols. 133–34.

29. Lady Beauclerk to Newcastle [n.pl.], June 10, 1760, BL, Add. MS 32,907, fol. 133.

30. Lady Beauclerk to Newcastle [n.pl., n.d.], BL, Add. MS 32,992, fols. 154–55.

31. Grafton to Newcastle, Euston, Nov. 24, 1760, BL, Add. MS, 32,915, fol. 43.

32. List of Queen's Officers [Sept. 7–8, 1761], BL, Add. MS 32,928, fols. 48–49. Lady Mary Coke's journal makes it clear that Miss Beauclerk was still a Maid of Honour in 1768: see "Journal, Feb. 8, 1768," in *Letters and Journals of Lady Mary Coke*, 4 vols. (Edinburgh, 1889–96), 2:185. See also Donald Adamson and Peter Beauclerk Dewar, *The House of Nell Gwyn: The Fortunes of the Beauclerk Family, 1670–1974* (London, 1974), 222–23.

33. See George R. An Establishment of List Containing all Payments to be made for the Civil List Affairs of our Kingdom of Ireland . . . Accounted Payable from the 25th day of October, last inclusive 1760, [1763], BL, M/297, Syon MSS, reel 18, fol. 11v. I would like to acknowledge the generosity of the duke of Northumberland for allowing me to consult his papers.

34. Newcastle was very aware of this. See Newcastle to Devonshire, Most Secret, Newcastle House, Apr. 5, 1761, BL, Add. MS 32,926, fol. 192. Newcastle's declining power is echoed in a fall in patronage requests. He lists only six applications made to him for the highly desirable places in the new queen's household—and none of his candidates was successful: see BL, Add. MS 32,925, July 20, 1761, fols. 211–12; List of Queen's Officers [Sept. 7–8, 1761], BL, Add. MS 32,928, fols. 48–49.

35. Lady Beauclerk to Hester Pitt, Somerset House [Nov. 1754–Dec. 1761], PRO, 30/8/19, fols. 10–11.

36. Since some letters contain several patronage requests, I have chosen to concentrate on the number of requests Newcastle received and not the number of letters.

37. Harriett Lane to Newcastle, Bingley House, June 4, 1754, BL, Add. MS 32,735, fols. 380r–v.

38. See BL, Add. MS 32,928, fol. 48; BL, M/297, Reel 18, vol. 35, fol. 11v.

39. Anne Jackson to duchess of Newcastle, Arlington Street, June 21, 1754, BL, Add. MS 32,735, fol. 534r–v.

40. Portland to duchess of Newcastle, Berkeley Square, Feb. 14, 1770, BL, Add. MS 33,082, fol. 97.

41. The Gordon family historian describes her uncharitably, as "a most persuasive and unscrupulous wirepuller" who used a combination of "patriotism and blatant self-advancement" to achieve her ends: George Gordon, *The Last Dukes of Gordon and their Consorts, 1743–1864* (Aberdeen, 1980), 25.

42. Katherine, Duchess of Gordon, to Newcastle, Grosvenor Street, Oct. 24, 1758, BL, Add. MS 32,885, fol. 66.

43. Katherine, Duchess of Gordon, to Newcastle, Gordon Castle, Nov. 26, 1759, BL, Add. MS 32,899, fols. 128–29.

44. Katherine, Duchess of Gordon, to Newcastle, London, Mar. 3, 1760, BL, Add. MS 32,903, fols. 57–58.

45. Anne, Duchess of Hamilton, to Newcastle, Bury, Nov. 30, 1759, BL, Add. MS 32,899, fol. 209.

46. Maria Constantia Nethercott to Newcastle, Tynemouth, Mar. 26, 1762, BL, Add. MS 32,936, fol. 157r–v.

47. Lady Forbes to Newcastle, New Bond Street, Sept. 9, 1755, BL, Add. MS 32,859, fol. 42r–v.

48. Lady Deskfoord to Newcastle, Banff Castle, Oct. 9, 1758, BL, Add. MS 32,884, fol. 297.

49. Kinnoull to Newcastle, Bradsworth, Oct. 28, 1758, BL, Add. MS 32,885.

50. Ladies Jane and Margaret Leslie, Memorial to the King [Mar. 1756], BL, Add. MS 32,863, fol. 292.

51. Andrew Leslie to Newcastle [n.pl.], Mar. 15, 1756, BL, Add. MS 32,863, fols. 294–95; Rothes to Newcastle, Brook Street, Mar. 15, 1756, ibid., fols. 290–91.

52. List of Salaries and Pensions, 1754–62, BL, Add. MS 33,044, fols. 1–10; List of Persons in Receipt of Pensions from the Crown, 1754–61, Bod.L, MS North d.61; George R. An Establishment . . . for our Kingdom of Ireland [1763], BL, M/297, Syon, MSS, reel 18, fols. 3–14. This last figure does not include a number of trusts that were to be shared between children of both sexes.

53. Namier, *Structure of Politics*, 187.

54. See Boissevain, *Friend of Friends*, 154–64.

55. Ragnild Hatton, "George I as an English and a European Figure," in Paul Fritz and David Williams, eds., *The Triumph of Culture: 18th Century Perspectives* (Toronto, 1972), 192–98.

56. *The Evidence . . . in the Trial wherein the Rt. Hon. John, Earl of Sandwich, was Plaintiff, and J. Miller, Defendant* (London, 1773); N. A. M. Rodger, *The Insatiable Earl: A Life of John Montagu, 4th Earl of Sandwich* (London, 1993), 167, 188.

57. For the duke of York and Mary Anne Clarke (the Wardle affair), see I. R. Christie, *Wars and Revolutions: Britain, 1760–1815* (Cambridge, MA, 1982), 302; Sir Charles Grant Robertson, *England Under the Hanoverians*, 15th ed. (London, 1948), 440, 442.

58. Ann Boscawen to duchess of Newcastle, Whichwood (sic) Forest, Aug. 18, 1760, BL Add. MS 32,910, fol. 101.

59. Lady Cromertie to the duchess of Newcastle [n.pl.], July 3 [1758], BL, Add. MS 32,881, fols. 157r–v.

60. Marlborough to Newcastle, [n.pl], Nov. 14, 1758, BL, Add. MS 32,885, fol. 330; Newcastle to Marlborough, Nov. 15, 1758, ibid., fols. 344r–v. The letter to the duchess of Marlborough does not seem to have survived. In an undated note to his wife, Newcastle tells her to let the duchess of Marlborough know, "I will certainly obey the Dutchess of Marlhs. Commands, as far as it is in My power": Newcastle to duchess of Newcastle, Newcastle House, [Nov. 14–15, 1755], BL, Add. MS 33,076, fol. 25.

61. G. E. Cokayne, *The Complete Peerage of England, Scotland, Ireland, Great Britain and the United Kingdom*, ed. Vicary Gibbs et al., 12 vols. (London, 1910–53), 6:596–97, 600; *Collins's Peerage of England: Genealogical, Biographical and Historical*, 6th ed., ed. Sir Egerton Brydges, 9 vols. (London, 1812), 8:143. See also Newcastle to Lady Howe, Newcastle House, Sept. 5, 1759, BL, Add. MS 32,895, fols. 197–98.

62. For her ability to secure the borough for her younger son in 1758, despite Newcastle's best efforts, see my "'That epidemical Madness': Women and Electoral Politics in the late Eighteenth Century," in Hannah Barker and Elaine Chalus, eds., *Gender in Eighteenth-Century England: Roles, Representations and Responsibilities* (Harlow, 1997), 164–65.

63. Lady Howe to Newcastle [n.pl.], Sept. 20, [1757], BL, Add. MS 32,874, fol. 187.

64. The extent of Lady Yarmouth's political involvement has been consistently underrated by historians and deserves further study. I hope to examine it in more detail elsewhere.

65. Newcastle to duchess of Newcastle, Kensington [Mar.–May 1756], BL, Add. MS 33,075, fol. 72.

66. Newcastle to duchess of Newcastle, Newcastle House, June 20, 1754, BL, Add. MS 33,075, fol. 3v; Newcastle to the duchess of Newcastle, Treasury Chambers [n.d., Spring 1755?], ibid., fol. 23.

67. Lady Katherine Pelham to Newcastle, Whitehall, Jan. 12, 1759, BL, Add. MS 32,887, fol. 121.

68. Lady Katherine Pelham to Newcastle, Greenwich House, Aug. 27, 1757, BL, Add. MS 32,873, fol. 319.

69. Namier's examination of politics at Harwich is still outstanding: see Namier, *Structure of Politics*, 358–89.

70. Ibid., 370–73; Lady Katherine Pelham to Newcastle [n.pl.], July 14, 1758, BL, Add. MS 32,881, fol. 319.

71. Namier, *Structure of Politics*, 372.

72. Newcastle to Lady Katherine Pelham, Newcastle House, Feb. 5, 1761, BL, Add. MS 32,918, fol. 279v.

73. Lady Katherine Pelham to Newcastle, London, Feb. 12 [1761], ibid., fols. 471v–472.

74. For example, Norman Sykes, *Church and State in England in the XVIIIth Century* (Cambridge, 1934), 63–65.

75. Stephen Taylor, "The Government and the Episcopate in the Mid-Eighteenth Century: The Uses of Patronage," in Charles Giry-Deloison and Roger Mettam, eds., *Patronages et clientélismes, 1550–1750 (France, Angleterre, Espagne, Italie)* (London, c. 1995), 191–205.

76. A. C. H. Seymour, *The Life and Times of Selina Countess of Huntingdon*, 2 vols. (London, 1839); Alan Harding, "The Countess of Huntingdon and her Connexion in the Eighteenth Century" (University of Oxford D.Phil. thesis, 1992). For the most recent examination of Queen Caroline's patronage activities, see Stephen Taylor, "Queen Caroline and the Church of England," in Stephen Taylor, Richard Connors, and Clyve Jones, eds., *Hanoverian Britain and Empire: Essays in Honour of Philip Lawson* (Cambridge, 1998). I must also thank Stephen Taylor for allowing me to consult his excellent *New Dictionary of National Biography* article on Queen Caroline prior to publication.

77. *The Clergyman's Intelligencer: or, A Compleat Alphabetical List of All the Patrons in England and Wales* (London, 1745); John Ecton, updated by Browne Willis, *Thesaurus Rerum Ecclesiasticarum: Being an Account of the Valuations of all the Ecclesiastical Benefices in the Several Dioceses of England and Wales*, 2d ed. (London, 1754). I would like to thank Stephen Taylor for sharing his insights into female ecclesiastical patronage with me and for making me aware of these sources.

78. Although most of the untitled women are identified as "Mrs.," as opposed to "Widow" or "Miss," both of which are used occasionally, this usage owes more to eighteenth-century convention than to actual marital status.

79. For the dioceses of Oxford and Norwich below, see Ecton, *Thesaurus Rerum Ecclesiasticarum*, 348–62, 282–348.

80. Ibid., 290, 295.

81. See my " '. . . & if I were in Parliament': Women, Electoral Privilege and Practice in the Eighteenth Century," in Kathryn Gleadle and Sarah Richardson, eds., *Women in British Politics, 1750–1850: The Power of the Petticoat* (London, 2000).

82. Present State of Elections for England and Wales [1754], BL, Add. MS 32,995, fol. 76; Cornish Boroughs and the Principal Interests [1760], BL, Add.

MS 32,999, fol. 301; Mr. Harris' State of the Case of the Burrough of Ashburton for Sr Wm Yonge [1753–54], BL, Add. MS 33,061, fols. 206–7.

83. Deskfoord to Newcastle, Banff Castle, Mar. 6, 1760, BL, Add. MS 32,903, fol. 110.

84. I discuss this and Lady Irwin's involvement in contested elections in the burgage borough of Horsham, cited below, in " . . . & if I were in Parliament."

85. Abstract of Voters at Aldborough belonging to the duke of Newcastle [c. 1754], BL, Add. MS 33,061, fols. 204–5. While Newcastle's women voters would not have voted themselves, it is intriguing that they are categorized in this way. For Horsham, see William Albery, *A Parliamentary History of the Ancient Borough of Horsham, 1295–1885, With Some Account of Every Contested Election, and So Far as can be Ascertained, a List of Members Returned*, intro. Hillaire Belloc (London, 1927), 93–97.

86. Anne Lister was still doing this in Yorkshire as late as 1833. See Jill Liddington, *Female Fortune: Land, Gender and Authority: The Anne Lister Diaries and Other Writings, 1833–36* (London, 1998), 51.

87. See, for instance, Sir Roger Newdigate's parliamentary notes on the Oxfordshire election of 1754 for Feb. 22, 1755, where he records the case of Thomas Holloway, whose landlady threatened to evict him from his farm if he did not vote as she wished. WCRO, Warwick, CR 136 B2526, B/D. I would like to thank Lord Daventry for permission to consult the Newdigate papers.

88. W. Vachell to Lady Portsmouth, Abbington, Sept. 16, 1746, ERO (Audley End Papers), D/Dby C42/5.

89. Ibid. See also W. Vachell to Lady Portsmouth, Abbington, Sept. 2, 1746, ERO, D/DBy C42/6. Her correspondence with Vachell, July–Aug. 1751 (letters nos. 11, 12, 12+), charts her negotiations with Lord Effingham for the purchase of the house, parklands, and presentation. By Mar. 8, 1752 (no. 20), the sale seems to have been agreed.

90. Newcastle to Lady Portsmouth, Newcastle House, June 10 1760, BL, Add. MS 32,907, fols. 137r-v.

91. Lady Portsmouth to Newcastle, Hurstbourne, June 11, 1760, ibid., fols. 160–61.

92. Newcastle to dean of Lincoln, Newcastle House, June 12, 25, 1760, ibid., fols. 184–85, 351–52.

93. Newcastle to Portsmouth, Claremont, July 9, 1760, BL, Add. MS 32,908, fol. 152.

94. Portsmouth to Newcastle, Hurstbourne, June 27, 1760, BL, Add. MS 32,907, fol. 417; Newcastle to Portsmouth, Claremont, July 9, 1760, BL, Add. MS 32,908, fol. 152.

CHAPTER 2

1. "Sir Cecil Wray," *Dictionary of National Biography* (Oxford, 1967–68 ed.), 21:989.

2. Lovers of Truth and Justice, *History of the Westminster Election con-*

taining Every Material Occurrence from its Commencement on the First of April to the Final Close of the Poll on the 17th May, to which is prefixed A Summary Account of the Late Parliament (London, 1784), 99.

3. Joan Perkin, *Women and Marriage in Nineteenth-Century England* (Chicago, 1989), 308.

4. See, for instance, Elaine Chalus, "'That epidemical Madness': Women and Electoral Politics in the Late Eighteenth Century," in Elaine Chalus and Hannah Barker, eds., *Gender in Eighteenth-Century England: Roles, Representations, and Responsibilities* (London, 1998); Judith Schneid Lewis, *Sacred to Female Patriotism: Gender, Class and Politics in Late Georgian Britain* (forthcoming).

5. Linda Colley, *Britons: Forging the Nation: 1707–1837* (London, 1992), 246.

6. Ibid., 242–50.

7. Amanda Foreman, *Georgiana: Duchess of Devonshire* (London, 1998).

8. M. D. George, "Fox's Martyrs: The General Election of 1784," *Transactions of the Royal Historical Society*, 4th series, 21 (1939):165.

9. Anon., *County of Down Election: The Patriotic Miscellany or Mirror of Wit, Genius, and Truth, Being a Correct Collection of all the Publications During the Late Contested Election Between the Hon. Colonel John Meade and the Right Hon. Lord Viscount Castlereagh* (London, 1805), 52–53, 55.

10. Colley, *Britons*, 242.

11. Chatsworth MSS 610.1. Chatsworth House, Derbyshire.

12. Hugh Stokes, *The Devonshire House Circle* (London, 1917), 192.

13. Linda Colley, "The Apotheosis of George III: Loyalty, Royalty, and the British Nation, 1760–1820," *Past and Present* 102 (1984).

14. L. G. Mitchell, *Charles James Fox* (Oxford, 1992), 70.

15. Stella Tillyard describes Fox as having the second most famous face of the eighteenth century (after David Garrick). "Fox found his way onto handkerchiefs, jugs, snuff boxes and packs of cards," she reminds us. He remains, of course, a visible part of twentieth-century London, owing to his burial in Westminster Abbey, and because he was "sculpted for the lobby of the House of Commons, and cast in bronze to sit amongst the polluted evergreens of Bloomsbury Square, plump in senatorial robes and covered in pigeon droppings." See Tillyard, *Aristocrats: Caroline, Emily, Louisa, and Sarah Lennox, 1740–1832* (New York, 1994), xxv.

16. Joanna Innes, "Politics and Morals: The Reformation of Manners Movement in Later Eighteenth Century England," in *The Transformation of Political Culture: England and Germany in the Late Eighteenth Century*, ed. Eckhart Hellmuth (London, 1990), 61.

17. *History of the Westminster Election*, 103.

18. Brian Masters, *Georgiana, Duchess of Devonshire* (London, 1981), 75.

19. Foreman, *Georgiana*, 90.

20. Nicholas Penny, ed., *Reynolds* (London, 1986), 289.

21. William Combe, *An Interesting Letter to the Duchess of Devonshire* (London, 1778), 53–54.

22. Ibid., 63.

23. Georgiana, Duchess of Devonshire, to her mother, Dowager Countess Spencer, Feb. 8, 1784. Chatsworth MSS 598.

24. Duke of Portland to duchess of Devonshire, Apr. 10, 1784. Chatsworth MSS 612.

25. Iris Leveson-Gower, *The Face Without a Frown: Georgiana, Duchess of Devonshire* (London, 1944), 112.

26. *History of the Westminster Election*, 226.

27. See, for instance, Lord Spencer to Richard Brinsley Sheridan, Jan. 6, 1784, BL, Althorp MSS G4; Lord Spencer to his mother, the dowager countess, Apr. 8, 1784, BL, Althorp MSS F11.

28. Lord Spencer to the dowager Countess Spencer, June 14, 1784, BL, Althorp MSS F11. Though a "violent" reformer in Spencer's words, Sloper was an unreliable Foxite. In fact, he had voted against the India Bill for reasons of his own, and consequently offered to resign his seat. Spencer did not accept the resignation on the basis that Sloper generally agreed with him politically, though he might not on every individual bill, and that Sloper was a man "on whose integrity I think I may very safely depend." Sir Lewis Namier and John Brooke, *History of Parliament: The House of Commons, 1754–1790* (Oxford, 1964), 3:445.

29. I have been unable to trace the birthdate of her daughter Caroline, who died unmarried. Her other two daughters were born in 1786 and 1789, while the son and heir was not born until 1791.

30. Vicary Gibbs, ed., *The Complete Peerage of England, Scotland, Ireland Great Britain and the United Kingdom* (13 vols. 1949), 11:411n.

31. The head of this family, the third Viscount Grimston (in the peerage of Ireland) had represented St. Albans only since December when the family's candidate, Radcliffe, had died. During the course of the spring campaign Lord Grimston decided to stand for the county instead and was elected. The Mr. Grimston who was elected for St. Albans was his younger brother.

32. Lady Spencer to Mrs. Howe, Mar. 30, 1784. BL, Althorp MSS F53.

33. Mark Girouard, *Historic Houses of Britain* (New York, 1979), 51.

34. Namier and Brooke, *Parliament* 1:309.

35. 2d Earl Spencer to Dowager Countess Spencer, Apr. 1, 1784. BL, Althorp MSS F11.

36. Lady Spencer to Mrs. Howe, Apr. 2, 1784. BL, Althorp MSS F54.

37. Lady Spencer to Mrs. Howe, May 3, 1784. BL, Althorp MSS F54.

38. Mr. Sloper to Lord Spencer, Apr. 8, 1784. BL, Althorp MSS G4.

39. Mr. Sloper to Lord Spencer, Apr. 12, 1784. BL, Althorp MSS G4.

40. Dowager Countess Spencer to Mrs. Howe, May 3, 1784. BL, Althorp MSS F54.

41. Sloper was, however, a member of that larger group of inter-related "friends" of whom Lady Spencer was the center. In 1774 Sloper had married a Miss Amelia Shipley, daughter of the Bishop of St. Asaph. The Bishop and his wife were great friends of Lady Spencer's: indeed Mrs. Shipley was a distant cousin. One of Mrs. Sloper's sisters married another Spencer dependant:

Sir William Jones, eventually to win fame as an Orientalist and jurist, but who began his professional life in 1765 at Althorp as tutor to the future second earl. Spencer and his sisters remained devoted to Jones, Georgiana helping him achieve his Indian position in 1783.

42. Lord Spencer to the dowager Lady Spencer, May 3, 1784. BL, Althorp MSS F11.

43. The traditional dichotomy of public/private, which cloistered women in the latter "sphere," has also come to seem naive. Amanda Vickery and Lawrence E. Klein, among others, have appropriately problematized the "separate spheres." See Vickery, "Golden Age to Separate Spheres? A Review of the Categories and Chronology of English Women's History," *HJ* 36 (1994); Klein, "Gender and the Public/Private Distinction in the Eighteenth Century: Some Questions About Evidence and Analytic Procedure," *Eighteenth-Century Studies* 29 (1995).

44. "At all events, St. Albans is a great comfort," she wrote her mother in April after returning to Westminster. "Other elections go on ill—but let Northampton and Westminster and York succeed, we shall not be disgraced." Chatsworth MSS. 610.5. As we know, the Foxites lost both Northampton and York.

45. Foreman, *Georgiana*, 141. Sir Lewis Namier estimated that there had been only nine thousand voters in 1760. This is a phenomenal level of growth if both figures are accurate. See Namier, *The Structure of Politics at the Accession of George III* (London, 1973), 80.

46. *History of the Westminster Election*, 434.

47. Leveson-Gower, *Face Without a Frown*, 105. The pun on the word "member" was a very commonly used one, even outside the unsavory environs of Covent Garden. See, for instance, a letter to the highly respectable Sir Thomas Acland, upon his defeat for the County of Devon in 1818. Acland MSS Devonshire Record Office 1148M/Box 21 (iii). Of course, this usage facilitates and emphasizes the connection between masculinity and political power, so this pun is no joke.

48. Chatsworth MSS 610.1.

49. Voters could of course decide not to vote at all, in which case they were declared "neuter."

50. Quoted in Stokes, *Devonshire House*, 202.

51. *History of the Westminster Election*, 227.

52. See Foreman's account in *Georgiana*, 149. See also the letter of Lord John Cavendish to the dowager Lady Spencer of April 14, 1784, in which he promises that her daughters and the other female canvassers will no longer engage in this cross-class intimacy, but will stay in their carriages where they belong, or simply look on from a window, where they could be seen but not spoken to. BL, Althorp MSS F121. Foreman (as above) believes that Georgiana ignored these orders. Cavendish's letter was sparked by Lady Spencer's complaints and was clearly designed to placate her: the Fox campaign may never have intended to change the strategy of the female canvassers.

53. Quoted by E. A. Smith, "The Election Agent in English Politics, 1734–1832," *EHR* 84 (1969): 15.

54. Donald McAdams, "Electioneering Techniques in Popular Constituencies," *Studies in Burke and His Time* 14 (1972–73): 33–34.

55. Georgiana Battiscombe, *The Spencers of Althorp* (London, 1984), 93.

56. *History of the Westminster Election*, 345.

57. Frank O'Gorman, "Campaign Rituals and Ceremonies: The Social Meaning of Elections in England, 1780–1860," *Past and Present* 135 (1992): 109.

58. Ibid., 109.

59. Ibid., 84.

60. *Squire Osbaldeston, His Autobiography*, E. D. Cuming, ed. (London, 1926). Squire Osbaldeston was twenty years old at the time of the election—his manuscript autobiography was published many years after his death.

61. *Complete Peerage* 11:270–270n.

62. Lady Clermont to Lady Spencer, July 12, 1784. BL, Althorp MSS F123.

63. Georgiana, Duchess of Devonshire to Lady Elizabeth Foster, Oct. 18, 1783. Chatsworth MSS 547.

64. Georgiana, Duchess of Devonshire to her mother, dowager Lady Spencer, Mar. 20, 1784. Quoted in *The Anglo-Saxon Review, A Quarterly Miscellany*, ed. Lady Randolph Spencer Churchill (London, 1899), 2:73.

65. *Georgiana: Extracts from the Correspondence of Georgiana, Duchess of Devonshire*, ed. earl of Bessborough (London, 1955), 78; dowager Lady Spencer to Harriet, Lady Duncannon, July 23, 1788. BL, Althorp MSS F39.

66. Duchess of Rutland to anonymous correspondent, Mar. 27, 1784. Pitt MSS. PRO 30/8/174/2.

67. Officially he was said to have died of liver disease and a violent fever. Unofficially he had "created a record for dining out never equalled by any subsequent viceroy." Two years before Rutland's premature demise the duke of Leinster noted that "provided he gets his skin full of claret," his fellow duke cared "little about anything else." *The Complete Peerage* 11:270–270n.

68. R. G. Thorne, *The House of Commons, 1790–1820* (London, 1986), 2:458.

69. Anonymous letter to Lord Wentworth [1790], Braye of Stanford Park MSS, Leicester Record Office, 23D57/3428.

70. John Lambert to Isabella, Duchess of Rutland, Feb. 6, 1788. Pitt MSS, PRO 30/8/174/2.

71. Duchess of Rutland to Pitt, Apr. 7, 1790. PRO 30/8/174/2 fols. 247–48.

72. Thorne, *House of Commons* 2: 458–59.

73. Penny, ed., *Reynolds*, 392.

74. Her mother was Ann Casey, illegitimate daughter of Sir Cecil Wray. This must have been the candidate's grandfather. The candidate himself could hardly have been the grandfather of Albinia, who was born in 1738.

75. *The Complete Peerage* 2:403. Her eldest son, later the fourth earl, in fact turned out to be a talented administrator. Hobart, Tasmania, is named for him.

76. BL, Add. MS. 37926.

77. *Anglo-Saxon Review* 2 (1899): 33–34.

78. *The Complete Peerage* 3:535. According to Amanda Foreman, Mrs. Crewe's virtuous reputation not only flew in the face of the odds, but also in the face of facts. She believes Mrs. Crewe at the very least had an affair with Sheridan. Foreman, *Georgiana*, 213.

79. Stokes, *Devonshire House*, 147.

80. Penny, ed., *Reynolds*, 243.

81. In this case, however, politics made incompatible bedfellows. Jockey left her husband in 1788, eloping with Fox's friend Lord John Townshend on the eve of the by-election in Westminster, in which Lord John was the Foxite candidate. The question of whether or not the duchess of Devonshire would canvass for Townshend was complicated—certainly in her mother's eyes—by this elopement.

82. Stokes, *Devonshire House*, 148 and 148n.

83. Duchess of Rutland to William Pitt, Apr. 7, 1790. Pitt MSS. PRO 30/8/174/2 fols. 247–48.

84. Georgiana, Duchess of Devonshire to Charles James Fox. [1804] Granville MSS, PRO 30/29/6/7 fol. 1158.

85. Georgiana, Duchess of Devonshire to Philip Francis, Nov. 29, 1798. BL, Add. MSS 40763.

86. Judith Schneid Lewis, *In the Family Way: Childbearing in the British Aristocracy, 1760–1860* (New Brunswick, NJ, 1986), 211.

87. Lord John Cavendish to Dowager Lady Spencer, Apr. 14, 1784. BL, Althorp MSS F121.

88. Dowager Lady Spencer to Harriet, Lady Duncannon, Mar. 26, 1786. BL, Althorp MSS F39.

89. A. S. Turberville, *The House of Lords in the Age of Reform: 1784–1837* (London, 1958), 393.

90. BL, Add. MSS 37926 fol. 44.

91. BL, Add. MSS 37926 fol. 38.

92. BL, Add. MSS 37926 (Dec. 1785).

93. BL, Add. MSS 37926 fol. 38.

94. Penny, ed., *Reynolds*, 388.

95. Lavinia, Countess Spencer to dowager Lady Spencer, June 24, 1793. BL, Althorp MSS F29.

96. See Foreman, *Georgiana*, 174–76.

97. *The Historical and the Posthumous Memoirs of Sir Nathaniel William Wraxall, 1772–1774*, ed. Henry B. Wheatley, in five volumes (London, 1884), 3:347.

98. See for instance, the "Coalition Minuet" and "A Concise Description of Covent Garden at the Present Westminster Election," *History of the Westminster Election*, 94, 434.

99. Bessborough, ed., *Georgiana*, 74. Wray was attacked as a "turn coat," appropriately enough, by the tailors, because he owed his Westminster seat to Fox in the first place.

100. Edmund Burke, *Reflections on the Revolution in France* (New York, 1961), 90.
101. *History of the Westminster Election*, 225.
102. Ibid., 117, 252.
103. See, for instance, ibid., 311.
104. Ibid., 345.
105. Bessborough, ed., *Georgiana*, 82.
106. *History of the Westminster Election*, 171. Georgiana appeared in verses four through eight. The final verse, number ten, cannot be overlooked. "Now this Judas [Wray, presumably] was a *lanky* man; and when he would have spoken, a certain quivering came over him, yea even from the crown of his head to the soles of his feet, and he fell flat on his back, even as a flounder."
107. Dorothy George, *English Political Caricatures: A Study of Opinion and Propaganda, vol. 1: to 1792* (Oxford, 1959), 186.
108. *History of the Westminster Election*, 314.
109. Donna Andrews, *London Debating Societies: 1776–1799* (London, 1994), vii–viii, 74.
110. Ibid. See in particular 75, 146.
111. Ibid., 358.
112. Andrews, *London*, 159, 231. These debating societies were profit-oriented—people paid to attend, and so topics were selected to draw wide audiences. Nevertheless, one should not exaggerate the seriousness of these debates. Gender-related topics were usually popular, perhaps only on the principle that sex sells. In other words, these debates may have had the flavor of TV talk shows. After a 1786 debate on whether Ladies, "in this enlightened age," should have the right to vote and even be elected to Parliament, the *Morning Herald* reported, "It is utterly impossible, for the limits of an advertisement in a due degree to express the exquisite entertainment the debate on the above question afforded: serious argument, sterling wit, and genuine humour, powerfully contended for the approbation of a splendid and numerous assemblage of persons," who nevertheless "decided in the affirmative." Ibid., 181.
113. *History of the Westminster Elections*, 353.
114. Ibid., 312.
115. Ibid., 352.
116. Wraxall, *Memoirs* 3:218.
117. Ibid.
118. *History of the Westminster Election*, 310.
119. Leveson-Gower, *Face without a Frown*, 103.
120. Andrews, *London*, 193, 256, 316, and 343.
121. See for instance, Randolph Trumbach's article, "London's Sodomites: Homosexual Behavior and Western Culture in the Eighteenth Century," *Journal of Social History*, Fall 1977, esp. 15. In his discussion of "the fop" Philip Carter criticizes Trumbach's tendancy to confuse social conduct with sexual orientation. Whatever the truth of the early eighteenth century,

surely by 1784 it would be appropriate to relate the two, as seen in the development of the "man-milliner" construct. See Carter's "Men About Town: Representations of Foppery and Masculinity in Early Eighteenth-century Urban Society," in Chalus and Barker, eds., *Gender*, 31–57.

122. Wraxall, *Memoirs* 3:395.

123. Quoted by Vincent Carretta, *George III and the Satirists from Hogarth to Byron* (Athens, GA, 1990), 281.

124. John Brewer has recently pointed out that what "we would now regard as aggressive male heterosexuality" was regarded as "effeminacy" in the eighteenth century, because the latter term connoted "unbridled passion, display, vanity, and private interests" while sacrificing these elements in the interests of "public duty" was thought to be the essence of masculinity. Thus the chaste Pitt was more masculine than the rakish Fox. See Brewer, *The Pleasures of the Imagination: English Culture in the Eighteenth Century* (London, 1997), 80–81.

125. Fox was, of course, a cartoonist's dream. Linda Colley provides us with this cartoon, "Cheek by Joul or the Mask," an anonymous print, in *Britons*, 247. My own personal favorite, also from 1784, is Rowlandson's "The Covent Garden Nightmare," a parody of Fuseli's recent painting. This has been reproduced in Michael Wynn Jones, *The Cartoon History of Britain* (New York, 1971), 74. Carretta provides us with two such cartoons: the anonymous "A Ministerial Fact," from 1786 in which Fox is portrayed as a woman who tried to murder the king, and Cruickshank's "Frith the Madman Hurling Treason at the King," from 1790; see Carretta, *George III*, 276, 288.

126. Gerald Newman, *The Rise of English Nationalism: A Cultural History, 1740–1830* (New York, 1987), 216, 218.

127. Phyllis Deutsch, "Moral Trespass in Georgian London: Gaming, Gender, and Electoral Politics in the Age of George III," *HJ* 39 (1996): 640, 655, and 637.

128. *History of the Westminster Election*, 313–14.

129. George, *Political Caricatures*, "Carlo Khan's entry into St. Stephens," 186.

130. Penny, ed., *Reynolds*, 379.

131. *History of the Westminster Election*, 445.

132. *Anglo-Saxon Review* 2 (1899): 34–35.

133. M. W. Patterson, *Sir Francis Burdett and His Times (1770–1844)* (London, 1931), 1:137. Fox and the duchess were to die within six months of each other.

134. Leveson-Gower, *Face without a Frown*, 97–98.

CHAPTER 3

1. Janet Ross, *Three Generations of English Women. Memoirs and Correspondence of Susannah Taylor, Sarah Austin and Lady Duff Gordon*, 2 vols. (London, 1888), 1: 8; Claire Tomalin, *The Life and Death of Mary Wollstone-*

craft (London, 1992 [first pub. 1974]), 129; Dorothy A. Stansfield, *Thomas Beddoes MD., 1760–1808. Chemist, Physician, Democrat* (Dordrecht, 1984), 55, 73; Margaret Eliot Macgregor, "Amelia Alderson Opie: Worldling and Friend," *Smith College Studies in Modern Languages* 14, nos. 1–2 (1933): 15.

2. Tomalin, *Life*, chap. 11; M. Ray Adams, "Helen Maria Williams and the French Revolution," in E. L. Griggs, ed., *Wordsworth and Coleridge. Studies in Honor of George McLean Harper* (New York, 1962), 87–117.

3. John Milton Baker, *Henry Crabb Robinson of Bury, Jena, The Times and Russell Square* (London, 1937), 59. Buck was waiting to hear news of the fate of Brissot.

4. Ada Earland, *John Opie and His Circle* (London, 1911), 169.

5. Eliza Fletcher, *Autobiography of Mrs Fletcher of Edinburgh, With Selections from her Letters and other Family Memorials* (Carlisle, 1874), 63, 78.

6. *MR* 5 (1810): 204.

7. The "middle class" is of course, as Dror Wahrman has recently explicated, a highly unstable and ambiguous classification: Dror Wahrman, *Imagining the Middle Class. The Political Representation of Class in Britain, c. 1780–1840* (Cambridge, 1995). The families analyzed in this chapter come primarily from what we might describe as the "professional" classes—doctors, solicitors, writers, academics, publishers, educationists, ministers, painters, and the like.

8. Catherine Hall, "Private Persons versus Public Someones: Class, Gender and Politics in England, 1780–1850," in Catherine Hall, *White, Male and Middle Class. Explorations in Feminism and History* (Oxford, 1992), 151–72. The neglect of middle-class female politics is in sharp contrast to the recent burst of interest in the political activity of upper-class women. See, for example, K. D. Reynolds, *Aristocratic Women and Political Society in Victorian Britain* (Oxford, 1998); and Elaine Chalus, "'That Epidemical Madness': Women and Electoral Politics in the Late Eighteenth Century," and Amanda Foreman, "A Politician's Politician: Georgiana, Duchess of Devonshire and the Whig Party," both in Hannah Barker and Elaine Chalus, eds., *Gender in Eighteenth-Century England. Roles, Representations and Responsibilities* (London, 1997), pt. 3.

9. Such a tendency runs throughout Frank K. Prochaska, *Women and Philanthropy in Nineteenth Century England* (Oxford, 1980), for example.

10. Lawrence Klein, "Gender and the Public/Private Distinction in the Eighteenth Century: Some Questions about Evidence and Analytic Procedure," *Eighteenth Century Studies* 29, no. 1 (1995): 97–109; for a discussion of the problems inherent in identifying "middle class" with "separate spheres" see Wahrman, *Imagining the Middle Class*, chap. 11.

11. See Kathryn Gleadle, "'Our Several Spheres': Middle-Class Women and the Feminisms of Early Victorian Radicalism," in Kathryn Gleadle and Sarah Richardson, eds., *Women in British Politics, 1780–1860: The Power of the Petticoat* (Basingstoke, 2000), 134–52.

12. Kathleen Wilson, *The Sense of the People. Politics, Culture and Imperialism in England, 1715–1785* (Cambridge, 1995).

13. J. Habermas, *The Structural Transformation of the Public Sphere: An Enquiry into a Category of Bourgeois Society*, trans. T. Burger (Cambridge, MA, 1989). An excellent overview of these developments may be found in Derinda Outram, *The Enlightenment* (Cambridge, 1995), chap. 2; see also Margaret C. Jacob, "The Mental Landscape of the Public Sphere: A European Perspective," *Eighteenth-Century Studies* 28, no. 1 (1994): 95–113.

14. Joan Landes, *Women and the Public Sphere in the Age of the French Revolution* (Ithaca, NY, 1988), provides a pessimistic analysis of the implications for women; see also Ann Bermingham, "Introduction. The Consumption of Culture, Image, Object, Text," in Ann Bermingham and John Brewer, eds., *The Consumption of Culture 1600–1800. Image, Object, Text* (London, 1995), 9–11. For more positive assertions as to women's consumption of cultural opportunities see Amanda Vickery, *The Gentleman's Daughter. Women's Lives in Georgian England* (New Haven, CT, 1998), chap. 7.

15. Elizabeth Fox-Genovese, "Women and the Enlightenment," in C. Koonz and S. Stuard, eds., *Becoming Visible. Women in European History* (Boston, 1987), 272; see also the argument developed in Landes, *Women and the Public Sphere*. For an account of the changing shifts in concepts of virtue during the Enlightenment consult Jane Rendall, "Virtue and Commerce: Women in the Making of the Adam Smith's Political Economy," in Ellen Kennedy and Susan Mendus, eds., *Women in Western Political Philosophy. Kant to Nietzche* (Brighton, 1987), esp. 44–77.

16. Such a "decentered" approach to the impact of and reception to Enlightenment ideas has long been called for by scholars of the British Enlightenment. See Roy Porter, "The Enlightenment in England," in Roy Porter and Mikulas Teich, eds., *The Enlightenment in National Context* (Cambridge, 1981), 1–18; Roy Porter, *English Society in the Eighteenth Century* (London, 1990), 83; Mark Philp, *Godwin's Political Justice* (London, 1986), 125–29.

17. For a more extended discussion see Kathryn Gleadle, *The Early Feminists. Radical Unitarians and the Emergence of the Women's Rights Movement, c. 1831–51* (Basingstoke, 1995), 64–67. A clear explanation of the "feminocentric" basis of Enlightenment historical enquiry is given in Karen Offen, "Reclaiming the European Enlightenment for Feminism," in Tjitske Akkerman and Siep Stuurman, eds., *Perspectives on Feminist Political Thought in European History* (London, 1998), 85–103; and Sylvana Tomaselli, "The Enlightenment Debate on Women," *History Workshop Journal* 20 (1985): 101–24.

18. See for example Joseph Priestley, "Of Politeness," in id., *Lectures on History and General Policy* (Birmingham, 1788), 429–31; or Robert Aspland, *The Beneficial Influence of Christianity on the Character and Condition of the Female Sex* (London, 1812), 27. See also n. 16 above.

19. "On the Rights of Woman," *The Cabinet, By a Society of Gentlemen* 2 (1795): 38–39; a point also made by Mary Robinson, *Letter to the Women of England on the Injustice of Mental Subordination* (London, 1799), 89n.

20. Rendall, "Virtue and Commerce," 44–45, 71–72. The pages of dissent-

ing journals abound with the obituaries of women praised for their perfect fulfillment of domestic duties.

21. Useful surveys of Unitarian educational thought and practice may be found in H. McLachlan, *The Unitarian Movement in the Religious Life of England. Its Contribution to Thought and Learning. 1700–1900* (London, 1934); and R. K. Webb, "The Unitarian Background," in Barbara Smith, ed., *Truth, Liberty, Religion: Essays Celebrating Two Hundred Years of Manchester College* (Oxford, 1986).

22. For an extended discussion of the Unitarian promotion of female education see Ruth Watts, *Gender, Power and the Unitarians in England 1760–1860* (London, 1998).

23. Letter from Mary Wollstonecraft to Joseph Johnson, Sept. 13, 1787, in Ralph M. Wardle, ed., *Collected Letters of Mary Wollstonecraft* (London, 1979), 159; MR 5 (1810): 203; Gina Luria, "Mary Hays's Letter and Manuscripts," *Signs* 3, no. 2 (1977): 526.

24. Mary Hays, *Letters and Essays, Moral and Miscellaneous*, ed. Gina Luria (London, 1974 [first pub. 1793]), 92.

25. Fox-Genovese, "Women and the Enlightenment," 260–61.

26. Gleadle, *The Early Feminists*, 24–27.

27. Ross, *Three Generations* 1:27.

28. Luria, "Introduction," in Hays, *Letters and Essays*, 6.

29. Robinson, *Letter to the Women of England*, 92–93.

30. Fletcher, *Autobiography*, 91; Ross, *Three Generations* 1:13. A. L. Barbauld educated teenage girls in her home, but refused to become involved in a project to establish a ladies' college. Lucy Aikin, ed., *The Works of Anna Laetitia Barbauld. With a Memoir by Lucy Aikin*, 2 vols. (London, 1825), xvi–xviii.

31. See for example Harriet Martineau, *Autobiography*, 3 vols. (London, 1983, [first pub. 1877]), 1:104; Henry Solly, *These Eighty Years or, The Story of an Unfinished Life* (London, 1893), 1:158; Sophia De Morgan, *Three Score Years and Ten. Reminiscences of the Late Sophia Elizabeth de Morgan*, ed. Mary A. De Morgan (London, 1895), xxviii.

32. MR 5 (1810): 249; Brook Aspland, *Memoir of the Life, Works and Correspondence of the Rev. Robert Aspland of Hackney* (London, 1850), 249n; MR 8 (1813): 341–42; 4 (1809): 52; 7 (1812): 109, 114; Helen Plant, "Catherine Cappe of York (1744–1821): a Unitarian Case Study," *Women's History Notebooks* 6:1 (Winter 1999): 18–23.

33. For a full analysis of the terms and implications of these acts see James E. Bradley, *Religion, Revolution and English Radicalism* (Cambridge, 1990), esp. 50–58, 84–85.

34. John Seed, "Gentlemen Dissenters: the Social and Political Meanings of Rational Dissent in the 1770s and 1780s," *HJ* 28, no. 2 (1985): 299–325; Anthony Lincoln, *Some Political and Social Ideas of English Dissent 1763–1800* (New York, 1971).

35. G. J. Barker-Benfield, "Mary Wollstonecraft: Eighteenth Century Commonwealthwoman," *Journal of the History of Ideas* 50 (1989): 101–2;

see also Hays, *Letters and Essays*, 9–10 for Hays's argument for disestablishment and full civic rights.

36. Kelly, *Women*, 30–31; Moira Ferguson, *Subject to Others. British Women Writers and Colonial Slavery, 1670–1834* (Routledge, 1992), 159.

37. Aikin, ed., *Works* 2:353–77.

38. Ibid., 185–87; although see the point made by McCarthy and Kraft, that the poem may have been written as an outburst to Wollstonecraft's criticisms of Barbauld in the *Vindication*, and should not be seen as representing Barbauld's "considered judgement" on the issue: William McCarthy and Elizabeth Kraft, eds., *The Poems of Anna Laetitia Barbauld* (Athens, OH, 1994), 289n.

39. For full biographical details, see Tomalin, *Life*; see also Gary Kelly, *Revolutionary Feminism. The Mind and Career of Mary Wollstonecraft* (Basingstoke, 1992), 28.

40. Stansfield, *Thomas Beddoes*, 109–10, 190; John Edmund Stock, *Memoirs of the Life of Thomas Beddoes* (London, 1811), 68, 391.

41. John Jebb, "Theological Propositions and Miscellaneous Observations. With General Maxims of Reason and Religion," in John Disney, *The Works, Theological, Medical, Political and Miscellaneous of John Jebb. With Memoirs of the Life of the Author*, 3 vols. (London, 1788), 2:180.

42. Ruth Watts, "The Unitarian Contribution to Education in England from the Late Eighteenth Century to 1853" (Ph.D. thesis, Univ. of Leicester, 1987), 76.

43. Thomas Holcroft, *Memoirs of the Late Thomas Holcroft, Written by Himself*, 3 vols. (London, 1816), 3:241–42; John Gale Jones, *Sketch of a Political Tour through Rochester, Chatham, Maidstone, Gravesend* (London, 1796), 91.

44. See Jones, *Sketch*, 91; Kelly, *Revolutionary Feminism*, 136.

45. Unitarian-leaning journals such as the *Christian Miscellany; or Religious and Moral Magazine* (1792) and the *MR* favorably reviewed the *Vindication*; and the work was followed by a number of other feminist disquisitions. These works, which varied considerably in their debt to Wollstonecraft, included Mary Hays, *Letters and Essays, Moral and Miscellaneous* (1793); Mary Robinson, *Letter to the Women of England on the Injustice of Mental Subordination* (1799); and Mary Ann Radcliffe, *The Female Advocate; or, an Attempt to Recover the Rights of Women from Male Usurpation* (1799). Throughout the 1790s, feminist articles continued to appear in dissenting publications, such as the *Cabinet* (which expanded much further than had Wollstonecraft upon women's right to political representation) and the *Universalist's Miscellany; or Philanthropist's Museum* (1797).

46. Bradley, *Religion*, 12; for a recent discussion of the relationship between rational dissent and radicalism, see Martin Fitzpatrick, "Heretical Religion and Radical Political Ideas in Late Eighteenth-Century England," in Eckhart Hellmuth, ed., *The Transformation of Political Culture. England and Germany in the Late Eighteenth Century* (Oxford, 1990), 339–72.

47. Eliza Gould made arrangements to hear Priestley when in London,

MR 5 (1810): 204; the correspondence of the women of the intellectual, Unitarian family, the Collets, is highly suggestive. I am grateful to the descendants of the family for allowing me to consult the private MS collection.

48. See John Seed, "Theologies of Power: Unitarianism and the Social Relations of Religious Discourse, 1800-50," in R. J. Morris, ed., *Class, Power and Social Structure in British Nineteenth-Century Towns* (Leicester, 1986), 108-56, esp. 124.

49. Philp, *Godwin's Political Justice*, 126-27, 164ff; Gerald P. Tyson, *Joseph Johnson. A Liberal Publisher* (Iowa City, IA, 1979); R. K. Webb, "Flying Missionaries: Unitarian Journalists in Victorian England," in J. M. W. Bean, ed., *The Political Culture of Modern Britain: Studies in Memory of Stephen Koss* (London, 1987), 16-17.

50. Franklin Fox, ed., *Memoir of Mrs. Eliza Fox. To Which Extracts are Added from the Journals and Letters of Her Husband, the Late W. J. Fox* (London, 1860), 15n.

51. John Gascoigne, *Joseph Banks and the English Enlightenment. Useful Knowledge and Polite Culture* (Cambridge, 1994), 35; Allan Ruston, "The Non-Con Clubs and Some Other Unitarian Clubs, 1783-1914," *Transactions of the Unitarian Historical Society* 14, no. 3 (1969): 147-62.

52. Letter from Eliza Florance to W. J. Fox, Aug. 13, 1817, quoted in Fox, *Memoir*, 134-35.

53. Catherine Hutton Beale, ed., *Catherine Hutton and Her Friends* (Birmingham, 1895), 64-65. The study of science, a key element of Enlightenment culture (and one in which rational dissenters excelled) was extremely popular among middle-class women. As Ann Shteir's superb study has highlighted, it could be embraced by writers such as Priscilla Wakefield to create new educational genres, the family-based conversation, for example, which endowed women with intellectual authority, yet within a domestic setting. Ann B. Shteir, *Cultivating Women. Cultivating Science. Flora's Daughters and Botany in England. 1760 to 1860* (London, 1996); Priscilla Wakefield, *Mental Improvement; Or, the Beauties and Wonders of Nature and Art*, ed. Ann B. Shteir (East Lansing, MI, 1995 [first pub. 1794-97]). For the popularity of scientific lectures among women see also Aikin, ed., *Works* 2:67.

54. For example, Mrs. H. C. Knight, *Jane Taylor. Her Life and Letters* (London, 1880), 30, 97.

55. Betsy Rodgers, *Georgian Chronicle. Mrs. Barbauld and Her Family* (London, 1958), 130.

56. See Donna T. Andrew, "Popular Culture and Public Debate: London 1780," *HJ* 39, no. 2 (1996): 405-23.

57. Thomas Sadler, ed., *Diary, Reminiscences and Correspondence of Henry Crabb Robinson* (London, 1872), 1:21.

58. Rachel Lee, *Memoirs of R. F. A. Written by Herself* (n.d.), 32.

59. Wilson, *Sense*, 431n.

60. Jones, *Sketch*, 88.

61. Thomas Hardy, *Memoir of Thomas Hardy, Written By Himself* (London, 1832), 87-88.

62. Deborah McLeod, "Introduction," in Anne Plumptre, *Something New* (Peterborough, ON, 1996 [first pub. 1801]), ix–x.

63. *Memoirs of Mrs. Jebb* (London, 1812). For the work of John Jebb see Carl B. Cone, *The English Jacobins. Reformers in Late Eighteenth Century England* (New York, 1968), 54, 60.

64. *Christian Reformer* 11 (1844): 159.

65. Mary Scott, *The Female Advocate. A Poem Occasioned by Reading Mr. Duncombe's Feminead* (Los Angeles, 1984 [first pub. 1774]); Moira Ferguson, "'The Cause of My Sex': Mary Scott and the Female Literary Tradition," *Huntington Library Quarterly* 50, no. 4 (1987): 359–77; Majorie Reeves, *Pursuing the Muses. Female Education and Nonconformist Culture, 1700–1900* (London, 1997), 47–49.

66. Kelly, *Women*, 30; for a discussion of the role of women in contemporary France see Dena Goodman, "Enlightenment Salons: The Convergence of Female and Philosophic Ambitions," *Eighteenth Century Studies* 22 (1989): 329–50.

67. Ross, *Three Generations* 1:8, 18, 25; Macgregor, "Amelia Alderson Opie," 10. Such female-led salons continued to be of importance throughout the period. In Wakefield, for example, Mary Gaskell cultivated a similar coterie. Sadler, ed., *Diary* 2:220.

68. Fletcher, *Autobiography*, 289.

69. Ellen Gibson Wilson, *Thomas Clarkson. A Biography* (Basingstoke, 1989), 92–93; Sadler, ed., *Diary*, 17–18; Baker, *Henry Crabb Robinson*, 42–43.

70. Stansfield, *Thomas Beddoes*, 102–3.

71. Oswald G. Knapp, ed., *The Intimate Letters of Hester Piozzi and Penelope Pennington (1788–1821)* (London, 1914), 188.

72. J. E. Cookson, *The Friends of Peace. Anti-war Liberalism in England, 1793–1815* (Cambridge, 1982), 136.

73. Kelly, *Revolutionary*, 12.

74. See for example Robinson, *Letter to the Women of England*, 66.

75. For a clear discussion of these ideas see Jane Rendall, *The Origins of Modern Feminism. Women in Britain, France and the United States, 1780–1860* (Chicago, 1985), chap. 2.

76. See Outram, *The Enlightenment*, chap. 6.

77. See for example, Mary Robinson's fierce critique of male sexuality in her *Letter to the Women of England*, in which she lambasts men as "Sensual Egotists," 85. This was also a constant theme in Wollstonecraft's *Vindication of the Rights of Women* (Harmondsworth, 1988 [first pub. 1792]), in which she argues that "The passions of men have thus placed women on thrones," 146.

78. Wedd, *The Love-Letters*, 238.

79. Fletcher, *Autobiography*, 299, 181.

80. Ibid., 320, 58, 60, 63, 313, 328.

81. Obituary of Mrs. Jebb, *Morning Chronicle*, Jan. 27, 1812. It was written by George Dyer.

82. *Memoirs of Mrs Jebb*, 15; George Dyer, "On Liberty," *Poems* (London, 1792), 36n.

83. A. L. Barbauld's work, for example, could not be—and was not—seen in the context of her husband's activities, yet she does not appear to have been widely stigmatized for her support for radical politics. For full details of the life and reputation of Catherine Macaulay see Bridget Hill, *The Republican Virago. The Life and Times of Catharine Macaulay, Historian* (Oxford, 1992).

84. Lois G. Schwoerer has noted of female writers that by the mid-eighteenth century, "their polemical voice had faded, only to be revived stronger and more permanently by century's end." My work would suggest that the role of the rational dissenters was crucial in this transition. Lois G. Schwoerer, "Women's Public Political Voice in England, 1640–1740," in Hilda L. Smith, ed., *Women Writers and the Early Modern British Political Tradition* (Cambridge, 1998), 73.

85. Rodgers, *Georgian Chronicle*, 210.

86. Diana Bowstead, "Charlotte Smith's *Desmond*. The Epistolary Novel as Ideological Argument," in M. A. Scholefield and Cecilia Macheski, eds., *Fetter'd or Free? British Women Novelists, 1670–1815* (Athens, OH, 1986), 239–40.

87. Barker-Benfield, "Mary Wollstonecraft"; Wendy Gunther-Canada, "The Politics of Sense and Sensibility: Mary Wollstonecraft and Catherine Macaulay Graham on Edmund Burke's 'Reflections on the Revolution in France'," in Smith, ed., *Women Writers*, 126–47.

88. Such a view might be found in, among many others, Miriam Brody, "The Vindication of the Writes of Women: Mary Wollstonecraft and Enlightenment Rhetoric," in Maria J. Falco, ed., *Feminist Interpretations of Mary Wollstonecraft* (London, 1996), 104–23, esp. 106.

89. *Observations on a Pamphlet entitled "Thoughts on the Cause of the Present Discontents"* (1770). See Hill, *The Republican Virago*, 75–76.

90. Catherine Macaulay, *Observations on the Reflections of the Rt. Hon. Edmund Burke on the Revolution in France, in a Letter to the Rt. Hon, the Earl of Stanhope* (London, 1790), 7, 79. The pamphlet was published anonymously.

91. T. Moore to Rev. Mr. Barbauld, Nov. 29, 1790, quoted in Le Breton, *Memoir*, 194.

92. Aikin, ed., *Works* 2:374.

93. George Dyer, "On Liberty," 36–37.

94. For example, Helen Maria Williams, "Peru" (1784), see Moria Ferguson, *Subject to Others, British Women Writers and Colonial Slavery, 1670–1834* (London 1992), 189; A. L. Barbauld, "Corsica" (1769), see Anna Laetitia Le Breton, *Memoir of Mrs. Barbauld* (London, 1874), 34–35; J. G. A. Pocock, "Catharine Macaulay: Patriot Historian," in Smith, ed., *Women Writers*, 243–58.

95. William McCarthy and Elizabeth Kraft, eds., *The Poems of Anna Letitia Barbauld* (Athens, OH, 1994), 285n.; Ferguson, *Subject*, 164.

96. Ferguson, *Subject*, 176–77, 188, 194; Bowstead, "Charlotte Smith," esp. 237.

97. Robert Hole, "British Counter-revolutionary Popular Propaganda," in Colin Jones, ed., *Britain and Revolutionary France: Conflict, Subversion and Propaganda* (Exeter, 1983), 53–69; see also Anne Stott, "Hannah More: Evangelicalism, Cultural Reformation and Loyalism" (Ph.D. thesis, Univ. of London, 1998), 215–17, 223–24.

98. Knapp, ed., *The Intimate Letters of Hester Piozzi*, 81, 116.

99. Hays, *Letters and Essays*, 17.

100. Aikin, ed., *Works* 1:180–82; Rodgers, *Georgian Chronicle*, 117.

101. A. L. Barbauld, "Sins of Government, Sins of the Nation; or, A Discourse for the Fast, appointed on April 19, 1793," in Aikin, ed., *Works* 2: 390; Cookson, *Friends of Peace*, 119. Barbauld wrote another such discourse in 1794, "Reasons for National Penitence, Recommended for the Fast."

102. Hole, "British Counter-Revolutionary Propaganda," 57–58.

103. Ann Jebb, *Two Penny-Worth of Truth for a Penny; or A True State of Facts; with an Apology for Tom Bull in a Letter to Brother John* (London, 1793) (esp. p. 3); and *Two Penny-Worth More, of Truth for a penny. Being a Second Letter from Bull to Brother John* (London, 1793).

104. Laetitia Matilda Hawkins, *Letters on the Female Mind, Its Power and Pursuit. Addressed to Miss H. M. Williams, with Particular Reference to Her Letters from France* (London, 1793), 2 vols.

105. Kelly, *Women*, 33–38.

106. Le Breton, *Memoir*, 35.

107. Ross, *Three Generations* 1:8; Fletcher, *Autobiography*, 328.

108. *Analytical Review* 8 (1790): 419, 431. Wollstonecraft's use of "male" genres has received considerable scholarly attention. For a recent treatment see Tom Furniss, "Gender in Revolution: Edmund Burke and Mary Wollstonecraft," in Kelvin Everest, ed., *Revolution in Writing. British Literary Responses to the French Revolution* (Milton Keynes, 1991), 65–100.

109. Cited in Kelly, *Women*, 84.

110. Hays, *Letters and Essays*, 16.

111. Colley, *Britons*, 250–54.

112. William Godwin, *Memoirs of the Author of the Rights of Woman* (London, 1798); Janes, "On the Reception," 299–300; Rendall, *Origins of Modern Feminism*, 66–72.

113. Tomalin, *Life*, 293; Rodgers, *Georgian Chronicle*, 189.

114. For example, Elizabeth Heyrick, Amelia Opie, and Catherine Clarkson all became Quakers. Clarkson and Mary Hays both became involved in Romantic circles. Kenneth Corfield, "Elizabeth Heyrick; Radical Quaker," in Gail Malmgreen, ed., *Religion in the Lives of English Women* (London, 1982), 42; Macgregor, "Amelia Alderson Opie," 82ff; Edith J. Morley, ed., *The Correspondence of Henry Crabb Robinson with the Wordsworth Circle (1806–60)*, 2 vols. (Oxford, 1927), 1:49; for Hays see also Burton R. Pollin, "Mary Hays on Women's Rights in the *Monthly Magazine*," *Etudes Anglaises* 24 (1972): 271–82.

115. Quoted in Macgregor, "Amelia Alderson Opie," 27, 42.
116. Ross, *Three Generations* 1:17; Fletcher, *Autobiography*, 172, 181, 299; Michael Hurst, *Maria Edgeworth and the Public Scene. Intellect, Fine Feeling and Landlordism in the Age of Reform* (London, 1969), chap. 2.
117. See McCarthy and Kraft, *Poems*, 302n.
118. *MR* 3 (1808): 232. For an analysis of the radicals' viewpoint see Cookson, *Friends of Peace*, 29.
119. Quoted in McLeod, "Introduction," xiv; Sadler, *Diary* 1:156.
120. Beale, *Catherine Hutton*, 127.
121. A highly convincing starting point for the role of women in loyalist activity during the war may be found in Linda Colley, *Britons. Forging the Nation, 1707–1837* (New Haven, CT, 1992), 254–62.
122. The best overview of these developments remains Catherine Hall, "The Early Formation of Victorian Domestic Ideology," in Hall, *White, Male and Middle-Class*, 75–93.
123. Unitarianism's overt radicalism was further quelled by the 1811 Act of Toleration and the repeal of the Test and Corporation Acts in 1828. Tyson, *Joseph Johnson*, 184; Philp, *Godwin's*, 162–63. For a discussion of the greater conservatism of the Unitarians during these years, and the implication of this for their treatment of women, see Gleadle, *The Early Feminists*, 21–32.
124. Catherine Cappe, *Memoirs of the Life of the Late Mrs. Catherine Cappe. Written by Herself*, 2d ed. (London, 1823), 341; Plant, "Catherine Cappe."
125. Fletcher, *Autobiography*, 68–69.
126. Lee, *Memoirs*, esp. 30–33.
127. Philopatria (R. F. A. Lee), *Essay on Government* (London, 1808), 163.
128. *Annual Review* 7 (1808): 168–69; *MR* 4 (1809): 338–39.
129. A.L.B., "Thoughts on the Inequality of Conditions," *Athenaeum* 2 (1807): 14–19 (quotes taken from 17, 19).
130. The discussion of Heyrick's pamphlets draws heavily on Corfield, "Elizabeth Heyrick," 53–61.
131. Beale, *Catherine Hutton*, 3–5, 64, 67.
132. Ibid., 158–59, 206; Clare Midgley, *Women Against Slavery. The British Campaigns, 1780–1870* (London, 1992), 58, 99–100.
133. Beale, *Catherine Hutton*, 110, 156, 170–71, 199–200, 205, 232.
134. Reeves, *Pursuing the Muses*, 108.
135. Beale, *Catherine Hutton*, 170, 179, 248, 177, 195; for Mary Leman Grimstone see Gleadle, *The Early Feminists*, 37–38.
136. Rosamund and Florance Davenport Hill, *The Recorder of Birmingham. A Memoir of Matthew Davenport Hill. With Selections from His Correspondence* (London, 1878), 115.
137. The term "radical unitarian" was coined by Gleadle in *The Early Feminists*, where a full account of their feminism may be found.
138. Gleadle, "'Our Several Spheres'," and see also Sarah Richardson, "'Well-Neighboured Houses'; The Political Networks of Elite Women"; Si-

mon Morgan, "Beyond 'Woman's Mission': Women and the Anti-Corn Law League"; and Nadia Valman, "Women Writers and the Campaign for Jewish Civil Rights in Victorian England," all in Gleadle and Richardson, eds., *Women in British Politics*. For women's involvement in anti-slavery by far the best account is Clare Midgley, *Women Against Slavery*.

139. For further elaboration of this and related points see See A. J. Vickery, "Golden Ages to Separate Spheres: A Review of the Categories and Chronology of English Women's History," *HJ* 36, 2 (1993): 383–414.

140. Subsequent research into the role of middle-class women in the political reform societies of the post-Napoleonic period might well reveal rather different patterns of female politics.

141. See above n. 15.

142. Hall, "The Early Formations of Victorian Domestic Ideology." My comments should not, however, be seen to detract from the importance of this essay, which was first published in 1979.

CHAPTER 4

1. Joan Perkin, *Women and Marriage in Nineteenth-Century England* (London, 1989), 50–51, 70–72; John Habakkuk, *Marriage, Debt, and the Estates System: English Landownership 1650–1950* (Oxford, 1994), chaps. 2–3.

2. Lawrence Stone, *The Family, Sex and Marriage in England 1500–1800* (London, 1977), chap. 8; Judith Schneid Lewis, *In the Family Way: Childbearing in the British Aristocracy 1760–1860* (New Brunswick, NJ, 1986), 10–13.

3. Norman Gash, *Politics in the Age of Peel* (London, 1953), 219–23; Sarah Richardson, "The Role of Women in Electoral Politics in Yorkshire during the Eighteen-Thirties," *Northern History* 32 (1996): 133–51.

4. Chap. 1 above; K. D. Reynolds, *Aristocratic Women and Political Society in Victorian Britain* (Oxford, 1998), 17–18, 80, 142–46.

5. Elaine Chalus, "'That epidemical Madness': Women and Electoral Politics in the Late Eighteenth Century," in Hannah Barker and Elaine Chalus, eds., *Gender in Eighteenth-Century England* (London, 1997), 151–78; Frank O'Gorman, *Voters, Patrons, and Parties: The Unreformed Electoral System of Hanoverian England 1734–1832* (Oxford, 1989), 93.

6. Linda Colley, *Britons: Forging the Nation 1707–1837* (New Haven, CT, 1992), 242–80; chap. 2 above; Amanda Foreman, "A Politician's Politician: Georgiana, Duchess of Devonshire and the Whig Party," in Barker and Chalus, eds., *Gender*, 185–87.

7. Richard Edgcumbe, ed., *The Diary of Frances, Lady Shelley, 1818–1873* (London, 1913), 28–29, 31; Peter Quennell, ed., *The Private Letters of Princess Lieven to Prince Metternich 1820–1826* (London, 1937), 20–21.

8. Pat Jalland, *Women, Marriage and Politics, 1860–1914* (Oxford, 1986), 205–7; Reynolds, *Aristocratic Women*, 149–50.

9. Lady Granville, quoted in Alison Adburgham, *Silver Fork Society: Fashionable Life and Literature from 1814 to 1840* (London, 1983), 120.

10. K. D. Reynolds, "Politics Without Feminism: The Victorian Political Hostess," in Clarissa Campbell Orr, ed., *Wollstonecraft's Daughters: Womanhood in England and France 1780–1920* (Manchester, 1996), 95; the argument now appears in expanded form in Reynolds, *Aristocratic Women*, chap. 5.

11. Leonore Davidoff, *The Best Circles: Society, Etiquette and the Season* (London, 1973), 20–28; Marjorie Morgan, *Manners, Morals and Class in England, 1774–1858* (Basingstoke, 1994), 29–31, 92–93. But see also Michael Curtin, *Prosperity and Position: A Study of Victorian Manners* (New York, 1987), 302, which allots to hostesses a more subordinate and also a more segregated role in aristocratic society.

12. On this last point, there are differences over whether aristocratic women were insulated from the growing "separation of spheres" that is said to have affected bourgeois women, or were affected in much the same way, or indeed whether the experience of aristocratic women casts doubt on the whole notion of a "separation of spheres": cf. Reynolds, "Politics Without Feminism," 95–96; Hannah Barker and Elaine Chalus, "Introduction," in Barker and Chalus, eds., *Gender*, 21–24.

13. Chalus, "'That epidemical Madness'," 151–53, 170–72; Reynolds, *Aristocratic Women*, 7, 143, 155–56, 220–21. But cf. P. J. Jupp, "The Roles of Royal and Aristocratic Women in British Politics, c. 1782–1832," in Mary O'Dowd and Sabine Wichert, eds., *Chattel, Servant or Citizen: Women's Status in Church, State and Society* (Belfast, 1995), 104–5, 113.

14. Foreman's claim that "elite women played a greater part in the political life of the nation than anywhere else in Europe" ("Politician's Politician," 179) needs to be measured against the considerable literature on French women's participation in pre-revolutionary public life: see the useful survey by Dena Goodman, "Public Sphere and Private Life: Toward a Synthesis of Current Historiographical Approaches to the Old Regime," *History and Theory* 31 (1992): 1–20.

15. Michele Cohen, *Fashioning Masculinity: National Identity and Language in the Eighteenth Century* (London, 1996), 30–34, 42–50, 53, 66, 75–78; Colley, *Britons*, 250–52. For a more sanguine view of the place of women in the construction of English "politeness," see Lawrence E. Klein, "Gender, Conversation and the Public Sphere in Early Eighteenth-Century England," in Judith Still and Michael Worton, eds., *Textuality and Sexuality: Reading Theories and Practices* (Manchester, 1993), 100–115.

16. For attacks on the "feminine" aristocracy, see Gerald Newman, *The Rise of English Nationalism: A Cultural History, 1740–1830* (London, 1987); for defenses of the "masculine" aristocracy, see Colley, *Britons*, and Philip Harling, *The Waning of 'Old Corruption': The Politics of Economical Reform in Britain, 1779–1846* (Oxford, 1996). Both sides need to be considered.

17. See Susan Staves, *Married Women's Separate Property in England, 1660–1833* (Cambridge, 1990), on the limited advance of contractarian thought in one key area.

18. Susan Buchan, *Lady Louisa Stuart: Her Memories and Portraits* (London, 1932), 227–29.

19. Colley, *Britons*, 250; Edgcumbe, ed., *Diary of Lady Shelley*, 7–10; Gervas Huxley, *Lady Elizabeth and the Grosvenors: Life in a Whig Family, 1822–1839* (London, 1965), 89.

20. Jupp, "Royal and Aristocratic Women," 105–7; Lytton Strachey and Roger Fulford, eds., *The Greville Memoirs 1814–1860*, 8 vols. (London, 1938), 1:283, 2:156; Guy Le Strange, ed., *Correspondence of Princess Lieven and Earl Grey*, 3 vols. (London, 1890), 3:5.

21. Lewis, *In the Family Way*, 9–14, 30–31.

22. *The Reminiscences and Recollections of Captain Gronow*, 2 vols. (London, 1900), 1:33–34, 221–23.

23. Strachey and Fulford, eds., *Greville Memoirs* 1:208; E. Beresford Chancellor, *Memorials of St. James's Street, Together with the Annals of Almack's* (London, 1922), 230–31.

24. Strachey and Fulford, eds., *Greville Memoirs* 1:171.

25. Lord Holland to Lord Granville, Jan. 3, 1834, PRO, PRO 30/29/409.

26. Hon. Mrs. Hugh Wyndham, ed., *Correspondence of Sarah Spencer, Lady Lyttelton, 1787–1870* (London, 1912), 207.

27. Quoted by Perkin, *Women and Marriage*, 90–91.

28. Jalland, *Women, Marriage and Politics*, 196. See also Lady Shelley's regrets in Edgcumbe, ed., *Diary of Lady Shelley*, 404–5. Reynolds, "Politics Without Feminism," 98, notes that the leading political hostesses were all socially heterodox—Jews or divorcées, for example—and might not have been able to conduct such a successful social life among other aristocratic women.

29. *Reminiscences of Gronow* 1:31–33; [Charles White], *Almack's Revisited; or, Herbert Milton*, 3 vols. (London, 1828), 1:370–80, 2:193–94, 3:4–5; John Ashton, *Social England Under the Regency* (London, 1889), 384. See also [Marianne Spencer Hudson], *Almack's: A Novel*, 3 vols. (London, 1826).

30. Leonore Davidoff and Catherine Hall, *Family Fortunes: Men and Women of the English Middle Class, 1780–1850* (London, 1987), chaps. 1–3; see also Catherine Hall, "The Sweet Delights of Home," in Michelle Perrot, ed., *A History of Private Life, vol. IV: From the Fires of Revolution to the Great War* (Cambridge, 1990), 47–93.

31. For criticisms of Davidoff and Hall along these lines, see Colley, *Britons*, 261–81; Amanda Vickery, "Golden Age to Separate Spheres? A Review of the Categories and Chronology of English Women's History," *HJ* 36 (1993): 383–414; and Dror Wahrman, "'Middle-Class' Domesticity Goes Public: Gender, Class, and Politics from Queen Caroline to Queen Victoria," *JBS* 32 (1993): 396–432. Earlier in Davidoff's career, she saw the change in manners along functional as well as class lines: *Best Circles*, 33–36.

32. Muriel Jaeger, *Before Victoria* (London, 1956), 28–29.

33. The influence of *Coelebs* is often noted, though a systematic survey would still be useful. See, among others, Maurice J. Quinlan, *Victorian Prelude: A History of English Manners 1700–1830* (New York, 1941), 149–59.

34. Ibid., 56–64.

35. Jessica Gerard, *Country House Life: Family and Servants, 1815–1914*

(Oxford, 1994), 104-7, 115-21, makes the point that evangelicalism was never likely to separate the spheres in aristocratic families as strictly as it might in middle-class ones. But her account of cultural change in the aristocracy, while analytically and chronologically coherent, still seems to me to overstate the role of *embourgeoisement*: ibid., 276-80.

36. Jaeger, *Before Victoria*, 76-77.

37. Pamela Horn, *Ladies of the Manor: Wives and Daughters in Country-House Society 1830-1918* (Far Thrupp, 1991), 42-45, 49; Gerard, *Country-House Life*, 50-54. As Gerard comments, the somewhat humbler families examined by M. Jeanne Peterson in *Family, Love, and Work in the Lives of Victorian Gentlewomen* (Bloomington, IN, 1989) took women's education more seriously than did the aristocracy, yet some of Peterson's analysis still applies.

38. Edgcumbe, ed., *Diary of Lady Shelley*, 298.

39. F. K. Prochaska, *Women and Philanthropy in Nineteenth-Century England* (Oxford, 1980), esp. 41-42, 50-60; and id., *Royal Bounty: The Making of a Welfare Monarchy* (New Haven, CT, 1995), 72 (but improperly characterizing the argument in Wahrman, "'Middle-Class Domesticity'"). Cf. Brian Harrison's anti-aristocratic analysis in "Philanthropy and the Victorians," in his *Peaceable Kingdom* (Oxford, 1982), 229-31 (softened on 244), and similar in Davidoff, *Best Circles*, 56-57, and Reynolds, *Aristocratic Women*, 110-18.

40. Horn, *Ladies of the Manor*, 112-19; Gerard, *Country-House Life*, 122-26. Reynolds, *Aristocratic Women*, 102 n.6, argues that these considerations might apply to the "permanently resident, parochial gentry," but not to a "peripatetic national aristocracy."

41. Horn, *Ladies of the Manor*, 11, 114-15. Note also Greville's account of Lady Cowper's philanthropy in Strachey and Fulford, eds., *Greville Memoirs* 2:232-33.

42. Maud, Lady Leconfield, ed., *Three Howard Sisters* (London, 1955), 34-36, 81.

43. The best source for this episode is the Anson MSS., Staffordshire Record Office, P(P)/1/22; it would repay further study.

44. Duke of Bedford to Lord John Russell, Aug. 4, 1847, PRO, PRO 30/22/6E, fol. 9. Cf. the quite different interpretation offered by Reynolds, *Aristocratic Women*, 144-46; also Gash, *Politics*, 181-82.

45. On the women's petition, see Clare Midgley, *Women Against Slavery: The British Campaigns, 1780-1870* (London, 1992), 148-49, and Reynolds, *Aristocratic Women*, 125-27; the duchess of Sutherland deserves a proper biography.

46. Malcolm Elwin, *Lord Byron's Wife* (London, 1962), 54, 150, 178, 210-14, 223-27; Peter Mandler, *Aristocratic Government in the Age of Reform: Whigs and Liberals, 1830-1852* (Oxford, 1990), 185-86, 189, 192.

47. Nancy Mitford, ed., *The Ladies of Alderley* (London, 1938), 202, 207-8; *Dictionary of National Biography* 18:952-53. Another obvious candidate for a proper biography.

48. Cf. Gerard, *Country-House Life*, 136–37, arguing for a brief period of privatized philanthropic activity c. 1840, between Regency public life and the "enlarged" sphere of mid-Victorian philanthropy.

49. Alex Tyrrell, "'Women's Mission' and Pressure Group Politics in Britain (1825–60)," *Bulletin of the John Rylands University Library* 63 (1980–81): 194–230; Jane Rendall, *The Origins of Modern Feminism: Women in Britain, France and the United States, 1780–1860* (Basingstoke, 1985), esp. chap. 3; Midgley, *Women Against Slavery*; Kathryn Gleadle, *The Early Feminists: Radical Unitarians and the Emergence of the Women's Rights Movement, 1831–51* (Basingstoke, 1995). See also Vickery, "Golden Age to Separate Spheres?," 398–401.

50. Horn, *Ladies of the Manor*, 131–32.

51. Noted by Janet Dunbar, *The Early Victorian Woman* (London, 1953), 140–43, despite her assumption that all "women reformers" were basically middle class. Murray was thus able to succeed where Mrs. Montagu, the eighteenth-century blue-stocking, had failed: not noted by Jaeger, *Before Victoria*, 124–25.

52. Prochaska, *Women and Philanthropy*, 174–80.

53. Lord Robert Grosvenor to Lady Westminster, Apr. 24, 1838, Bod.L, MS. c. 440, fol. 107.

54. The Howard sisters' relations with the duke can be followed in Leconfield, ed., *Three Howard Sisters*, and also in Chatsworth House, Derbyshire, Chatsworth MSS., esp. 6th duke's ser., 2993, 3674–75, 3911, and the quote from 2d ser., 1/o.

55. Chancellor, *Memorials*, 261–64; Prochaska, *Women and Philanthropy*, 52–55.

CHAPTER 5

I would like to acknowledge with gratitude the financial support given by the British Academy in the preparation of this chapter. I would also like to thank the Mistress of Girton College Cambridge for the use of the Parkes and Davies Papers.

1. John Stuart Mill to Priscilla McLaren, Dec. 12, 1868, in Francis E. Mineka and Dwight N. Lindley, eds., *The Later Letters of John Stuart Mill, 1849–1873*, 4 vols. CW 16:1521, also reprinted in *The Times*, Dec. 23, 1868, cited in Bruce L. Kinzer, Ann P. Robson, and John M. Robson, eds., *A Moralist In and Out of Parliament: John Stuart Mill at Westminster, 1865–8* (Toronto, 1992), 113, and 270–71.

2. Leslie Goldwin Smith, "Female Suffrage," *Macmillan's Magazine* 30 (June 1874): 148.

3. Barbara Bodichon to Helen Taylor, Aug. 1, 1869, MT 12, no. 50, fols. 127–32.

4. Lady Amberley to Helen Taylor, July 9, 1869, MT 19, no. 19, fols. 41–42.

5. Elizabeth Garrett Anderson to Helen Taylor, June 4, 1869, MT 14, no. 13, fols. 30–32.

6. Lydia Becker, "Women's Suffrage *versus* Mr Goldwin Smith," *WSJ* Oct. 1, 1874, 136.

7. Brian Harrison, *Separate Spheres. The Opposition to Women's Suffrage in Britain* (London, 1978), 39.

8. Ann P. Robson, "The Founding of the National Society for Women's Suffrage 1866-1867," *Canadian Journal of History* 8 (1973): 1-22; Barbara Caine, "John Stuart Mill and the English Women's Movement," *Historical Studies* 18 (1978): 52-67. See also Barbara Caine, "Feminism, Suffrage and the Nineteenth Century English Women's Movement," *Women's Studies International Forum* 5 (1982): 537-50; Andrew Rosen, "Emily Davies and the Women's Movement 1862-67," *JBS* 19 (1979): 101-21. The only overall narrative of the movement remains Helen Blackburn, *Women's Suffrage. A Record of the Women's Suffrage Movement in the British Isles with Biographical Sketches of Miss Becker* (New York, 1970 [first pub. 1902]).

9. Caine, "John Stuart Mill and the English Women's Movement," 57; see, for instance, the series of Mill's letters to George Croom Robertson from May 1871 to Dec. 1872 on the management of the London National Society for Women's Suffrage, in Mineka and Lindley, eds., *Later Letters, CW* 17.

10. See Ann Robson, "No Laughing Matter: John Stuart Mill's Establishment of Women's Suffrage as a Parliamentary Question," *Utilitas* 2 (1990): 88-101; Kinzer, Robson, and Robson, *A Moralist In and Out of Parliament*, chap. 4.

11. Mill to John Elliot Cairnes, May 26, 1867, *Later Letters, CW* 16:1271.

12. *EWR* 10 (Jan. 1869): 140-45.

13. The only analyses of Parliamentary divisions to date are those of Brian Harrison, *Separate Spheres*, chap. 2; and Martin Pugh, "The Limits of Liberalism: Liberals and Women's Suffrage," in Eugenio F. Biagini, ed., *Citizenship and Community. Liberals, Radicals and Collective Identities in the British Isles, 1865-1931* (Cambridge, 1996), 45-65.

14. For instance, see Kathryn Dodd, "Cultural Politics and Women's Historical Writing. The Case of Ray Strachey's *The Cause*," *Women's Studies International Forum* 13 (1990): 127-37.

15. Goldwin Smith, "Female Suffrage," 148.

16. Jane Rendall, "'A Moral Engine'?: Feminism, Liberalism, and the *English Woman's Journal*," in Rendall, ed., *Equal or Different Women's Politics 1800-1914* (Oxford, 1987), 112-38; Barbara Caine, *Victorian Feminists* (Oxford, 1992), chap. 2.

17. For relevant discussions of Mill, see Stefan Collini, *Public Moralists. Political Thought and Intellectual Life in Britain* (Oxford, 1991), chap. 4; John Gibbins, "J. S. Mill, Liberalism, and Progress," in Richard Bellamy, ed., *Victorian Liberalism. Nineteenth-century Political Thought and Practice* (London, 1990), 91-109; Susan Mendus, "The Marriage of True Minds: the Ideal of Marriage in the Philosophy of John Stuart Mill," in Susan Mendus and Jane Rendall, eds., *Sexuality and Subordination. Interdisciplinary Studies of Gender in the Nineteenth Century* (London, 1989), 171-91; Gail Tulloch, *Mill and Sexual Equality* (Boulder, CO, 1989). Useful anthologies in-

clude Andrew Pyle, ed., *The Subjection of Women. Contemporary Responses to John Stuart Mill* (Bath, 1995), and Ann P. Robson and John M. Robson, eds., *Sexual Equality. Writings by John Stuart Mill, Harriet Taylor Mill, and Helen Taylor* (Toronto, 1994).

18. Mill, *The Subjection of Women* (1869) in John M. Robson, ed., *Essays on Equality, Law and Education* (Toronto, 1984), *CW* 21:265.

19. Mill, "Modern French Historical Works," in John M. Robson, ed., *Essays on French History and Historians* (Toronto, 1985), *CW* 20:45-47. For discussion of Millar and the eighteenth-century background, see Jane Rendall, "Clio, Mars and Minerva: the Scottish Enlightenment and the Writing of Women's History," in Thomas M. Devine and John R. Young, eds., *Eighteenth Century Scotland. New Perspectives* (East Linton, 1999), 134-51.

20. Harriet Taylor and J. S. Mill, "The Case of Anne Bird," repr. from *Morning Chronicle*, Mar. 13, 1850, in Robson and Robson, eds., *Sexual Equality*, 69, and also ibid., xxi-ii.

21. Ibid., xxxii-iii.

22. John Stuart Mill, *Principles of Political Economy with Some of their Applications to Social Philosophy* (1848), ed. Donald Winch (Harmondsworth, 1970), 125-26.

23. Harriet Taylor Mill and J. S. Mill, "Women's Rights," and Harriet Taylor Mill, "The Enfranchisement of Women" [first publ. *Westminster Review*, 1851], in Robson and Robson, eds., *Sexual Equality*, 161-203.

24. J. S. Mill, *Considerations on Representative Government* (1861) in id., *Utilitarianism, Liberty, Representative Government* (London, 1910), 290.

25. Entries in Bessie Rayner Parkes's diary, Nov. 3 and 4 and Dec. 13, 1849, PPG, 1, fols. 4, 12 and 13; and Barbara Leigh Smith, "Abstract of Mill's principles of political economy," Bodichon Papers, Girton College.

26. Parkes to Bodichon, Jan. 5, 1858[1859], PPG, 5, fol. 86.

27. [Bessie Rayner Parkes], "The Opinions of John Stuart Mill," *EWJ* 6 (Sept. and Nov. 1860): 1-10, and 193-201, here 7.

28. "The Enfranchisement of Women," *EWJ* 13 (July 1864): 289-95; Emily Davies to Barbara Bodichon, Dec. 28, 1862, and Aug. 21, 1866, fols. 303 and 316, Davies Papers, Girton College.

29. Davies to Anna Richardson, May 10, 1865, "Family Chronicle," Davies papers, Girton College, fols. 421-22.

30. Davies to Anna Richardson, July 5, 1865, ibid., fol. 427.

31. Ibid., fols. 423-24; Andrew Rosen, "Emily Davies and the Women's Movement," 107-9; Helen Taylor, "Parliamentary Suffrage for Women," in Robson and Robson, eds., *Sexual Equality*, 211-12.

32. Emily Davies to Mr Tomkinson, Nov. 10, 1865, "Family Chronicle," fol. 439.

33. Davies to Bodichon, Aug. 21, 1866, Bodichon Papers, Girton College Cambridge, fol. 316.

34. Robson, "The Founding of the National Society for Women's Suffrage 1866-67," 13-22.

35. Jane Rendall, "Citizenship, Culture and Civilisation: the Languages of British Suffragists 1866-74," in Caroline Daley and Melanie Nolan, eds., *Suffrage and Beyond: International Feminist Perspectives* (Auckland, 1994), 127-50, here 134-40.

36. Julia Wedgwood, "Female Suffrage in Its Influence on Married Life," *Contemporary Review* 20 (Aug. 1872): 370; and id., "Female Suffrage, Considered Chiefly with Regard to Its Indirect Results," in Josephine Butler, ed., *Woman's Work and Woman's Culture* (London, 1869), 255.

37. See Thomas Hare, *The Election of Representatives, Parliamentary and Municipal. A Treatise.* 3d ed. (London, 1865); F. B. Smith, *Making of the Second Reform Bill* (Cambridge, 1966), 212-13; Millicent Fawcett, "Proportional Representation," *Macmillan's Magazine* 22 (Sept. 1870): 376-82; and "A Short Explanation of Mr Hare's Scheme of Representation," *Macmillan's Magazine* 23 (Apr. 1871): 816-26; Barbara Bodichon, "Authorities & Precedents for Giving the Suffrage to Qualified Women," *EWR* 2 (Jan. 1867): 64-72; Jessie Boucherett to Helen Taylor, June 4 [1867], MT 12, fols. 162-65; [Jessie Boucherett?], "Debate on the Enfranchisement of Women," *EWR* 4 (1867): 207.

38. Millicent Fawcett, "Free Education in its Economic Aspects," in Henry Fawcett and Millicent Garrett Fawcett, *Essays and Lectures on Social and Political Subjects* (London, 1872), 64.

39. Julia Wedgwood, "Female Suffrage in its Influence on Married Life," 365-66; id., "Female Suffrage, Considered Chiefly with Regard to its Indirect Results," 278-89.

40. In my analysis of parliamentary affiliations I have followed *The Dictionary of National Biography*; F. H. McCalmont, *The Parliamentary Poll Book of All Elections from the Reform Act of 1832 to October 1900*, 5th ed. (London, 1900); M. Stenton and S. Lees, eds., *Who's Who of British Members of Parliament*, 4 vols. (Brighton, 1976-81), 1-2. Where doubt exists as to the degree of advanced radicalism I have taken as a guide inclusion in J. O. Baylen and N. J. Gossmann, eds., *Biographical Dictionary of British Radicals*, 4 vols. (Brighton, 1984).

41. Becker to Stephen Heelis, May 29, 1868, Lydia Becker's Letter-Book, M50/1/3, fols. 198-99, MCL.

42. *EWR* 4 (July 1867): 199. The Conservative Jessie Boucherett had hoped for more from Disraeli.

43. Robson, "No Laughing Matter," 97-101.

44. But see Sandra Holton, *Suffrage Days. Stories for the Women's Suffrage Movement* (London, 1996); Rendall, "Citizenship, Culture and Civilisation," 134-40.

45. "I have been thrown into such low spirits by being very much laughed at, at Gladstone's party the other night as my poor little Committee somehow found its way into the London papers." She had recently founded a women's suffrage committee in the small Gloucestershire village of Stroud. Lady Amberley to Helen Taylor, Feb. 16, 1871, MT 19, no. 39.

46. Jonathan Parry, *The Rise and Fall of Liberal Government in Victorian Britain* (New Haven, CT, 1993), 7.

47. Ibid., 3.

48. Biagini, ed., *Citizenship and Community*; Eugenio F. Biagini and Alastair Reid, eds., *Currents of Radicalism. Popular Radicalism, Organised Labour and Party Politics in Britain, 1850–1914* (Cambridge, 1991).

49. Ann Robson, "A Bird's Eye View of Gladstone," in Bruce L. Kinzer, ed., *The Gladstonian Turn of Mind: Essays Presented to J. B. Conacher* (Toronto, 1985); Christopher A. Kent, *Brains and Numbers: Elitism, Comtism and Democracy in Mid-Victorian England* (Toronto, 1975).

50. Kathryn Gleadle, *The Early Feminists. Radical Unitarians and the Emergence of the Women's Rights Movement, 1831–1851* (Basingstoke, 1995), 64–70.

51. "Witness," "Effects of Legislating upon Love," *The National. A Library for the People* (1839): 327, quoted in Gleadle, *Early Feminists*, 69.

52. Margot Finn, *After Chartism. Class and Nation in English Radical Politics, 1848–1874* (Cambridge, 1993), 160.

53. Ibid., 166–67.

54. Rendall, "'A Moral Engine?'," 118–19.

55. *EWR* 10 (Apr. 1872): 113.

56. Parkes to Leigh Smith, Nov. 25, 1851, and Mar. 27, 1852, PPG, 5, fols. 59 and 60; Bessie Rayner Parkes to Joseph Parkes, Nov. 11, 1851, PPG, 2, fol. 39; Margaret Howitt, ed., *Mary Howitt, An Autobiography*, 2 vols. (London, 1889), 2:78–81.

57. Mill to George Croom Robertson June 1, 1871, *Later Letters*, CW 17:1823–24.

58. The first translation of *The Duties of Man* (London, 1862), was by Emilie (Ashurst) Venturi, who took an active part in the women's movement, especially the campaigns for reform of the law affecting married women's property and the repeal of the Contagious Diseases Acts. See also, for instance: "Are Duties and Rights the Same?," *EWR* 27 (July 1875): 301–6; Kate Amberley, "The Claims of Women," *Fortnightly Review* 15 o.s., 9 n.s. (Jan. 1871): 110, which cites Venturi's translation of the *Duties of Man*, chap. 6; "Mazzini on the Franchise for Women," *WSJ* 9 (Nov. 1, 1871): 95.

59. The general relationship between the anti-slavery movement and the women's movement is not discussed here in detail but has been authoritatively reviewed in Clare Midgley, *Women Against Slavery. The British Campaigns, 1780–1870* (London, 1992), chaps. 8–9; and id., "Anti-Slavery and Feminism in Britain," *Gender and History* 5, no. 3 (1993): 343–62.

60. Simon Morgan, "Domestic Economy and Political Agitation: Women and the Anti-Corn Law League," in Kathryn Gleadle and Sarah Richardson, eds., *Women in British Politics 1780–1860: The Power of the Petticoat* (Basingstoke, 2000); A. Tyrrell, "'Woman's Mission' and Pressure Group Politics (1825–1860)," *Bulletin of the John Rylands Library* 63 (1980): 194–230.

61. A. Tyrrell, "Making the Millennium: the Mid-Nineteenth Century Peace Movement," *HJ* 20, no. 1 (1978): 75–95.

62. I owe this interpretation of Manchester politics to Antony David Tay-

lor, "Modes of Political Expression and Working-Class Radicalism 1848–1874: the London and Manchester Examples" (2 vols., PhD thesis, Manchester, 1992); see also H. J. Hanham, *Elections and Party Management. Politics in the Time of Disraeli and Gladstone*, 2d ed. (Sussex, 1978), 308–12; Peter Clarke, *Lancashire and the New Liberalism* (Cambridge, 1971), 27–29.

63. Taylor, "Modes of Expression" 1:357; on Potter, a Unitarian and member of a leading Manchester family, formerly an activist of the Anti-Corn Law League and Complete Suffrage Union, and the founder of the Cobden Club, see the entry in *Dictionary of British Radicals*, ed. Baylen and Gossmann, 2:418–22; on Bright, there is little biographical information, but see ibid., 126–28; Harrison, *Dictionary of British Temperance Biography*, and obituary in the *Manchester Guardian*, Nov. 9, 1899.

64. Taylor, "Modes of Expression" 2:490–504; F. E. Gillespie, *Labor and Politics in England 1850–1867* (New York, 1966 [first pub. 1927]), 243–57.

65. Midgley, *Women Against Slavery*, 152–53.

66. Holton, *Suffrage Days*, 11.

67. Parkes to Mary Swainson, June 5, 1851, PPG, 3 fol. 23.

68. Parkes to Leigh Smith, Apr. 21, Dec. 16 and 24, 1847, Mar. 30 and Nov. 14, 1851, PPG, 5, fols. 8,17, 18, 21 and 58; "Bernard," "Eyes and no eyes," *Hastings and St Leonard's News*, Apr. 27, 1849, refers to a lecture by Elihu Barrett which Parkes attended. Generally, see Jane Rendall, "Friendship and Politics: Barbara Leigh Smith Bodichon (1827–91) and Bessie Rayner Parkes (1829–1925)," in Mendus and Rendall, eds., *Sexuality and Subordination*, 136–70.

69. Jane Rendall, "'A Moral Engine?'," 129–32.

70. Accounts differ as to the date of the committee's foundation; see Sandra Holton, *Suffrage Days*, 21–22, and 254 n.25; Sylvia Pankhurst, *The Suffragette Movement. An Intimate Account of Persons and Ideals* (London, 1977 [first pub. 1931]), 30–31; Helen Blackburn, *Women's Suffrage*, 59. On Becker, see Audrey Kelly, *Lydia Becker and the Cause* (Lancaster, 1992).

71. Manchester Committee for the Enfranchisement of Women [Manchester, 1867], M50/1/9/1, MCL. On the last years of the career of Ernest Jones, and also on Edward Hoosen in these years, see Antony David Taylor, "Ernest Jones: His Later Career and the Structure of Manchester Politics 1861–1869" (MA thesis, Univ. of Birmingham, 1984); id., "'The Best Way to Get What He Wanted': Ernest Jones and the Boundaries of Liberalism in the Manchester Election of 1868," *Parliamentary History* 16 (1997): 185–204.

72. Kyllmann, a German native, was a founder of the Union and Emancipation Society, and a friend of George Jacob Holyoake, with an interest in co-operatives; Mill, *Later Letters*, CW 15:810; on Rusden, see Becker to Taylor, Jan. 8, 1868, MT 12, fols. 80–83.

73. *MET*, Nov. 20 and 27, 1867; for a more detailed discussion of this election, see Jane Rendall, "Who Was Lily Maxwell? Women's Suffrage and Manchester Politics, 1866–7," in Sandra Holton and June Purvis, eds., *Votes for Women* (London, 1999), 57–83.

74. Lydia Becker to Mary Smith of Carlisle, May 20, 1868, Lydia Becker's

Letter-Book, fols. 138–39, M50/1/3, MCL; *First Annual Report of the Executive Committee of the Manchester National Society for Women's Suffrage* (Manchester, 1868), 4–5.

75. G. M. Trevelyan, *The Life of John Bright* (London, 1913), 379–80.

76. Sandra Holton, *Suffrage Days*, 20–25; June Hannam, "'An Enlarged Sphere of Usefulness': the Bristol Women's Movement c. 1860–1914," in Madge Dresser and Philip Ollerenshaw, eds., *The Making of Modern Bristol* (Tiverton, 1996).

77. Holton, *Suffrage Days*, 38–40; Mill to George Croom Robertson, Oct. 20 and 31, 1871, *Later Letters*, CW 17:1843 and 1849.

78. *MET*, Feb. 12, 1868.

79. Ibid., Apr. 2 and 20, 1867.

80. Ibid., Feb. 12, 1868, and other unidentified cuttings in M50/1/9/1, MCL; Lydia Becker to Helen Taylor, Feb. 12 [1868], MT 12, fols. 11–12; Lydia Becker to Jessie Boucherett Apr. 1, 1868, M50/1/3, fols. 40–41, MCL.

81. See, for more details of this campaign, Blackburn, *Women's Suffrage*, 71–88; Jane Rendall, "The Citizenship of Women and the Reform Act of 1867," in Catherine Hall, Keith McClelland, and Jane Rendall, *Defining the Victorian Nation. Class, Race, Gender and the Reform Act of 1867* (Cambridge, 2000). It was pursued on two grounds: firstly, that there was significant evidence that in medieval and early modern England, property had given women the right to exercise the parliamentary vote or to send deputies; secondly, on the legal technicality that the Act of 1867 by using the term "man" and not "male person" had generically included "woman."

82. *MET*, Apr. 15, 1868; *The Guardian*, Apr. 15, 1868; *Birmingham Daily Post*, May 9, 1868; *Birmingham Daily Gazette*, May 11, 1868; *Birmingham Journal*, May 16, 1868. Extracts from these newspapers form part of the collection of newspaper cuttings, M50 1/9/1–2, MCL.

83. Becker to Mary Johnson, May 29, 1868, Lydia Becker's Letter-Book fol. 193–94, M50/1/3, MCL. This letter-book gives a very detailed account of her direction of this campaign from March to November 1868.

84. *The Scotsman*, Oct. 1, 1868; Priscilla McLaren to John McLaren, June 9, 1868, National Library of Scotland MS 24793, fols. 122–23.

85. M50 1/9/1–2 contains numerous cuttings on the progress of this campaign, and the examples given could be multiplied, though not all cuttings have been identified.

86. *Northern Daily Express*, Apr. 1, 1869; *Newcastle Daily Chronicle*, Apr. 1, 1869; *Newcastle Daily Journal* Apr. 1 and 2, 1869; *Leeds Mercury*, Apr. 6, 1869. See also accounts of her meetings in Rochdale, *MET*, Feb. 13, 1869; in Gateshead, *The Tribune*, Apr. 3, 1869; in Carlisle, *Carlisle Journal*, Apr. 6, 1869; in Cheetham, *Manchester City News*, Apr. 17, 1869. Extracts are in M50 1/9/1–2, MCL.

87. G. C. Brodrick, *Report of Speeches on the Abolition of Tests* (London, 1866), 11, quoted in Christopher Harvie, *The Lights of Liberalism. University Liberals and the Challenge of Democracy, 1860–86* (London, 1976), 89.

88. Ibid., 304.

89. *List of Petitions presented to Parliament for the Enfranchisement of Qualified Women* [1867] M50/1/9/1, MCL.

90. Josephine Butler to James Bryce, Feb. 9, 1869, and Mar. 16 [1869], Bryce MS 160, fols. 44–51, Bod.L; Butler to Charles Pearson, Feb. 23, 1869, MS Eng. lett. d. 186, fols. 206–8, Bod.L.

91. Emily Davies to Anna Richardson, Aug. 1, 1867, "Family Chronicle," fols. 532–33, Davies Papers, Girton College.

92. Charles Pearson, "On Some Historical Aspects of Family Life," in Josephine Butler, ed., *Women's Work and Women's Culture,* 154. Pearson was a former disciple of F. D. Maurice, and from 1869 to 1871 lectured in modern history in Trinity College Cambridge.

93. John Boyd Kinnear, "The Social Position of Women in the Present Age," in Butler, ed., *Women's Work and Women's Culture,* 331–67, here 363–64; on Kinnear see Christopher Harvie, "John Boyd Kinnear, 1828–1920," *Journal of the Scottish Labour History Society* 3 (1970): 25–33.

94. T. W. Wemyss Reid, *The Life, Letters and Friendships of Richard Monckton Milnes, 1st Lord Houghton,* 2 vols., 2d ed. (London, 1869), 2:178–79.

95. S. Hutchinson Harris, *Auberon Herbert. Crusader for Liberty* (London, 1943), 130–31; Mill's correspondence with Herbert, *Later Letters, CW* 17:1808, 1822, 1869, 1945; Lady Florence May's correspondence with Helen Taylor, MT 14, fols. 124–58.

96. Lydia Becker to Elizabeth Wolstenholme, Apr. 26, and to Albert Rutson, May 26, 1868, Lydia Becker's Letter-Book, fols. 71–72 and 185–86, M50/1/3, MCL.

97. See the report of the Edinburgh women's suffrage meeting of Jan. 17, 1870, *EWR,* Apr. 1870, 91–98. It was estimated that around 1,200 were present, including 5 MPs and Sir Alexander Grant, principal of the University of Edinburgh.

98. Sir Henry Jones and John Muirhead, *The Life and Philosophy of Edward Caird* (Bristol, 1991 [first pub. 1921]), 96–101, 113–14.

99. Becker to T. E. Cliffe Leslie, May 22, 1868, Lydia Becker's Letter-Book, M50/1/3 fol. 149, MCL.

100. G. M. Trevelyan, *Sir George Otto Trevelyan. A Memoir* (London, 1932), 68–69.

101. John Morley, "Condorcet's Plea for the Citizenship of Women. A Translation," *Fortnightly Review,* n.s. 7 (May 1870): 719–24.

102. Millicent Fawcett, *What I Remember* (London, 1924), 86; *WSJ* 12 (Feb. 1, 1871): 17; Emily Davies to Lydia Becker, Jan. 17–Feb. 4, 1867, M50/1/2/1–7, MCL.

103. David Rubinstein, *A Different World for Women. The Life of Millicent Garrett Fawcett* (Brighton, 1991), 8; Justine Whiteley, "Millicent Garrett Fawcett, 1867–1894: An 'Excellent Guerrilla Partisan'" (MA thesis, Univ. of York, 1999), 28.

104. *The Rev. F. D. Maurice on Female Suffrage* [from the *Spectator* of Mar. 5, 1870].

105. Charles Kingsley, "Women and Politics," *Macmillan's Magazine* 20 (1869): 557.

106. F. D. Maurice, "Introductory Lecture. Plan of a Female College for the Help of the Rich and the Poor," *Lectures to Ladies on Practical Subjects* [1855] 3d ed. (Cambridge, 1857), 13; see also *The Life of Frederick Denison Maurice Chiefly Told in His Own Letters*, ed. Frederick Maurice, 2 vols. (London, 1884), 61, 86–87.

107. *The Rev. F. D. Maurice on Female Suffrage*, 2; Frank Maulden McLain, *Maurice, Man and Moralist* (London, 1972), 110–13.

108. Charles Kingsley, "On English Literature. Introductory Lecture given at Queen's College, London, 1848," in *The Works of Charles Kingsley*, vol. 20, *Literary and General Lectures and Essays* (London, 1880), 265.

109. Charles Kingsley, *The Massacre of the Innocents! An Address delivered by the Rev. Charles Kingsley, F. S. A., Rector of Eversley, At the First Public Meeting of the Ladies National Association for the Diffusion of Sanitary Knowledge, Reprinted from the English Woman's Journal* (London, [1859]).

110. Rendall, "'A Moral Engine?'," 128.

111. Harriet Taylor Mill, "Enfranchisement of Women," in Robson and Robson, eds., *Sexual Equality*, 202; Mill, *Subjection of Women*, CW 21:330.

112. Kingsley, "Women and Politics," 554–55, 557.

113. Charles Kingsley, to Mrs. Peter Taylor, May 27, 1870, and to John Stuart Mill, n.d., in *Charles Kingsley. His Letters and Memories of His Life*, ed. by his wife, 2 vols. (London, 1877), 2:326–28.

114. Mill to Charles Kingsley, July 9, 1870, *Later Letters*, CW 17:1742–44.

115. *Reasons for and Against the Enfranchisement of Women* (London, 1866), quoted in Patricia Hollis, "Women in Council: Separate Spheres, Public Space," in Jane Rendall, ed., *Equal or Different. Women's Politics 1800–1914* (Oxford, 1987), 192.

116. See especially Lawrence Goldman, "The Social Science Association, 1857–1886: a Context for Mid-Victorian Liberalism," *EHR* 101 (1986): 95–134, and "'A Peculiarity of the English?' The Social Science Association and the Absence of Sociology in Nineteenth-Century Britain," *Past and Present* 114 (1987): 133–71. Also see, Kathleen McCrone, "The National Association for the Promotion of Social Science and the Advancement of Victorian Women," *Atlantis* 8, no. 1 (1982): 44–66; Eileen Janes Yeo, *The Contest for Social Science. Relations and Representations of Gender and Class* (London, 1996), chap. 6.

117. Yeo, *Contest for Social Science*, 127–35.

118. Maria Luddy, "Isabella M. S. Tod," in Mary Cullen and Maria Luddy, eds., *Women, Power and Consciousness in 19th Century Ireland* (Dublin, 1995), 200.

119. Goldman, "The Social Science Association, 1857–1886," 104.

120. *Hansard Parliamentary Debates*, n.s. 1, o.s. 196, June 7, 1869, cols. 1973–76.

121. *EWR* 12 (July 1869): 279; for discussion of the support for this bill, see

Martin Pugh, "The Limits of Liberalism: Liberals and Women's Suffrage 1867–1914," 49.

122. *Hansard Parliamentary Debates*, 3d ser., 201, cols. 229–34, May 4, 1870; cols. 607–14, May 12, 1870.

123. Ibid., 201, cols. 229–34, May 4, 1870.

124. For Sir John Gray, this speculation rests on R. V. Comerford, *The Fenians in Context. Irish Politics and Society 1848–82* (Dublin, 1985), 142–44. Sir John Gray was present at the meeting held in Dublin on April 18, 1870, at which both the Fawcetts spoke, *EWR* n.s. 3 (July 1870): 193–95. For McLaren, see the entry by Jeffrey Williams in Baylen and Gossmann, eds., *Biographical Dictionary of British Radicals*; J. B. Mackie, *The Life and Work of Duncan McLaren*, 2 vols. (London, 1888), 2:102–5.

125. For the sources for the analysis which follows, see n. 38.

126. The complete list, with constituencies, is: Edward Baines (Leeds); Sir Thomas Bazley (Manchester); Joseph Cowen (Newcastle); Robert Dalguish (Glasgow); Henry Fawcett (Brighton); Francis Goldsmid (Reading); Sir John Gray (Kilkenny); J. T. Hibbert (Oldham); G. Hodgkinson (Newark); W. G. Langton (West Somerset); H. G. Liddell (Northumberland South); Duncan McLaren (Edinburgh); John Francis Maguire (Cork); W. P. Urquhart (Westmeath); D. Robertson (Berwickshire); W. Stacpoole (Ennis); James Stansfeld (Halifax); C. R. Talbot (Glamorganshire); Peter Taylor (Leicester).

127. Mill to Charles Kingsley, July 9, 1870, *Later Letters*, CW 17:1744.

128. *EWR* n.s. 3 (July 1870): 181.

129. *Hansard Parliamentary Debates*, 3d ser., 201, cols. 607–14, 618–20, May 12, 1870.

130. Ibid., 3d ser., 201, cols. 204–5, May 4, 1870.

131. Goldwin Smith to Thorold Rogers, May 18, 1970, uncatalogued Thorold Rogers Papers, Box 3, f. 629, Bod.L.

132. Goldwin Smith to James Bryce, June 5 [1874], Bryce MS 16, fols. 34–35, Bod.L.

133. For unfavorable reactions to Smith's article, see Charles Pearson to Charles Eliot Norton, Aug. 10 [1874], in John Tregenza, *Professor of Democracy. The Life of Charles Henry Pearson, 1830–1904. Oxford Don and Australian Radical* (Carlton, Victoria, 1968), 73; John Elliot Cairnes, "Woman Suffrage: A Reply," *Macmillan's Magazine* 31 (Sept. 1874): 3–24.

134. Pugh, "The Lights of Liberalism," 56; Harrison, *Separate Spheres*, chap. 2.

135. Jonathan Spain, "Trade Unionists, Gladstonian Liberals, and the Labour Law Reforms of 1875," in Biagini and Reid, eds., *Currents of Radicalism*, 109–33; Keith McClelland, "Rational and Respectable Men: Gender, the Working Class and Citizenship in Britain 1850–1867," in Laura Frader and Sonya Rose, eds., *Gender and the Reconstruction of Working Class History in Modern Europe* (Ithaca, NY, 1995), 280–93; Anna Clark, "Gender, Class and the Nation: Franchise Reform in England, 1832–1928," in James Vernon, ed., *Rereading the Constitution. New Narratives in the Political History of England's Long Nineteenth Century* (Cambridge, 1996), 250–53.

136. *WSJ*, Apr. 1, 1886. I owe this reference to Heloise Brown.

137. The Bill of 1885 also passed its second reading, but with no hope of going further.

138. Harrison, *Separate Spheres*, 35.

139. Priscilla McLaren to John McLaren, June 9, 1868, National Library of Scotland MS 24793, fols. 122–23.

CHAPTER 6

I would like to thank Krista Cowman, Andrew Davies, Sandra Holton, Susan Kinglsey Kent, James Thompson, James Vernon, and the participants in the two conferences on women and politics held at the Center for the History of Freedom. I gained much from presenting the paper to seminar groups at the Institute of Historical Research (London), the University of East Anglia, and the University of Liverpool. I would also like to thank the Fawcett Library at London Guildhall University for permission to quote from manuscripts in their possession, and the British Academy for the generous support of their Research Leave Scheme.

1. A. L. Lowell, *The Government of England*, 2 vols. (London, 1908), 2:65.

2. For instance see John Garrard, "Parties, Members and Voters after 1867: a Local Study," *HJ* 20 (1977): 145–63; James Vernon, *Politics and the People: A Study in English Political Culture, c. 1815–1867* (Cambridge, 1993).

3. C. O'Leary, *The Elimination of Corrupt Practices in British Elections* (Oxford, 1962), esp. 177 and 233.

4. D. Richter, *Riotous Victorians* (Athens, OH, 1981), 165.

5. K. T. Hoppen, "Grammars of Electoral Violence in Nineteenth-Century England and Ireland," *EHR* 109 (1994): 597–620 (esp. 605).

6. This theme is explored at length in Jon Lawrence, *Speaking for the People: Party, Language and Popular Politics in England, 1867–1914* (Cambridge, 1998), esp. chap. 7.

7. For good examples of the use of such military metaphors see Emmeline Pethick-Lawrence's writings prior to the disruption of Lloyd George's 1908 speech to the Women's Liberal Federation at the Albert Hall in *Votes for Women*, Dec. 3, 1908, and *The Times*, Dec. 3, 1908.

8. On changing attitudes toward public forms of interpersonal violence during the nineteenth century see V. A. C. Gatrell and T. B. Hadden, "Criminal Statistics and their Interpretation," in E. A. Wrigley, ed., *Nineteenth-Century Society: Essays in the Use of Quantitative Methods for the Study of Social Data* (Cambridge, 1972); V. A. C. Gatrell, "The Decline of Theft and Violence in Victorian and Edwardian England," in V. A. C. Gatrell, B. Lenman and G. Parker, eds., *Crime and the Law: the Social History of Crime in Western Europe since 1500* (London, 1980). D. Woods, "Community Violence," in John Benson, ed., *The Working Class in England, 1875–1914* (London, 1985), notes that some forms of male violence, especially within the home, were still much more widely tolerated, though see M. J. Weiner,

"The Victorian Criminalization of Men," in P. Spierenburg, ed., *Men and Violence: Gender, Honor and Rituals in Modern Europe and America* (Columbus, OH, 1998).

9. Discussed at length in Lawrence, *Speaking for the People*, 180–93.

10. Lowell, *Government of England*, 61–62; Jon Lawrence, "The Decline of Popular Politics?," *Parliamentary History* 13 (1994): 333–37.

11. See Jeff Hearn, *Men in the Public Eye: Critical Studies in Masculinities* (London, 1992), 128–30; for a discussion of the politics of male (partial) democracy see Jon Lawrence, "Class and Gender in the Making of Urban Toryism, 1880–1914," *EHR* 108 (1993): 629–52.

12. For a discussion of these themes see Lawrence, *Speaking for the People*, 188–90, which pays particular attention to late Victorian and Edwardian celebrations of the military and political adventurer Colonel Fred Burnaby, who fought Chamberlain's followers in Birmingham much as he fought the "Mahdi's" followers in the Sudan.

13. Peter Clarke, *Hope and Glory: Britain, 1900–1990* (London, 1997), 41.

14. *South London Observer*, Oct. 30, 1900.

15. For discussion of competing views of manliness in politics see Boyd Hilton, "Manliness, Masculinity and the Mid-Victorian Temperament," in Lawrence Goldman, ed., *The Blind Victorian: Henry Fawcett and British Liberalism* (Cambridge, 1989); Stefan Collini, *Public Moralists: Political Thought and Intellectual Life in Britain, 1850–1930* (Oxford, 1991), 186–96; and Catherine Hall, "Competing Masculinities: Thomas Carlyle, John Stuart Mill and the Case of Governor Eyre," in her *White, Male and Middle-Class: Explorations in Feminism and History* (Cambridge, 1992).

16. See Alan Sinfield, *The Wilde Century: Effeminacy, Oscar Wilde and the Queer Moment* (London, 1994), and R. Dellamora, *Masculine Desire: the Sexual Politics of Victorian Aestheticism* (Chapel Hill, NC, 1990), 193–217.

17. Thorough ticketing could help prevent this, but only if all seats were reserved to ticketholders, and tickets went only to known supporters—both conditions were rarely followed. For a discussion of the very different atmosphere at the heavily ticketed set-piece meetings addressed by the parties' national leaders see H. C. G. Matthew, "Rhetoric and Politics in Great Britain, 1860–1950," in P. J. Waller, ed., *Politics and Social Change in Modern Britain: Essays Presented to A. F. Thompson* (Brighton, 1987).

18. Vernon, *Politics and the People*, 217, 225–30, 249.

19. Chap. 2 above; on aristocratic women's involvement in party politics see also chap. 4 above; and K. D. Reynolds, *Aristocratic Women and Political Society in Victorian Britain* (Oxford, 1998). See also Dorothy Thompson, "Women, Work and Politics in Nineteenth-Century England: the Problem of Authority" in J. Rendall, ed., *Equal or Different: Women's Politics, 1800–1914* (Oxford, 1987). On middle-class women and politics in the late eighteenth and early nineteenth centuries see chap. 3 above and also Kathryn Gleadle, *The Early Feminists: Radical Unitarians and the Emergence of the Women's Rights Movements, 1831–51* (Basingstoke, 1998).

20. For a review of the debate relating to female involement in eight-

eenth-century food riots see E. P. Thompson, "The Moral Economy Reviewed," in his *Customs in Common* (London, 1993), 305–36; on the early nineteenth century see Anna Clark, "Queen Caroline and the Sexual Politics of Popular Culture in London, 1820," *Representations* 31 (1990): 47–68; Dorothy Thompson, "Women and Radical Politics: a Lost Dimension," in J. Mitchell and A. Oakley, eds., *The Rights and Wrongs of Women* (London, 1976).

21. Anna Clark, *The Struggle for the Breeches: Gender and the Making of the British Working Class* (Berkeley, 1995), 158–74; Jon Fulcher, "Gender, Politics and Class in the Early Nineteenth-Century English Reform Movement," *Historical Research* 67 (1994): 58–74.

22. Clark, *Struggle for the Breeches*; Sally Alexander, "Women, Class and Sexual Difference in the 1830s and 1840s," in her collection *Becoming a Woman and Other Essays in 19th and 20th Century Feminist History* (New York, 1995), esp. 110–15, 121–25; Barbara Taylor, *Eve and the New Jerusalem: Socialism and Feminism in the Nineteenth Century* (London, 1983).

23. Clark, *Struggle for the Breeches*, 197–263; though see Alexander, "Women, Class and Sexual Difference," for a more skeptical view of the potential for egalitarian forms of plebeian politics in the early nineteenth century.

24. See Anna Clark, "Gender, Class and the Constitution: Franchise Reform in England, 1832–1928," in James Vernon, ed., *Re-reading the Constitution: New Narratives in the Political History of England's Long Nineteenth Century* (Cambridge, 1996). On the post-1867 "male democracy" see Keith McClelland, "Masculinity and the Representative Artisan in Britain, 1850–1900," in M. Roper and J. Tosh, eds., *Manful Assertions: Masculinity in Britain Since 1800* (London, 1991); id., "Rational and Respectable Men: Gender, the Working Class and Citizenship in Britain, 1850–1867," in L. Frader and S. Rose, eds., *Gender and the Reconstruction of Working Class History in Modern Europe* (Ithaca, NY, 1995); also Lawrence, "Class and Gender."

25. For good examples from the Black Country see *Wolverhampton Express and Star*, July 5, 1892, July 16, 1895, Jan. 15, 1906. Annie Kenney recalls campaigning in a poor part of North Staffordshire where all the women painted themselves "dolly blue" (the local Liberal color); see Kenney, *Memories of a Militant* (London, 1924), 109.

26. *Wakefield Journal and Examiner*, Nov. 20, 1868; on the complex symbolism of "chairing" a successful candidate, see F. O'Gorman, "The Social Meaning of Elections: Campaign Rituals and Ceremonies in England During the Eighteenth and Nineteenth Centuries," *Past and Present* 135 (1992): 79–115; Vernon, *Politics and the People*, 95–98, 231. "Chairing" was carrying the winning candidate about the constituency raised shoulder-high on a chair. At Wolverhampton in 1874 a "riotous gang of factory girls" played a prominent part in an election riot which closed the polls early, *Wolverhampton Chronicle*, Feb. 11, 1874.

27. The Durham miners' leader, John Wilson, recalls being chased out of a

Leicestershire pit village by "a band of women" who suspected his motives for spreading trade unionism. See also Henry Snell, *Men, Movements and Myself* (London, 1938), 60; Frank Hodges, *My Adventures as a Labour Leader* (London, 1924), 24.

28. Linda E. Walker, "The Women's Movement in England in the Late Nineteenth and Early Twentieth Centuries" (PhD thesis, Univ. of Manchester, 1984), chaps. 1–3; Pat Jalland, *Women, Marriage and Politics, 1860–1914* (Oxford, 1986).

29. R. F. Foster, *Randolph Churchill: a Political Life* (Oxford, 1981), 215–16; R. G. Martin, *Lady Randolph Churchill: a Biography, 1854–1895* (London, 1969), 164–67; Beatrix Campbell, *The Iron Ladies: Why do Women Vote Tory?* (London, 1987), 8–23.

30. Walker, "The Women's Movement"; id.,"Party Political Women: a Comparative Study of Liberal Women and the Primrose League, 1890–1914," in J. Rendall, ed., *Equal or Different: Women's Politics, 1800–1914* (Oxford, 1987); J. H. Robb, *The Primrose League, 1883–1906* (New York, 1942); Martin Pugh, *The Tories and the People, 1880–1935* (Oxford, 1985), chap. 3; Campbell, *Iron Ladies*, 8–23; Gillian Scott, "The Working-Class Women's Most Active and Democratic Movement: the Women's Cooperative Guild from 1883 to 1950" (PhD thesis, Univ. of Sussex, 1988); June Hannam, "Women and the ILP, 1890–1914," in D. James, T. Jowitt, and K. Laybourn, eds., *The Centennial History of the Independent Labour Party* (Halifax, 1992); Karen Hunt, *Equivocal Feminists: the Social Democratic Federation and the Woman Question, 1884–1911* (Cambridge, 1996). For a good local study, which brings out *men's* equivocal attitudes toward female activism, see Krista Cowman, "'Engendering Citizenship': the Political Involvement of Women on Merseyside, 1890–1920" (D. Phil. thesis, Univ. of York, 1995), esp. chaps. 4 and 8.

31. It should be noted, on the other hand, that both the Liberal and Conserative parties continued to refuse to recognize women as members.

32. Walker, "Women's Movement," 22–27.

33. For instance, Emmeline Pankhurst, *My Own Story* (New York, 1914), 15.

34. See Christabel Pankhurst, *Unshackled: the Story of How Women Won the Vote* (London, 1987 [first pub. 1959]), 43–44; E. Sylvia Pankhurst, *The Suffragette Movement: an Intimate Account of Persons and Ideals* (London, 1931), 167–68.

35. *The Times*, Oct. 23, 1908; see also Elizabeth Robins, *The Convert* (London, 1980 [first pub. 1907]), 114.

36. For instance, Sandra Stanley Holton, *Feminism and Democracy: Women's Suffrage and Reform Politics in Britain, 1900–1918* (Cambridge, 1986); id., "In Sorrowful Wrath: Suffrage Militancy and the Romantic Feminism of Emmeline Pankhurst," in H. L. Smith, ed., *British Feminism in the Twentieth Century* (Aldershot, 1990); id., "The Suffragist and the 'Average Woman'," *Women's History Review* 1 (1992): 9–24; Krista Cowman, "'The Stone-Throwing Has Been Forced Upon Us': the Function of Militancy

Within the Liverpool WSPU, 1906–14," *Transactions of the Lancashire and Cheshire Historical Society* 145 (1996 for 1995): 171–92.

37. Holton, "In Sorrowful Wrath"; id., *Suffrage Days: Stories from the Women's Suffrage Movement* (London, 1996), esp. chaps 2 and 9; B. Harrison, "The Act of Militancy: Violence and the Suffragettes, 1909–1914," in his *Peaceable Kingdom: Stability and Change in Modern Britain* (Oxford, 1982)—though this does *not* eschew the "court of judgement" approach; Martha Vicinus, *Independent Women: Work and Community for Single Women, 1850–1920* (Chicago, 1985), chap. 7; Lisa Tickner, *The Spectacle of Women: Imagery of the Suffrage Campaign, 1907–14* (Chicago, 1988); Ann Morley and Liz Stanley, *The Life and Death of Emily Wilding Davison* (London, 1988), esp. chap. 5; Laura Mayall, "Creating the 'Suffragette Spirit': British Feminism and the Historical Imagination," *Women's History Review* 4 (1995): 319–44.

38. For instance, Claire Eustance, "Protest from Behind the Grille: Gender and the Transformation of Parliament, 1867–1918," *Parliamentary History* 16 (1997): 107–26 (Special Issue 4, E. H. H. Green, ed., *An Age of Transition: British Politics, 1880–1914*); Claire Eustance, "Meanings of Militancy: the Ideas and Practice of Political Resistance in the Women's Freedom League," in M. Joannou and J. Purvis, eds., *The Women's Suffrage Movement: New Feminist Perspectives* (Manchester, 1998); Cowman, "Stone-Throwing"; Sandra Holton, "Manliness and Militancy: the Political Protest of Male Suffragists and the Gendering of 'Suffragette' Identity," in A. V. John and C. Eustance, eds., *The Men's Share? Masculinities, Male Support and Women's Suffrage in Britain, 1890–1920* (London, 1997); Ian Fletcher, "'A Star Chamber of the Twentieth Century': Suffragettes, Liberals, and the 'Rush the Commons' Case," *JBS* 35 (1996): 504–30.

39. Grey was not technically a minister at this point, but it was widely recognized that the fall of the Conservative Government was imminent—the Liberals took office in December.

40. C. Pankhurst, *Unshackled*, 49–52; S. Pankhurst, *Suffragette Movement*, 189; E. Pankhurst, *My Own Story*, 46–50; *Votes for Women*, Dec. 3, 1908.

41. E. Pankhurst, *My Own Story*, 48.

42. Teresa Billington-Greig, *The Militant Suffrage Movement: Emancipation in a Hurry* (London, 1911); this chronology is confirmed by contemporary accounts; see, for instance, *The Times*, Jan. 5, 6, 9, and 10, 1906 (meetings involving Churchill, Asquith, and Campbell-Bannerman). The original tactic was not wholly abandoned, though it was rarely pursued with much success—see *The Times*, June 16, 1906 (Asquith at Northampton); *Votes for Women*, Nov. 12, 1908 (Haldane at Glasgow).

43. E. Pankhurst, *My Own Story*, 234–35; C. Pankhurst, *Unshackled*, 51 and 59; and *The Times*, Jan. 6, 1906, where a suffragette at Churchill's meeting argues that "the methods adopted to raise the question were unconstitutional and unfair, but if they waited until the close of the meetings they would not be answered."

44. *Votes for Women*, Apr. 30, 1909; he also suggests that the WSPU persisted much longer with their original strategy of non-interruption, as does S. Pankhurst, *Suffragette Movement*, 212.

45. E. Pankhurst, *My Own Story*, 234–35.

46. *The Times*, Oct. 10, 1906; Emmeline Pethick-Lawrence, *My Part in a Changing World* (London, 1938), 158.

47. *The Times*, Oct. 10, 1906, Dec. 6, 1907; also *Votes for Women*, Dec. 1907 (Gladstone at Leeds).

48. H. M. Swanwick, *I Have Been Young* (London, 1935), 197 and 217. For classic examples of "serial" interruption in practice see *The Times*, Nov. 18 and 22, 1907; Evelyn Sharp, *Unfinished Adventure: Selected Reminiscences from an Englishwoman's Life* (London, 1933), 138; and, of course, accounts of Lloyd George's Albert Hall meeting in 1908 (see below).

49. Jane Marcus, *Suffrage and the Pankhursts* (London, 1987), 9.

50. For a strong discussion of this theme see Vicinus, *Independent women*, 262–68.

51. For analyses of why, ideologically, it was so important for the suffragettes to avoid recourse to male tactics of violence and disorder see Holton, "In Sorrowful Wrath," esp. 20–21; and id., "Manliness and Militancy."

52. See *Votes for Women*, Dec. 3, 1908, Apr. 16 and 30, 1909.

53. For instance, E. Pankhurst, *My Own Story*, 16, 48, 66, 81, 119, 213–14, 266. Also Viscountess Rhondda (Margaret Haig), *This Was My World* (London, 1933), 129; Mary Richardson, *Laugh a Defiance* (London, 1953), 8; *Votes for Women*, Dec. 1907.

54. For instance, Rhondda, *My World*, 122–23; *The Times*, Nov. 21 and Dec. 3, 1907.

55. For a skit on the attachment to "party flags" see R. Tressell, *The Ragged-Trousered Philanthropists* (London, 1965), 533–36; on the importance of party colors see Vernon, *Politics and the People*, esp. 83–85, 107–13, 164–67.

56. For good early examples see *The Times*, Jan. 5, 9, and 10, 1906; and on the Grey meeting in 1905, E. Pankhurst, *My Own Story*, 50, and C. Pankhurst, *Unshackled*, 50.

57. Though in times of great political excitement, such as war, even these meetings were not immune from disruption; see Lawrence, *Speaking for the People*, 183–90.

58. On the politics of such meetings see Matthew, "Rhetoric and Politics"; also the contemporary account of Henry Jephson, *The Platform: Its Rise and Progress*, 2 vols. (London, 1892), 2:555–72.

59. Billington-Greig, *Militant Suffrage Movement*, 41–46.

60. Additionally, Viscountess Rhondda recalls how Welsh members sometimes declined to get involved in WSPU activities in their own commuity for fear of the social consequences. Indeed, during 1910 she agreed to campaign in Scotland to spare her father's feelings; Rhondda, *My World*, 140, 144. See also Leah Leneman, "A Truly National Movement: the View From Outside London," in Joannou and Purvis, eds., *Women's Suffrage Movement*, 44.

61. For good examples see *The Times*, Nov. 8, 1907 (Harcourt at Batley), and June 3, 1909 (Burns at Whitechapel).

62. *Votes for Women*, Dec. 3, 1909.

63. For a different approach see the discussion of Molony's intervention at the 1908 Dundee by-election in the next section.

64. Teresa Billington-Greig, "Suffragist Tactics: Past and Present," *Fortnightly Review* 82 (July 1, 1907): 65–76; this reworks themes from her essay "The Militant Policy of Women Suffragists," *Teresa Billington-Greig Papers* (Fawcett Library, London Guildhall University), Box 404, 7/TSBG/G3 (Nov. 1906). See also Claire Eustance, "'Daring to be Free': the Evolution of Women's Political Identities in the Women's Freedom League, 1907–1930" (D. Phil. thesis, Univ. of York, 1994), esp. 148–52 and 169–71.

65. See "Women, Votes and Violence," *Teresa Billington-Grieg Papers*, Box 404, 7/TSBG/G3 (Apr. 18, 1913)—she also argued that violence was in any case often counter-productive.

66. Billington-Greig, *Militant Suffrage Movement*, 37, and more generally, 1–4 and 140–42.

67. Robins, *The Convert*, 157–59; Teresa Billington-Greig, "The Woman with the Whip" [1907], repr. in Carol McPhee and Ann FitzGerald, eds., *The Non-Violent Militant: Selected Writings of Teresa Billington-Greig* (London, 1987), 125–30; *Women's Franchise*, July 18, 1907; and A. E. Metcalfe, *Woman's Effort: a Chronicle of British Women's Fifty Years Struggle for Citizenship, 1865–1914* (Oxford, 1917), 81, 161–62. Many autobiographies touch on the subject, some more frankly than others; see esp. Pethick-Lawrence, *My Part*, 250; S. Pankhurst, *Suffragette Movement*, 286, 297, 313, and 342; Richardson, *Laugh a Defiance*, 9–10.

68. *The Times*, Dec. 8, 1908—Emmeline Pethick-Lawrence wrote denouncing sexual assaults; see also Swanwick, *I Have Been Young*, 198. For a sustained discussion of the sex-war dimension to suffrage politics see Susan Kingsley Kent, *Sex and Suffrage in Britain, 1860–1914* (London, 1990), esp. chap. 6.

69. For instance see *Women's Franchise*, Jan. 9 and 23 and Oct. 8, 1908; C. Pankhurst, *Unshackled*, 78; Robins, *The Convert*, 167–69. On the WSPU training in how to handle a hostile crowd see Kenney, *Memories of a Militant*, 104. Evelyn Sharp recalls that a working man who helped her to her feet after a rough ejection in Norwich commented, "I admire your pluck, mum"; Sharp, *Unfinished Adventure*, 138.

70. See S. Pankhurst, *Suffragette Movement*, 262; Rhondda, *My World*, 124–25; Isabella Ford to Milicent Fawcett, Feb. 14, 1908, *Fawcett Papers*, Box 89 (Fawcett Library).

71. Pethick-Lawrence, *My Part*, 160–61.

72. For a classic discussion of the suffragettes from this perspective see Stephen Reynolds, Bob Wooley, and Tom Wooley, *Seems So! A Working-Class View of Politics* (London, 1911), chap. 2. Reynolds (one suspects) argues "we do not approve, but we thank them for the sport provided," ibid., 17.

73. *The Times*, May 6, 8, and 9, 1908; S. Pankhurst, *Suffragette Movement*, 281. Molony was demanding an apology for alleged insults to the WFL. For subsequent criticism of Miss Molony within the WFL, apparently for organizing political disruption in Haggerston, see *Women's Freedom League*, National Executive Committee minutes, Nov. 24, 1908 (Fawcett Library), Box 54, FL6/1/1.

74. *The Times*, May 9, 1908.

75. S. Pankhurst, *Suffragette Movement*, 221—which stresses that Christabel Pankhurst relied on more than physical charms to control a crowd; her secret was "her crisply-phrased audacity" and her power as a speaker; Robins, *The Convert*, 115, 155, 176–77, 179; and id., "Votes for Women," in D. Spender and C. Hayman, eds., *How the Vote Was Won and Other Suffragette Plays* (London, 1985), 61, 65–66 present a similar analysis. See also Maroula Joannou, "Suffragette Fiction and the Fictions of Suffrage," 103–10; June Purvis, "Cristabel Pankhurst and the Women's Social and Political Union," 161—both in Joannou and Purvis, eds., *Women's Suffrage Movement*; and Jane Eldridge Miller, *Rebel Women: Feminism, Modernism and the Edwardian Novel* (London, 1994), 134–35.

76. Evelyn Sharp recalled quelling a near riot at one meeting by catching a rotten egg hurled from the crowd (without breaking it), a feat which perhaps takes the idea of needing to be a "good sport" a little far: Sharp, *Unfinished Adventure*, 132.

77. Many had in fact learned their politics as itinerant propagandists for the ILP in the 1890s; see Walker, "Women's Movement," 66–71, perhaps the only precedent for women speakers to confront the roughest aspects of popular politics.

78. Elizabeth Gaskell, *North and South* (London, 1988 [first pub. 1855]), 234–35.

79. Holton, "In Sorrowful Wrath," 21; Vicinus, *Independent Women*, 263–64; also Diane Atkinson, "Six Suffragette Photographs," in Joannou and Purvis, eds., *Women's Suffrage Movement*, 93.

80. F. K. Prochaska, *Women and Philanthropy in Nineteenth-Century England* (Oxford, 1980); Anne Summers, "A Home from Home: Women's Philanthropic Work in the Nineteenth Century," in Sandra Burman, ed., *Fit Work for Women* (London, 1979).

81. For classic, if retrospective, "maternalist" representations of Mrs. Pankhurst see Kenney, *Memories*, 41–42, 192; C. Pankhurst, *Unshackled*, 21–22, 28–31, 36–39; on Mrs. Pankhurst's ability to quell even the most hostile meeting see ibid., 78, 100; Ethel Smyth, *Female Pipings in Eden* (London, 1933), 194; Rhondda, *My World*, 124–25. On the use of dress to project a "controlled sexuality" in contrast to the "uncontrolled" and "unruly" male polity see Vicinus, *Independent Women*, 264.

82. See Michelle Myall, "'No Surrender!': the Militancy of Mary Leigh, a Working-Class Suffragette," 173–87 and Leneman, "Truly National Movement," 46–47, both in Joannou and Purvis, eds., *Women's Suffrage Movement*.

83. "The Militant Policy of Women Suffragists," *Teresa Billington-Greig Papers*, Box 404, 7/TSBG2/G3, 8; also Holton, "In Sorrowful Wrath," 20–22, and Atkinson, "Six Suffragette Photographs," 90–91. This theme is explored more fully in Section IV below.

84. Constance Lytton and "Jane Warton," *Prisons and Prisoners* (London, 1914); *Votes for Women*, Oct. 15, 1909; see also Vicinus, *Independent Women*, 271–77; Mary Jane Corbett, *Representing Femininity: Middle-Class Subjectivity in Victorian and Edwardian Women's Autobiographies* (Oxford, 1992), 165–69; June Purvis, "The Prison Experiences of the Suffragettes in Edwardian Britain," *Women's History Review* 4 (1995): 118–20.

85. E. Pankhurst, *My Own Story*, 129 (quoting from her defense at the first conspiracy trial of 1908). Her epigram that "If men will not do us justice, they shall do us violence" was no less frequently quoted; for instance see Smyth, *Female Pipings*, 198, and, significantly, Lytton, *Prisons and Prisoners*, 36.

86. S. Pankhurst, *Suffragette Movement*, 195.

87. For discussions of this theme see Kent, *Sex and Suffrage*; Holton, "In Sorrowful Wrath"; Brian Harrison, *Separate Spheres: the Opposition to Women's Suffrage in Britain* (London, 1978), esp. 73–78 and 114–15.

88. *Women's Franchise*, July 11, 1907 and Dec. 3, 1908.

89. Ibid., Dec. 26, 1907.

90. See chap. 5 above.

91. Holton, "In Sorrowful Wrath," esp. 20–22.

92. "The Militant Policy of Women Suffragists," *Teresa Billington-Greig Papers*, Box 404, 7/TSBG2/G3, 8.

93. Accounts of such incidents are by no means *confined* to suffrage sources. These were not simply fabricated stories of solace; for instance, see *The Times*, Nov. 12, 1907, and Dec. 7, 1908.

94. *The Times*, Sept. 4, 1908 (from Zeneide Mirovitch, a Russian journalist in London). For similar sentiments from a male "militant" see *Women's Franchise*, Dec. 17, 1908 (the socialist Joseph Clayton).

95. *Women's Franchise*, Oct. 8, 1908. See also Rhondda, *My World*, 146–47 on being rescued from a hostile Scottish crowd by three golf caddies.

96. Richardson, *Laugh a Defiance*, 54–55—she describes the Hyde Park "mob" in graphic terms and claims they wore locks of suffragettes' hair as trophies in their lapels.

97. For examples see *Women's Franchise*, Jan. 23, Oct. 15, and, Dec. 17, 1908; *The Times*, Dec. 7, 1908. For useful discussions of these issues see Joanna de Groot, "'Sex' and 'Race': the Construction of Language and Image in the Nineteenth Century," in S. Mendus and J. Rendall, eds., *Sexuality and Subordination: Interdisciplinary Studies of Gender in the Nineteenth Century* (London, 1989); Hall, *White, Male and Middle-Class*, chap. 10; id., "'From Greenland's Icy Mountains . . . to Afric's Golden Sand': Ethnicity, Race and Nation in Mid-Nineteenth-Century England," *Gender & History* 5 (1993): 212–43; John Tosh, "What Should Historians Do With Masculinity? Reflections on Nineteenth-Century Britain," *History Workshop Journal* 38

(1994): esp. 193–98; Clare Midgley, ed., *Gender and Imperialism* (Manchester, 1997).

98. See especially S. Strauss, *Traitors to the Masculine Cause: The Men's Campaigns for Women's Rights* (Westport, CT, 1982), 195–233; John and Eustance, eds., *The Men's Share?*; and chap. 7 below.

99. For instance, Cowman, "Stone-Throwing," 175, 177–78, and 180.

100. Hannah Mitchell, *The Hard Way Up: the Autobiography of Hannah Mitchell, Suffragette and Rebel* (London, 1977), 128, and 139; also S. Pankhurst, *Suffragette Movement*, 193. For a typically jaundiced retrospective account of this socialist minority see Teresa Billington-Grieg's notebook "Early Days, 1903-4-5," *Teresa Billington-Grieg Papers*, Box 244, item TBG 76. For contemporary accounts of male socialist "bodyguards" see *Women's Franchise*, Oct. 15, 1908; *Votes for Women*, Dec. 1907 and Oct. 29, 1908; *Labour Record*, Nov. 1906.

101. This was undoubtedly the prime motive stressed by groups such as the Men's League for Women's Suffrage, which organized a "Stewards Corps" to defend women against "outrages" which were an "affront to male honour"; see *Women's Franchise*, Jan. 9 and 28, Apr. 9, July 2, Oct. 8 and 15, and Dec. 17, 1908.

102. For instance, *The Times*, Nov. 23, 1907 (Gladstone at Leeds), Nov. 13, 1908 (Birrell at City Temple); Mitchell, *Hard Way Up*, 138. For a contemporary *celebration* of one of these incidents see *Votes for Women*, Dec. 1907 (Gladstone at Leeds).

103. *Women's Franchise*, Feb. 27, 1908.

104. C. Pankhurst, *Unshackled*, 117–18, 135, 195, and 220; even so she still *excused* these male reactions, suggesting that they were hardly surprising when one considers that men had to watch women violently ejected or forcibly fed—she seems to assume that it would be against the nature of "honorable" masculinity not to react to such outrages with violence.

105. *Women's Franchise*, Jan. 2, 1908. Later in the campaign it became commonplace to organize all-woman bodyguards to protect famous speakers from arrest; see for instance, E. Pankhurst, *My Own Story* (Glasgow, 1914), 340–42. For an early and apparently spontaneous example see *Women's Franchise*, Oct. 31, 1907, in which Emma Sproson describes an incident at Bilston in April 1907 where local women formed a bodyguard to protect militants from an unruly male crowd.

106. On the implications of such male "apostasy" within Parliament—long the most hallowed of male political spaces—see Eustance, "Behind the Grille," 122–26.

107. For graphic accounts of their fate at such meetings see C. Pankhurst, *Unshackled*, 135–42; Pethick-Lawrence, *My Part*, 235–36; *The Times*, July 31 and Oct. 11, 1909.

108. On this point see Sandra Holton's careful consideration of the equivocal status of male militancy in the post-1911 phase of the campaign in "Manliness and Militancy," esp. 122–28.

109. S. Pankhurst, *Suffragette Movement*, 296–97, suggests that elaborate

plans were laid to ensure that reporters and photographers would see the sorry condition of women ejected from the meeting.

110. This point was more or less acknowledged in her autobiographical account of the movement; see C. Pankhurst, *Unshackled*, 153.

111. *The Times*, Sept. 25, 1909. Many historians have recently emphasized the "reactive" quality of suffragette militancy, see esp. Morley and Stanley, *Emily Wilding Davison*.

112. For good discussions of these different tactics see *Votes for Women*, Apr. 30, 1909; Pethick-Lawrence, *My Part*, 159–61; E. Pankhurst, *My Own Story*, 81–82, 88, and 265–66; C. Pankhurst, *Unshackled*, 68, 78, 83, and 137; S. Pankhurst, *Suffragette Movement*, 212, 262, and 286; Richardson, *Laugh a Defiance*, 7–12, 31, and 54–55.

113. Sharp, *Unfinished Adventure*, 137–38. Also Pethick-Lawrence, *My Part*, 191; Swanwick, *I Have Been Young*, 193 and *Votes for Women*, Apr. 30, 1909.

114. *The Times*, Sept. 18, 1909, notes that some women were allowed on the platform. The paper estimates that Asquith drew an audience of approximately 13,000 (including the over-spill meeting in the Curzon Hall). See also *Votes for Women*, Oct. 29 and Dec. 24, 1908; C. Pankhurst, *Unshackled*, 117 and 121; Pethick-Lawrence, *My Part*, 228.

115. S. Pankhurst, *Suffragette Movement*, 193, 275; Mitchell, *Hard Way Up*, 138; E. Pankhurst, *My Own Story*, 235; Sharp, *Unfinished Adventure*, 138.

116. *Votes for Women*, Dec. 1907, Apr. 2 and 30, 1909; *The Times*, Dec. 2, 1907, Oct. 23, 1908; C. Pankhurst, *Unshackled*, 193–94.

117. *Votes for Women*, Dec. 1907; *The Times*, Nov. 23, 1907, and July 19, 1909.

118. *Votes for Women*, Dec. 3, 1908; though ticketing was common at party meetings, it was rare for all seats to be ticketed unless the speaker was a great celebrity, and even rarer for the seats to be restricted solely to party members.

119. See *Votes for Women*, Nov. 26, 1908 (Grey at Scarborough), Dec. 3, 1908 (Birrell at Warrington); also ibid., Apr. 30, 1909, and E. Pankhurst, *My Own Story*, 234–35 and 242.

120. For instance, *Votes for Women*, Oct. 29, Nov. 12 and 26, Dec. 24, 1908, Mar. 5, 1909; *The Times*, Oct. 11, 1909.

121. For useful accounts of each see *Manchester Guardian*, Dec. 7, 1908, and Swanwick, *I Have Been Young*, 197–98 (Albert Hall); S. Pankhurst, *Suffragette Movement*, 342–43 (Black Friday); Eunice Murray, "Suffrage Scrapbook No. 2" (Fawcett Library), 3 and 15 (Black Friday and Llanystumdwy).

122. S. Pankhurst, *Suffragette Movement*, 309. She claims that the window-breaking policy was intensified after "Bloody Friday" as "a painless method of securing arrest" (ibid., 359).

123. Pethick-Lawrence, *My Part*, 233.

124. C. Pankhurst, *Unshackled*, 153, 166, 169. On male violence in 1912 and the shift to "terrorist" tactics, see ibid., 226.

125. *The Times*, Sept. 23, 1912. During 1912 *The Times* reported 17 cases of suffragette disruption at cabinet ministers' meetings; in 1908 they had reported 30 and in 1909, 42 ("repeat" disturbances, as at the Dundee by-election, counted as only one case). Clearly the politics of disruption had *not* been abandoned, though they had, perhaps, been down-played within the struggle.

126. Vicinus, *Independent Women*, 268–76; Corbett, *Representing Femininity*, 163–69; Purvis, "Prison Experiences," 112–24; Marcus, *Suffrage and the Pankhursts*, 1–2.

127. See Kent, *Sex and Suffrage*, 18, 20, 148–49, 154–56, and 196.

128. C. Pankhurst, *Unshackled*, 73; see also E. Pankhurst, *My Own Story*, 88, 90–93.

129. *Votes for Women*, Nov. 12, 1908. Violent disruption of suffragette meetings was a constant problem throughout the campaign; for early examples see *The Times*, Nov. 30, Dec. 3 and 6, 1907, Oct. 14, 1909.

130. For instance, Lowell, *Government of England* 1:64.

131. See *Parliamentary Debates*, 4th ser., 80 (1900), cols. 940–986, "Right of Free Speech: Disturbances Directed Against Opponents of the War in South Africa."

132. For instance, see Emrys Hughes, ed., *Keir Hardie's Speeches and Writings: From 1888 to 1915* (3d ed., Glasgow, n.d. [1928?]), 122; Ramsay MacDonald, *Socialism and Government*, 2 vols. (London, 1909), 1: xxvi and 108; id., *Parliament and Revolution* (Manchester, 1919), repr. in B. Barker, ed., *Ramsay MacDonald's Political Writings* (London, 1972), 221–22; Philip Snowden, *An Autobiography*, 2 vols. (London, 1934), 1:169 (attacking Grayson's populism). Though giving evidence to the Home Office in 1909, both Hardie and MacDonald argued that they would rather see meetings disrupted than encourage increased police intervention in party politics; see *Report of the Departmental Committee on the Duties of the Police With Respect to the Preservation of Order at Public Meetings*, 2 vols. (PP1909 Cd4674, XXXVI), 2, Q1799 and Q1857.

133. *Parliamentary Debates*, 4th Ser., 198 (1908). Advocates of reform included Cecil (Marylebone, E.), cols. 2169, 2336; Ward (Stoke), cols. 2329–30; Vivian (Birkenhead), col. 2331; and Maddison (Burnley), cols. 2334–35; those defending tradition included: Radford (Islington, E.), col. 2169; Harmsworth (Droitwich), col. 2329; Wedgwood (Newcastle-under-Lyme), cols. 2330–31; Thorne (West Ham), cols. 2331–32; and Crooks (Woolwich), cols. 2334 and 2337–38.

134. See *Committee on the Duties of the Police*, 2 vols. (PP1909, Cd4674, XXXVI) 1:95, 97–98; 2; also Pethick-Lawrence, *My Part*, 212.

135. Though the intensified "guerrilla" campaign mounted after 1912 certainly made it difficult for many to recognize this aspect of the "militant" movement.

136. For a full discussion of the campaign see Lawrence, *Speaking for the People*, 255–56.

137. *Daily Herald*, Nov. 25, 1912.

138. The subject of the author's present research into "The British Way of Voting Transformed"; see also Michael Dawson, "Liberalism in Devon and Cornwall, 1910–1931: 'the Old Time Religion'," *HJ* 38 (1995): 425–37, esp. 425 and 432–37.

139. Susan Kingsley Kent, *Making Peace: the Reconstruction of Gender in Inter-War Britain* (Princeton, NJ, 1993).

CHAPTER 7

1. See chap. 6 above.
2. See chap. 5 above and S. Strauss, *'Traitors to the Masculine Cause.' The Men's Campaigns for Women's Rights* (Westport, CT, 1982).
3. See K. Hunt, *Equivocal Feminists* (Cambridge, 1996) for the views of those in the Social Democratic Federation; and L. Ugolini, "Independent Labour Party Men and Women's Suffrage in Britain 1893–1914" (Ph.D. thesis, Univ. of Greenwich, 1997).
4. An exception to this neglect is K. Cowman, "'A Party Between Revolution and Peaceful Persuasion.' A Fresh Look at the United Suffragists," in M. Joannou and J. Purvis, eds., *The Women's Suffrage Movement. New Feminist Perspectives* (Manchester, 1998), 77–88. I am grateful to Krista Cowman for letting me read this chapter in draft.
5. C. Law, *Suffrage and Power. The Women's Movement 1918–1928* (London, 1997), 1–2.
6. See chap. 5 above.
7. See chap. 8 below.
8. S. S. Holton, "Now you see it, now you don't: the Women's Franchise League and its place in the contending narratives of the women's suffrage movement," in Joannou and Purvis, eds., *The Women's Suffrage Movement*, 31.
9. M. A. Butler and J. Templeton, "The Isle of Man and the First Votes For Women," *Women and Politics* 4, 2 (1984): 33–47.
10. Fawcett Library, London Guildhall University, Box 396.11(06).
11. For details of the workings of the men's societies see A. V. John and C. Eustance, eds., *The Men's Share? Masculinities, Male Support and Women's Suffrage in Britain 1890–1920* (London, 1997) and A. V. John, "Between the Cause and the Courts: The Curious Case of Cecil Chapman," in C. Eustance, J. Ryan, L. Ugolini, eds., *A Suffrage Reader. Themes and Directions in the Study of British Suffrage History* (London, 2000). Jacob's wife Agnes Larkom joined the Women's Freedom League and Actresses' Franchise League.
12. A. V. John, *"Chwarae Teg": Welsh Men's Support for Women's Suffrage* (Aberystwyth, 1998), 2.
13. *Men's League for Women's Suffrage Monthly*, July 1910.
14. John, "Between the Cause."
15. See chap. 5 above.
16. J. R. DeVries, "Challenging Traditions. Denominational Feminism in

Britain, 1910–1920" in B. Melman, ed., *Gender Identities in War and Peace 1870–1930* (London, 1998), 270.

17. See J. Tosh, "The Making of Masculinities. The Middle Class in Late Nineteenth-Century Britain," in John and Eustance, eds., *The Men's Share?*, 47–51.

18. Quoted in J. Beckett and D. Cherry, eds., *The Edwardian Era* (London, 1987), 19.

19. It is instructive to compare the gendered autobiographies and reminiscences of partners who were both active in women's suffrage. For example, Frederick Pethick-Lawrence later recalled the suffrage period as one which accorded him "the privilege of friendship with some of the most glorious women that have ever lived," Bod.L, Evelyn Sharp Nevinson Papers, MSS Eng. Lett. c277, fol. 170. June Balshaw has noted how women's suffrage was portrayed in his autobiography as "a short period in his life, covering four slim chapters, while in Emmeline's it is presented as her life's main focus. J. Balshaw, "Sharing the Burden. The Pethick Lawrences and Women's Suffrage," in John and Eustance, eds., *The Men's Share?*, 154.

20. G. Savage, "'. . . Equality from the Masculine Point of View . . .' The Second Earl Russell and Divorce Law Reform in England," *Journal of the Bertrand Russell Archive*, n.s. 16 (1996): 67–84. I am grateful to Lesley Hall for this reference.

21. Viscountess Rhondda, *This Was My World* (London, 1933), 229–30.

22. *Men's League for Women's Suffrage Monthly*, June, July 1910. See too L. Tickner, *The Spectacle of Women* (London 1987), 111–15.

23. *Men's League for Women's Suffrage Monthly*, July 1910. Compare this with the account in the *Daily Chronicle* by Harold Owen quoted in B. Green, *Spectacular Confessions. Autobiography, Performative Activism, and the Sites of Suffrage 1905–1938* (London, 1997), 10–11. Green comments on Owen's apparent reservations about the feminization of modern public space.

24. Evelyn Sharp Nevinson Papers, Bod.L, MSS Eng. Misc. d270.

25. M. E. Gawthorpe, "Votes For Women. How They Were Won" (pamphlet, London, n.d.).

26. S. Paget, *Sir Victor Horsley. A Study of His Life and Work* (London, 1919), 203–7.

27. E. Robins, *Way Stations* (London, 1913), 289.

28. A. Kenney, *Memories of a Militant* (London, 1924), 218–19; M. Richardson, *Laugh a Defiance* (London, 1953), 148; E. S. Pankhurst, *The Suffragette Movement* (London, 1931, 1977 ed.) paid tribute to individual men, especially Keir Hardie.

29. E. Pethick-Lawrence, *My Part in a Changing World* (London, 1938), 290.

30. Bod.L, Henry Woodd Nevinson Papers, Diaries, MSS Eng. Misc. e617/1, Jan. 19, 1912.

31. L. E. N. Mayhall, "'Creating the Suffragette Spirit.' British Feminism and the Historical Imagination," *Women's History Review* 4 (1995): 319–44.

See too H. Kean, "Searching for the Past in Present Defeat: the Construction of Historical and Political Identity in British Feminism in the 1920s and 1930s," *Women's History Review* 3 (1994): 57–80; and Green, *Spectacular Confessions* chap. 4, which draws attention to the impact the rise of fascism had on the way suffrage memories were shaped.

32. See chap. 6 above.
33. F. Brockway, *Inside the Left* (London, 1942), 28–29.
34. H. W. Nevinson, *More Changes, More Chances* (London, 1925), 322–24. He was threatened with suspension by the *Daily News* but this threat was withdrawn when fellow journalists looked likely to resign in protest. A few months later Nevinson and his fellow journalist H. N. Brailsford chose to resign because of the paper's attitude toward suffrage.
35. *Glamorgan Free Press*, May 14, 1909.
36. A. V. John, "Men, Manners and Militancy. Literary Men and Women's Suffrage," in John and Eustance, eds., *The Men's Share?*, 101.
37. H. Carter, ed., *Women's Suffrage and Militancy* (London, 1911), 43, 56.
38. See, for example, *Cambrian News*, Oct. 9, 30, 1908; Oct. 15, 1909.
39. *Westminster Gazette*, May 7, 1914.
40. Fawcett Library, London Guildhall University, Hugh Franklin and Elsie Duval Papers, 226, Folder 4.
41. Robins, *Way Stations*, 24.
42. Nevinson Diaries, e617/1, Nov. 16, 1911.
43. For this incident see John, "Chwarae Teg," 7–8.
44. The MLWS claimed to be the first society to take this decision. It was then adopted by the NUWSS and Women's Freedom League. *Men's League for Women's Suffrage Monthly*, June 1912.
45. S. S. Holton, "Manliness and Militancy. The Political Protest of Male Suffragism and the Gendering of the 'Suffragette Identity'," in John and Eustance, eds., *The Men's Share?*, 110–34.
46. Hugh Franklin and Elsie Duval Papers, Box 227.
47. Nevinson Diaries, e617/1, Mar. 8, 1912.
48. Hugh Franklin and Elsie Duval Papers, 226, Folder 4.
49. C. Eustance, "Citizens, Scotsmen, 'bairns.' Manly Politics and Women's Suffrage in the Northern Men's Federation, 1913–20," in John and Eustance, eds., *The Men's Share?*, 182–205.
50. Balshaw, "Sharing the Burden," 135–57 and A. V. John, *Elizabeth Robins. Staging A Life. 1862–1952* (London, 1995), chap. 7.
51. B. Winslow, *Sylvia Pankhurst. Sexual Politics and Political Activism* (London, 1996); J. Schneer, *George Lansbury* (Manchester, 1990).
52. Correspondence with Krista Cowman, to whom I am grateful.
53. Museum of London, Suffragette Fellowship Collection, Book of Suffragette Prisoners, 58.87/65.
54. University of Wales, Bangor. Bangor and District Women's Suffrage Society. Minute Book, 25800; P. Ellis Jones, "The Women's Suffrage Movement in Caernarfonshire," *Transactions of the Caernarvonshire Historical Society* 48 (1987): 75–112.

55. It is interesting, though, to note that it tended to be daughters rather than sons who supported suffrage parents. K. Bradley, "Faith, Perseverance and Patience: the History of the Oxford Suffrage and Anti-Suffrage Movements" (Ph.D. thesis, Oxford Brookes Univ., 1997).
56. Nevinson Diaries, e617/3, Jan. 28, 1913.
57. Quoted in A. Rosen, *Rise Up, Women!* (London, 1974), 224-26.
58. For example, J. Vellacott Newberry, "Antiwar Suffragists," *History* 62 (1977): 411-25.
59. Sandra Holton has, however, pointed to the US links with the Daily Herald League. See S. S. Holton, *Feminism and Democracy. Women's Suffrage and Reform Politics in Britain 1900-1918* (Cambridge, 1986), 128.
60. I. Fletcher, "'A Star Chamber of the Twentieth Century': Suffragettes, Liberals and the 1908 'Rush the Commons' Case," *JBS* 35 (1996): 506.
61. Nevinson's Diaries from e618/1, Dec. 3, 1914, onward provide an invaluable personal account of the evolution of the society which can be set alongside *Votes For Women*.
62. Evelyn Sharp Nevinson Papers, MSS Eng. Lett. c277, fol. 12.
63. Editorial signed by the executive in *Votes For Women*, Feb. 1918.
64. Ibid., July 10, 1914.
65. I am currently working on a triple biography of Evelyn Sharp, Margaret Wynne Nevinson, and Henry Nevinson.
66. For this speech and its repercussions see *Votes For Women*, July 10, 1914; Nevinson Diaries, e618/3, July 7, 10, 16, 1914, Oct. 9, 1914.
67. *Westminster Gazette* May 7, 1914. His wife, Lady Winifred, had become vice-president of the Littlehampton branch of the NUWSS in 1913. In 1920 Sir Harry would parody the pre-war militants in his novel *Mrs. Warren's Daughter* which extended Shaw's play, presenting Vivie Warren as a suffragette whose activism involved her cross-dressing.
68. Nevinson Diaries, e618/2, May 13, 1914.
69. *Westminster Gazette*, May 11, 1914.
70. *Votes For Women*, Feb. 6, 1914.
71. Cowman, "A Party Between Revolution," 80.
72. John, *Elizabeth Robins*, 171.
73. *Votes For Women*, Feb. 6, 1914.
74. Ibid.
75. Melman, *Borderlines*, esp. 1-9.
76. Nevinson Diaries, e618/3, Oct. 17, 1914.
77. Ibid., e620/3, Jan. 23, 1918.
78. He signed a number of his editorials. Nevinson also wrote on women's suffrage in other newspapers.
79. Nevinson Diaries, e619/3, Jan. 30, 1916.
80. Ibid., e619/1, July 26, 1915.
81. Ibid., e619/2, Oct. 24, 1915; *Votes For Women*, Oct. 29, 1915.
82. Nevinson Diaries, e619/1, May 25, 1915.
83. L. Housman, *The Unexpected Years* (London, 1937), 298. See too Mayhall, "Creating the Suffragette Spirit."

84. Nevinson Diaries, e618/3, Nov. 21 1914; see *Votes For Women* for frequent reports and announcements of entertainment, etc.

85. Evelyn Sharp recalled how "We made it as unlike an institution as possible," one of the first arrivals apparently commenting, "Why, it's just like a West End gentleman's club, with no religious instruction." After a suffragist spoke on the relations of the sexes and absurdity of sex war, one of the audience was heard to say of her husband, "Well, I've bore with 'im sixteen year—but I'm going home now to tell 'im what I *do* think of 'im!" Quoted in E. Sharp, "Our Club" in id., *The War of All the Ages* (London, 1915), 53, 57.

86. *Votes For Women*, Dec. 1918.

87. Nevinson Diaries, e618/4, Nov. 30, 1914. See too G. Braybon and P. Summerfield, *Out of the Cage. Women's Experiences in Two World Wars* (London, 1987), 109–10.

88. *Votes For Women*, July 17, 1916.

89. Cowman, "A Party Between Revolution," 84.

90. W. E. Adams, *Memoirs of a Social Atom* (London, 1968 [first pub. 1903]), 196.

91. Nevinson Diaries, e618/4, June 25, 1915. The fact that much of the detailed knowledge of the United Suffragists comes from Nevinson's diaries does need to be taken into account in evaluating this society.

92. Ibid., e619/3, Apr. 14, 1916.

93. Ibid., e620/1, Aug. 19, 1916.

94. Ibid., e620/1, Dec. 15, 1916. Compare this with Emmeline Pankhurst's written comment about the NUWSS: "so staid, so willing to wait, so incorrigibly leisurely." E. Pankhurst, *My Own Story* (London, 1914), 485. See Holton, *Feminism and Democracy*, chap. 7, for the co-operation between women's suffrage groups at this time.

95. The National Council for Adult Suffrage had slightly more male than female members. Nevinson's Diaries for 1916–17 are useful for chronicling these developments.

96. Ibid., e620/1, Sept. 24, 1916.

97. Editorial by Nevinson in *Votes For Women*, Feb. 1917, quoting the *Westminster Gazette*. For details see M. Pugh, *Women and the Women's Movement in Britain 1914–59* (London, 1992), 36–38; S. S. Holton, *Suffrage Days. Stories from the Women's Suffrage Movement* (London, 1996), 225–26.

98. Nevinson Diaries, e620/3, Feb. 6, 1918.

99. For a useful examination of the limitations of the legislation, see C. Law, "The old faith living and the old power there: the movement to extend women's suffrage," in Joannou and Purvis, eds., *The Women's Suffrage Movement*, 201–14.

100. Nevinson Diaries, e620/3, Feb. 16, 1918.

101. Ibid., e620/3, Apr. 28, 1918. Fales Library, New York University Library, Elizabeth Robins Papers, Series 1, Box 6, Diary, Apr. 28, 1918.

102. E. Sharp, *Hertha Ayrton 1854–1923. A Memoir* (London, 1926), 273.

103. Ibid., 241.
104. Cowman, "A Party Between Revolution," 86.
105. See chap. 8 below.

CHAPTER 8

1. Barbara Caine, *English Feminism, 1780–1980* (Oxford, 1997), 173–255. H. L. Smith, "British Feminism in the 1920s," in H. L. Smith, ed., *British Feminism in the Twentieth Century* (Aldershot 1990), 124–43. Martin Pugh, *Women and the Women's Movement in Britain 1914–1959* (London, 1992), presents a rather more complex picture.
2. Pugh, *Women's Movement*, 312.
3. Caine, *English Feminism*; Smith, ed., *British Feminism*; Pugh, *Women's Movement*.
4. Quoted in Caine, *English Feminism*, 183.
5. Shirley M. Eoff, *Viscountess Rhondda. Equalitarian Feminist* (Columbus, OH, 1991), 64.
6. Ibid., 132, quoted from *Time and Tide*.
7. E.g. by Olive Banks, *Faces of Feminism* (Oxford 1981).
8. Eoff, *Rhondda*, 174.
9. Sylvia Pankhurst, *The Suffrage Movement* (London, 1977 [first pub. 1931]).
10. Pugh, *Women's Movement*.
11. Pankhurst, *Suffrage*, 607–8.
12. Susan Kingsley Kent, *Making Peace. The Reconstruction of Gender in Interwar Britain* (Princeton, NJ, 1993). Sandra M. Gilbert, "Soldier's Heart: Literary Men, Literary Women and the Great War," in Margaret R. Higonnet et al., *Behind the Lines. Gender and the two World Wars* (New Haven, CT, 1987), 197–226. This interpretation has been ably criticized by S. Cullen, "Gender and the Great War. British Combatants, Masculinity and Perceptions of Women, 1918–39" (D. Phil. thesis Oxford University, 1999).
13. Eoff, *Rhondda*, 149.
14. Andro Linklater, *An Unhusbanded Life. Charlotte Despard: Suffragette, Socialist and Sinn Feiner* (London, 1980), 249.
15. *The Vote*, July 6 1928, 212, quoted in Cheryl Law, *Suffrage and Power. The Women's Movement, 1918–28* (London, 1997), 224.
16. Sandra Stanley Holton, *Feminism and Democracy* (Cambridge, 1986).
17. Millicent Garrett Fawcett, *The Women's Victory—and After: Personal Reminiscences, 1911–1918* (London, 1920).
18. E.g. Caine, *English Feminism*, 173.
19. Chap. 6 above; and *The Times*, Oct. 30, 1924.
20. Quoted in Law, *Suffrage*, 227.
21. Ray Strachey, *The Cause. A Short History of the Women's Movement in Great Britain* (London, 1978 [first pub. 1928]).
22. Caine, *English Feminism*, 197.
23. Strachey, *Cause*, 367.

24. D. and G. Butler, *British Political Facts, 1900–1994* (London, 1994), 213–19.
25. *The Times*, Nov. 16, 1922.
26. *The Times*, Dec. 7, 1923.
27. *The Times*, Dec. 8, 1923.
28. *The Times*, Oct. 30, 1924.
29. *The Times*, May 30, 1929.
30. Ibid. Election Day Report from the North-East.
31. Ibid. Report from Greater London.
32. Ibid. Report from the Midlands.
33. Ibid. Report from Scotland.
34. *The Times*, May 31, 1929.
35. Sam Davies, *Liverpool Labour. Social and Political Influences on the Development of the Labour Party in Liverpool, 1900–1939* (Liverpool, 1996), 190.
36. E.g. J. Blondel, *Voters, Parties and Leaders* (London, 1965).
37. Vicky Randall, *Women and Politics. An International Perspective* (London, 1987).
38. Ibid. 69–70.
39. Among others, D. Butler and D. Stokes, *Political Change in Britain: the Evolution of Political Choice* (2d ed. London, 1974), 160. I. Crewe et al., *The British Electorate, 1963–87: A Compendium of Data from the British Election Studies* (Cambridge, 1991), 6.
40. J. Lovenduski et al., "The Party and Women," in A. Seldon and S. Ball, eds., *Conservative Century. The Conservative Party since 1900* (Oxford, 1994), 611–35.
41. Chap. 9 below; John Turner, "The Labour Vote and the Franchise after 1918: an Investigation of the English Evidence," in P. Denley and D. Hopkin, eds., *History and Computing* (Manchester, 1987); J. Rasmussen, "Women in Labour: the Flapper Vote and Party System Transformation in Britain," *Electoral Studies* 3,1 (1984). For a critique see Duncan Tanner, *Political Change and the Labour Party, 1900–1918* (Cambridge, 1990), 308.
42. Tanner, *Political Change*, 308.
43. Randall, *Women and Politics*, 70–76.
44. Pat Thane, "The Women of the British Labour Party and Feminism, 1906–1945" in Smith, ed., *British Feminism*, 124.
45. J. Mark-Lawson et al., "Gender and Local Politics: Struggles over Welfare Policies, 1918–1939," in L. Murgatroyd et al., eds., *Localities, Class and Gender* (London, 1985), 67–90.
46. Patricia Hollis, *Ladies Elect. Women in English Local Government, 1865–1914* (Oxford, 1987).
47. Michael Savage, *The Dynamics of Working Class Politics: The Labour Movement in Preston, 1880–1940* (Cambridge, 1987).
48. Davies, *Liverpool Labour*, 186–88.
49. Pamela M. Graves, *Labour Women. Women in British Working Class Politics, 1918–1939* (Cambridge, 1994).

50. Pugh, *Women*, 125.
51. Ibid.
52. Pat Thane, "Women, Liberalism and Citizenship, 1918–1930," in E. Biagini, ed., *Citizenship and Community. Liberals, Radicals and Collective Identities in the British Isles 1865–1931* (Cambridge, 1996), 68.
53. Ibid; *Liberal Women's News*, Apr. 1925.
54. For details see Thane, "Women of the British Labour Party"; Graves, *Labour Women*.
55. See chap. 9 below; and see Pugh, *Women's Movement*, 124–29.
56. Graves, *Labour Women*, 22–40, 154–80; Thane, "Women, Liberalism and Citizenship."
57. Law, *Suffrage*, 113.
58. Brian Harrison, *Separate Spheres. The Opposition to Women's Suffrage in Britain* (London, 1978), 229.
59. Graduates, male and female, could vote both in their constituencies and for a separate list of university candidates, who were elected by proportional representation. This practice was abolished in 1948.
60. Butler and Butler, *Facts*, 167–68.
61. I am grateful to Janet Howes, who is completing a Ph.D. thesis at Anglia Polytechnic University, for this information.
62. Davies, *Liverpool Labour*, 247–361.
63. In Liverpool Labour women and the local WCA drew increasingly apart in the 1920s. Davies, *Liverpool Labour*, 176.
64. Pugh, *Women's Movement*, 70–71.
65. Maggie Andrews, *The Acceptable Face of Feminism. The Women's Institute as a Social Movement* (London, 1997).
66. Pugh, *Women's Movement*, 240–41.
67. Law, *Suffrage*, 232–37.
68. Also Andrews, *Womens Institutes*; Caitlin Beaumont, "Women and Citizenship: a study of non-feminist women's societies and the women's movement in England, 1928–1950" (Ph.D. diss. Warwick Univ. 1997).
69. Jacqueline R. deVries, "Challenging Traditions: Denominational Feminism in Britain, 1910–1920," in Billie Melman, ed., *Borderlines. Genders and Identities in War and Peace, 1870–1930* (London, 1998), 265–84. Sheila Fletcher, *A. Maude Royden. A Life* (Oxford, 1989).
70. I am grateful to Sue Innes (University of Edinburgh) for this information.
71. Pugh, *Women's Movement*, 241–42.
72. Caine, *English Feminism*, 200.
73. Ibid., 176.
74. These extended the rights of women to sit on municipal and county councils. Hollis, *Ladies in Council*, 491.
75. Fawcett, *Women's Victory*, 165.
76. Nurses Registration Act, 1919.
77. Elizabeth Peretz, "Maternal and Child Welfare in England and Wales Between the Wars: A Comparative Regional Study" (Ph.D. diss. Middlesex

Univ., 1992). Davies, *Liverpool Labour*, 173-81. Mark-Lawson, "Gender and local politics." Thane, "Women, Liberalism," 68. Caine, *English Feminism*, 176, 200. Peretz, *Maternal Welfare*.

78. A. Leathard, *The Fight for Family Planning* (London, 1980); Julie Grier, "Eugenics and Birth Control: Contraceptive Provision in North Wales, 1918-1939," *Social History of Medicine* 11, 3 (Dec. 1998): 443-59.

79. Law, *Suffrage*, 82-84. Carol Dyhouse, "Women Students and the London Medical Schools, 1914-39: The Anatomy of a Masculine Culture," *Gender and History* 10, 1 (1998): 110-32.

80. Fawcett, *Women's Victory*, 162-65.

81. Ibid., 161.

82. Cordelia Moyse, "The Reform of Marriage and Divorce Law in England and Wales, 1909-1937" (Ph.D. diss. Univ. of Cambridge, 1996), 201-4.

83. Ibid., 211-20.

84. Ibid., 264n.1.

85. Ibid., 389.

86. Susan Pedersen, *Family, Dependence and the Origins of the Welfare State. Britain and France, 1914-1945* (Cambridge, 1993).

87. Olive Banks, *Faces of Feminism*, 169-71; Smith, "British Feminism in the 1920s," in Smith, ed., *British Feminism*, 124-43.

88. This had occurred at Oxford in 1921.

89. Law, *Suffrage*, 143.

90. Moyse, "Marriage and Divorce," 111.

91. Law, *Suffrage*, 85.

92. Ibid., 193-218.

93. *The Woman Teacher*, July 9, 1926, 305, quoted in Law, *Suffrage*, 212-13.

94. Law, *Suffrage*, 213.

95. Moyse, "Marriage and Divorce," 111.

96. B. Harrison, *Prudent Revolutionaries* (Oxford, 1987), 273-300. Olive Banks, ed., *The Biographical Directory of British Feminists, Vol. 1. 1800-1930* (Brighton, 1985), 95-99.

97. Pugh, *Women's Movement*, 70-71.

98. For further examples see P. Thane, "Women in the British Labour Party and the Construction of State Welfare, 1906-1939," in S. Koven and S. Michel, eds., *Mothers of a New World. Maternalist Politics and the Origins of Welfare States* (London, 1993), 343-77; Peretz, *Maternal Welfare*.

99. Smith, ed., *British Feminism*.

100. Pugh, *Women's Movement*, 109.

101. Caine, *English Feminism*; Smith, ed., *British Feminism*.

102. *Labour Woman*, Feb. 1944.

103. Smith, ed., *British Feminism*.

104. J. Alberti, *Beyond Suffrage: Feminists in War and Peace, 1914-28* (London, 1989).

105. Mass Observation Archive, University of Sussex, Topic Collection, Family Planning 1944-49.

106. *Report, Royal Commission on Population*, Cmd.7695, *Parliamentary Papers*, 1948-49, vol. 19:156.

CHAPTER 9

1. On the 1997 general election result, see D. Butler and D. Kavanagh, *The British General Election of 1997* (Basingstoke, 1997), 295-325; and A. Geddes and J. Tonge, eds., *Labour's Landslide. The British General Election, 1997* (Manchester, 1997). On the general state of the Party, see P. Whiteley, P. Seyd, and J. Richardson, *True Blues. The Politics of Conservative Party Membership* (Oxford, 1994); J. Gray and D. Willetts, *Is Conservatism Dead?* (London, 1997); D. Kavanagh, *The Reordering of British Politics. Politics After Thatcher* (Oxford, 1997), 231-32.

2. E.g. I. Gilmour and M. Garnett, *Whatever Happened to the Tories? The Conservatives Since 1945* (London, 1997).

3. These themes are discussed at greater length in D. Jarvis, "Whatever Happened to the Tories? Some Reflections on the Recent History of Post-1867 Conservatism," *HJ* (forthcoming).

4. A striking example of this is C. Pattie and R. Johnston, "The Conservative Party and the Electorate," in S. Ludlam and M. J. Smith, eds., *Contemporary British Conservatism* (Basingstoke, 1996), 37-62, which contrives to ignore gender as a variable in an otherwise detailed analysis of the Party's electoral support.

5. P. Norris, "Mobilising the 'Women's Vote': the Gender-generation Gap in Voting Behaviour," *Parliamentary Affairs* 49 (1996): 333-42.

6. Richard Shannon's *The Age of Salisbury. 1881-1902* (London, 1996) is typical in this respect. His discussion of the influence of women within the Primrose League is limited to a single page, during which the League Dames are described with classic male ambivalence as "formidable" (120). The other volumes in the Longman's series are R. Stewart, *The Foundation of the Conservative Party, 1830-67* (London, 1978); R. Shannon, *The Age of Disraeli, 1868-1881; the Rise of Tory Democracy* (London, 1992); J. Ramsden, *The Age of Balfour and Baldwin, 1902-40* (London, 1978); id., *The Age of Churchill and Eden, 1940-57* (London, 1995); id., *The Winds of Change: Macmillan to Heath, 1957-75* (London, 1996).

7. E.g. J. Charmley, *A History of Conservative Politics, 1900-1996* (Basingstoke, 1996); B. Evans and A. Taylor, *From Salisbury to Major. Continuity and Change in Conservative Politics* (Manchester, 1996); R. Blake, *The Conservative Party From Peel to Major* (London, 1997).

8. These characteristics are discussed at greater length in D. Jarvis, "The Shaping of the Conservative Electoral Hegemony, 1918-39," in J. Lawrence and M. Taylor, eds., *Party, State and Society. Electoral Behaviour in Britain Since 1820* (Aldershot, 1997), 131-52.

9. R. Morris, *Tories. From Village Hall to Westminster: a Political Sketch* (Edinburgh, 1991), 103. The characterization of Thatcher as an "honorary man" is thoughtfully discussed in H. Young, *One of Us. A Biography of*

Margaret Thatcher (London, 1989), 303-12; and B. Campbell, *The Iron Ladies. Why Do Women Vote Tory?* (London, 1987), 233-47.

10. J. Lovenduski, P. Norris, and C. Burness, "The Party and Women," in A. Seldon and S. Ball, eds., *Conservative Century. The Conservative Party Since 1900* (Oxford, 1994), 611-35. See also S. Ball, "The National and Regional Party Structure" and "Local Conservatism and the Evolution of the Party Organisation," in ibid., 169-220 and 261-314.

11. Morris, *Tories*, 41-42.

12. E.g. A. J. Davies, *We, the Nation. The Conservative Party and the Pursuit of Power* (London, 1995), 153-54; Ramsden, *Churchill and Eden*, 124.

13. For a sardonic description of this ritual, see J. Varley, "No 'Lady Bountifuls': the Way to an Efficient Women's Organisation," *CAJ*, Jan. 1966.

14. This point is explored in greater detail in D. Jarvis, "The Conservative Party and the Politics of Gender, 1900-1939," in M. Francis and I. Zweiniger-Bargielowska, eds., *The Conservatives and British Society, 1880-1990* (Cardiff, 1996), 172-93.

15. E.g. M. Benney, A. P. Gray, and R. H. Pear, *How People Vote* (London, 1956), 17; H. Durant, "Voting Behaviour in Britain, 1945-64," in R. Rose, ed., *Studies in British Politics* (London, 1966), 125; The Gallup Poll, "Voting Behaviour in Britain," in ibid., 3d ed. (London, 1976), 211; D. Butler and D. Stokes, *Political Change in Britain: the Evolution of Political Choice*, 2d ed. (London, 1974), 160; I. Crewe, N. Day, and A. Fox, *The British Electorate, 1963-87: A Compendium of Data From the British Election Studies* (Cambridge, 1991), 6.

16. E.g. P. Norris, "Conservative Attitudes in Recent British Elections: An Emerging Gender Gap?," *Political Studies* 24 (1986): 120-28.

17. Two exceptions in this respect are M. Groot and E. Reid, "Women: If Not Apolitical, Then Conservative," in J. Siltanen and M. Stanworth, eds., *Women and the Public Sphere: A Critique of Society and Politics* (London, 1984), 130-32; and I. Zweiniger-Bargielowska, "Explaining the Gender Gap," in Francis and Zweiniger-Bargielowska, eds., *Conservatives and British Society*, 194-224.

18. A recent, but conspicuously unsuccessful, attempt to do so is G. E. Maguire, *Conservative Women. A History of Women and the Conservative Party, 1874-1997* (Basingstoke, 1998), reviewed by this author in *Twentieth Century British History* 10, 4 (1999): 540-51.

19. Ramsden, *Balfour and Baldwin*, 250-51; Shannon, *Age of Salisbury*, 120.

20. Campbell, *The Iron Ladies*.

21. Ibid., 298. Cf. Lovenduski et al., "The Party and Women," 611-12.

22. Campbell, *Iron Ladies*, 54-55 and 71-75; cf. P. Graves, *Labour Women* (Cambridge, 1994); and D. Weinbren, *Generating Socialism. Recollections of Life in the Labour Party* (Stroud, 1997), 157-63. Campbell's characterization of traditional Labour culture is given more credence in H. Wainwright, *Labour. A Tale of Two Parties* (London, 1987), esp. 162-87.

23. Jarvis, "Politics of Gender," 176–82.
24. Quoted in Zweiniger-Bargielowska, "Explaining the Gender Gap," 194.
25. P. Abrams and A. Little, "The Young Activist in British Politics," *British Journal of Sociology* 16, 4 (1965): 315–33; J. Holroyd-Doveton, *Young Conservatives. A History of the Young Conservative Movement* (Durham, NC, 1996), 153–59.
26. I am indebted at this point to Dr. Alison Jeffries for access to her unpublished work on Conservative individualism and gender.
27. M. Pugh, "Popular Conservatism in Britain: Continuity and Change," *JBS* 27 (1988): 254–82.
28. See, for example, G. Himmelfarb, "The Politics of Democracy," *JBS* 6 (1966).
29. J. Roper, *Democracy and Its Critics. Anglo-American Democratic Thought in the Nineteenth Century* (London, 1989); D. Jarvis, "British Conservatism and Class Politics in the 1920s," *EHR* 440 (1996): 65–68.
30. E. H. H. Green, *The Crisis of Conservatism. The Politics, Economics and Ideology of the British Conservative Party, 1880–1914* (London, 1995), 125.
31. E.g. South Oxfordshire Conservative Association AGM, Jun. 6 1925, ORO, S. Oxon Con I/3.
32. E. H. H. Green, "The Strange Death of Tory England," *20th Century British History* 2, 1 (1991): 67–88; and id., *The Crisis of Conservatism*.
33. M. Pugh, *Electoral Reform in War and Peace, 1906–18* (London, 1978), 26.
34. See, for example, B. Harrison, *Separate Spheres: The Opposition to Women's Suffrage in Britain* (London, 1972).
35. On the prevalence of these fears after 1918, see S. Kingsley Kent, *Making Peace. The Reconstruction of Gender in Inter-war Britain* (Princeton, NJ, 1993), 89–91.
36. M. Cowling, *The Impact of Labour, 1920–1924* (Cambridge, 1971), 427.
37. *CAJ*, June 1920, 6–8.
38. Jarvis, "Class Politics," 80–81.
39. D. Jarvis, "Mrs. Maggs and Betty. The Conservative Appeal to Women Voters in the 1920s," *20th Century British History* 5, 2 (1994): 129–52.
40. See, for example, D. H. Close, "The Collapse of Conservative Resistance to Democracy: Conservatives, Adult Suffrage and Second Chamber Reform, 1911–1928," *HJ* 20 (1977): 893–918.
41. Sanders diary, Dec. 12 1923, in J. Ramsden, ed., *Real Old Tory Politics. The Political Diaries of Robert Sanders, Lord Bayford, 1910–1935* (London, 1984), 211; J. A. R. Marriott, *Memories of Four Score Years* (London, 1946), 195; S. Ball, *Baldwin and the Conservative Party. The Crisis of 1929–1931* (London, 1988), 221.
42. Bridgeman diary, Oct. 1931, in P. Williamson, ed., *The Modernisation of Conservative Politics: The Diaries and Letters of William Bridgeman, 1904–35* (London, 1988), 250.

43. J. Turner, *British Politics and the Great War. Coalition and Conflict 1915-1918* (New Haven, CT, 1992), 414-18.
44. J. Turner, "Sex, Age and the Labour Vote in the 1920s," in P. Denley and D. Hopkin, eds., *History and Computing II* (Manchester, 1989), 243-54; J. Rasmussen, "The Political Integration of British Women: The Response of a Traditional System to a Newly Emergent Group," *Social Science History* 7 (1983): 61-95; and id., "Women in Labour," *Electoral Studies*, 1984, 47-63.
45. Ramsden, *Churchill and Eden*, 90.
46. On the "Eden factor," see J. Boyd-Carpenter, *Way of Life* (London, 1980), 123-24.
47. Jul. 4 1957, CCO 500/9, p. 5, CPA.
48. E. H. H. Green, "The Conservative Party, the State and the Electorate, 1945-64," in Lawrence and Taylor, *Party, State and Society*, 176-200.
49. Zweiniger-Bargielowska, "Explaining the Gender Gap," 195.
50. L. Peake, "Women in the Campaign and in the Commons," in Geddes and Tonge, *Labour Landslide*, 166; Zweiniger-Bargielowska, "Explaining the Gender Gap," 195.
51. Peake, "Women," 166.
52. Norris, "Mobilising the 'Women's Vote.'"
53. A. Clark, *The Tories: Conservatives and the Nation State, 1922-1997* (London, 1998), 380-81.
54. For a fuller discussion of the historiography of "popular Toryism," see Jarvis, "Conservatism and Class Politics," 60-61.
55. M. Pugh, *Women and the Women's Movement, 1918-59* (London, 1992), 124-25.
56. Doubts about the former are longstanding—see, for example, R. Blake, *The Conservative Party From Peel to Thatcher* (London, 1985), 164-66. Internal Conservative debates about the latter are brilliantly explored in E. H. H. Green, "Radical Conservatism: The Electoral Genesis of Electoral Reform," *HJ* 28 (1985): 667-92.
57. Jarvis, "Politics of Gender."
58. J. Robb, *The Primrose League, 1883-1906* (New York, 1942), 228.
59. Ibid., 115.
60. M. Pugh, *The Tories and the People, 1880-1935* (Oxford, 1985), 54-55.
61. Lovenduski et al., "The Party and Women," 618.
62. L. Walker, "Party Political Women: A Comparative Study of Liberal Women and the Primrose League, 1890-1914," in J. Rendall, ed., *Equal or Different? Women's Politics 1880-1914* (Oxford, 1987), 191.
63. Jarvis, "Shaping," 136-37.
64. South Oxfordshire Conservative Association AGM, Jun. 9 1928, ORO S. Oxon Con. I/3.
65. For details of the scope and activities of Women's Unionist Associations, see Pugh, *Women and the Women's Movement*, 124-29. Further light has been thrown on the WUAs in the 1920s in N. McCrillis, *The British Conservative Party in the Age of Universal Suffrage. Popular Conservatism, 1918-1929* (Columbus, OH, 1998), 46-82.

66. Ibid., 125.

67. R. Topping, "Women's Organisation. A Plea for Joint Associations," *CAJ*, Aug. 1920, 7–10; E. J. Forster, "The Separate System Supported," *CAJ*, Sept. 1920, 6–8; id., "A Woman Organiser," *CAJ*, Feb. 1921, 16–17.

68. Speech of Mrs. Harding, Stafford Women's Unionist Association, reported in the *Staffordshire Sentinel*, Oct. 30 1922; M. Maxse, *CAJ*, May 1924, 108–9. Cf. Jarvis, "Mrs Maggs and Betty," 137.

69. See Jarvis, "Politics of Gender."

70. Flintshire Conservative Association (CA) management committee, Sept. 4, 1930, Clwyd RO D/DM/307/8. See also Banbury CA, ORO. BCA I/3.

71. S. Ball, "Local Conservatism and the Evolution of the Party Organisation," in Seldon and Ball, *Conservative Century*, 270.

72. E.g. *The "Women's Party"* (National Union leaflet no. 3021).

73. CCO 500/9/2, p. 13, CPA, Bod.L.

74. Working Party Report on the State of Women's Organisations, July 4, 1957, 3. CPA CCO 500/9/2.

75. *The Right Way* 1 (Autumn 1954): 3.

76. J. Critchley, *A Bag of Boiled Sweets* (London, 1994), 32.

77. J. Holroyd-Doveton, *Young Conservatives: a History of the Young Conservative Movement* (Durham, NC, 1996), 153–59. On the longstanding social exclusivity of Conservative youth organizations, see Cuthbert Headlam diary, Feb. 9, 1931, in S. Ball, ed., *Parliament and Politics in the Age of Baldwin and Macdonald. The Headlam Diaries, 1923–35* (London, 1992), 201.

78. Conservative Women's National Association Committee (WNAC) working party, CPA 500/9/2.

79. R. Kelly, *Conservative Party Conferences. The Hidden System* (Manchester, 1989), 123–27.

80. Whiteley, Seyd, and Richardson, *True Blues*, 42–71.

81. The fallacy of describing Conservatism as a non-ideological belief system now seems finally to have been laid to rest. See for example J. D. Fair and J. A. Hutcheson, "British Conservatism in the Twentieth Century: An Emerging Ideological Tradition," *Albion* 19, 4 (1987): 549–78.

82. J. Lawrence, "Class and Gender in the Making of Urban Toryism, 1880–1914," *EHR* 108 (1993): 630–52.

83. For details, see Jarvis, "Mrs Maggs and Betty," 146–47.

84. *Home and Politics* 51 (1925): 11.

85. Elliot, *Toryism*, 124–27.

86. Ramsden, *Balfour and Baldwin*, 210.

87. Jarvis, "Mrs. Maggs and Betty," 48–50.

88. W. Elliot, *Toryism and the Twentieth Century* (London, 1927), 82–83.

89. I. Zweiniger-Bargiewloska, "Rationing, Austerity and the Conservative Party Recovery After 1945," *HJ* 37 (1994): 173–97.

90. I. Gilmour, *Inside Right* (London, 1977), 147.

91. Zweiniger-Bargiewloska, "Explaining the Gender Gap," 210–15.

92. E.g. CCO 506/14, Northern Area Young Conservatives Area Policy Group Report, "Society and the Individual," Section C, p. 1, CPA.

93. J. Barnes, *A Woman's Place* (London, 1960).
94. CCO 500/9/7, WNAC Course, Swinton 1961, group 2, CPA.
95. A classic example of this, albeit phrased in atypically frank language, remains Peregrine Worsthorne's assault on the "excessive freedom" of the 1970s: P. Worsthorne, "Too Much Freedom," in M. Cowling, ed., *Conservative Essays* (London, 1978), 141–54.
96. M. Durham, *Sex and Politics. The Family and Morality in the Thatcher Years* (Basingstoke, 1991).
97. On the ideological coherence or otherwise of "Thatcherism," see A. Gamble, *The Free Economy and the Strong State: The Politics of Thatcherism*, 2d ed. (London, 1994); S. Hall, *The Hard Road to Renewal* (London, 1988); B. Jessop et al., *Thatcherism* (London, 1988).
98. Gilmour, *Inside Right*, 151.
99. Durham, *Sex and Politics*, 131–38. See also Campbell, *Iron Ladies*, 174–76.
100. Whiteley, Seyd, and Richardson, *True Blues*, 254.
101. See Jeffries, "Conservatism and Gender," 12–14.
102. I. Crowther, "Mrs. Thatcher's Idea of the Good Society," *Salisbury Review* 3 (1987): 42.
103. Whiteley, Seyd, and Richardson, *True Blues*, 265.
104. Quoted in Morris, *Tories*, 82.
105. M. Cowling, *A Conservative Future* (London, 1997), 13–14.
106. D. Anderson and P. Mullen, eds., *Faking It: the Sentimentalisation of Modern Society* (London, 1998).
107. See, for example, S. Ball, "The Conservative Party and the Heath Government," in S. Ball and A. Seldon, eds., *The Heath Government, 1970–74: A Reappraisal* (London, 1996), 15.
108. A good example is the discussion of changing family life in D. Willetts, "Civic Conservatism," in J. Gray and D. Willetts, *Is Conservatism Dead?* (London, 1997), e.g. 103–15.
109. J. Gray, "The Undoing of Conservatism," in Gray and Willetts, ibid., 1–66.
110. The phenomenon of "Worcester woman" is discussed in Peake, "Women and the Campaign," 167. A crude American equivalent might be the "soccer mom."

Index

In this index an "f" after a number indicates a separate reference on the next page, and an "ff" indicates separate references on the next two pages. A continuous discussion over two or more pages is indicated by a span of page numbers, e.g., "57–59." *Passim* is used for a cluster of references in close but not consecutive sequence.

Aberdeen, Lord, 72
Aberdeenshire, 85
Abolition, *see* Anti-slavery movement
Academic liberalism, 180; and women's suffrage movement, 188–91
Acland, Eleanor, 246
Adams, Abigail, 8
Adams, W. E., 181
Address to the Opposers of the Repeal of the Corporation and Test Acts (Barbauld), 129
Adelaide, Queen, 163
Adoption Act, 278
Affluence, 308–9
Age of Marriage Act, 281
Albert Hall meetings, 220, 222, 235
Alderson, Amelia, 123, 133–34. *See also* Opie, Amelia Alderson
Allowances: family, 278
Almack's, 159–60, 163, 167
Amberley, Kate Stanley, 168, 178
Amberley, Viscount, 177f
Amelia of Hesse, Princess, 76
American colonies, 22, 118
American Revolution, 21, 115, 128
Analytical Review, The, 141
Anderson, Elizabeth Garrett, 169
Anderson, Louisa Garrett, 250
Anderson, Perry, 293
Andrew, Donna, 21, 24, 115, 117, 132
Anglican church, 184, 189, 232
Animal cruelty issues, 30, 54, 148
Anne, Queen, 74
Anti-Corn League, 182ff

Anti-slavery movement, 22, 26–30 *passim*, 139, 144, 164, 169
"Anti-Waste," 269
Appeal to the Electors of the United Kingdom, on the Choice of a New Parliament (Heyrick), 147
Arbuthnot, Charles, 107
Arbuthnot, Mrs., 155
Aristocracy, 2, 26, 90, 355nn12, 14; political power of, 16–17, 49–50, 153–54, 167; and patronage, 58–59, 70, 71–73; philanthropy and, 144, 164; and public sphere, 152–53; Georgian-era, 156–57; public-private spheres, 160–61; evangelicalism and, 161–63; morality of, 165–66
Arnott, Mr., 69
Ashburton, 85
Ashurst, William, 181
Ashurst family, 182
Asquith, 215, 220f
Asquith, Herbert H., 236, 238, 378n114
Associations, 22–27 *passim*, 50–51
Astor, Lady Nancy, 39, 44, 54
Astor, Lady Violet, 259, 269, 272–73
Athol, Louisa, 16
Aubrey House, 181
Audley End, 86
Authorship, 157, 162
Ayrton, Hertha, 244

Baillie Weaver, Gertrude Colmore, 244
Baillie Weaver, Harold, 244
Baines, Edward, 177f, 188, 197, 367n126

Index

Bangor (Wales), 242
Barbauld, A. L., 28, 128, 132, 137f, 141, 146, 347n30, 348n38, 351n83; political writing of, 129, 139–40, 143
Barmby, Catherine, 180
Barmby, Goodwin, 180f
Bass, M. T., 177
Bastardy Act, 278
Bastille, 123
Bateson, Mary, 61
Bath, 186
Bazley, Thomas, 188, 198, 367n126
Beauclerk, Lord Henry, 63, 332n19
Beauclerk, Martha, Lady Henry: patronage requests of, 57–58, 63–66
Beauclerk, Miss, 65
Beaufort, duke of, 103
Becker, Lydia, 169f, 187ff, 182, 185f, 191, 194
Bedale Ladies Amicable Society, 24–25
Beddoes, Rosamund, 134
Beddoes, Thomas, 129, 134
Bedford, duke of, 163–64
Beesly, E. S., 180
Begging letters, 105. *See also* Patronage
Belfast, 194
Belle Assemblee, La, 148
Berkeley, Grantley, 54
Besant, Annie, 280
Beveridge report, 39
Biagni, Eugenio, 179
Biggs, Caroline Ashurst, 169, 182
Billington-Greig, Teresa, 208–17 *passim*
Bingley Hall rally (Asquith), 215, 220f
Birley, Hugh, 188
Birley Lectures, 184
Birmingham, 148, 187, 196
Birth control, 274, 288
Blackburn, Helen, 185
"Black Friday" (1910), 222
Blair, Tony, 55, 311
Blanc, Louis, 181
Blickling, 105
Bodichon, Barbara Leigh Smith, 1f, 29, 168, 172, 175, 181, 189
Bolton, 196
Bondfield, Margaret, 39
Book clubs, 131f
Books, 20. *See also* Novels
Booksellers, 131
Boscawen, Ann, 78

Boscawen, Mr., 78
Boucherett, Jessie, 165, 172, 178
Bourne, J. M., 61
Bouverie, Edward Pleydell, 107, 198
Bouverie, Harriot Fawkener, 91, 103, 107–8, 111
Boycotting, 22–23
Brackley, Lord, 163
Braddock, Bessie, 264
Bradford, 25
Bradley, James E., 130
Brailsford, H. N., 238f
Brewer, John, 19
Brewster, Bertha, 240, 248, 250
Bright, Jacob, 31f, 170, 195f, 231; women's suffrage movement, 184–91 *passim*, 198–99
Bright, John, 177, 184f
Bright, Ursula Mellor, 185f
Brighton, 196
Bristol, 186, 196
British Household Survey, 262–63
British Nationality Act, 40
British Nonconformity, 125
Brittain, Vera, 284
Brockway, Fenner, 236
Brodrick, George, 190
Brokers: patronage, 62, 65, 76; women as, 69, 77–83
Brooks Walden manor, 86
Brougham, Henry, 134, 136
Bruce, Henry Austin, 194f, 198
Bryce, James, 189, 199
Buck, Catherine, 123, 134
Buck, Sarah, 134
Buck, William, 134
Buckinghamshire, Earl of (George Hobart), 105, 341n75
Burdett, Francis, 122
Burgess, Mrs. Ann, 25
Burghersh, Lady, 155
Burke, Edmund, 112–13, 138; *Reflections on the Revolution*, 137
Burlington, Lord, 165f
Burney, Dr., 106
Burney, Frances (Fanny), 106f
Burritt, Elihu, 183
Bury St. Edmunds, 134
Butchers, 13, 112
Bute, Lord, 66, 70, 82
Butler, George, 188ff

Butler, Josephine, 185, 189
Butler Education Act, 40
Byron, Lady Noel, 26, 164

Caine, Barbara, 169
Caird, Edward, 189
Cairnes, John Elliot, 191
Callington, 85
Cambridge, 268
Cambridge University, 86, 136, 188–89, 259, 279
Campaigns, campaigning: women's participation in, 7–8, 11, 16–17, 18, 206–7; 1784 Westminster, 89–95 passim; 1784 St. Albans', 96–99. See also Canvassing
Campbell, Bea: *The Iron Ladies*, 292
Canning, George, 17, 106
Cannon, John, 9
Canvassing: women and, 7–8, 11, 16–17, 18, 109, 112–13; in 1784 Westminster election, 89–95 passim, 104, 108, 120–21; in 1784 St. Albans election, 96–99; by duchess of Devonshire, 102–3, 113–14, 117; by aristocratic women, 154–55, 340n52
Cappe, Catherine, 128, 143, 145
Cappe, Newcombe, 128
Capper, Mary, 148
Cardiff, 248
Carlisle, 25, 326n74
Carlisle, Lady Rosalind, 16, 165
Carlo Khan, see Fox, Charles James
Caroline, Queen, 84, 205
Carpenter, Estlin, 181
Carpenter, Lant, 127
Carter, Mr., 73
Cartoons, cartoonists, 114, 120–21, 344n125
Castlereagh, Lord, 91, 105, 119
Cat and Mouse Act, 235
Cather, Lieutenant, 247
Catholic Emancipation, 158
Catholic Women's Suffrage Society (CWSS), 243, 277
Cavendish, John, 109, 340n52
CCWO, see Consultative Committee of Women's Organizations
Cecil, Lord Robert, 224
Cecil family, 97
Central Suffrage Society, 231

Century Club, 191
Chadwick, Edwin, 194
Chamberlain, Austen, 296
Chapman, Cecil, 231
Charities, charity, 24–25, 50, 162–63, 177
Chartists, Chartism, 22, 29, 180f, 184
Cheap Repository Tracts (More), 139
Chester, 25
Chichester, 131
Childbirth, 42, 284
Children, 145, 278, 286–87, 309
Child welfare, 44, 54, 274, 284
Chivalry, 217
Christianity, 24, 125–26, 149, 177
Christian Socialists, Socialism, 180, 191–92, 194, 271
Church: and patronage, 83–85
Churchill, Lady Randolph, 16, 206
Churchill, Winston, 54, 213, 240, 372n42
Church League for Women's Suffrage (CLWS), 232, 243, 271
Church of England, 161, 271
Citizenship, 6, 33, 193; rights of, 15, 30, 52, 146; women's, 172, 192, 195f; responsibilities of, 177, 288
City councils, 268, 273(table)
Civic Sermons to the People (Barbauld), 139
Civilization, 177
Civil service, 40, 61
Civil War (American), 180, 184, 189
Clark, Anna, 205
Clarke, Mary Anne, 77
Clark family, 186
Class, 112, 122, 217, 295; and women's movement, 214–15. See also Social status
Clayton, Joseph, 234, 239–40
Clergyman's Intelligencer, The, 84
Clients: patronage, 62, 71–76, 86
Club movement, 46, 300
Clubs, 21, 131–32, 232–33, 248. See also by name
CLWS, see Church League for Women's Suffrage
Coachmaker's Hall debate, 115f
Cobden, Richard, 183f
Coelebs in Search of a Wife (More), 50, 161
Coffee houses, 21, 325n64
Colley, Linda, 8f, 20, 23, 90, 92f

Colmore, Gertrude, 244
Coltman, Elizabeth (Eliza), 131–32, 147
Coltman, John, 147
Coltman, Mary Ann, 148
Combe, William, 95
Common sense, 307–8, 312
Communist Party, 269, 292
Community action, 23
Complete Suffrage Union, 184
Conciliation Bill, 230, 234, 238
Conciliation Committee, 230, 238
Condorcet, Marquis de, 191
Congregationalists, 271
Conscience, 4, 24
Conscription, 248
Conservatism, 44–45, 139, 303–4. *See also* Conservative Party
Conservative Agents' Journal, 296
Conservative Party, 45–46, 53f, 206, 223, 263, 269, 314; women's activism in, 46–47, 264f, 289–93; propaganda of, 47–48; freedom and, 48–49; and 1867 Reform Bill, 178, 187; women's suffrage and, 197, 253, 297–98; female membership in, 293–94, 300–305; and class issues, 295–96; women's support for, 299–300; on false freedoms, 306–8; and labor force, 309–10; and Princess Diana's death, 311–12; volunteerism in, 312–13
Conservative Primrose League, 16
Conservative Reform Bill (1867), 177–78, 187
Conservative Women's Reform Association, 277
Considerations on Representative Government (Mill), 174, 176
Constitutionalism, 30, 95
Consultative Committee of Women's Organizations (CCWO), 269, 281
Consumers: political symbols and, 22–23
Contagious Diseases Acts, 32, 185, 193
Contemporary Review, 191
Conyingham, Lady, 155
Cookson, J. E., 135
Co-operative Party, 269
Corn Laws, 30
Cornwall, 85
Cornwallis, Lord, 102
Correspondence networks, 133
Corrupt and Illegal Practices Act, 155

Corruption, 76–77, 93–94
Corrupt Practices Act (1883), 5, 16, 33, 89, 206
Council of Women Civil Servants, 41, 270
Courtauld, Samuel, 181
Courtney, Leonard, 189
Courts: arbitration, 275
Covent Garden, 100, 101–2, 117–22 *passim*
Coventry, 15
Cowen, Joseph, Jr., 181, 188
Cowen, Joseph, Sr., 177, 188, 197, 367n126
Cowling, Maurice, 311
Cowman, Krista, 246, 248
Cowper, Lady, 159
Cracroft, Bernard, 190
Cremer, William Randall, 32, 200
Crewe, Frances Anne Greville, 12, 91, 103–10 *passim*, 342n78
Crewe, John, 106
Criminal Law Amendment Act, 276
Critchley, Julian, 305
Cromertie, Lady, 78
Crooks, Will, 224
Crosskey, Henry, 181
Crowther, Ian, 48–49, 310
Cursory Remarks on the Evil Tendency of Unrestrained Cruelty (Heyrick), 148
CWSS, *see* Catholic Women's Suffrage Society

Daily Advertiser (newspaper), 12, 94
Damer, Mrs., 91
Darlington, countess of, 77
Dashwood, Dorothy, 84
Dashwood, Francis, 132
Daventry, 126
Davies, Emily, 1, 2, 172; and John Stuart Mill, 174–75; and suffrage movement, 176, 192; *Woman's Work and Woman's Culture*, 189–90
Davies, Llewellyn, 192
Dawson, George, 180f
Debating societies, 8, 21, 115, 324–25nn63, 64, 343n112; rational dissenters and, 131–32
Deceased Brother's Widow's Marriage Act, 276
Demonstrations, 221, 233f, 280–81

Department stores: boycotts against, 22–23
Derby, Lady, 16
Deskfoord, Lady, 74
Deskfoord, Lord, 85
Desmond (Smith), 137, 139
Despard, Charlotte, 217, 280
Deutsch, Phyllis, 119
Devonshire, 123
Devonshire, dukes of, 18, 165–66
Devonshire, Georgiana, Duchess of, 94, 98, 104–10 *passim*, 154, 343n106; and Charles James Fox's election, 11–13, 89f, 92, 117; political campaigning by, 13–14, 95–96, 122; as symbol, 19, 22, 113–14, 121; and Westminster canvassing, 100, 101–3; and social status issues, 111–12; public manners of, 119–20; *The Sylph*, 162
Devonshire, Louise, Duchess of, 121
Devonshire House, 161
D'Ewes, 7
Diana, Princess, 311–12
Dicey, Albert, 199
Dickinson, W. H., 249
Dilke, Charles Wentworth, 196
Discrimination: against rational dissenters, 128–29, 130
Disraeli, Benjamin, 169, 178
Disruption, 223f, 379nn125, 129, 208, 379n132; as tactic, 35–36, 201–3; purpose of, 209–10, 211–12; violence and, 215f, 220; male assistance in, 218, 221
Dissenters, *see* Rational dissenters
Division of labor, 172, 278
Divorce, 39, 42, 145, 276–78
Domesticity, domestic sphere, 16, 124, 127, 151, 161, 192, 205, 253, 288, 325n71; as political, 28, 133–37; legislation and, 40–41; Conservative Party and, 49, 306–7, 310–11; political activism and, 51–52; Enlightenment and, 125, 130; rational dissenters and, 126, 346–47n20; and legislation, 284–85; inter-war changes in, 286–87; outside employment and, 309–10
Douglas Jerrold's Weekly Newspaper, 149
Down, County, 91
Downshire, Margaretta, Marquessa of, 97

Downshire, Marquess of, 97
Dress, 22; and social status, 110–11
Drysdale, C. V., 234
Duncannon, Lady Harriet, 91, 96, 98, 109, 114
Dundee, 213
Dutton, Frederick, 113
Duval, Victor, 239
Dyer, George, 135, 138

East India Bill, 92, 93–94, 118
East London Federation, 241
Eates, Louise Mary, 242
Ecton, John: *Thesaurus Rerum Ecclesiasticarum*, 84
Eden, Anthony, 298
Edgefield, 84
Edgeworth, Maria, 143
Edinburgh, 51, 186, 196; Eliza Fletcher in, 136, 145; householder votes in, 187–88; academic liberalism in, 189, 190–91
Edinburgh Society for Women's Suffrage, 187
Education, 126–28, 192, 347n30, 357n37; reform of, 30, 44; rational dissenters, 130f; aristocratic philanthropy and, 163f
Edwardian era: suffrage campaign in, 34–35; political disruption in, 35–36; public meetings during, 201–2, 204, 221; Conservatives and, 295–96
Edwards, John, 241
Effingham, Lord, 86
Election Fighting Fund, 239
Elections, 28, 34, 55, 72, 102, 143, 175, 213, 279, 387n59; participation in, 7–8, 11, 16–17, 18, 115–16, 163, 195, 205–6; rate payers and, 32, 187, 321n16; and patronage, 78, 85–86; 1784 Westminster, 89–91, 92–93; 1784 St. Albans, 96–99; rituals, 205, 370nn25, 26; post–World War I, 257f, 260–62; women candidates in, 266, 268–69
Elite, 18, 49–50, 133, 355n14. *See also* Aristocracy; Nobility
Elizabeth I, Queen, 19
Eliza Cook's Journal, 149
Ellen Middleton (Fullerton), 162
Elliot, Walter, 308
Elliott-Lynn, Mrs., 280

Elmy, Elizabeth Wolstoneholme, 229. *See also* Wolstoneholme, Elizabeth
Emancipation, 27, 29–30
Empire, 61
Employment, 24; of married women, 40, 309–10; opportunities for, 279–80, 285–86
Enfield, William, 133
Enfranchisement, 39, 41, 130, 146; male support for, 129, 230; female, 150, 180, 294; women's movement and, 171–72, 195; support for, 198–99, 300
England, 32, 42, 76, 83, 321n18
English Woman's Journal, 29, 172–76 passim, 181, 192–93, 195
Englishwoman's Review (journal), 2, 170, 176, 178, 186
Enlightenment, 4f, 124–25, 130, 151, 171, 349n53
"Epistle to William Wilberforce" (Barbauld), 139
Equal Franchise Act, 2, 39, 295
Equality, 139, 307; gender, 129, 283, 325n71; wage, 276, 279, 285f
Equal Pay Act, 40
Essay on Government (Lee), 145–46
Essays on Reform (Rutson), 189
Essex Street Chapel, 136
Estlin, Mary, 186
Eustance, Claire, 240
Evangelicalism, 7, 26f, 142, 144, 151, 356–57n35; and aristocracy, 160, 161–63
Evans, Samuel, 209
"Expected General Rising of the French Nation in 1792, On the" (Barbauld), 139

Fabian Society, 241, 277
Factory Act, 278
Fairford, Lord, 97f
Faithfull, Emily, 178
Families, 19, 94, 181, 192, 278; political, 2, 8–16 passim, 59, 62, 89–99 passim; and patronage, 9–10, 66–67, 69, 73–75, 79–80; restructuring of, 135, 145; suffragist, 241–42, 383n55; social legislation and, 283f; changes in, 286–87, 288; and domesticity, 310–11
Fancy fairs, 163
"Farewell for Two Years to England, A" (Williams), 139

Farr, William, 194
Fashion: and politics, 110–11
Fawcett, Henry, 177, 189, 196f, 367n126
Fawcett, Millicent Garrett, 169, 176, 192, 249, 259, 273, 274–75, 280, 283; *The Women's Victory—And After*, 257–58
Fawkener, Everard, 107
Fawkener, Georgiana "Jockey" Poyntz, 107
Fawkener, Harriot, *see* Bouverie, Harriot Fawkener
Feathers: boycotts against, 22–23
Female Advocate (Scott), 133
Female benefit society, 145
Femininity, 119, 213–14, 216, 344n124
Feminism, 31, 35, 39, 44, 129, 255f, 279, 296, 313; organizations and, 41–42; Conservative Party and, 48, 307; Unitarianism and, 149–50; philanthropy and, 164–65; social issues and, 283–84
Fenn, Mr., 241
Ferguson, Rachel, 233
Fife, Lord, 102
Finn, Margot, 30, 181
Finsbury, 149
Fletcher, Archibald, 136
Fletcher, Eliza, 51, 123, 127, 134ff, 141–45 passim
Florence, Eliza, 131
Food, 23; and radical politics, 134–35
Forbes, Lady, 74
Foreman, Amanda, 12ff, 90
Fortnightly Review, 191
Forward Cymric Suffrage Union, 243, 248
Foundling Hospital, 24
Fox, Charles James, 8, 53, 106f, 118f, 338n15; election campaign of, 11, 12–13, 89–90, 112, 117, 122; and George III, 92–93; politics of, 93–94; and duchess of Devonshire, 95, 114; canvassers for, 102–3, 107–8; support for, 109, 113; political cartoons and, 120, 344n125
Fox, Henry, 67
Fox, William Johnson, 149, 181
Fox-Genovese, Elizabeth, 124
Fox-North coalition, 118
Franchise, 1, 2, 223; household, 180, 205, 229; municipal, 195f; violence and,

215–16; equal, 280–81; Conservative Party and, 295–96
Francis, Philip, 108
Franklin, Hugh, 240, 246
Freedom, 310; Conservative Party on, 48–49, 306–8, 313
Freeholders: as electoral patrons, 85–86
Free Presbyterians, 196
Free Trade Hall meeting (Manchester), 187, 220
French Revolution, 28, 123, 129, 134, 142; literary response to, 137–39, 140; Napoleon Bonaparte and, 143–44
Frend, William, 141
Friends of Italy, 181
Fry, Elizabeth, 148
Fullerton, Lady Georgiana: *Ellen Middleton*, 162
Fundraising, 65, 183

Gage, Lord, 76
Garrison, William Lloyd, 186
Gawthorpe, Mary, 34, 209, 214; "Votes for Men," 235
Gender, 129, 217, 250; and patronage requests, 67–69; and social status, 112–13, 114–15; 1780 issues of, 117–18, 122; complementarity of, 173–74; and public meetings, 203–4; equality of, 276, 283
Gender roles, 253, 257
George I, 74, 77, 331n2
George II, 63ff, 70, 76, 80ff
George III, 65, 70, 92–93, 118–19
George IV, 155
George, Dorothy, 12, 91
Gibson, John, 38
Gillespie, H. J., 244, 247
Gilmour, Ian, 310
Girls' Public Day-School Company, 26, 164
Girton College, Cambridge, 26, 164
Gladstone, William, 30, 32, 169, 179, 195f, 198, 361n45
Glasgow, 190
Glenarvon (Lamb), 162
Gloyn, Elizabeth, 185
Godwin, William, 129, 132, 142
Goldman, Lawrence, 194
Goldsmid, Francis, 198, 367n126

Gordon, Katherine, Duchess of, 85, 72–73
Gordon riots, 23
Gore-Langton, Lady Anna, 197
Gore-Langton, William, 197
Gorman, Teresa, 311
Gorst, John Edward, 178
Gould, Barbara, 244, 251
Gould, Eliza, 123, 348–49n47
Gould, Gerald, 244
Government, 61; local, 32–33, 321nn16, 17; social role of, 145–46
"Government, On" (James Mill), 14–15
Grafton, duke of, 65
Grand Whiggery, 165
Granville, Lady, 161
Gray, John, 197, 313, 367n126
Great Reform Act, 1, 5, 8, 14f, 29
Green, Ewen, 298
Green, James, 135
Greville, Frances Anne, *see* Crewe, Frances Anne Greville
Greville, Fulke, 106
Grey, Charles, 248
Grey, Edward, 208, 220, 372n39
Grimston, Lord, 97, 339n31
Grimston, Mary Leman, 148
Grimston family (Grimstons of Gorhambury), 96f
Gronow, Captain, 158
Grosvenor, Lord Robert, 165
Guardianships, 278
Guest, Lady Charlotte, 16
Guild of Girl Citizens, 280
Gurney, Lord Russell, 178

Habermas, Jurgen, 3, 124
Habitations, 301
Hack, Maria, 131
Hadfield, George, 177
Hague, William, 311
Hale, Margaret: *North and South*, 214
Halifax, 18
Hall, Catherine, 14, 124
Hamilton, Anne, Duchess of, 73
Hammersley, Mr., 84
Harben, Agnes, 243
Harben, Henry, 243
Harbord, Rebeccah, 84–85
Hardie, Keir, 32, 223
Hardwicks, Lord, 66–67, 78

Hardy, Thomas, 132, 134
Hare, Thomas, 176, 191
Harman, Harriet, 55
Harraden, Beatrice, 247–48
Harris, Barbara, 62
Harrison, Brian, 169
Harrison, Fred, 179–80
Hartley, David, 126
Harvie, Christopher: *The Lights of Liberalism*, 189
Harwich, 81–82
Hase, John, 85
Hastings, George, 195
Hatfield House, 97
Hawkins, Laetitia: *Letters on the Female Mind, Its Powers and Pursuits*, 140
Hawkshead, 25
Hays, Mary, 127, 135, 140f, 348n45; "Thoughts on Civil Liberty," 139
Health care, 44
Heath, John, 81
Henniker, Lady Mary, 301
Herbert, Auberon, 190, 196
Herbert, Lady Florence May, 190
Heyrick, Elizabeth, 28, 146, 352n114; *Appeal to the Electors of the United Kingdom, on the Choice of a New Parliament*, 147; *Cursory Remarks on the Evil Tendency of Unrestrained Cruelty*, 148
Hibbert, J. T., 177, 197, 367n126
Hill, Frank, 190f
Hill, Matthew Davenport, 148–49
Hinscliff, Claude, 232
Hinscliff, Gertrude, 232
History of the Conservative Party, A, 290
Hobart, Albinia, 12, 91, 103, 105–6, 110f
Hobart, George, Earl of Buckinghamshire, 105, 341n75
Hodgkinson, Grosvenor, 198, 367n126
Holcroft, Thomas, 129
Holden, Isaac, 177
Holdernesse, Lord, 67
Holland, Lady, 155, 161
Holland, Lord, 159
Holton, Sandra, 186, 199
Holywell, 96
Homeopathy, 30
Home Rulers, 196, 198
Homosexuality, 118

Hood, Admiral Lord, 12
Hood, Lady, 157
Hoosen, Edward, 184f
Horsham, 85
Horsley, Victor, 235, 237
Hostesses: political, 155, 356n28
Houghton, Lord, 190
Householders: as voters, 187–88, 205, 249–50, 321n19
Households: power in, 6–7; voting patterns in, 262–63
House of Commons, 17, 55, 154, 196, 229; viewing, 157–58; John Stuart Mill in, 168, 169–70; 1867 Reform Bill support, 177–78; women in, 272–73
House of Lords, 17, 31, 39, 154, 158, 233, 279
Housing Acts, 282
Housman, Laurence, 234, 248
Howard, Blanche, 165
Howard, Caroline, 165
Howard, Georgiana, 165
Howe, Lady, 79
Howitt's Journal, 149
How Women Can Use the Vote, 268
Hoxton, 126
Hubback, Eva, 281
Hughes, Mary, 128
Hughes, Thomas, 177, 192
Hull, 149
Humanitarianism, 28
Hume-Rothery, Mary, 185f
Humming Bird (journal), 148
Hunt, Margaret, 25
Huntingdon, Lady, 84
Hutton, Catherine, 144, 148
Hutton, William, 148
Hyde Park demonstration, 280–81

Illingworth, Alfred, 196
ILP, *see* Independent Labour Party
Importance des Opinions Religeuses, De L' (Neckers), 128
Independence, 3, 39, 127
Independent Labour Party (ILP), 32f, 37, 183, 218, 239, 241, 375n77
India, 61, 93–94
Individualism, 127, 130, 172
Industrial Courts Act, 275
Infanticide Act, 277
Infants, 278. *See also* Children

Inheritance, 2, 7, 9, 84, 86, 275, 320n15
Intellectual communities, 126
Intercourse: unlawful, 276
Intoxicating Liquors (Sales to Young Persons under 18) Act, 278, 283
Inversion: rituals of, 102
Ireland, 22, 196; Home Rule in, 31, 198; pensions and, 75f; women's suffrage and, 196f
Ireland, Alexander, 184, 186
Irish civil list, 75–76
Iron Ladies, The (Campbell), 292
Irwin, Lord, 85
Isle of Man, 229

Jacobitism, Jacobins, 21f, 133
Jacobs, Herbert, 37, 230ff, 234
Jaeger, Muriel, 162
Jebb, Ann, 133–40 *passim*
Jebb, John, 129, 133, 136f
Jenkinson, Charles, 70
Jersey, Lady, 16, 155, 159, 163
Jessop, G. L., 244
Jewish League for Women's Suffrage, 232
Joel, W. L., 296
Johnson, Joseph, 128f, 131, 137
Johnston, Harry, 245–46, 383n67
Jollie, Helen, 241
Jones, Ernest, 184f, 188
Jones, John Gale, 129, 132
Junior Imperial League, 304
Jurors, 39
Justices of the Peace, 39, 42

Kay-Shuttleworth, James, 164
Kencote St. George, 84
Kendal, duchess of, 77
Kenney, Annie, 208, 214f, 235
Kensington Ladies Debating Society, 175
Kimber, Edward, 21
King, Peter Lock, 178
Kingsley, Charles, 31, 192f
Kingsway Hall meeting, 245
Kinnear, John Boyd, 190
Kinnoull, Lord, 74
Kintore, Lord, 74
Kossuth, Lajos, 181f
Kyllmann, Max, 185, 363n72

Labor force, 174, 224, 309–10
Labor movement, 241, 278

Labouchere, Henry, 177
Labour Party, 45, 47, 53, 55, 239, 251, 254, 274, 282, 284, 290, 294, 308; goals of, 42, 43–44; women's support of, 261–65 *passim*, 270, 298–99
Ladies Charitable Society, 24
Ladies' Gallery, 54
Ladies National Association for the Diffusion of Sanitary Knowledge, 192f
Lady Patronesses, 159
Lady's Gallery (Parliament), 221
Lamb, Caroline, Lady, 154; *Glenarvon*, 162
Lambert, John, 105
Lancashire, 18, 184, 200, 264
Lancaster, 15
Land, *see* Property
Landowners, *see* Property holders
Lane, Harriett, 69
Langham Place, 172, 175f
Lansbury, George, 32, 224–25
Lawes and Resolutions of Women's Rights, The, 6
Lawson, Wilfred, 196
League Dames, *see* Primrose League
League of the Church Militant, 271
League of Nations, 275
Leatham, W. H., 177
Lectures to Ladies (Maurice), 192
Lee, Rachel (Philopatria), 28, 132; *Essay on Government*, 145–46
Leeds, 25, 188, 196
Leeds Mercury (newspaper), 178, 188
Leeds University, 218
Legal system, 42–43
Legislation: domesticity and, 40–41; women's associations and, 273–82; and women voters, 282–83
Legitimacy Act, 283
Leicester, 131–32
Leicester House, 79
Leicestershire, 104
Leigh, Mary, 214
Leslie, Lady Jane, 74–75
Leslie, Lady Margaret, 74–75
Leslie, Thomas Cliffe, 191
Letters on the Female Mind, Its Powers and Pursuits (Hawkins), 140
Letters Written in France (Williams), 139
Lex Parliamentaria, 8
Liberalism, 30–37 *passim*, 179f, 184, 265;

and women's suffrage, 182–83, 199–200; Manchester radical, 185, 187; academic, 188–91; and Social Science Association, 194–95; urban, 196–97. *See also* Liberal Party
Liberal Men's Association for Women's Suffrage, 240
Liberal Registration Societies, 187
Liberal Party, 179, 196, 223f, 230, 269, 370n25; in Manchester, 31, 185; and women's suffrage, 37f, 179–80, 188, 197–98, 218, 220–21; and 1867 Reform Bill, 177f, 187; women in, 264–65; and WNLF, 265–66
Liberal Women's News, 265
Liberal Women's Suffrage Union, 246
"Liberty, On" (Robinson), 139
"Liberty and Fame introducing Female Patriotism in Britania" (Rowlandson), 113
Liddell, H. G., 194, 197, 367n126
Lieven, Princess, 154f, 158–59
Lights of Liberalism, The (Harvie), 189
Lincolnshire, 22
Linton, W. J., 180
Lister, Anne, 18
Literary and Philosophical Societies, 131–32
Literature, 20, 30, 214; radical, 137–41
Liverpool, 25, 241, 264, 268
Llandaff, Bishop of, 101–2
Llanystumdwy (1912), 222
Lloyd George, David, 212, 220, 222, 230, 236, 238f
Lobbying, 220
Locke, John, 126, 127
Loder, Mrs., 84
London, 8, 21f, 24, 118, 186, 190; debating societies in, 115, 132; radicalism in, 131, 181; women's suffrage movement in, 188–89
London Chronicle (newspaper), 94
London Committees for Women's Suffrage, 182
Londonderry, Lady, 16, 155
London Graduates' Union, 232
London National Society for Women's Suffrage, 176, 190f
London Society for Women's Suffrage, 169
London University, 234

Long Parliament, 7
Lowell, A. L., 201f
Lower class, 112. *See also* Working class
Lucas, Margaret Bright, 185
Lyttelton, Lady Sarah, 159
Lyttelton, W. H., 159
Lytton, Lady Constance, 215
Lytton, Lord, 230

Macartney, Frances, 106
Macaulay, Catherine, 28, 137, 141; *Observations on the Reflections of the Rt. Hon Edmund Burke, on the Revolution in France*, 138
Macdowell, Paula, 20
McIlquham, Harriet, 229
Mackintosh, James, 134
McLaren, Duncan, 177, 187–88, 190, 197, 367n126
McLaren, John, 187
McLaren, Priscilla Bright, 168, 185, 200
Macmillan, Alexander, 189, 191
Macmillan, Chrystal, 281
Macmillan governments, 309
Macmillan's Magazine, 191, 199
Maddison, Fred, 224
Magdalene College, Cambridge, 86–87
Magistrates, 39, 42, 320n15
Magoliouth family, 242
Maguire, John Francis, 197, 367n126
Maidstone, 217
Major, John, 48, 310
Male Electors' League for Women's Suffrage, 229
Maling, Sarah Jane, 134, 143
Manchester, 194; women's suffrage movement and, 182–90 *passim*, 196; radical liberalism in, 180–87 *passim*, 200
Manchester Abolitionists, 51
Manchester Examiner and Times (newspaper), 184, 186
Manchester Free Trade Hall, 208
Manchester Men's League, 231, 243
Manliness, manhood, 3, 203, 217, 228, 237
Manners, 110–11
Manning, Adelaide, 189
Marcus, Jane, 209
Marie Antoinette, 112–13
Marine Society, 24

Marlborough, duchess of, 16, 79
Marlborough, duke of, 79
Marlborough, Sarah, Duchess of, 95
Marriage, 4, 37, 40, 172f, 190, 192, 283f, 286; aristocratic, 154, 158; and suffrage, 199–200, 242; separation from, 276–77; and employment, 309–10
"Marriage, On" (Mill), 173
Martineau, Harriet, 27
Mary, Queen, 6
Mary of Hesse, Princess, 76
Masculinity, 3f, 157f, 238, 256, 343–44nn121, 124; and politics, 13, 18; and Parliament, 53–54; in 1780s, 117–18, 119; and disruption tactics, 202–3; and suffragists, 219, 228; and violence, 225, 377n104; men's societies and, 232–33; World War I and, 247, 257
Masson, David, 190
Maternity, *see* Motherhood
Maternity and Child Welfare Act, 42, 274
Matrimonial Causes Act, 39, 277
Maurice, Frederick Denison, 175; *Lectures to Ladies*, 192
Maxwell, Lily, 185, 187
Mayhall, Laura, 236
Mazzini, Giuseppe, 30, 181f
Mechanics Institute, 188
Medical College for Women, 26, 164
Mellor, Ursula, *see* Bright, Ursula Mellor
Men's Committee for Justice to Women, 234
Men's International Alliance for Woman Suffrage, 231
Men's League for Women's Suffrage (MLWS), 34, 37f, 218f, 230–35 *passim*, 241f, 243f, 377n101, 382n44; and WSPU, 238f
Men's Liberal Society for the Parliamentary Enfranchisement of Women, 232
Men's Political Union for Women's Enfranchisement (MPU), 34, 37, 231–32, 243f; opposition to, 239–40, 246
Men's Society for Women's Rights, 232
Miall, Edward, 196
Middle class, 41, 192, 214, 254, 355n12; radicalism of, 30, 123–24, 150, 181; women's movement and, 171–72; masculinity of, 232f
Middlesex, 122
Middleton Stoney, 163

Mid-Glamorgen, 209
Midgley, Claire, 27
Midwives Act (1902), 273
Midwives Amending Act, 274
Militancy, 35, 37, 217, 243, 377n105; WSPU, 34, 208–9, 240; suffragette, 207–8, 212–13, 220, 222, 226; role of, 211–12; male assistance in, 218–19, 251; male supporters and, 237–38
Military: and patronage, 63, 73
Mill, James: "On Government," 14–15
Mill, John Stuart, 31, 52, 172–81 *passim*, 199, 231; and women's suffrage, 1–2, 37, 171, 182, 186, 190ff, 196, 198; works of, 168, 173–74, 176, 193; in House of Commons, 169–70, 177
Millar, John, 172–73
Milnes, Richard Monckton, 190
Milton, Lady, 16
Ministers of the Crown, 17
Minorities, 30, 54, 176
Missionary movement, 27
Mistresses, 76f
Mitchell, Hannah, 34, 214, 218
Mitchell, J. Malcolm, 234
MLWS, *see* Men's League for Women's Suffrage
Modernization, 61, 173
Molony, Miss, 213, 375n73
Morality, 48, 173, 310; of Charles James Fox, 93f; aristocracy, 165–66; of affluence, 308–9
More, Hannah, 26f; works of, 50, 139, 161
Morley, John, 191, 199
Morley, Samuel, 196
Morning Chronicle, The (newspaper), 12
Morning Herald, The (newspaper), 94
Morris, Rupert, 290–91
Motherhood, 29, 44, 64, 135–36, 199, 307
Moullin, Charles Mansell, 237
Mowlam, Mo, 55
MPs, 15, 43f, 52, 55, 148, 266(table)
MPU, *see* Men's Political Union for Women's Enfranchisement
Municipal Franchise Bill and Act, 170, 195
Murray, Amelia, 164, 358n51
Murray family, 242
Muswell Hill, 181
Myers, Frederick, 188f

Namier, Lewis, 9, 19, 61, 81
Napoleon I (Napoleon Bonaparte), 143–44
Narrative of a Residence in France (Plumptre), 143
National Childbirth Trust, 5
National Council for Adult Suffrage, 249, 384n95
National Council for Equal Citizenship, 271
National Council for the Unmarried Mother and Her Child, 278
National Council of Women (NCW), 267, 269, 281
National Insurance Act, 39–40
Nationalists, 196
National Reform Union, 31, 184ff
National Society for Women's Suffrage, 185, 188
National Union, 46, 300
National Union of Societies for Equal Citizenship (NUSEC), 41, 268f, 270f; and public policy issues, 275–82 *passim*
National Union of Women's Suffrage Societies (NUWSS), 2, 34, 229–34 *passim*, 239, 241f, 251, 257, 267f, 384n94; and World War I, 243, 249
National Union of Women Teachers, 41, 270
National Union of Women Workers, 267
National Women's Suffrage Society, 186
NCW, *see* National Council of Women
Neal, Mary, 248
Necker, Jacques: *De L'Importance des Opinions Religeuses*, 128
Nethercott, Maria Constantia, 73–74
Nevinson, H. W., 236, 238f, 247, 249ff, 383n78; and United Suffragists, 243f, 245–46
Newcastle, 9–10, 20, 77–78, 181, 188
Newcastle, duchess of, 10, 71–72, 78, 80
Newcastle, duke of (Thomas Pelham-Holles), 61, 79, 85, 331n2; and Lady Beauclerk, 57, 58–59, 63, 64–65; patronage requests of, 66–78 *passim*, 87–88, 333n34, 335n60; and Katherine, Duchess of Gordon, 72–73; and Lady Katherine Pelham, 80–82; and Lady Portsmouth, 86–87

Newell, Mrs., 84
Newell, William, 84
New English Law of Property, 277
Newman, Francis, 181
New Poor Law (1835), 205
New Privilege of Citizenship, The, 268
New Right, 310
Newspapers, 12, 20f
Newton, Sir Henry, 74
Nichol, Elizabeth Pease, 187
Nicholson, Emma, 305
Nicole, Miss, 98
Nicole, Mr., 98
Nicole, Mrs. Sam, 98
Nightingale, Florence, 164–65
Nobility, 18
Non-Con Club, 131
Nonconformist Enlightenment, 28, 135, 147ff
Nonconformists, 182, 196
Non-party political organizations: activism in, 267–73
Norris, Pippa, 299
North, Mrs. Jane, 25
North, Lady, 10
North, Lord, 75, 92
Northampton, 96
North and South (Hale), 214
Northern Men's Federation, 240, 243
North London, 243
Northumberland, duchess of, 70, 82
Northumberland, duke of, 70
North of England Council for Promoting the Higher Education of Women, 188
North Warwickshire, 187
Norwich, 20, 22; female patrons in, 84–85; radical politics in, 123, 132, 133–34
Novels, 21, 157, 162
Nurses, 274
NUSEC, *see* National Union of Societies for Equal Citizenship
NUWSS, *see* National Union of Women's Suffrage Societies

Observations on the Reflections of the Rt. Hon Edmund Burke, on the Revolution in France (Macaulay), 138
O'Connell, Daniel, 177
O'Donoghue, 177
O'Gorman, Frank, 102
Oldham, 196

Old Sarum, *see* Salisbury, Lady, Mary Amelia
Oliphant, Laurence, 177
Olive Leaf Circles, 183
One Penny-Worth More (Jebb), 140
Opie, Amelia Alderson, 143, 352n114. *See also* Alderson, Amelia
Opie, John, 143
Orford, Lady, 85
Oxford, 84, 86–87, 302
Oxford University, 188–89, 259
Oxford Women's Suffrage Society, 242

Palmerston, Lady, 16, 159
Pamphleteering, pamphlets, 20, 28, 140, 148, 234–35, 268
Pankhurst, Christabel, 37f, 208f, 213f, 218–23 *passim*, 242, 250f, 375n75; and male supporters, 238f, 240–41, 246
Pankhurst, Emmaline, 209, 229, 280f, 376n85
Pankhurst, Richard Marsden, 185, 229
Pankhurst, Sylvia, 215, 225, 235, 241, 249, 256, 258–59
Parkes, Bessie Rayner, 1f, 29, 184, 192–93; and John Stuart Mill, 172, 174f; radical unitarians and, 181f
Parliament, 5, 17, 154, 160, 187, 220, 222, 249, 324n59; voting for, 7–8; women in, 39, 55, 254, 266(table), 274; masculinity of, 53–54, 157; and patronage, 60, 81–82; and George III, 92–93; viewing of, 157–58, 221; influencing elections to, 238–39
Parry, John, 179
Patriotism, 92, 113
Patronage(s), 9–10, 18, 25, 164, 333n34; and political power, 16, 105; requests for, 57–59, 63–67, 69–73, 87–88; system of, 60–62; types of, 62–63; gender and, 67–69; pensions and, 73–76; corruption in, 76–77; ecclesiastical, 83, 84–85; and elections, 85–86; Regency period, 159–60
Pauperism, 176–77
Paxton, Joseph, 165
Peace movement, 144
Peace Society, 184
Peake, Lucy, 299
Pearson, Charles, 189f
Pease, Elizabeth, 184

Peck, Linda Levy, 60, 62
Peckham, 213
Peel, Jonathan, 178
Peerages, 9, 17, 39, 279
Pelham, Henry, 72, 80f
Pelham, Lady Katherine, 10; as broker, 80–82
Pelham family, 72, 331n2
Penberthy, Mrs., 265
Pensions, 42, 276; requests for, 64f, 72, 74–75; numbers and amounts of, 75–76
People's Suffrage Federation, 227
Perkin, Joan, 89
Peterloo massacre, 23, 204
Pethick-Lawrence, Emmeline, 245, 374n68; and WSPU, 213, 222, 235–42 *passim*
Pethick-Lawrence, Frederick, 208–9, 239–45 *passim*, 251, 381n19
Peyt, George: *Lex Parliamentaria*, 8
Philanthropy, 24, 26, 28, 150, 176, 193, 326–27nn74, 76; and public sphere, 142, 151; radicalism and, 144–48; and aristocracy, 160f, 162–64; and feminism, 164–65
Philips family, 191
Phillips, Richard, 148
Philopatria, *see* Lee, Rachel
Pierce, Mrs., 25
Piozzi, Hester Thrale, 139
Pitt, Dr., 79
Pitt, William, 12–13, 53, 65, 95, 97, 113, 332n19; and debating societies, 21, 115; and 1784 election, 92f; supporters of, 103, 108–9; and duchess of Rutland, 104f; chastity of, 116–17; masculinity of, 117–18, 119; political cartoons and, 120f
Platt, John, 177
Playfair, Lyon, 190, 196
Plumptre, Annabella, 133
Plumptre, Anne, 133; *Narrative of a Residence in France*, 143
Pochin, Henry, 187
"Poem on the Bill, The" (Williams), 128
Poetry: political, 138–39
Policewomen, 279–80
Politeness, 156–57
Political culture: reforming, 224–25; women and, 253–54
Political economy, 176–77, 183f

Political meetings: disruption of, 201, 202–3, 209–15 *passim*, 220; women at, 208, 221–22; violence and, 211–12, 216, 218–19; militancy at, 212–13, 220–21
Political parties, 210, 272; activism in, 43, 52–53, 205–6; and suffragettes, 220–21; women's participation in, 263–67
Political power, 2, 8–9, 15; duchess of Rutland, 104–5; aristocracy, 153–54
Political rights, 113–14, 126
Political societies, 132–33
Politics, 22, 33, 97, 125, 199, 254; as male, 3, 4–5, 18; parish, 6–7; and families, 10–11, 59; participation in, 11–14, 16–17, 26, 43, 52–55; female exclusion from, 14–15; popular debate in, 19–20; street, 35, 222; Tory, 46–47; patronage and, 70–71, 84f; rational dissenters and, 130–31; of domestic sphere, 133–37; and evangelicalism, 161–62; street-corner, 205–6; violence and, 215–16, 223–24, 257; reform of, 224–25
Poor Law, 278
Poor law boards, 32, 321n16
Poor Law Guardians, 195
Populism, 184
Portland, dowager duchess of, 91
Portland, duchess of, 12, 91, 322n34
Portland, duke of, 71–72, 122
Portsmouth, Lady, 86–87
Potter, Thomas Bayley, 184f, 187
Poverty, 147
Press, 11–12, 178; on election results, 260–63
Preston, 15, 264
Pretenders, 22
Price, Elizabeth, 128
Price, Richard, 129, 144
Priestly, Joseph, 125, 127, 144, 148, 348–49n47
Priestman family, 186
Primrose League, 33, 35, 45f, 52, 206, 293, 295, 389n6; social status and, 300–301; power relations of, 301–2
Principles of Political Economy (Mill), 173–74
Prisoners: force-feeding of, 215, 222–23, 240
Private sphere, 4, 19, 165; domestic womanhood and, 16, 125; and public life, 158–59, 160
Prochaska, Frank K., 25, 162–63
Propaganda, 128, 213, 375n77; Conservative, 47–48; in 1784 Westminster election, 91, 112–13, 114; cartoons as, 120–21; radical, 139–40; suffragette movement, 215, 222–23; by men's societies, 234–35
Property, 39, 83, 190; and political power, 8f, 15; ownership of, 86, 153–54, 277
Property holders, 8, 24; aristocratic women as, 153–54; and voting rights, 196, 229, 253, 364n81
Prostitution, 276
Protestant Party, 269
Proxies, 85–86
Public baths, 44
Public meetings, 207; disruption of, 202–3, 209–10, 215, 224; women at, 203–4; ticketing and, 221–22
Public Meetings Bill, 224
Public policy: enfranchisement and, 273–82
Public sphere, 3, 16, 21, 124; behavior in, 109–10, 118; participation in, 142–43, 149–50; philanthropy and, 144–48, 151, 163–65; aristocracy in, 152–53, 155–57, 167; private influence in, 158–59; evangelicalism in, 161–62; possession of, 220–21, 234
Publishing, publishers, 20–21, 131, 157
Pugh, Martin, 200, 254, 300

Quakerism, 28, 142, 148, 183, 186, 352n114
Queen's College, Harley Street, 164, 192
Queen's Hall, 233

Radicalism, 54, 123, 130, 177, 207, 217, 257, 351n83; Unitarians as, 28, 29–30, 53, 149–50, 353n123; and women's suffrage, 37, 171, 180–82, 191; Enlightenment, 124–25; and formal associations, 131–32; and political societies, 132–33; domesticity and, 133–37, 205; literature and, 137–41; and philanthropy, 142, 144–48, 151; French Revolution and, 143–44; Manchester, 183–

84. *See also* Rational dissenters; Unitarians, Unitarianism
Rank, 8, 10, 17, 67
Rate payers, 30, 32, 187, 321n16
Rathbone, Eleanore, 41, 255–56, 267f, 278
Rational dissenters, 125, 129, 349n53; and education, 126–28; political activism and, 130–31, 143f, 183; formal associations and, 131–32; and domestic sphere, 133–37, 346–47n20; literature of, 138–41, 351n84; and women's suffrage, 181, 196. *See also* Unitarians, Unitarianism
Ray, Martha, 77
Rayner, Elizabeth, 128
Rebel Women (Sharp), 244
Reform Act (1832), 150, 323n43
Reform Act (1918), 273
Reform Acts, 5, 158
Reform Bill and Act (1867), 31, 169, 177–78, 187, 193
Reform League, 177, 179
Regency Period, 18, 26; political influence during, 158–60
Registration courts, 187, 190
Reid, Alistair, 179
Reid, Mrs., 131–32
Religion, 24, 128; and political participation, 4, 27; and aristocracy, 26, 161–63, 165–66
Rent payers, 85
Representation of the People Bill and Act, 37, 39, 249, 256, 260, 268, 295, 302
Republicanism, 31
Reynolds, Joshua, 106
Reynolds, Kim, 15–16, 17, 155f
Rhondda, Viscountess, 39, 233, 255, 373n60, 376n95
Rhys family, 242
Richardson, Mary, 217, 235, 248
"Rights of man" debate, 115
"Rights of Women, The" (Barbauld), 129
Right Way (newspaper), 304
Riots, 23, 142, 144, 237, 325n68
Robb, Janet, 301
Roberts, John, 81–82
Robertson, George Croom, 169
Robins, Elizabeth, 212, 235, 237f, 242, 246

Robinson, Henry Crabb, 132, 134
Robinson, Mary, 28, 127, 348n45, 350n77; "On Liberty," 139
Robson, Ann, 169, 170, 173
Robson, John, 173
Roch, Walter, 239
Rodney, Admiral, 73–74
Rogers, Nicholas, 23
Rogers, Thorold, 190, 199
Roland, Madame, 141
Roman Catholics, 264, 270–71
Romanticism, 28, 142
Rothes, Lord, 75
Rowlandson, Thomas: "Liberty and Fame introducing Female Patriotism in Britania," 114
Royal Chelsea Hospital, 116
Royal Commission on Population, 287
Royston, 132
Rusden, R. D., 185, 187
Russell, Earl, 233
Russell, Lady John, 16
Rutland, duke of, 80, 103, 105, 341n67
Rutland, Isabella, Duchess of, 91, 103–8 *passim*
Rutson, Albert, 190; *Essays on Reform*, 189
Rylands, Peter, 196

Sacheverell riots, 23
St. Albans, 11; 1784 election in, 92, 96–99, 113, 340n44
St. Joan's Social and Political Union, 270–71, 276f
Sales of Offices Prevention Act, 77
Salic law, 113
Salisbury, 148
Salisbury, Earl of, 97
Salisbury, Lady, 155
Salisbury, Lady, Mary Amelia, 16, 91, 111; and St. Albans election, 96, 97–98, 99, 113
Salisbury, Lord, 295
Salisbury, Mrs., 12
Salons, 30, 133–34
Salvation Army, 27
Sanby, Mr., 87
Sandwich, Lord, 77
"Sanitary mission," 192, 193–94
Savage, Michael, 264
Sayers, James, 120–21

Scarborough, 108
Scatcherd, Alice, 229
School boards, 32, 195
Schools, 26, 163f
Scotland, 72, 85, 173, 196f, 275
Scott, Mary, 148; *Female Advocate*, 133
Scrimshaw, Mrs. Boothby, 10
Scurr, John, 244
Second Reform Act, 2, 16
Secret Ballot Act (1872), 16, 206
Sennett, Maud Arncliffe, 240
Separation: from marriage, 276–77
Set-piece meetings, *see* Political meetings; Public meetings
Seward, Anna, 148
Sex Discrimination Act, 40
Sex Disqualification (Removal) Act, 39, 42, 274–75
Sexuality, 4, 119, 126
Shackleton, Elizabeth, 20, 22, 324n59
Shaen, William, 180
Shall I have the Parliamentary Vote!, And, 268
Sharp, Evelyn, 221, 247ff, 250f, 374n69, 375n76, 384n85; *Rebel Women*, 244
Shaw-Lefevre, George, 178, 194
Sheffield, 196
Shelley, Lady, 155, 162
Shephard, William, 129
Sheridan, Richard, 106
Sherwood, Richard, 229
Shoreditch Liberal meeting, 216
Short, Claire, 55
Sidgwick, Henry, 188f
Silk weavers, 26, 164
Sins of Government, Sins of the Nation (Barbauld), 139–40
Six Million Women Can Vote, 268
Six Point Group, 41, 269
Sloper, William, 96–97, 98f, 339–40nn28, 41
Smith, Barbara Leigh, 174, 182, 184, 193–94. *See also* Bodichon, Barbara Leigh Smith
Smith, Charlotte, 138; *Desmond*, 137, 139
Smith, Leslie Goldwin, 32, 168f, 199f
Social clubs: Regency Period, 159–60
Social Darwinism, 32
Socialism, socialists, 31, 35, 52, 149, 191, 217, 241, 297, 307f

Social issues, 145, 193–94, 283–84
Socialist Democratic Federation, 33
Social Science Association, 31, 165, 175, 194–95, 197
Social status, 2, 15, 295; and political power, 8–9; and political participation, 13, 16f; and patronage, 69, 78; and canvassing, 101–3, 109–10; dress and behavior and, 110–11; and duchess of Devonshire, 111–12, 120; and gender, 112–13, 114–15; and Primrose League, 300–301
Society for Charitable Purposes, 24
Society for Promoting Reform in the Marriage and Divorce Laws of England, 233
Society for Promoting the Employment of Women, 165
Society of Friends, 186. *See also* Quakerism
"Song for the London Volunteers" (Barbauld), 143
South African War, 223–24
Southey, Robert, 134
South Place Chapel, 149, 181
Southwark, 248
Soviet Union, 307
Sparham St. Mary, 85
Special Register Bill, 249
Spencer, Countess, 161
Spencer, Earl, 96
Spencer, Lady Georgiana, *see* Devonshire, Georgiana, Duchess of
Spencer, Lady Lavinia, 11, 106, 109, 111; and St. Albans election, 91, 96ff, 113
Spencer, Lord, 109
Spencer, second Earl, 122
Spencer family: and St. Albans election, 96–99
Spitalfields: silk weavers at, 26, 164
Stacpoole, William, 197–98, 367n126
Stair, Lady, 72
Standard of living, 308–9
Standing Joint Committee of Industrial Women's Organizations, 277
Stanley, Kate, *see* Amberly, Kate Stanley
Stanley of Alderly, Lady Henrietta, 26, 164
Stanley of Alderley, Lord, 26
Stansfeld, James, 177, 180f, 197, 367n126
Stead, W. T., 237

Steele, Anne, 148
Steinthal, Saul A., 181, 185
Stella House, 181
Stephen, James Fitzjames, 199
Stone, Lawrence, 9
Strachey, Ray, 1, 259
Street corners: politics of, 205–6
Stuart, James, 188
Stuart, Lady Louisa, 111, 157, 162
Subjection of Women (Mill), 168, 171, 193
Suffolk, Earl of, 86
Suffrage, suffrage movement, 30, 33, 186, 204, 256, 259, 361n45, 376n85; John Stuart Mill and, 1–2, 168f, 171, 174, 191; radical unitarians on, 29, 181; male, manhood, 31, 238; Edwardian era, 34–35; male support of, 36–38, 229–43, 250–51; pre- and post-World War I, 38–39; political support for, 169f, 175–76, 224–25; Liberal party and, 179–80; Manchester and, 184–85; academic liberalism in, 188–91; Christian Socialists and, 191–92; married women, 199–200; during World War I, 247–50
Suffragettes, suffragists, 33; militancy of, 207–8, 211–13, 217, 220–22, 226; disruption by, 35–36, 216, 379nn125, 129; as political sport, 213–14; violence against, 215, 222–23; males supporters of, 218–19, 227–28; families of, 241–42; expectations of, 255–59
Suffragist Churchwoman's Protes Committee, 232
Sugar boycotts, 22
Summary jurisdiction (Separation and Maintenance Act), 281
Sutherland, duchess of, 16, 26, 27, 163–64
Swanwick, Helena, 34, 209
Swing Riots, 237
Sylph, The (Georgiana, Duchess of Devonshire), 162

Tariff Reform League, 300
Taxation, 116
Taylor, Clementia, 176, 181f, 193
Taylor, Harriet, 172ff, 181, 190f, 193
Taylor, Helen, 168f, 172, 174ff
Taylor, Peter, 177, 181, 197, 367n126

Taylor, Susannah, 127, 133, 141, 143
Taylor, William, 134
Temperance, 27
Test and Corporation Acts, 29, 128f, 138, 150, 353n123
Tests Act, 180, 188–89, 191
TGs, *see* Townswomen's Guilds
Thatcher, Margaret, 40, 46, 290, 299, 310
Thesaurus Rerum Ecclesiasticarum (Ecton), 84
Third Reform Act, 31f, 295
Thorne, Will, 224
"Thoughts on Civil Liberty" (Hays), 139
Ticketing, 202, 221–22, 223, 369n17, 378n118
Time and Tide (journal), 255, 282
Times, The (newspaper), 21, 178
Tod, Isabella, 194
Toryism, Tories, 3, 18, 87, 105; and suffrage support, 37, 230; female, 45f, 47–48; canvassing by, 109–10. *See also* Conservative Party
Townshend, Charles, 81f
Townswomen's Guilds (TGs), 41, 270–71, 272, 282
Trades unionism, 32, 43, 278
Training school, 163
Trevelyan, George Otto, 177, 191
Trimmer, Sarah, 161
Trumbach, Randolph, 118
Tucker, Josiah, 8
Turberville, A. S., 109–10
Turner, John, 298
Two Penny-Worth of Truth (Jebb), 140

Union and Emancipation Society, 184, 191, 363n72
Union of Jewish Women, 271, 277
Unitarian Christian Tract Society, 128
Unitarian New College, 127
Unitarians, Unitarianism, 28, 128, 136, 143f, 151; radical, 29–30, 31, 53, 149–50, 183, 197, 353n123; and education, 126f; formal associations and, 131f; women's movement and, 172, 180, 181–82, 197
United Liberal Party, 185, 188
United States, 186. *See also* Civil War (American)
United Suffragists (US), 34, 37, 228, 241, 251f; organization of, 243–45; policies

of, 245–47; during World War I, 247–50
Upper class, see Aristocracy
US, see United Suffragists

Vagrancy Laws (1824), 147
Vegetarianism, 30
Vere Bertie, Lord, 105
Vernon, Admiral, 22
Vernon, James, 14
Victoria, Queen, 15, 164
Victorian era, 154–55, 204
Village Politics (More), 139
Vindication on the Rights of Man (Wollstonecraft), 137
Vindication on the Rights of Women (Wollstonecraft), 130
Violence, 225, 368n8, 377n104; and suffragist movement, 36, 212–13 *passim*, 236, 259, 374n68, 375n76, 376nn84, 95, 377nn104, 105; WSPU disruptions and, 209f; and political campaigns, 211–12, 215–16, 220, 223–24, 257
Virtue, 125, 157
Vivian, H. H., 224
Volunteers, voluntarism, 197, 206, 274; Conservative Party, 293–94, 312–13
Voters, 78, 101, 112, 187, 195; registration of, 190, 268; property holders as, 229, 321n19, 364n81; and World War I, 249–50; women as, 259–63, 303
Votes: ownership of, 85–86
"Votes for Men" (Gawthorpe), 235
Votes for Women (newspaper), 240, 245, 247ff
Voting rights, 1f, 7–8, 44, 177, 257–58, 267, 272; World War I and, 249, 253

Wages: equality in, 40, 276, 279, 285f
Wakefield, 25, 205, 370n26
Waldegrave, Ladies, 91
Wales, 27, 32, 42, 83, 128, 242, 321n18, 373n60
Walker, Linda, 302
Walpole, Horace, 101, 139
Ward, Mrs. Humphrey, 33
Ward, John, 224
Wardle affair, 77
Warrington, 126
Warton, Jane, see Lytton, Lady Constance

Watts, Susanna, 147–48
WCAs, see Women's Citizens Associations
WCG, see Women's Co-operative Guild
Webbe, A. J., 244
Webster family, 244
Wedderburn, David, 190
Wedgwood, Julia, 176, 189
Welfare, 39–40, 42, 44, 283f, 326n74
Wellington, duke of, 155, 160
Westlake, John, 195
Westminster, 15, 154; 1784 election in, 11–13, 14, 89–90, 92, 100–103, 112–15, 120, 122; masculinity of, 53–54
Westminster Forum, 115, 117–18
Westminster Gazette (newspaper), 245f
Westminster School of Eloquence, 115–16
West Riding (Yorkshire), 18
WFL, see Women's Freedom League, 212
Whalley, 25
Whigs, 22, 27, 92, 106–8, 110; and Charles James Fox, 12, 91; and duchess of Devonshire, 13–14, 95; political patronage and, 72, 87
Whitworth, Benhamin, 187
WIs, see Women's Institutes
Widows' and Orphans' Pensions, 42
Wilde, Oscar, 203
Wilkes, John, 20f, 22f, 53
Williams, Helen Maria, 12, 28, 123, 138, 140f; works by, 128, 139
Willis's Rooms, 167
Wilson, Alice, 186
Wilson, George, 183f
Wilson, Harold, 40
Wilson, Kathleen, 20, 22, 124
Windham, William, 133, 143
Wives: and divorce, 39, 276–77; political, 136–37
WNAC, see Women's National Advisory Committee
WNLF, see Women's National Liberal Federation
Wollstonecraft, Mary, 1, 8, 115, 123–29 *passim*, 135, 138, 142, 348n45; *Vindication on the Rights of Women*, 130; *Vindication on the Rights of Man*, 137
Wolstenholme, Elizabeth, 184f, 200
Woman Citizen's Club, 248
Woman's mission, 176, 183

Woman's Suffrage Journal, 182
Woman's Work and Woman's Culture (Davies), 189–90
Women's Citizens Associations (WCAs), 267f, 279
Women's Co-operative Guild (WCG), 41–42, 206, 271, 274, 277
Women's Disabilities Bill, 196
Women's Disabilities Removal Bill, 170
Women's Emancipation Bill, 275
Women's Franchise League, 229, 276
Women's Freedom League (WFL), 212f, 241, 248, 257, 277, 279; class issues, 214–15; on violence, 216, 218–19
Women's Institutes (WIs), 41, 46, 269–70, 272
Women's Labour League, 33
Women's Liberal Federation, 16, 33, 35, 52, 206, 212, 220
Women's Liberal Unionist Association, 26, 164
Women's movement: and class, 171–72, 214–15
Women's National Advisory Committee (WNAC), 298
Women's National Liberal Federation (WNLF), 265–66, 276
Women's rights, 115–16, 151, 210, 233; 1780s, 118, 122; radicalism and, 130, 149–50
Women's Sanitary Improvement and Health Visitors Union, 41, 271
Women's Social and Political Union (WSPU), 2, 34, 37, 201–2, 207, 213, 225, 229, 257, 373nn44, 60; militancy of, 208–9; disruption by, 209–10, 223f; class issues, 214–15; and men's societies, 232, 234–35; male supporters and, 238–41, 251; Pankhursts and, 242–43
Women's Suffrage Bill, 200, 229
Women's Unionist Association, 302
Worcester, 22
Work, workplace, 270, 278. *See also* Labor
Workers' Suffrage Federation, 249
Working class, 164, 174, 192, 248, 264, 295; non-political organizations for, 206, 271
Workington, 25
World War I, 5, 41, 257, 276, 280; and United Suffragists, 247–50
World War II, 40f, 253, 286
Wraxall, Nathaniel, 111, 119, 121
Wray, Sir Cecil, 12, 89, 103, 105, 116, 341n74, 342n99, 343n106; political propaganda of, 91, 112f, 121
Writers, 162; rational dissenters as, 131, 351n84; radicalism in, 137–41
WSPU, *see* Women's Social and Political Union

Yarmouth, Lady, 10, 76, 80
YCs, *see* Young Conservatives
York, 22, 24–25
York, duke of, 77
York Herald (newspapers), 18
Yorkshire, 7, 18, 181
Young Conservatives (YCs), 293, 304–5
YWCA, 276, 281

Zangwill, Edith, 244
Zangwill, Israel, 38, 244
Zweiniger-Bargielowska, Ina, 298–99, 308